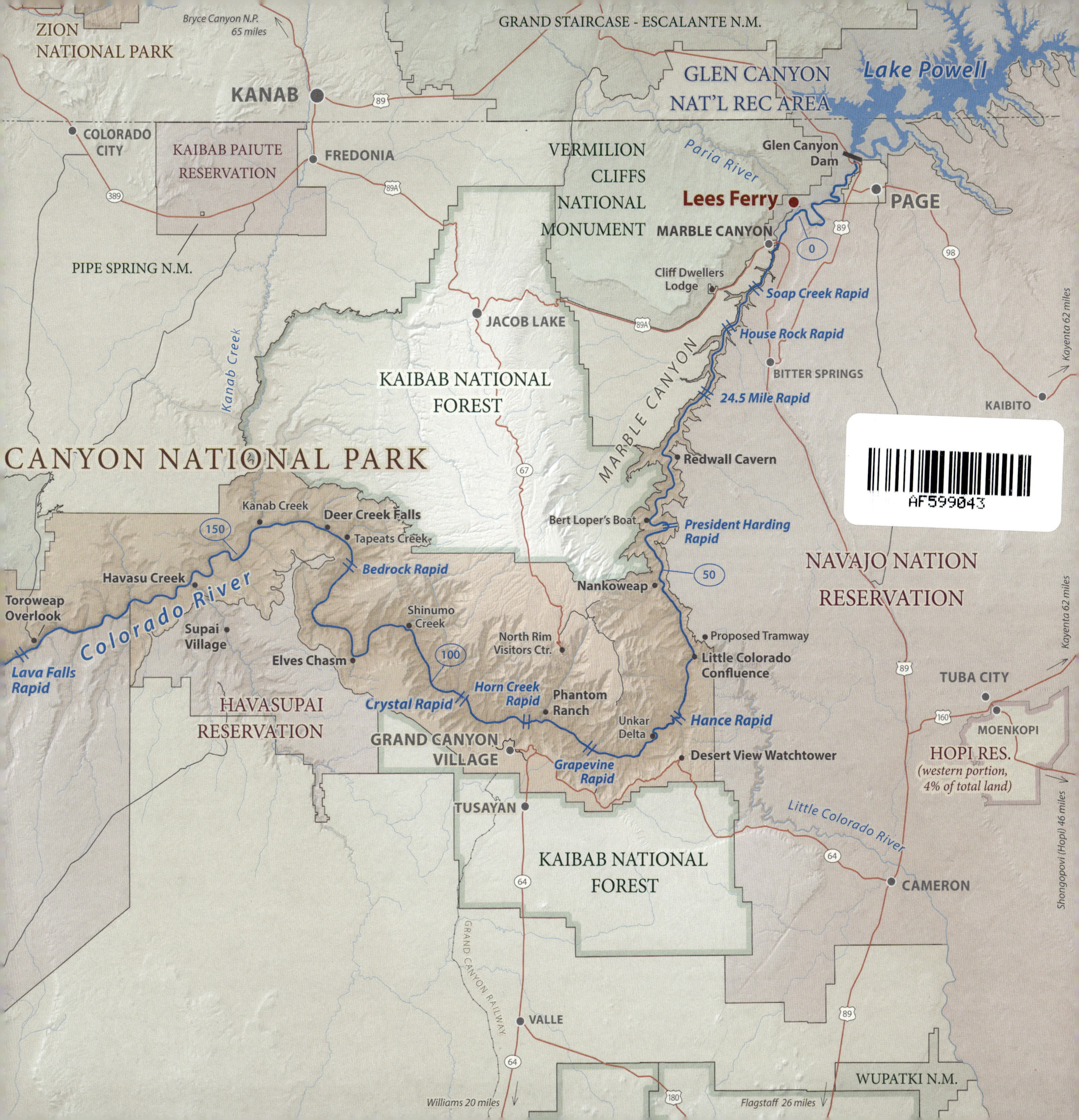
ZION NATIONAL PARK
Bryce Canyon N.P. 65 miles
GRAND STAIRCASE - ESCALANTE N.M.
KANAB
GLEN CANYON NAT'L REC AREA
Lake Powell
COLORADO CITY
KAIBAB PAIUTE RESERVATION
FREDONIA
VERMILION CLIFFS NATIONAL MONUMENT
Paria River
Glen Canyon Dam
Lees Ferry
PAGE
MARBLE CANYON
PIPE SPRING N.M.
Cliff Dwellers Lodge
Soap Creek Rapid
JACOB LAKE
House Rock Rapid
Kanab Creek
BITTER SPRINGS
KAIBAB NATIONAL FOREST
MARBLE CANYON
24.5 Mile Rapid
Kayenta 62 miles
KAIBITO
CANYON NATIONAL PARK
Redwall Cavern
AF599043
Kanab Creek
Deer Creek Falls
Tapeats Creek
Bert Loper's Boat
President Harding Rapid
Bedrock Rapid
NAVAJO NATION RESERVATION
Havasu Creek
Colorado River
Nankoweap
Toroweap Overlook
Shinumo Creek
Supai Village
North Rim Visitors Ctr.
Proposed Tramway
Little Colorado Confluence
Elves Chasm
Lava Falls Rapid
TUBA CITY
Horn Creek Rapid
Phantom Ranch
Crystal Rapid
HAVASUPAI RESERVATION
Unkar Delta
Hance Rapid
MOENKOPI
GRAND CANYON VILLAGE
Desert View Watchtower
HOPI RES. (western portion, 4% of total land)
Grapevine Rapid
TUSAYAN
Little Colorado River
Shongopovi (Hopi) 46 miles
KAIBAB NATIONAL FOREST
CAMERON
GRAND CANYON RAILWAY
VALLE
WUPATKI N.M.
Williams 20 miles
Flagstaff 26 miles

THE GRAND CANYON

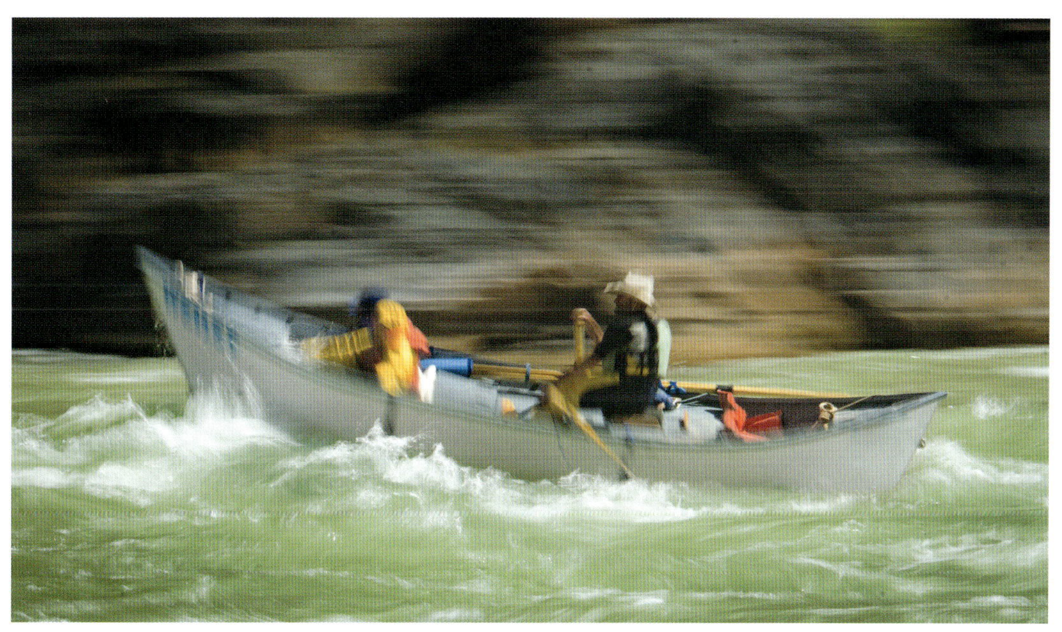

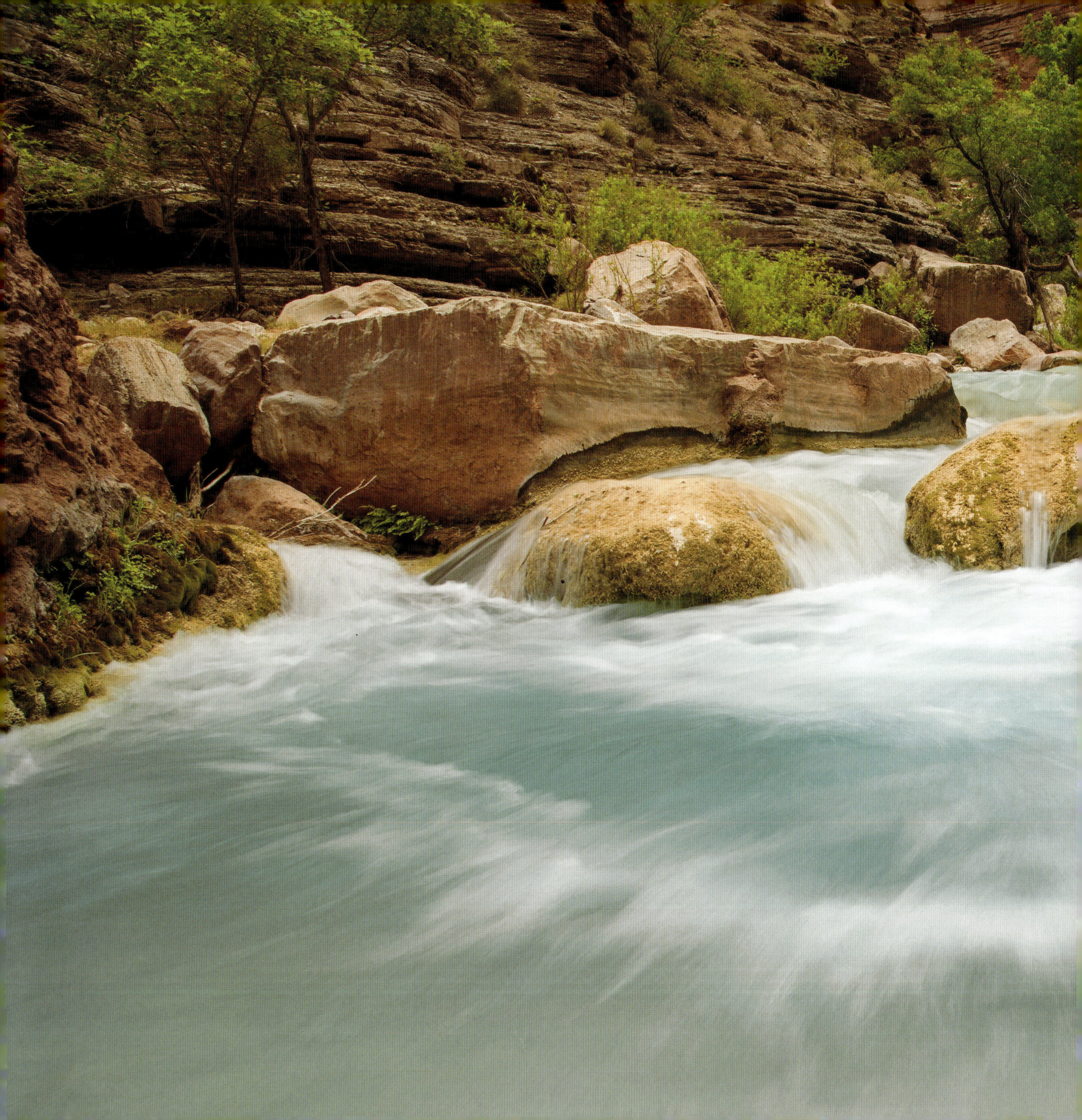

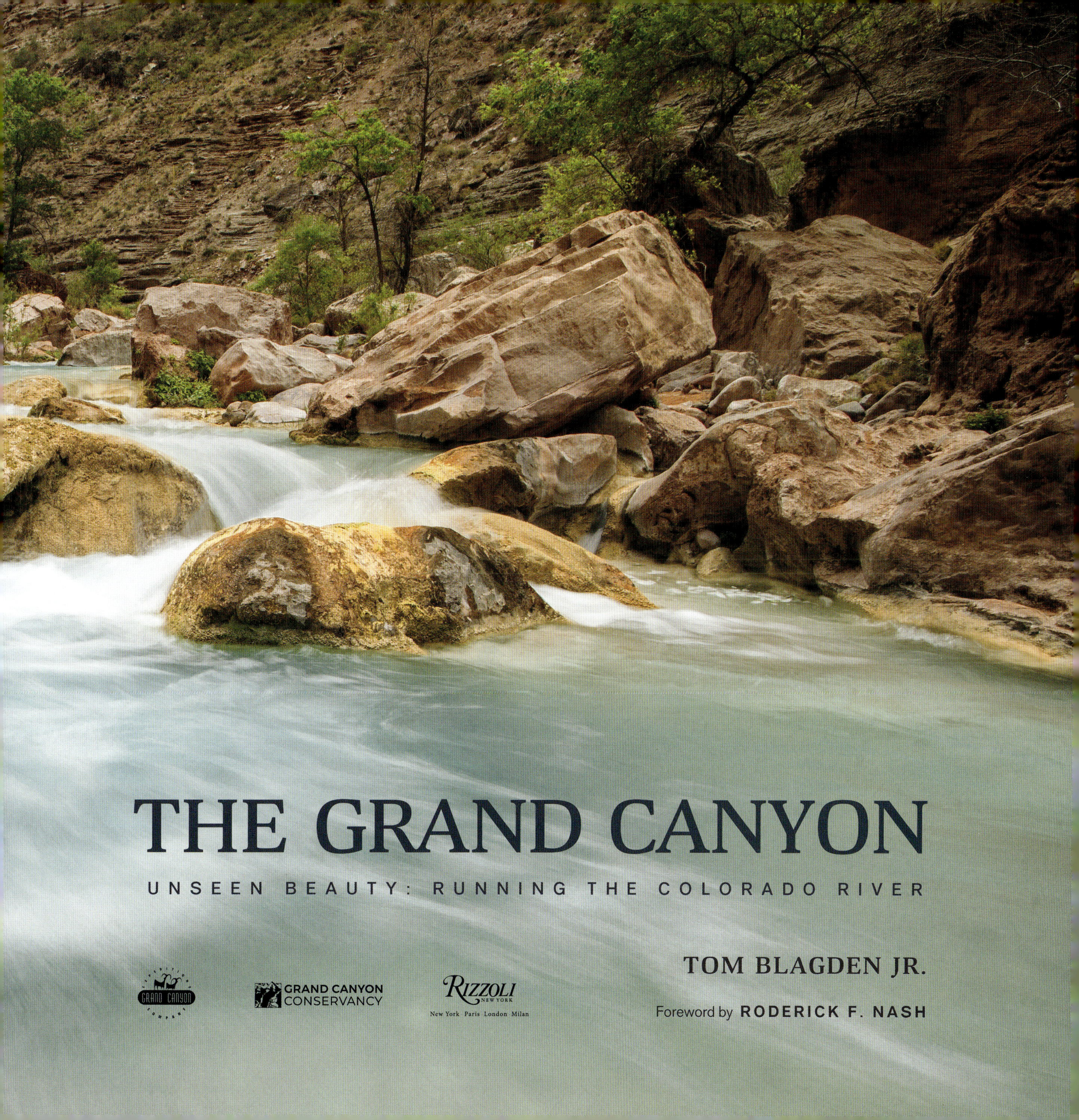

THE GRAND CANYON

UNSEEN BEAUTY: RUNNING THE COLORADO RIVER

TOM BLAGDEN JR.

Foreword by RODERICK F. NASH

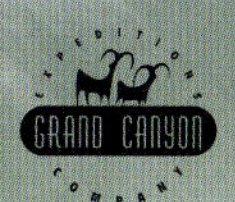

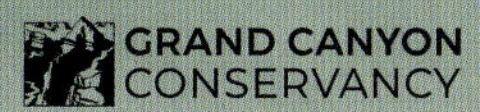

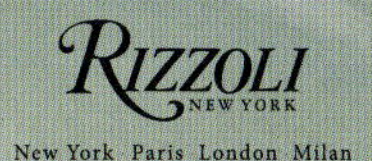

New York Paris London Milan

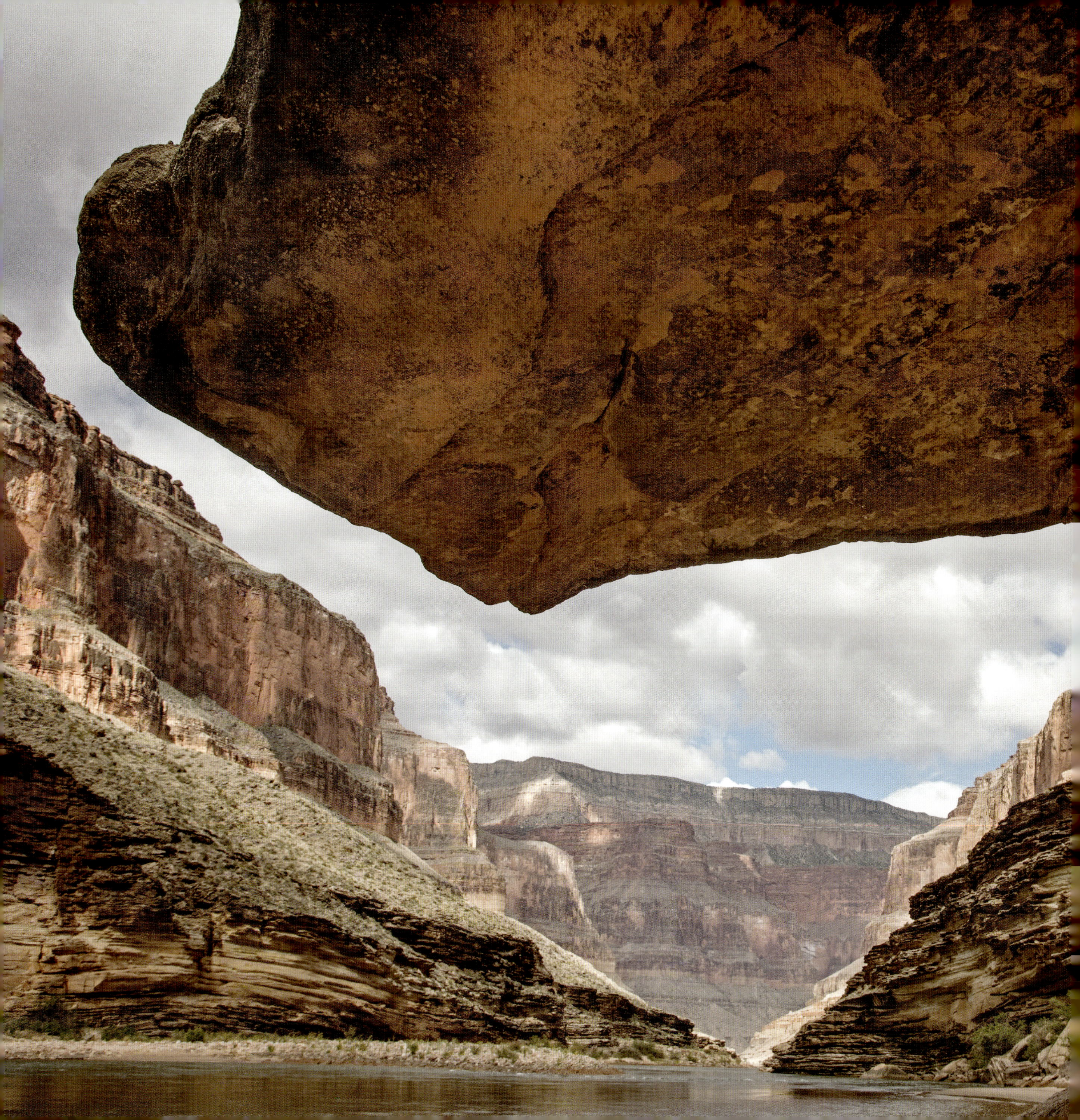

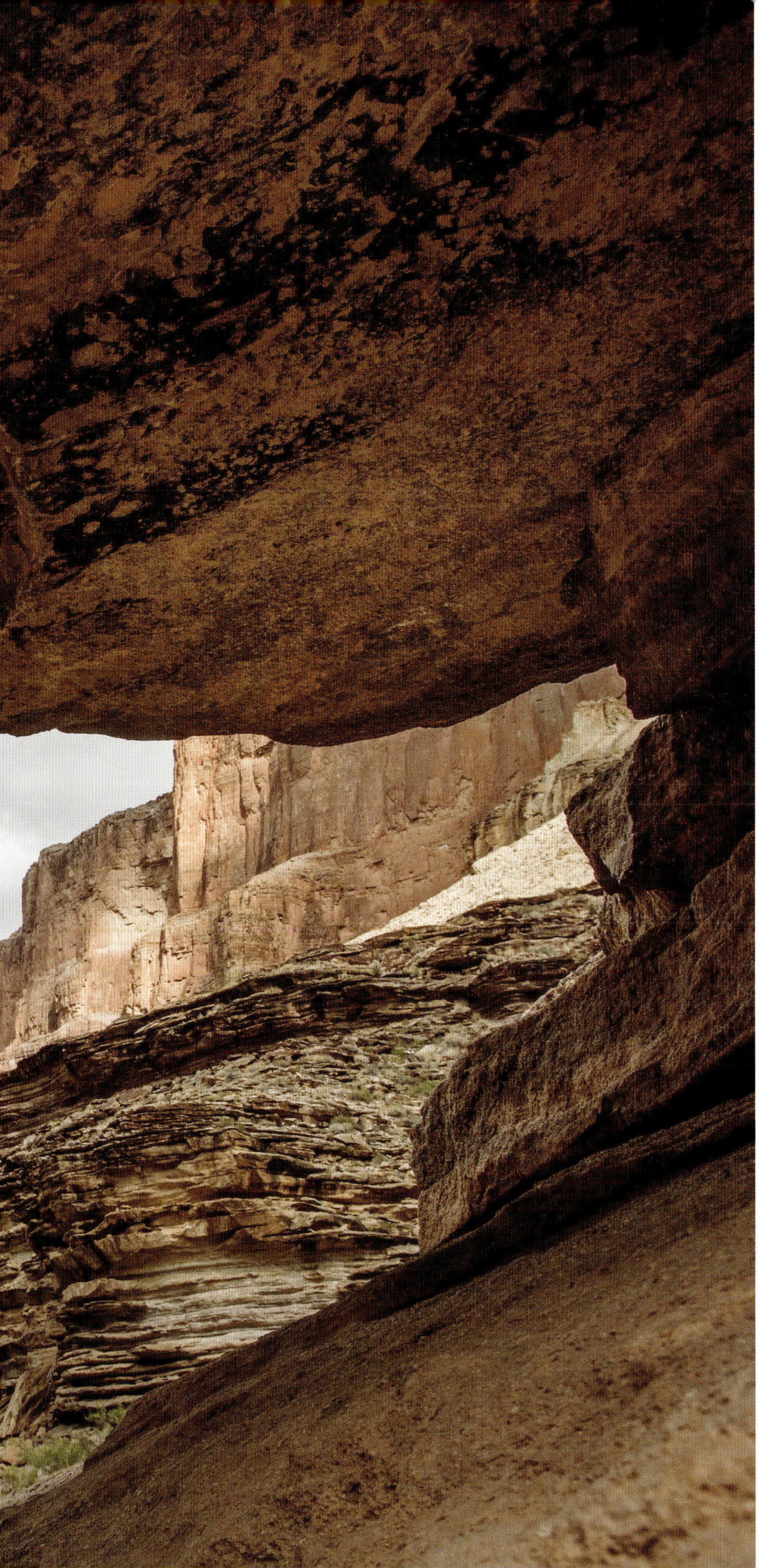

Contents

I've still got the black-and-white photograph of that first switchback on the Bright Angel Trail dropping off the South Rim. It was 1947, and the mules lined up perfectly for the Kolb Studio photographer. I was eight years old, and I rode just behind the wrangler. My father was farther back in the string. I recall not being completely sold about what the adults had promised: a big river at the end of the trail into the desert. But seven dusty miles later, down where Pipe Creek enters the Colorado River,

A Fierce GEOGRAPHY

RODERICK F. NASH

I sat on a rock and ate the best orange in the world. The river was indeed big and colored with sediment since there were no upstream dams then. I did not see any boats pass by; records indicate that in the entire year of 1947 a total of four people ran the river! Floating by Pipe Creek recently, I saw a lot of mule riders and walkers. They still eat oranges and sit on the same rock. • What's most amazing about the wildness of the Grand Canyon is its location. It's in the temperate latitudes, surrounded by freeways, not far from major cities such as Flagstaff, Arizona, St. George, Utah, and Las Vegas, Nevada.

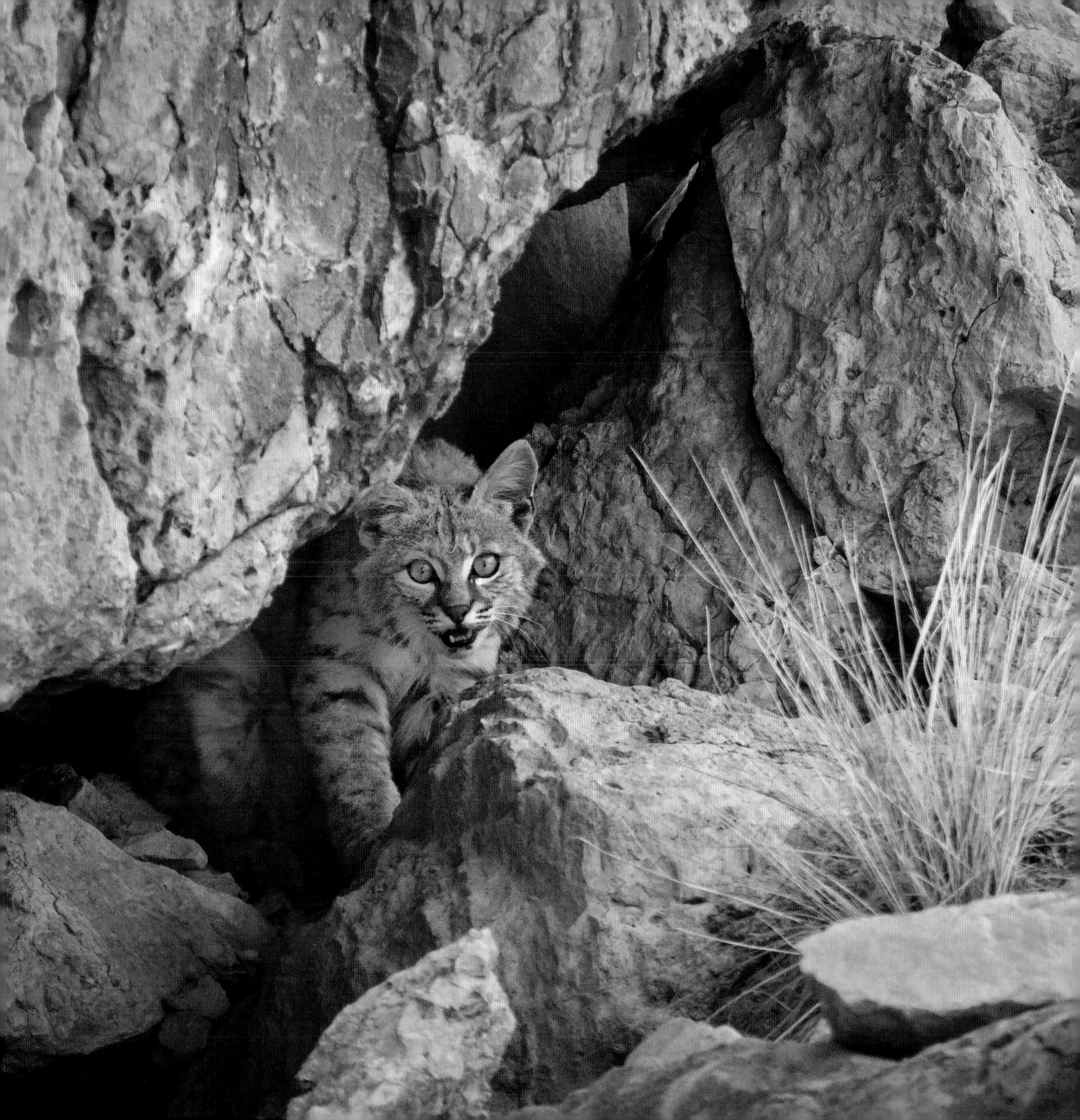

Millions of visitors drive to its rims annually. Yet when you push a boat off the beach at Lees Ferry or drop over the rim with a backpack, you are entering one of the most intense wildernesses on the planet. It has been said that more people have walked on the moon than have completed a continuous backpack of the entire Grand Canyon below the rim. From a river perspective, you see no cars for 225 miles and no buildings for the entire passage of 277 river miles. The complexity of the massive side canyons boggles the mind. Sheer walls of rock block travel off both the rim and the river. Up until 1950, only 100 people had floated the Colorado through the Grand Canyon and they did not go far from the water. Native access was hindered by the same fierce geography and took place in only a few areas, such as Unkar Delta. Put another way, no human has ever stood on most of Grand Canyon National Park.

It's exciting to me that a lot of the country in Tom Blagden's photographs is unexplored and truly wild. Sure, the water in the river is released by an upstream dam (Glen Canyon), but once freed from the reservoir (Lake Powell), it behaves in a wild way—moving sand and rocks, blasting through rapids, slowly carving a deeper canyon. With the aid of gravity water recovers its wildness, and as you go down the river you tend to think less about the dam. River running exploded in popularity in the 1960s; more than 30,000 people now make the trip annually and more would if they could get permits. They are, in the words of the Wilderness Act of 1964, "visitors who do not remain." In general, they stick close to the boats and the points of interest that are now often called "attractions." The pace of a river trip, now tightly regulated, is too fast to permit much exploration. Relatively few canyoneers have followed the example of off-trail pioneer Harvey Butchart and worked their way into remote and difficult terrain. They follow drainages; the vertical walls are unclimbed.

But so much of the Canyon has not been seen from the ground. Case in point one: In 1956, a horrible midair collision of two commercial planes occurred over the eastern Grand Canyon. The death toll was 128—everyone on board. The crash site was incredibly isolated and hard to reach. Searchers brought out only a few bodies; a mass funeral on the rim honored the unfound. Larger pieces of the aircraft were helicoptered away. Many small ones used to glint on the cliffs if the sun was right. Some still do.

Case in point two: A few years ago, friends on a noncommercial river trip found themselves with enough time to hike up a side canyon from their camp. It was tough going, climbing a ridge and then descending through ledges into the bottom of the drainage. Suddenly, they saw something that did not look natural: a wing of an airplane jammed into the rocks! Getting closer, they determined there was a backbone in the pilot's seat. They took note of the aircraft identification number and contacted the National Park Service. Research revealed that the aircraft had been missing for several years despite extensive aerial searches. The family of the pilot was glad to have closure on the event. Significant is the fact that the wreck was reached by hiking, not rock climbing, and it was only a mile from the river. It is likely that no one had ever been there. Wild country!

As a professor of American history, I have been especially interested in national parks, thinking about them as a remnant of the frontier, a way to keep the New World new. The big, wild public park, after all, was an American invention, an impressive blend of the democratic idea, the presence of large tracts of public land, and the rise of appreciation for wild country. Beginning with the establishment of Yellowstone in 1872, parks were an original American contribution to world civilization. Just a decade after Yellowstone, in 1882, Senator Benjamin Harrison from Indiana introduced a bill to establish a national park

▲ Bobcat opposite Dinosaur Camp

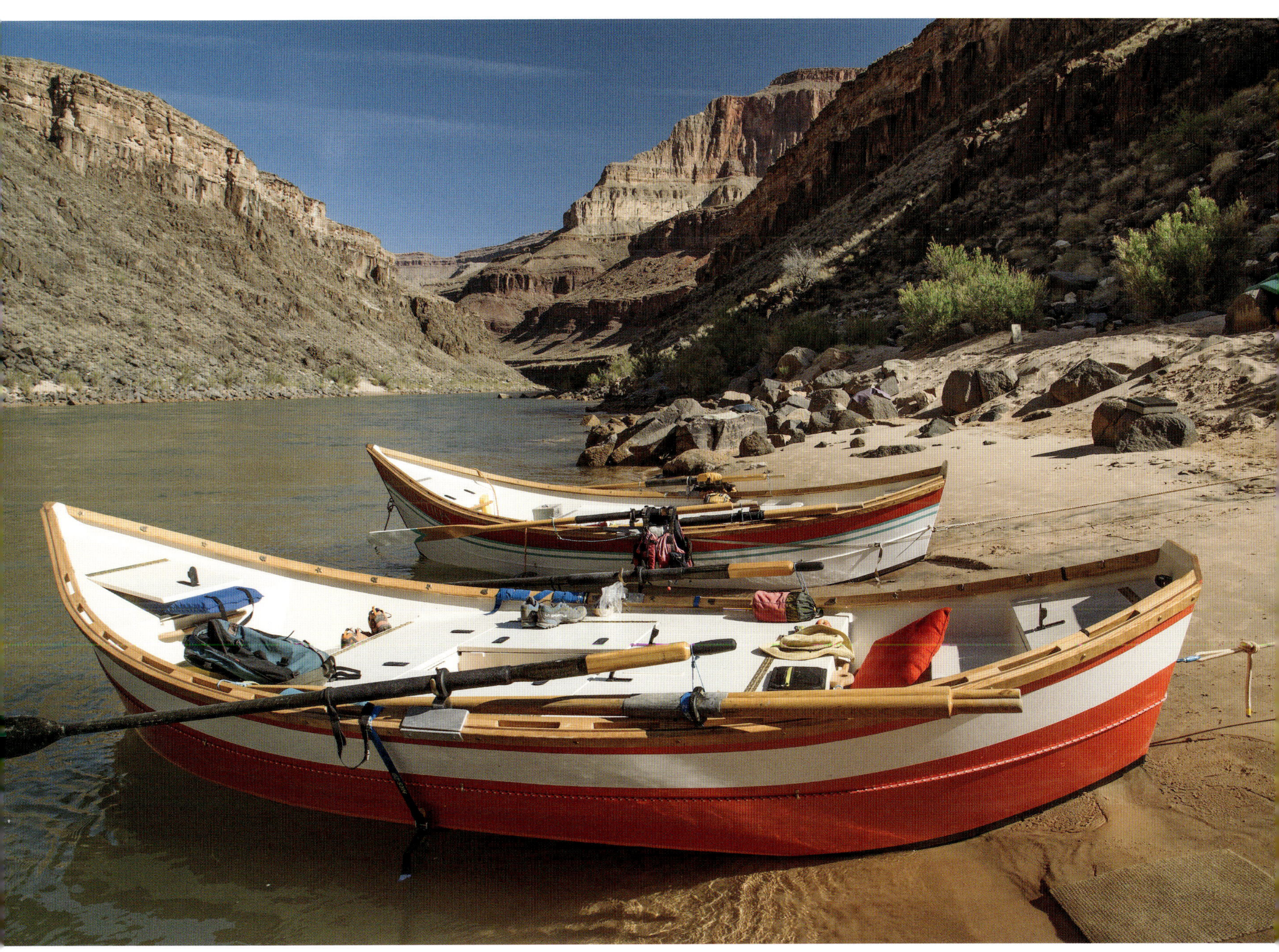

Owner-built dories on their maiden voyage

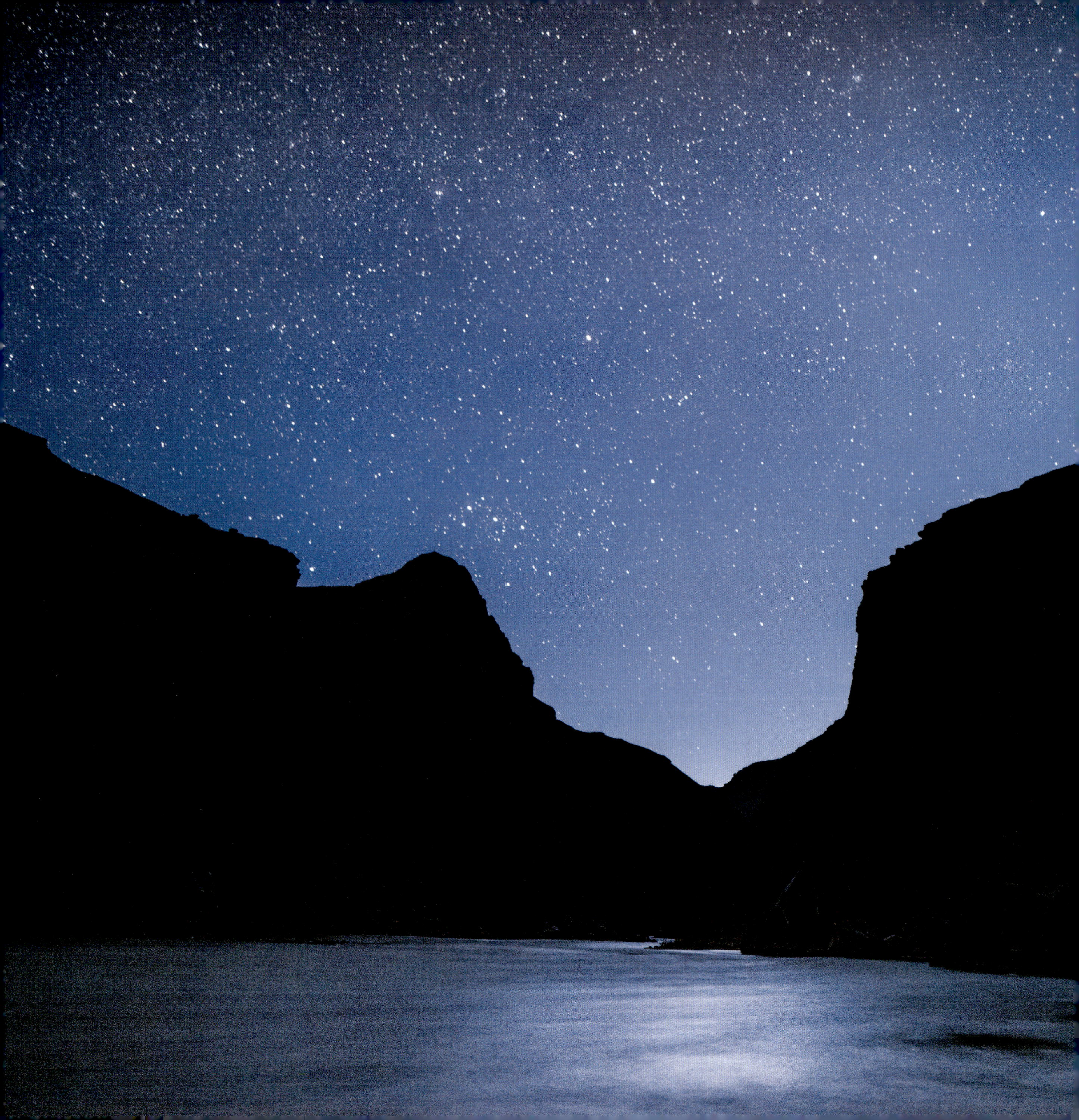

in Grand Canyon. It died before reaching the floor of Congress, but Harrison was not done. An enthusiastic outdoorsman, he had visited Yellowstone several times and loved the idea of national parks. In 1890, Harrison, now president of the United States, signed the bill creating the second national park: Yosemite. In 1893, Harrison used the new Forest Reserve Act to give the first protection to a portion of the Grand Canyon. Another president, Theodore Roosevelt, established a Grand Canyon Forest Reserve in 1906 and two years later designated the central portion of the Canyon a national monument. This crazy-quilt federal-land policy received some organization when President Woodrow Wilson signed a bill on February 26, 1919, establishing Grand Canyon National Park. Part of the motivation for the book you are holding is a centennial celebration of that action in 2019.

National park status was a great step forward, but serious problems remained. One was that protection did not include the whole Grand Canyon from Lees Ferry 277 miles downstream to the Grand Wash Cliffs. The second problem was a loophole left in the act that permitted "government reclamation projects" in the Canyon. This meant dams—big ones—to generate hydropower. When I started running the river in the 1960s, construction at two sites was underway. I recall looking at the scaffolding and drill holes on the walls and thinking, "They can't be serious!" But the engineers wanted linked reservoirs from the headwaters of Lake Mead (Hoover Dam had been completed in 1936) all the way to the base of Glen Canyon Dam (1963). One way to think of the impact of such a project is to realize that almost every point of view Tom Blagden used for his photography in this book would be hundreds of feet under the water of a reservoir.

In 1967 the stage was set for a showdown battle over national parks and designated wilderness areas. People who applauded Hoover Dam during the Great Depression but were not so sure about Glen Canyon Dam drew a line in the sand when it came to damming the Grand Canyon. Leading the charge was the Sierra Club's executive director, David Brower, and board member Martin Litton, who was also my river-boating mentor. Tensions ran high; full-page ads in national newspapers compared the Grand Canyon to the Sistine Chapel. Sacred space was involved. The Canyon was a treasure not only of Arizona and the United States, but also the entire world. My book, *Wilderness and the American Mind*, transcended its scholarly origins and became, for some people, a manifesto. I remember one Sierra Club strategy meeting when I excused myself to catch a flight. Brower stopped me at the door. "There will always be another airplane," he said quietly. Everyone at the table knew what he left unsaid: the Grand Canyon was unique. I returned to my seat. The dam battle ended the next summer, in 1968, when Congress passed a hydropower bill that expressly forbid dams in the Grand Canyon. The old loophole was closed and the big-dam era in American history ended. In 1975, the other problem was resolved when an enlargement act protected all non–Native American land in the river corridor. Unfortunately, rim to river mechanized tourist transports (helicopters and tramways) have been or could be developed on the Hualapai and Navajo Reservations.

I was scheduled to lead a commercial river trip through the Grand Canyon in June 1983, and it was very uncomfortable standing on a clearly vibrating Glen Canyon Dam the day before the launch. The crew went up there after rigging out at Lees Ferry because we knew Lake Powell was full and the dam was in trouble. In his masterful book *The Emerald Mile: The Epic Story of the Fastest Ride in History through the Heart of the Grand Canyon*, Kevin Fedarko told the story: a huge winter snowfall in the

Star-filled sky over the river, 110 Mile Camp

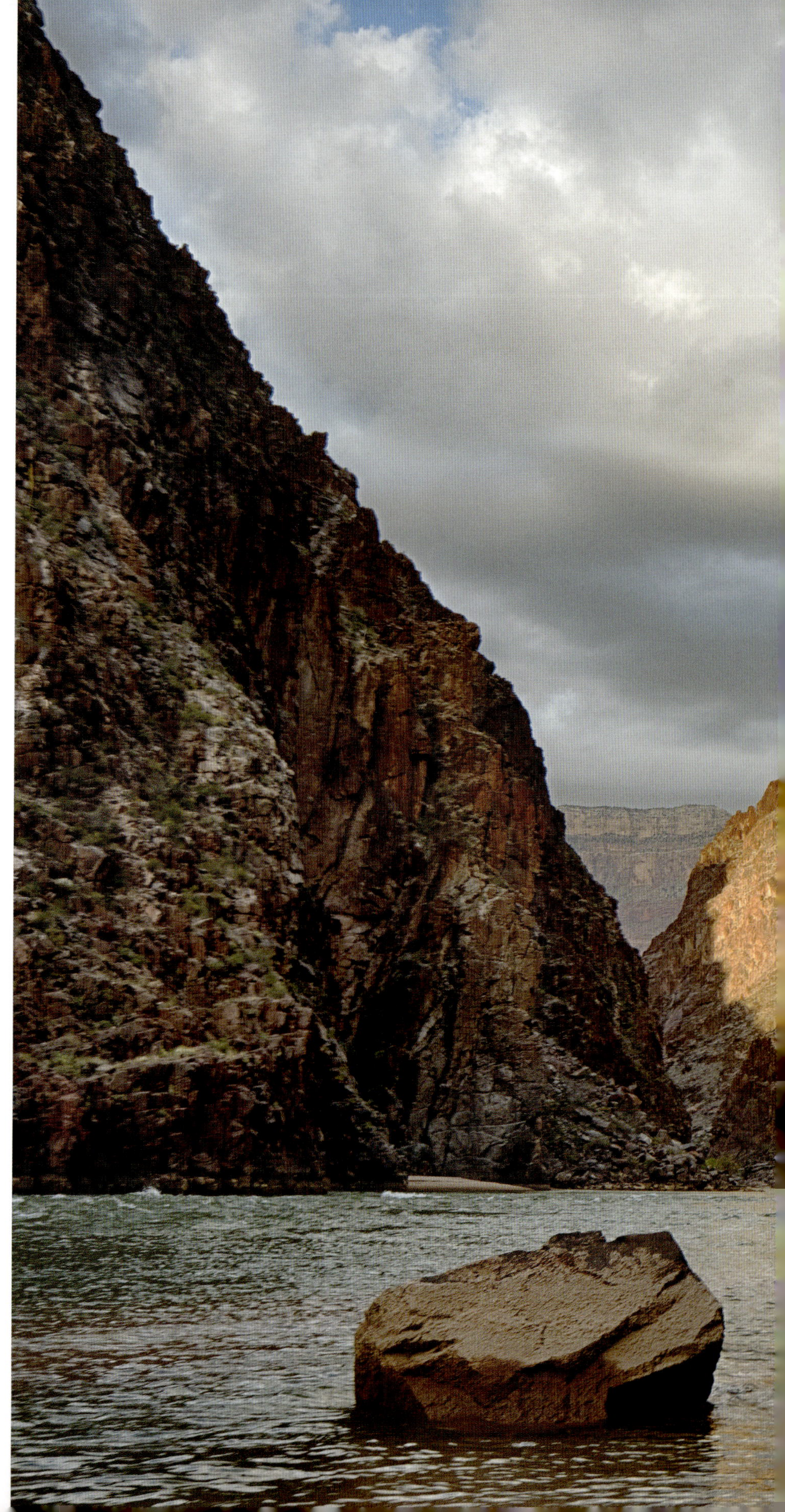

View downriver from Trinity Camp

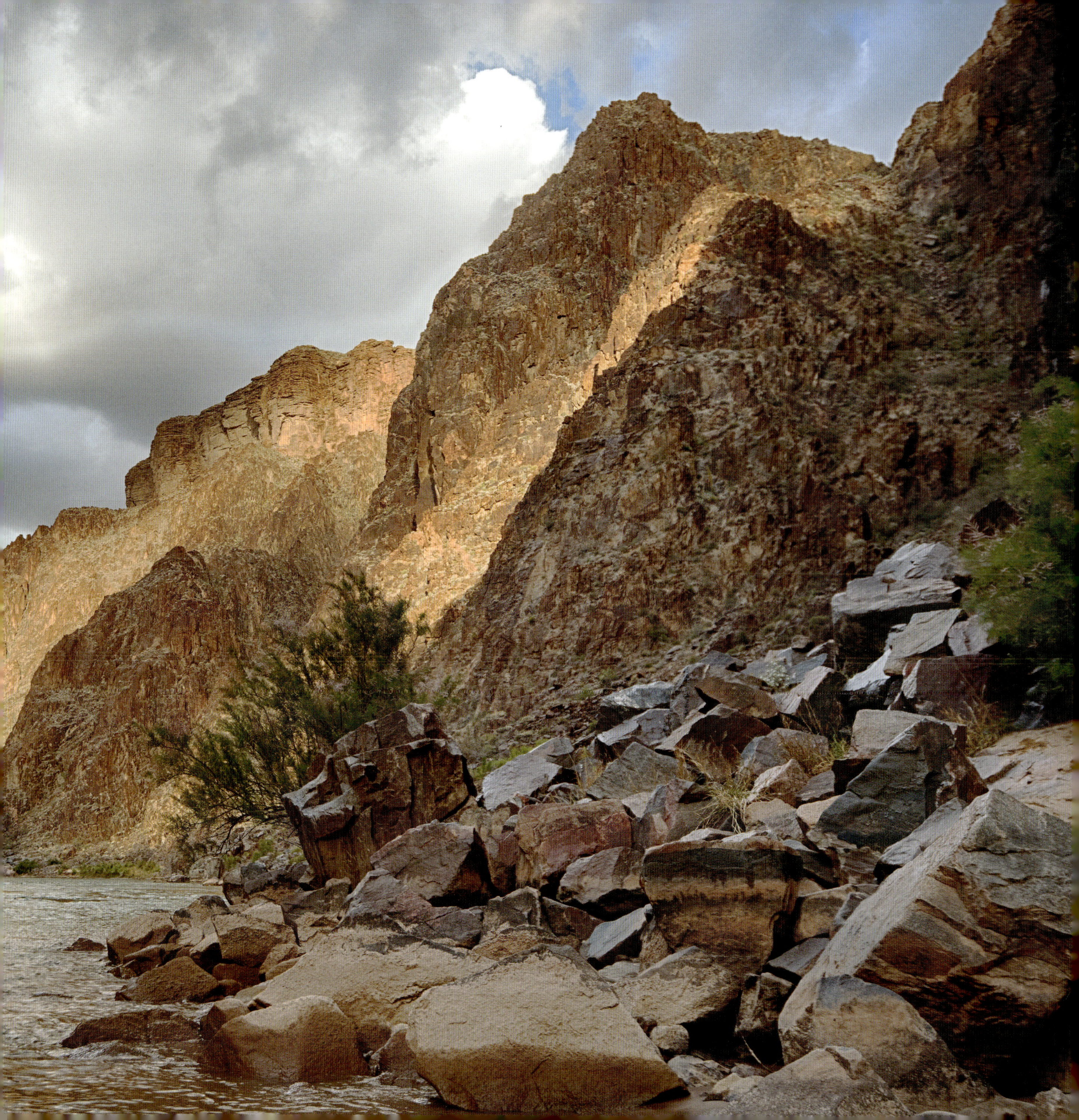

West, a reservoir already filled to capacity, no option for the engineers other than to let as much water as possible through, around, and over the dam. It's one thing to talk about the possibility of dam failure in a government office; it's quite another to be on the river in a small boat below that dam. After our trip started, we did not need the plastic bags rangers dropped from helicopters to tell us the river was on the rise—fast! Frankly, we were scared; we were the guides but we didn't know what was around the next bend. We talked with our group about evacuation, but also about the exhilaration of feeling the power of a chained giant flexing its wild muscles. A flow of 100,000 cubic foot per second had not blown through the Canyon since the pre-dam 1950s. We did not expect to live long enough to see it again. My friend and boating colleague Kenton Grua seized the opportunity and used his dory *Emerald Mile* to run the whole 277 miles in a little more than 36 hours. His three-person crew passed my boats in camp at Parashant Wash (mile 198). We were taking two weeks to make the same passage. Martin Litton, owner of Grand Canyon Dories, flew his plane over us at 205 Mile Rapid and dipped his wing in acknowledgment.

I turn 80 this year, and I'm fortunate to still be able to go with the flow. The gods willing, I'll row my dory, *Canyon Dancer*, through the Canyon in September, searching as always for the magic in moving water. Most of us who have spent a lot of time on rivers think they are alive. Some go further to regard them as oppressed minorities in a human-dominated planet. Why not extend rights to rivers so that life, liberty, and the pursuit of happiness—in the rivers' terms—could be represented in our legal system? America has made such moral leaps in the past (with the abolition of slavery, for instance); maybe it's time for natural rights to be extended to the rights of nature. National parks and designated wildernesses are ways to balance the needs and wants of our species with those of the rest of nature. Wild places have value—even if, like most of the Grand Canyon, we never visit them—as symbols of unselfishness and evidence of our capacity to restrain and share. Protecting the Canyon and places like it are gestures of planetary modesty on the part of the world's most dangerous animal.

For me, after years below the rim, the most important takeaway is humility. The Grand Canyon reminds us constantly that we are merely specks in the history of the earth and universe. When asked, I tell people the hardest thing about running the Canyon is not the rapids; it's being confronted with what I call the weight of cosmic time. The whole earth story is on display here, right back to the rocks that formed when the molten planet cooled, before life and evolution began. In this context we are not very significant, but, along with destructiveness, we have developed the capacity to recognize and protect wild beauty. Grand Canyon National Park—and the book you are holding—evince that truth.

A boatman plunging into Lava Rapid

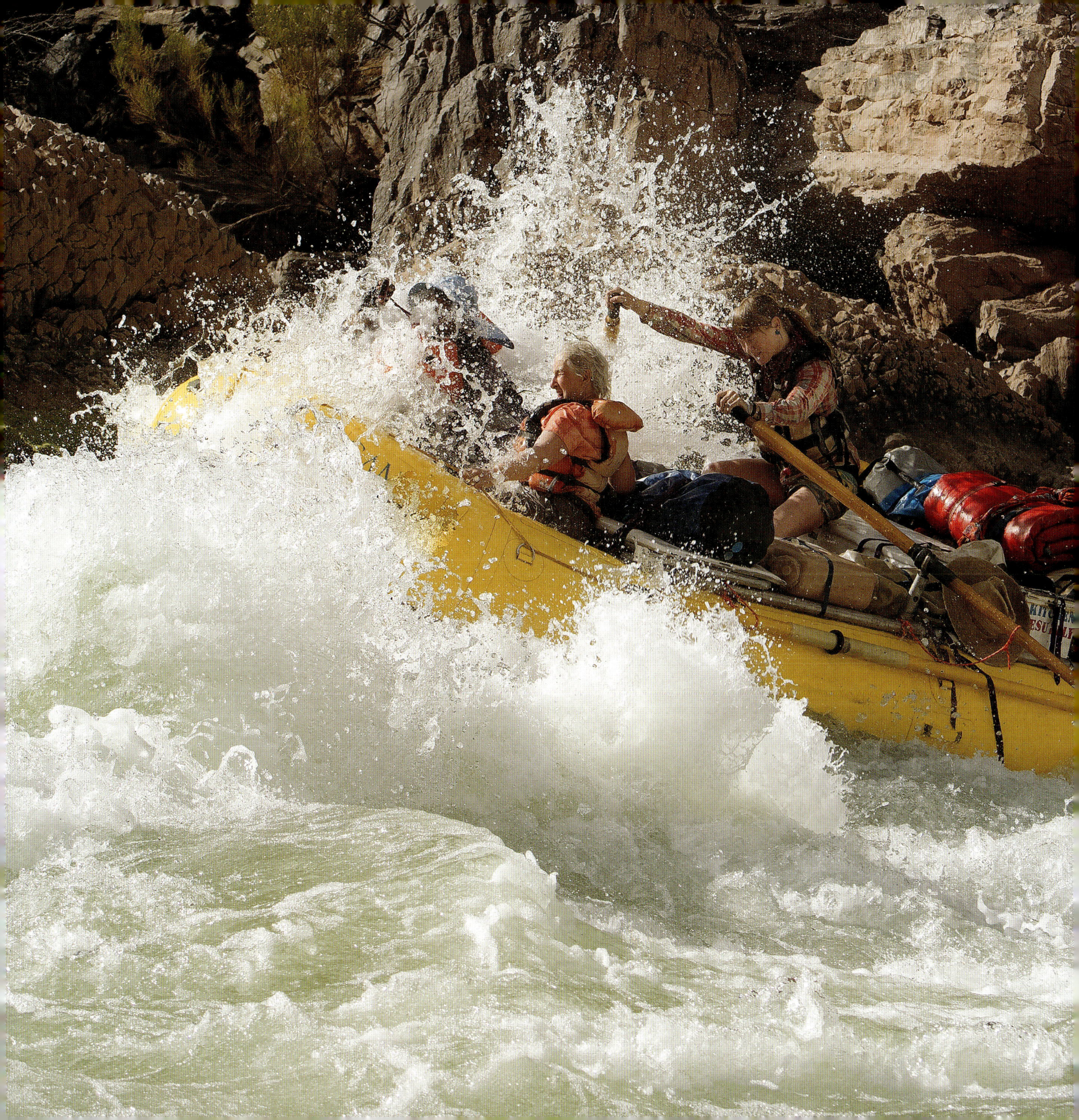

Embarking on the waters of the Colorado River through the Grand Canyon rapidly evaporates all expectations. Nothing in our paradigm of daily life prepares us for this journey. The experience could not differ more from anything we define as normal, as it seems to reach beyond our sense of scale and human perception. It is truly a canyon of contrast. Most enter seeking another check on their adventure list, only to emerge a different person. • Early on one trip I asked a single woman in her 30s

Canyon of CONTRAST

TOM BLAGDEN JR.

why she had signed up and come by herself. She emotionally explained that she had just lost her husband prematurely to cancer, and, with it, her zest for life. She said she had come to see if life was still worth living, to see if the Canyon would snap her out of her depression. I was stunned and didn't know what to say. Over the course of the following week she began to embrace the experience, do all the hikes, swim in the creeks, marvel at the scenery, and interact with her fellow adventurers. By the end she was smiling and laughing; she had found herself by being drawn out of herself. The Canyon had worked its magic.

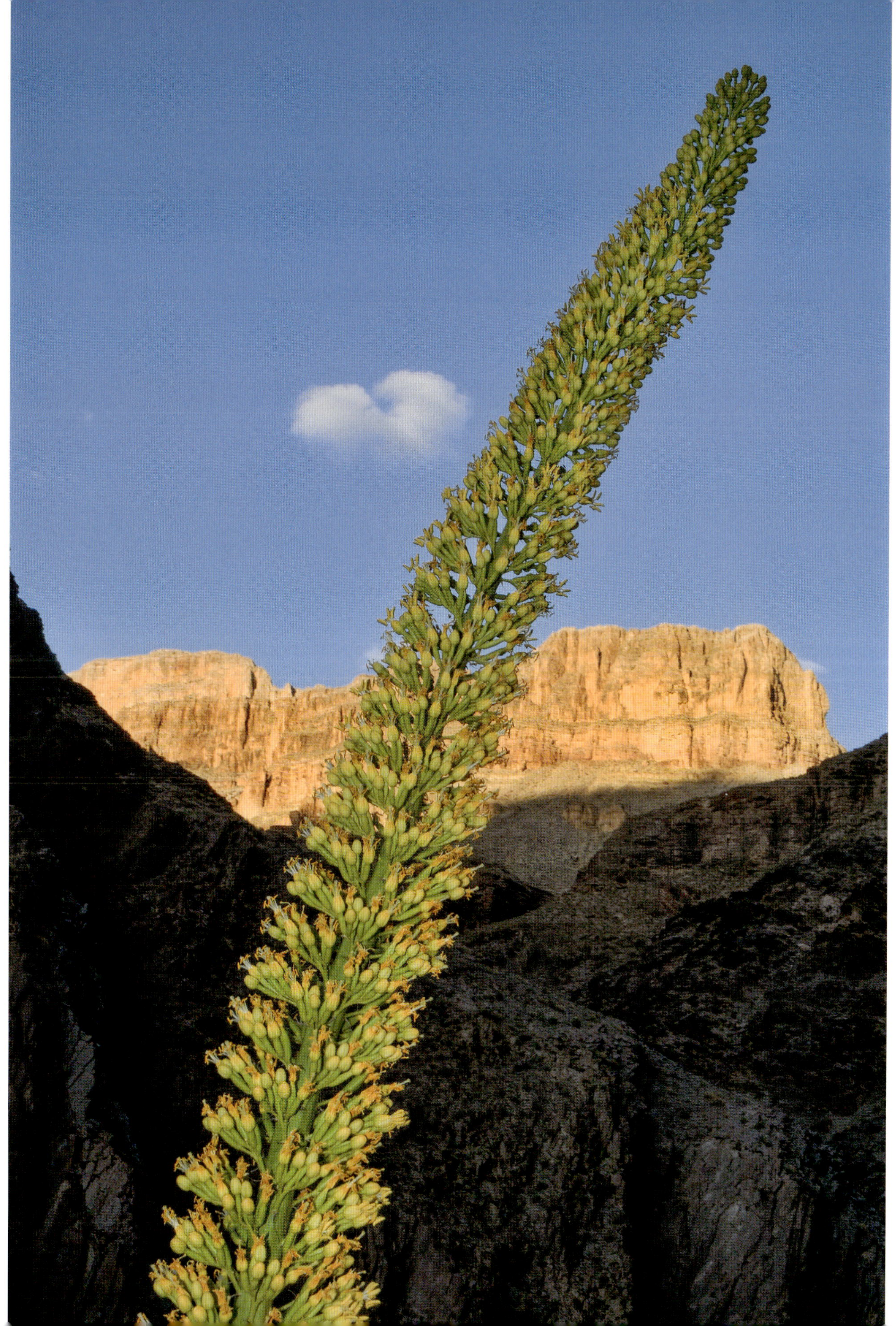

▲ Utah century plant in bloom

► View upriver from Tequila Camp below Lava Falls Rapid

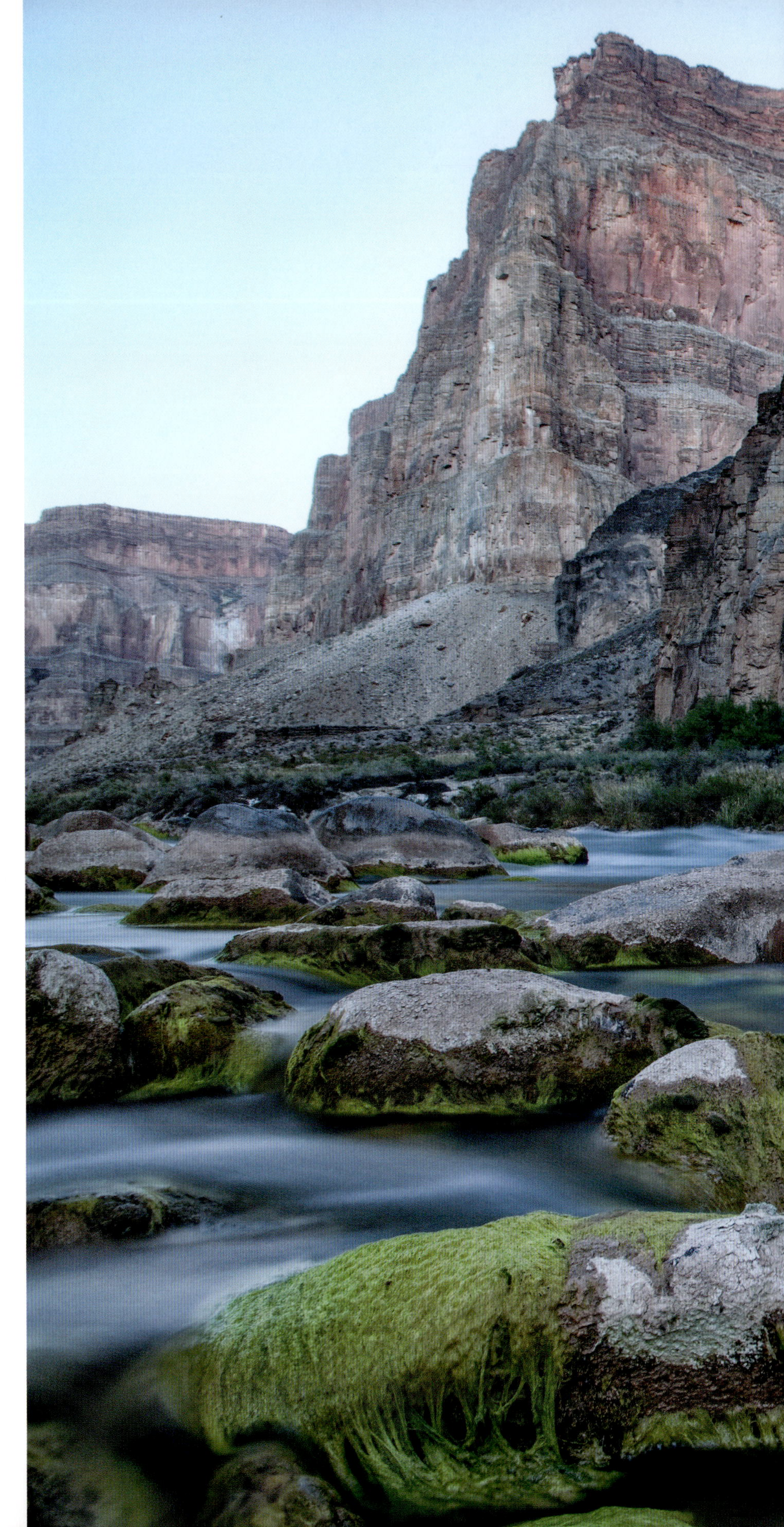

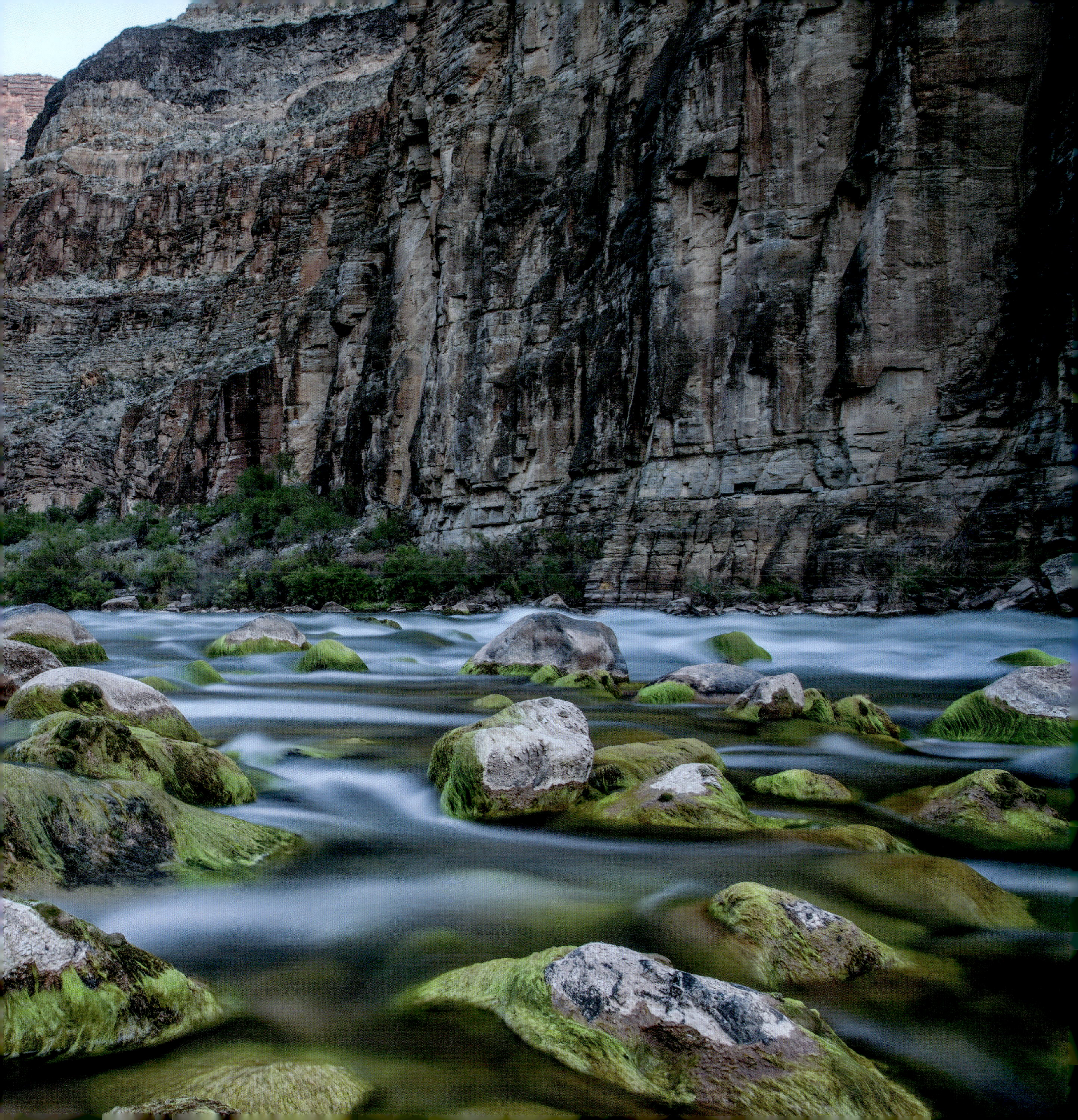

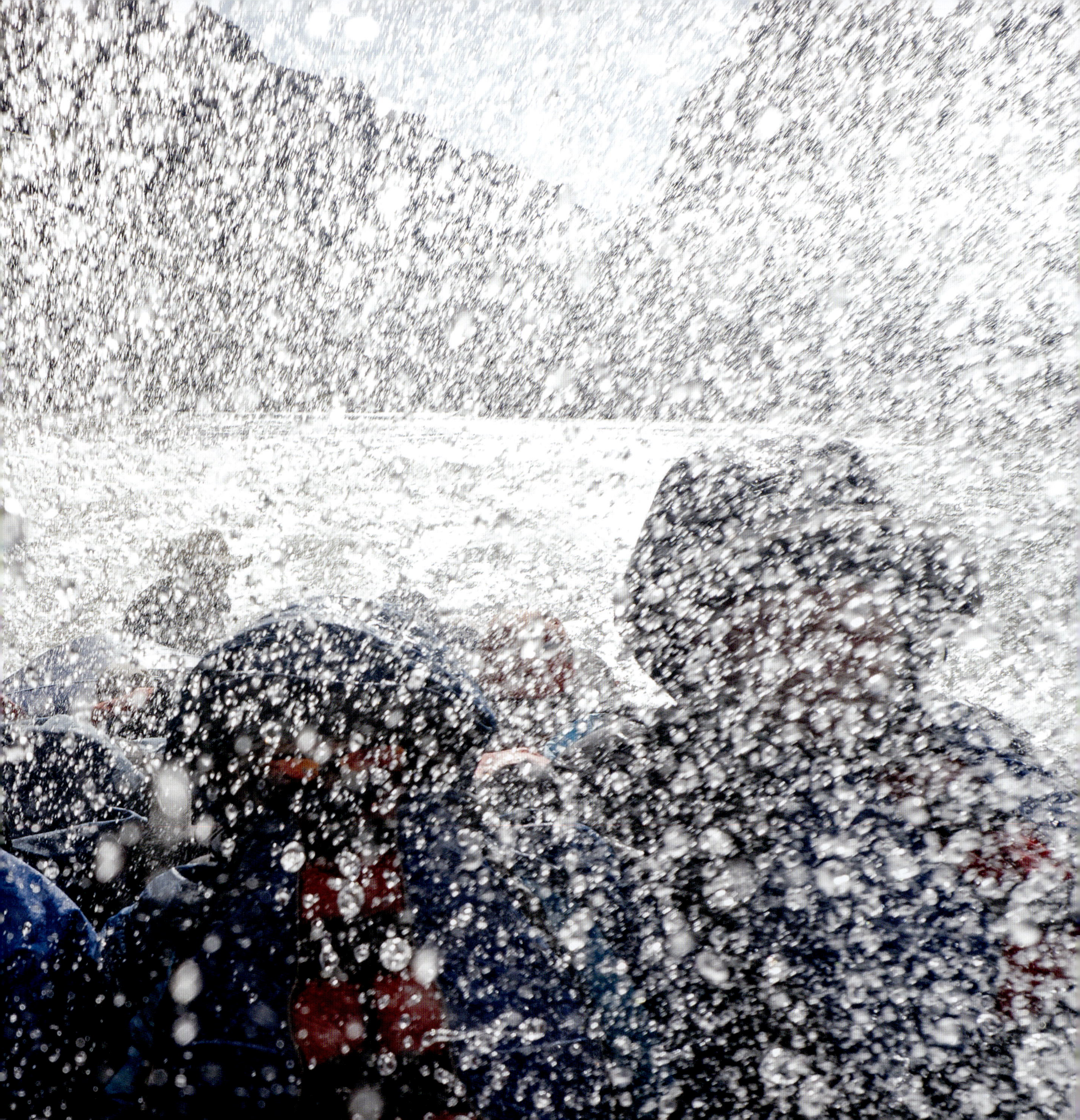

I feel privileged to have experienced rafting the Grand Canyon so many times, and the journey always reaches a different part of me. Once we shove off at Lees Ferry there's no turning back for 277 miles. We can't call home, we can't check emails, our kids are out of touch, and the only current events are the currents we're in. But there are also no bills to pay, no unwanted phone solicitations, no leaf blowers, and no news of world chaos. River time takes over and we go with the flow and one another. All that matters is the moment, defined by water and rock and weather. We learn the value of disconnecting from life as we normally know it and instead are immersed in the immediate.

A significant part of what makes a raft or dory trip through the Grand Canyon so impressionable is the almost constant contrast and fluctuation around us. The numbingly cold water practically arrests the heart and cripples the brain. The frigid dunking of more than 150 rapids soaks us to the core, only to have the baking sun desiccate us in a matter of minutes. Quiet, meditative stretches of river terminate in deafening rapids that instantly erase any harbored thoughts we may have. Vivid reflections dance on the water's surface, only to disintegrate into roiling rapids and tumultuous waves. The river's soft waters relentlessly carve their way through almost two billion years of hard rock, whose edges in places are worn as smooth as glass by the silty liquid sandpaper. Vertical cliffs constantly loom above, yet they are composed of horizontal layers of myriad hue and texture.

Our own presence, dwarfed by the massive canyon walls, is rendered fragile and insignificant. The landscape is timeless, yet we barely exist in its presence. Our delicate emotions are huge and profound surrounded by this seemingly eternal cathedral of stone and vibrant river, yet our vocabulary fails us in contrast to the depth of our impressions. The intellect struggles to grapple with the complex geology while our senses are infused by the aesthetics of our surroundings. We notice everything in the moment, but true understanding seems beyond our grasp. We travel this sinewy river through the desert, yet try to mentally process that it was all once at the bottom of the sea. For the most part, it remains beyond our capacity to comprehend its origins. The Grand Canyon has evolved and will continue to evolve. For all its stable, monumental presence, the Canyon is a testament to the power of change and earthly forces. The Canyon is nature at its grandest, and we embrace the mystery that goes with it.

Rafting the Grand Canyon slows us down. The power is in the details, both subtle and bold. We aren't just passive passengers but rather participants with senses fully engaged. The rock walls display countless abstract textures and patterns. Reflections oscillate with every ripple. The rapids each sing a different chorus, some thunderous and deep throated, others lyrical and rhythmic. The dynamic light reverberates off canyon walls, imbuing them with shifting colors in each passing hour. The cliffs glow in the full moon as if they were internally lit, or stars crowd a moonless night sky framed in entirety by the canyon walls.

The various trips tend to blend together, but certain memories and experiences are indelible: lying in my sleeping bag under an immaculate desert night sky and projecting reflections on the day and wonderment into the cosmos; the remarkable and rare sighting of a bobcat as it hunts along the river and gazes at us from its refuge under a large boulder (see page 7); two bighorn rams butting heads over territory and hierarchy as the deep sound echoes off the canyon wall; witnessing the immensity of Redwall Cavern and imagining the power of the unbridled river that carved it out over millions of years; marveling at the raw power of Lava Falls Rapid swallowing dories completely from sight and then spitting them

Rafters in the impact zone

Comanche Point

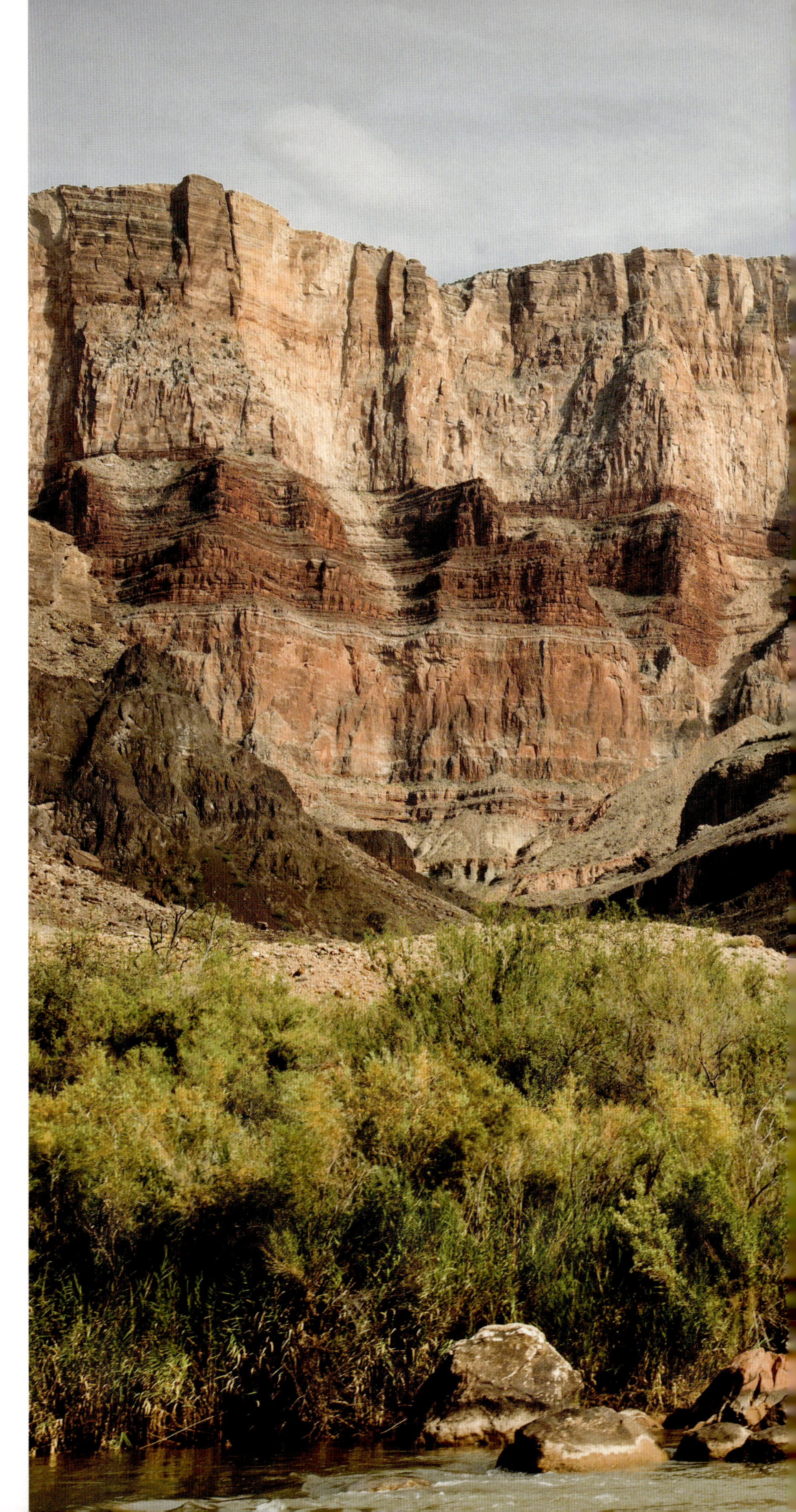

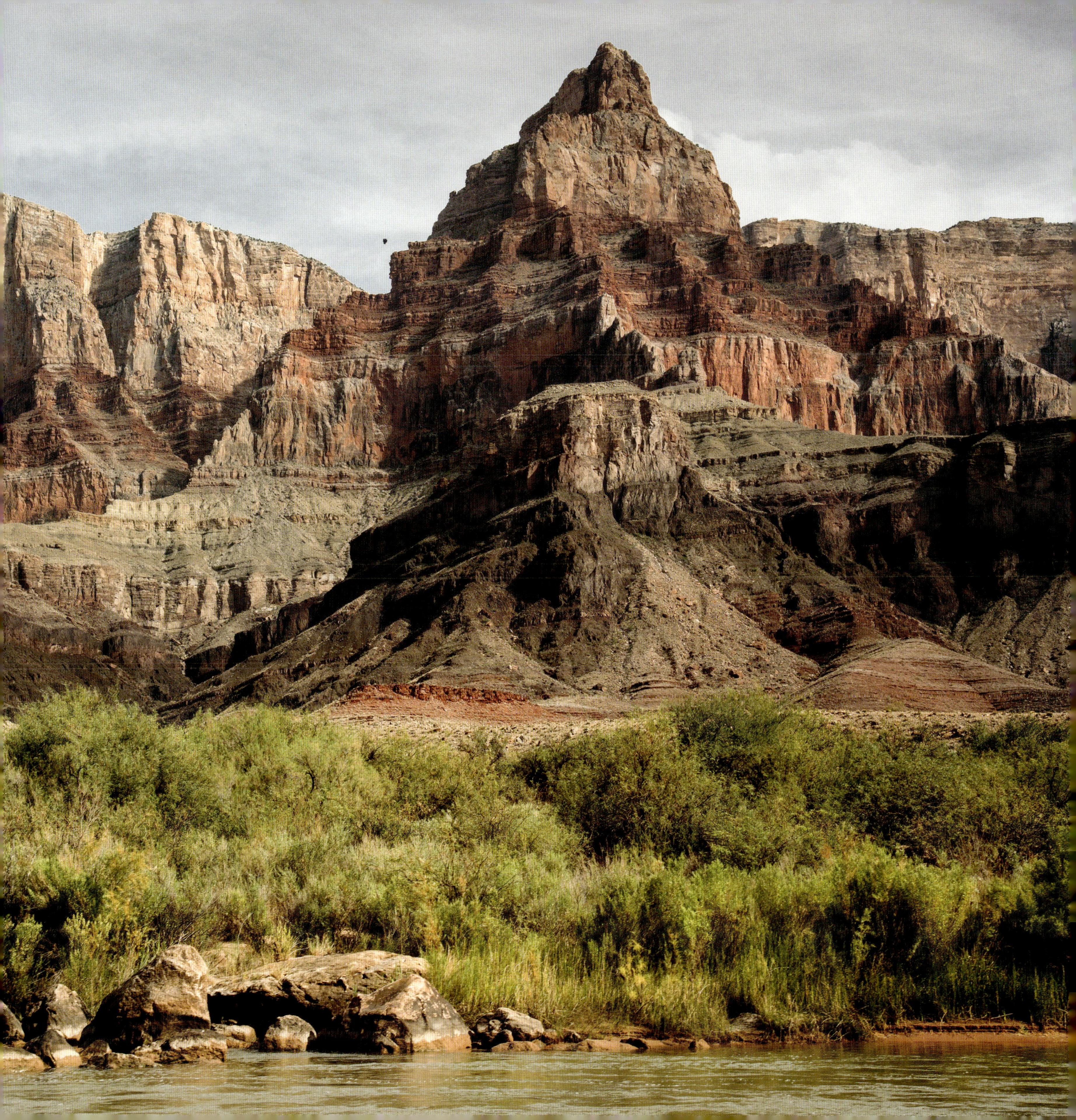

out still intact; witnessing swarms of violet-green swallows feeding on an insect hatch over the water, only to see one detonate in a cloud of feathers right off our bow as a plummeting peregrine falcon claims its meal; watching a kingfisher desperately trying to evade an attacking peregrine by repeatedly diving underwater at the peregrine's every swooping assault, finally to escape exhausted into a bush on the far shore; canyon slopes erupting in a profusion of wildflower blooms from unusually abundant spring rains; discovering that the upper part of Saddle Canyon is almost unrecognizable after a flash flood scoured out massive boulders and most of the vegetation; having the deep silence of a slot canyon punctuated by a chorus of frogs and then the lyrical, wistful call of a canyon wren reverberating off the stone walls; seeing seven condors at once, one of the rarest birds in North America, riding thermals along the cliffs; drifting silently through The Narrows, enraptured as a Native American boatman plays his flute while deeply moved participants' tears flow with the river; and committing the ashes of a dear friend who loved the Canyon to its river spirit, followed by the emergence of a perfect rainbow arcing over the water, rim to rim (see pages 60–61).

Other humorous and dramatic memories endure just as meaningfully: waking up after an unexpected night rainstorm to see tentless sleepers scattered about, rolled up burrito-style in tarps like giant blue insect larvae from another planet; seeing faces masked with sand, like mimes, after a night sandstorm engaged with their desert moisturizer; a passenger's preference for facing the big rapids wearing a nor'easter hat and swim mask—Ahab confronting Moby Dick; a woman going to the potty at night, placing her flashlight on the ground and unknowingly projecting her whole silhouette on a massive scale on the canyon wall behind, IMAX style, for the whole camp to see; the contrast of having to restrict personal belongings to a small waterproof bag despite the seemingly unlimited supply of beer and alcohol; watching the elders of the group, in their 70s, set the pace such that nobody younger dared complain; consoling many photographers at the demise of their equipment to water and sand; a cot perched at the river's edge for coolness, only to have the occupant awake, surrounded by rising waters; experiencing a big raft flex and whiplash so violently in a rapid that the motor sheared off and disappeared to the river bottom; decades-old logs perched a dozen feet up on giant river boulders, a testament to a pre-dam, wilder river; and the ever-present crafty ravens scanning the scene for an opportunity to burglarize our belongings and food.

Most visitors to the Grand Canyon see it from above, perched on the rim, where they experience primarily a series of finite, static views in contrast to extensive wilderness. As the Grand Canyon's creator, only the river itself can give us that. From above we are at a loss for scale. In the 1500s, the Canyon's first non-American discoverer, the Spaniard García López de Cárdenas, thought the river on first sighting to be tiny. We also tend to think of the Grand Canyon as being the same age as the Colorado River, six million years, yet geologically speaking it is 70 million years. In terms of human history, which is all we usually ask of ourselves, the Canyon is relatively unchanged in its course and depth—10 to 18 miles wide and more than a mile deep at the extremes.

A place so big, so long, so wide, and so very old defies understanding. We sense the power of earthly forces and water, but we cannot truly fathom the Canyon's meaning. There is, however, a culture of the Canyon that comes closest to grasping both its physical and spiritual layers: the cadre of river boatmen. To float the Colorado River through the Grand Canyon is to surrender oneself to their knowledge and formidable skill. In an age of specialization,

California condor

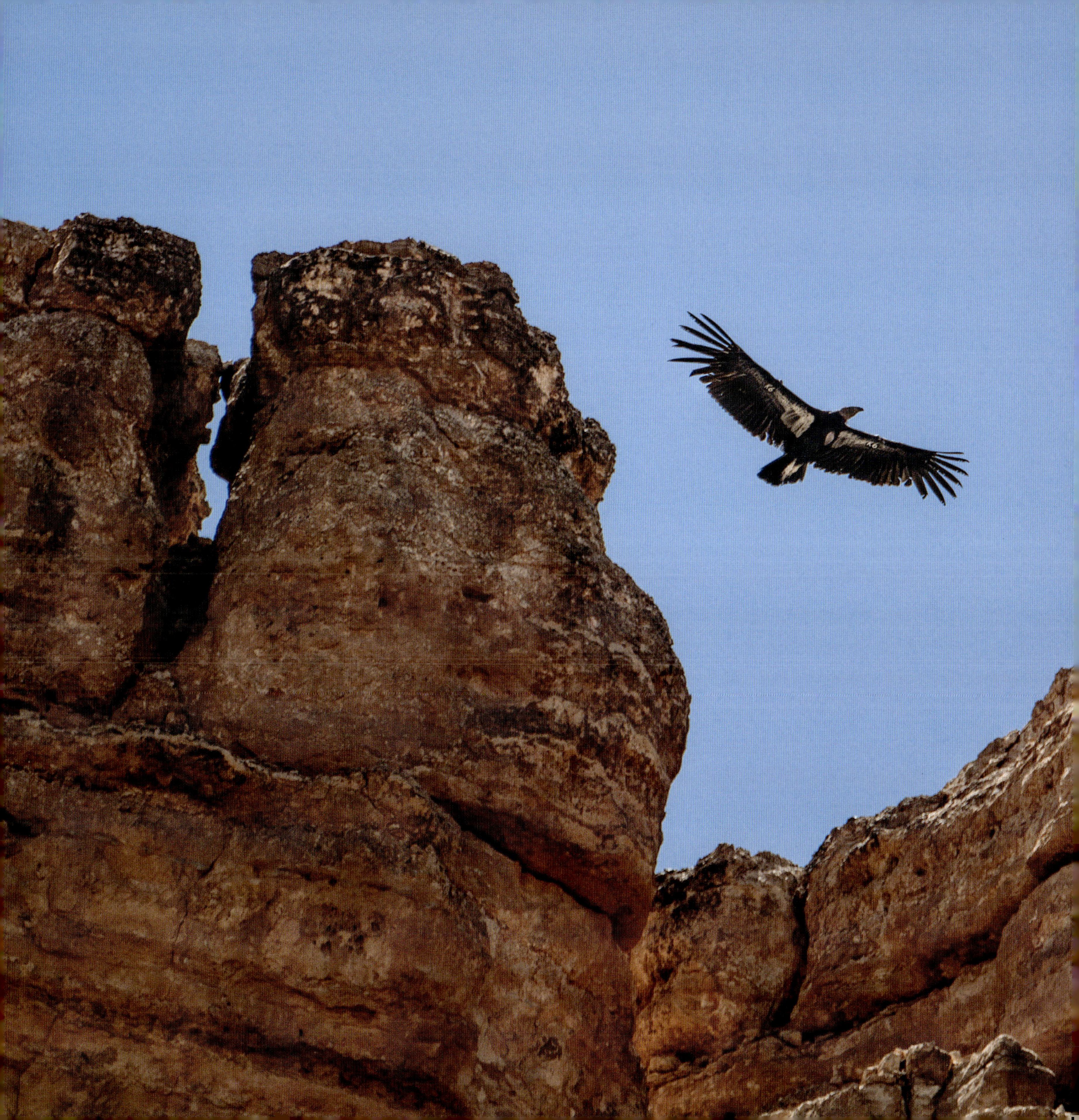

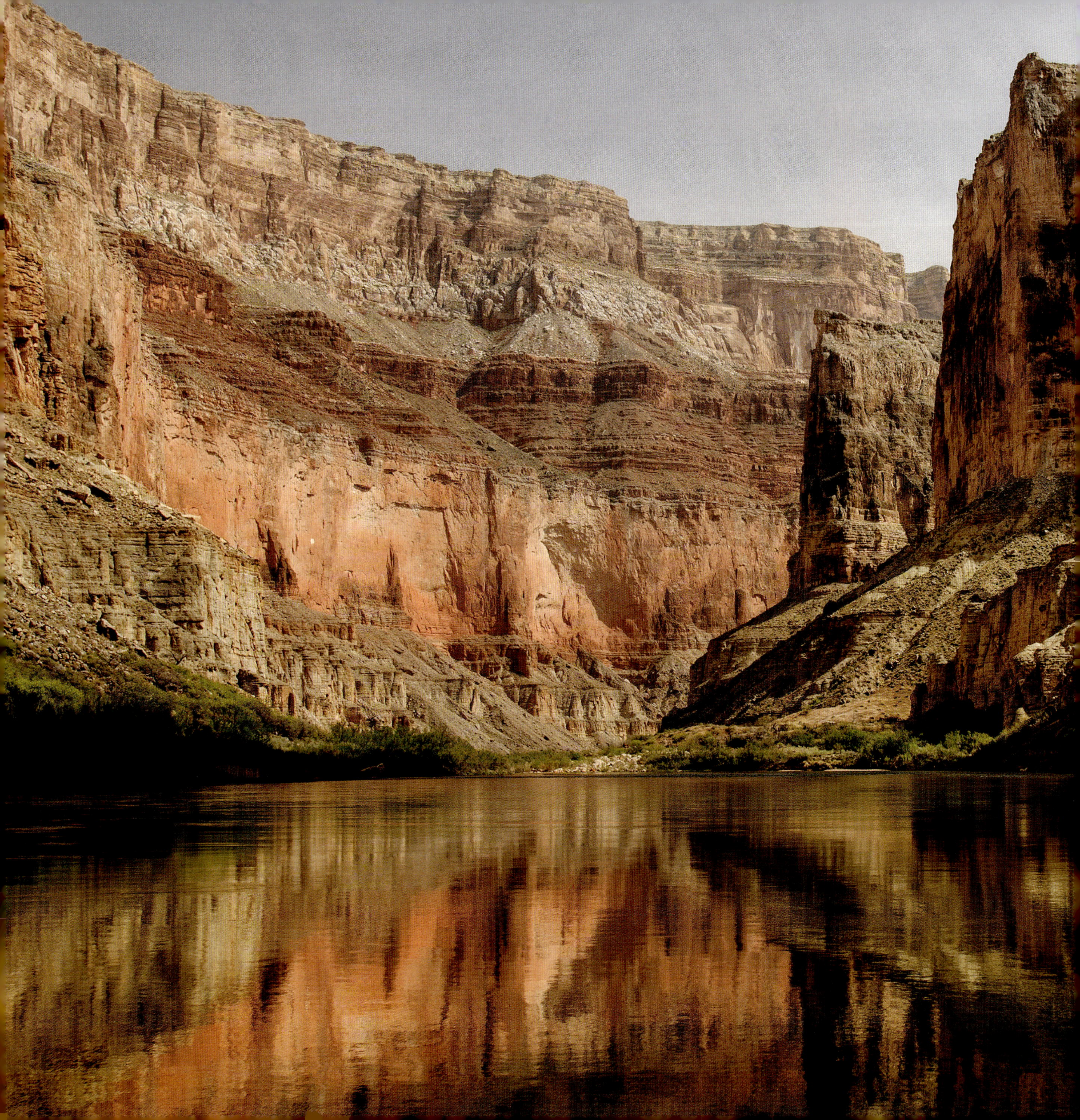

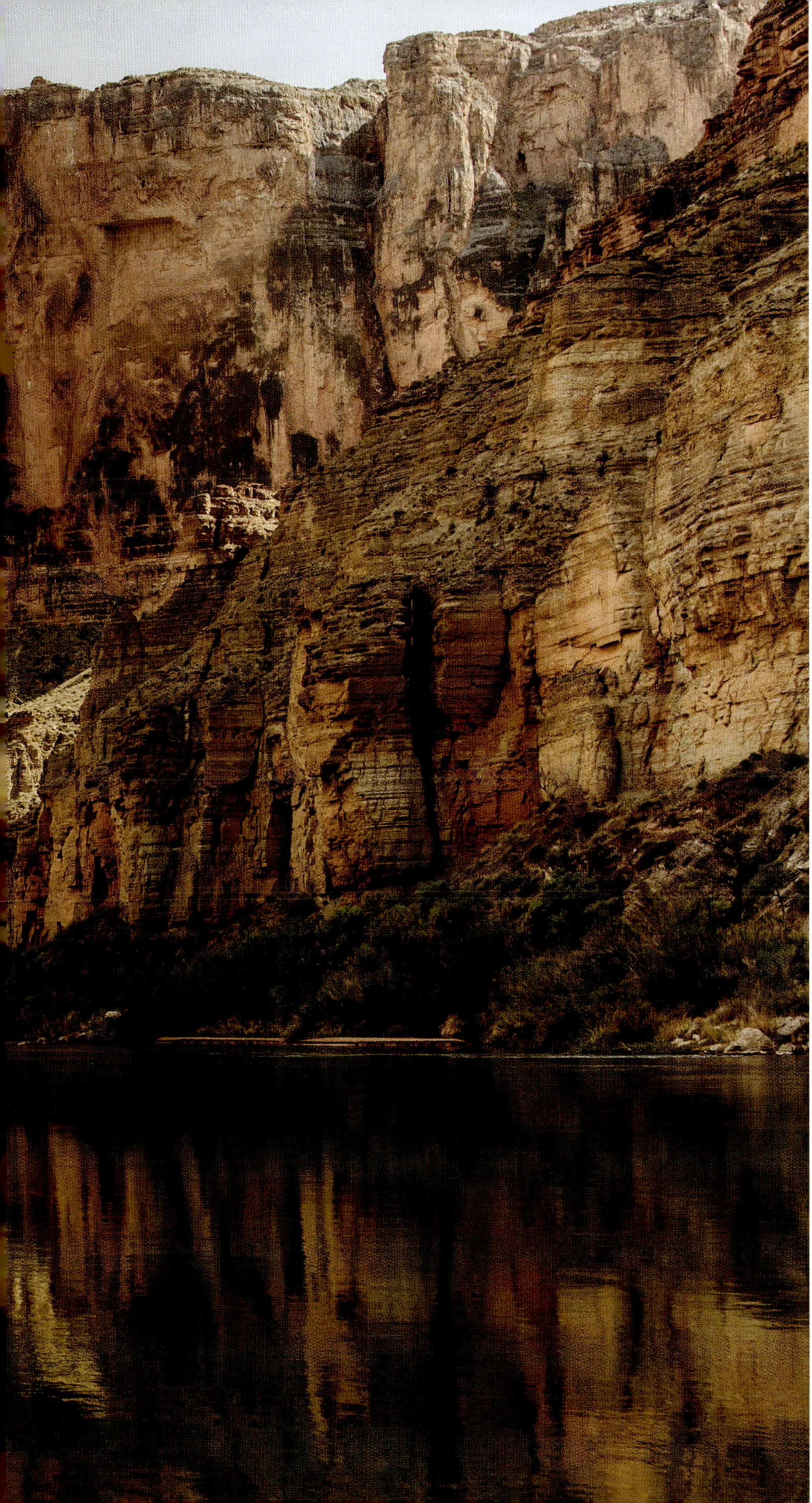

View downriver just above mile 50

all the boatmen I've known are highly trained generalists who can not only command an oar boat or motor raft through life-threatening rapids, but also render discourses on geology, history, archaeology, conservation, and nature, often with a dash of philosophy or irreverent humor . . . or both! These boatmen, many of whom are multigenerational professionals, are veterans of the river. They embody and exude an informed sense of place.

As if all this weren't exceptional enough, I remain in awe of their social skills as they orchestrate a disparate group of strangers into a bonded team eager for the next minute, hour, and day. They can fix an engine in the middle of a rapid, cook a complicated meal on a sand beach, treat most wounds, and even serenade us with a song on guitar. Their lives are full and passionate, and we willingly absorb every contagious ounce of it. After a lifetime of adventure, I can say there are few folks I respect more than boatmen, and "boatmen" definitely includes both genders. I've seen some come up through the ranks as "swampers" (assistant boatmen) and be mentored by the veterans in a relationship of trust and hard work. Now I have the honor of rafting the river with them at the helm of their own boats. They are a tight community unto themselves, the brother and sisterhood of the traveling river, the "church of the flowing water." They reveal a whole new world to us. The river is part of their psyche; it defines who they are and where they belong, their sanctuary, sometimes to the extent that the outside world brings even greater adjustments and challenges.

At times I feel reasonably self-satisfied at having completed more than a dozen photographic trips down the Grand Canyon, only to be instantly humbled when I realize that a veteran boatman might do 10 to 12 trips in a season. That's a minimum of 2,770 miles of the Colorado River in a single year! And some have been doing it for 30 years. Do the math; that's a lot of canyon. You've got to love it and love sharing it!

In contrast to the depth of a boatman's knowledge of the Canyon is the ignorance of John Wesley Powell, who

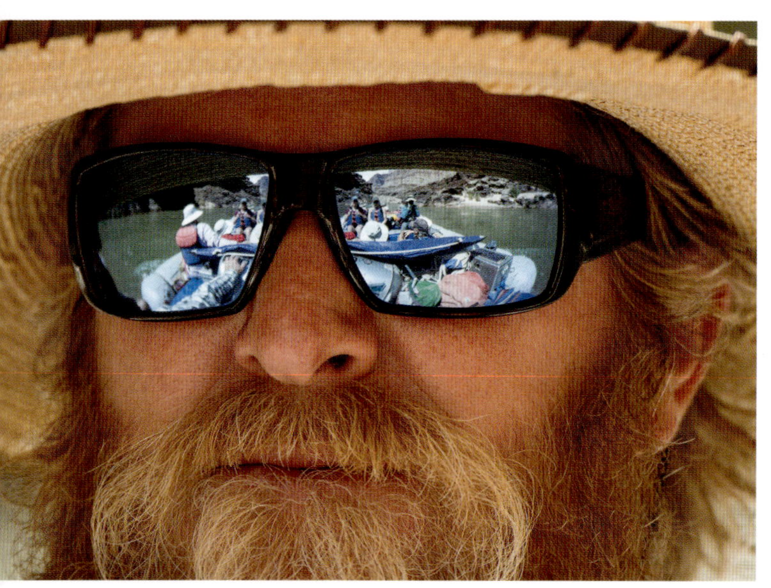

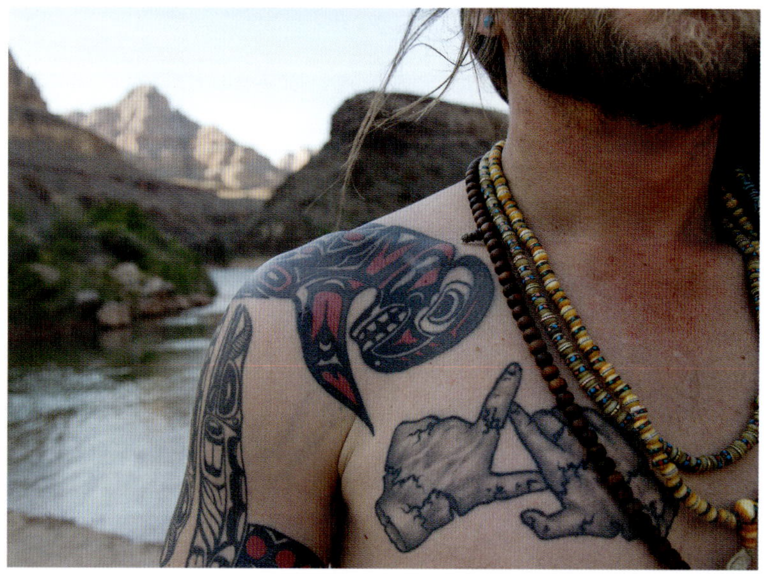

▲ River boatmen Duffy Dale (left) and Jared "Beav" Weaver (right) ▶ Raft plunging into the rapids

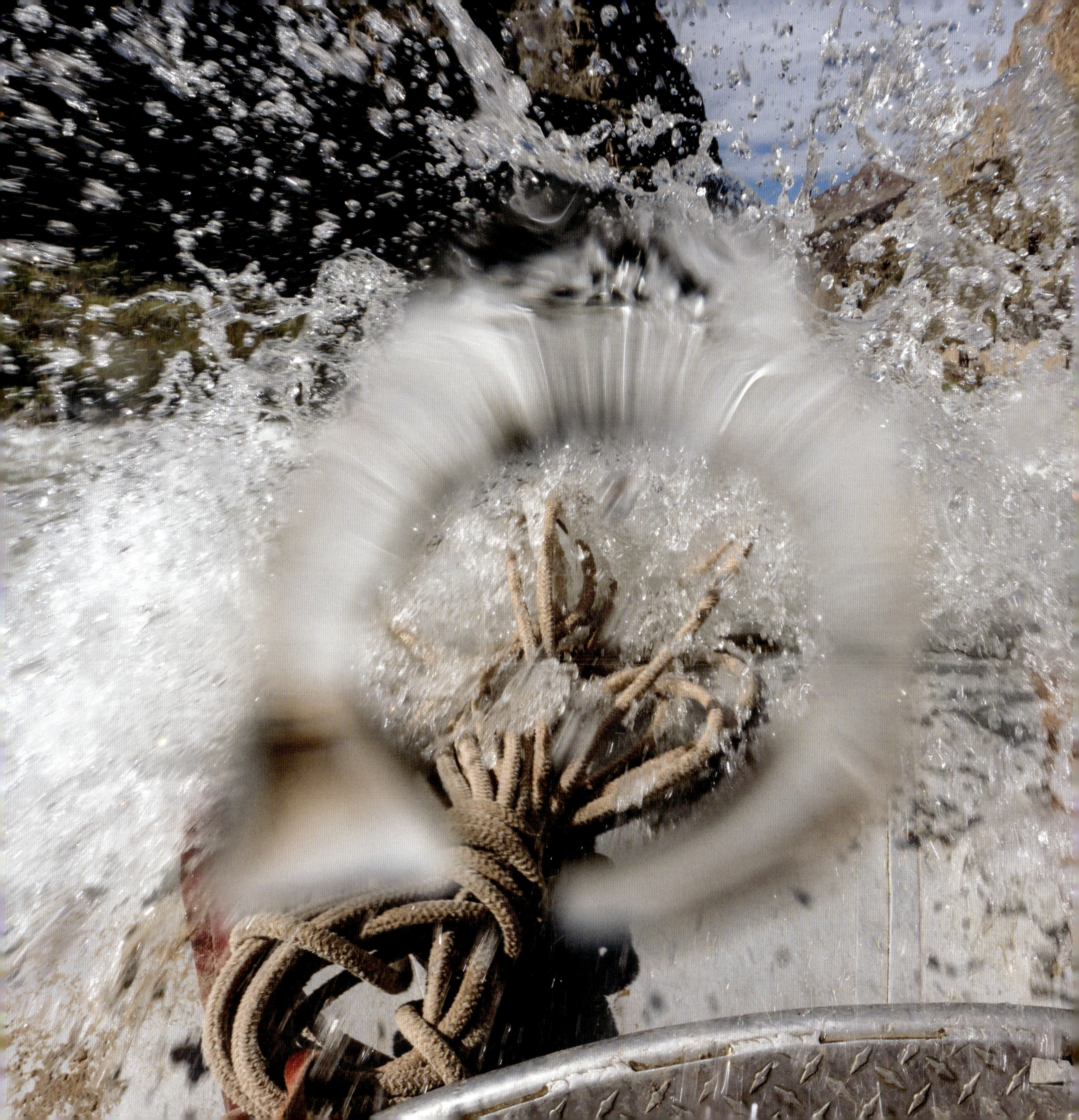

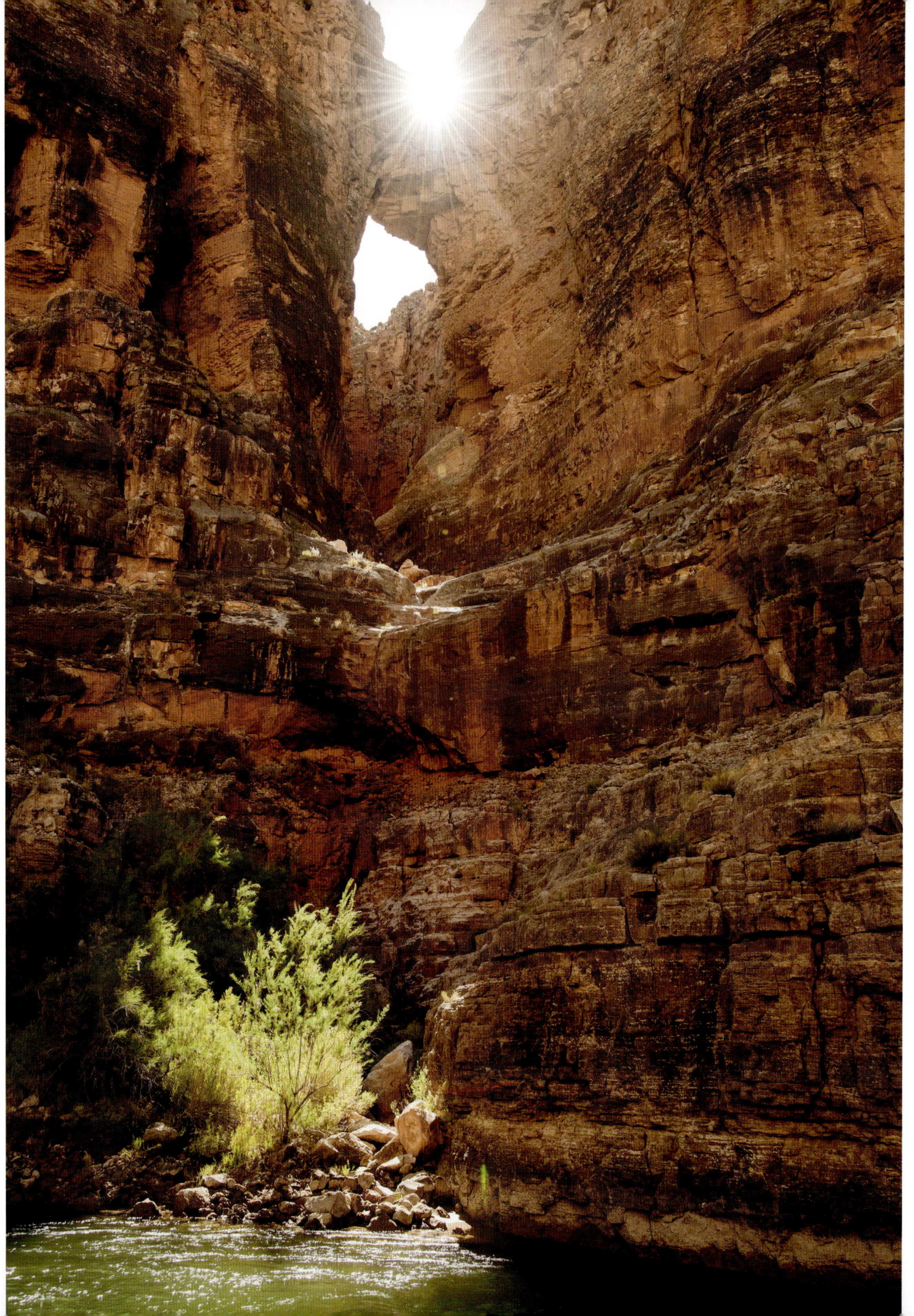

in 1869 made the first descent down the Grand Canyon. He went as an explorer-scientist to study the Canyon, the West's last huge blank on the map. Powell knew almost nothing of the river: the number of rapids, their intimidating size, nor the extreme length of the Canyon. His crew had no experience on a major river, and their boats were ill designed for rapids and quick maneuvering. He literally did not know what was around the next corner. Ten men started the trip on the Green River; three months and 1,000 miles later, six exited the Grand Canyon, emaciated but having survived one of the greatest wilderness discoveries in the history of America. In a combination of extraordinary leadership, determined will, and a heavy dose of optimism and good luck, Powell, despite having only one arm and small stature, pulled off a monumental feat of exploration. He measurably impacted our national spirit and pride in documenting the last great mystery of the American West. Powell was considered a visionary, as much for his romantic sensibilities as for his science. In his determination to measure and map the Grand Canyon, he also poetically described its grandeur and was deeply moved by its many moods and scenery. Trusting the government over the private sector in managing the country's resources, Powell prophetically declared water and the river as a precious commodity and predicted the challenge of rationing its use wisely. In advocating and fighting for this cause in Washington, DC, Powell became one of America's earliest conservationists.

Perhaps the most compelling contrast, arguably contradiction, of the Canyon lies within its perception as an iconic wilderness. In reality, the Grand Canyon is one of the most transformed and managed "wildernesses" in the country. What feels wild is anything but. Every drop of river water is controlled in the Canyon. It all started primarily with the damming of the Colorado River, first in 1936 at the bottom end with the Hoover Dam and then in 1963 at the top end with the Glen Canyon Dam, which flooded a canyon as beautiful and striking as the Grand itself. The Colorado River within the Grand Canyon became the equivalent of a hobbled racehorse. A river running unimpeded and free was now in a vise grip, with its waters allocated by the power and irrigation needs of seven states that service some 36 million people in several cities, including Las Vegas, Los Angeles, San Diego, Salt Lake City, Denver, Boulder, Phoenix, Tucson, and Albuquerque. The Glen Canyon Dam created one of the largest reservoirs in the country and set the stage for Grand Canyon National Park to be subjected to the policies of a stew of federal agencies, including the Bureau of Reclamation, Department of the Interior, Department of Energy, Environmental Protection Agency, Department of Agriculture, Bureau of Indian Affairs, and, finally, the National Park Service. There are probably others I left out.

The Glen Canyon Dam has been and is still altering the ecology of the Grand Canyon. The formerly wildly fluctuating waters from spring snowmelts and heavy rainstorms are now relegated to controlled dam releases of moderate levels. The naturally warm waters of summer are replaced by waters hundreds of feet below the surface of the dam at temperatures of 48 to 52 degrees. This has radically affected the native aquatic species, as has the lack of the pre-dam flooding on the native plant species and the distribution of sand and silt. It's a whole new game where more than 150 invasive plants, such as tamarisk and Russian olive, are colonizing the Canyon, and introduced trout are outcompeting the indigenous warm-water species. If you add climate change and increasing droughts to the equation, park managers are faced with the daunting challenge of having to work with the "new now" versus trying to resurrect the "that was then."

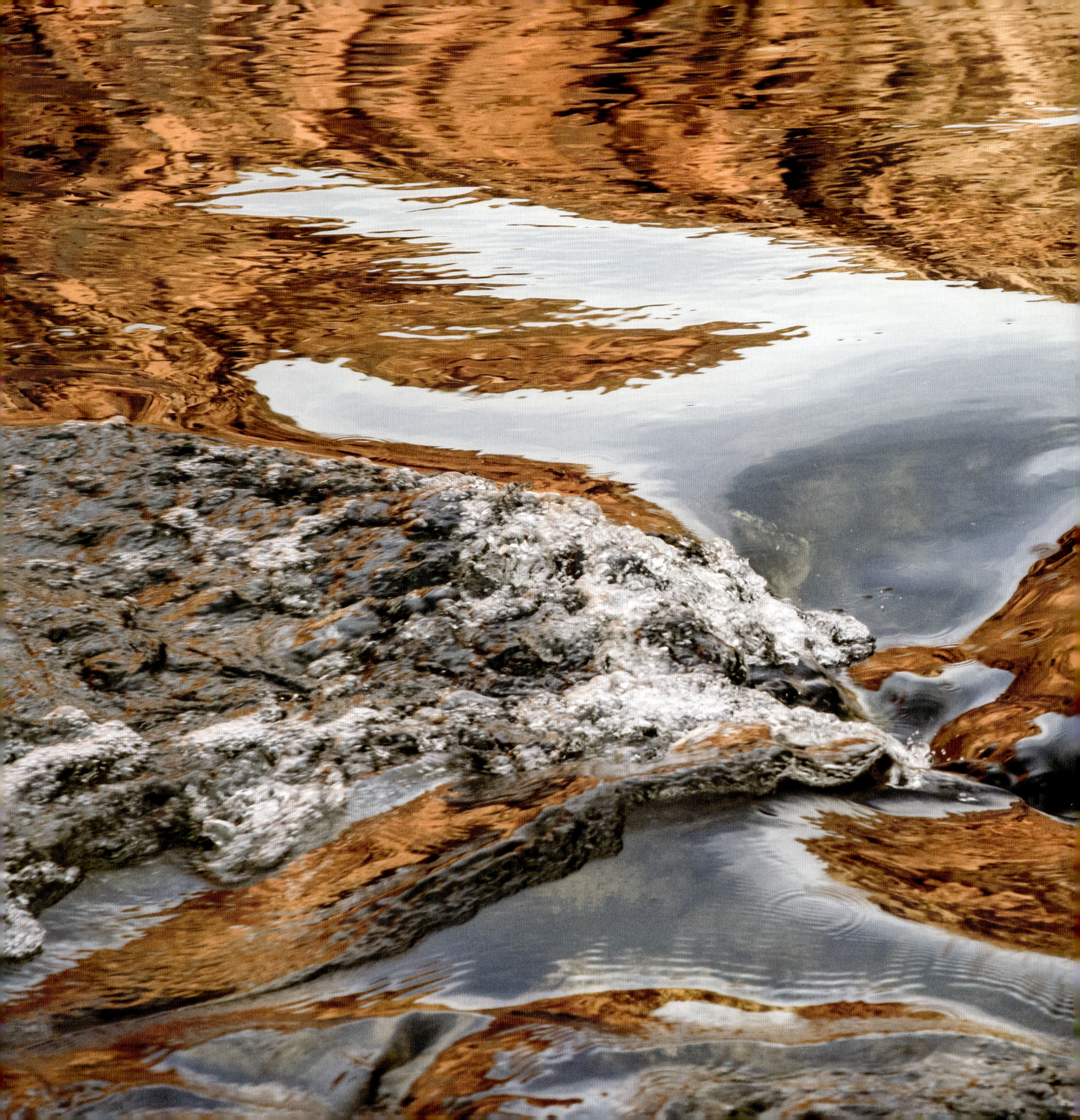

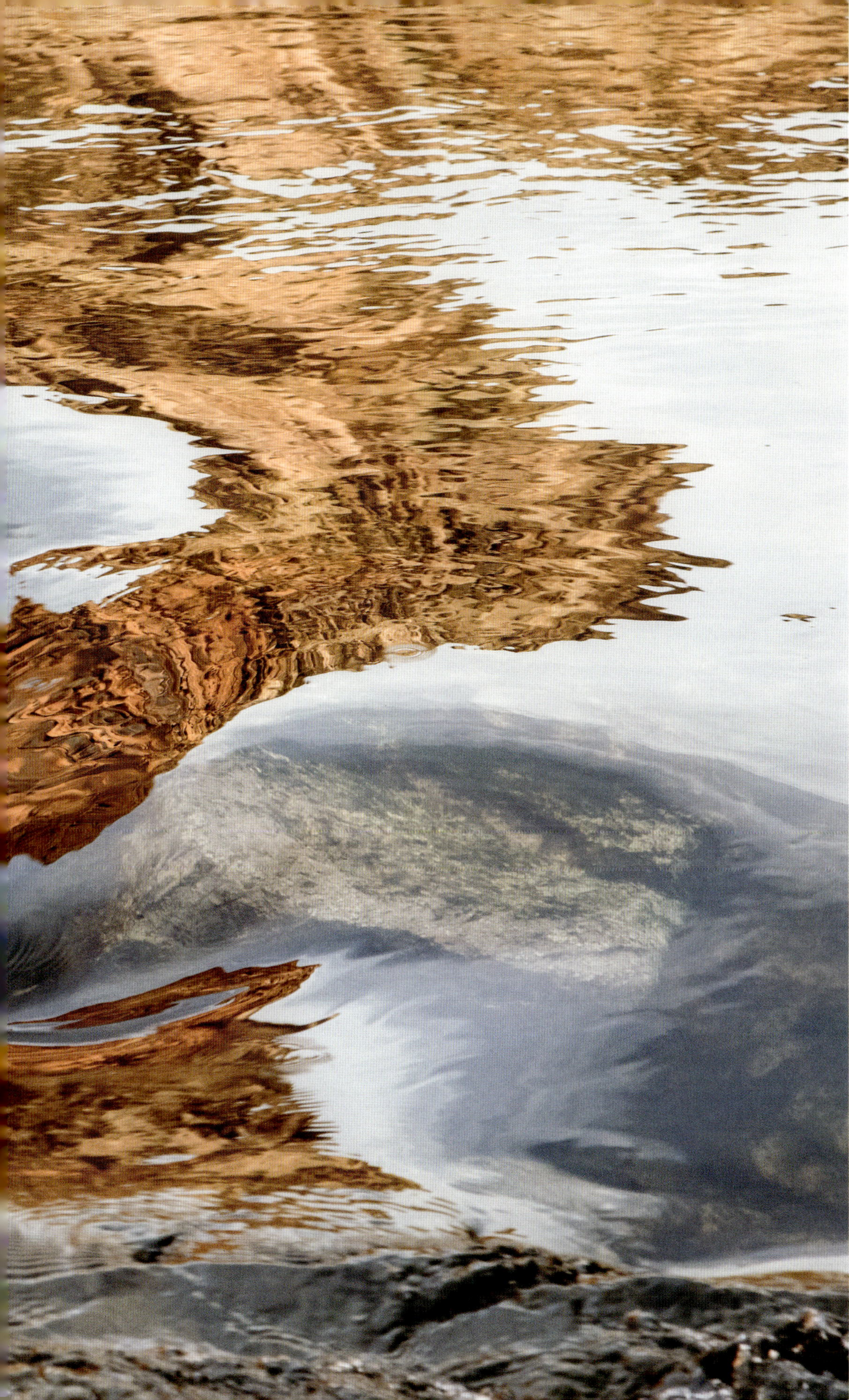

Rapid and reflections

The dams are just part of the problem. The Grand Canyon and Colorado River are under assault from a number of threats. Just outside its borders the park has uranium mines on both rims, several of which are active, with more than 800 others under claim. One of those, the Canyon Mine, is near Grand Canyon Village on the South Rim. These mines have the potential of contaminating the water, both in tributaries and subsurface springs, some of which are already unfit to drink. Past history has revealed that wherever there was money to be had, attempts were made to exploit the Grand Canyon: selling bat guano from caves, building a proposed railroad through the Canyon, and mining everything from copper and zinc to asbestos.

Today, with six million visitors per year, the development pressure outside the park has only increased. One of the most shocking proposals is to build a tramway from the rim down to the Little Colorado River that would allow up to 10,000 visitors a day to experience the depths of the Canyon without setting foot on a trail or in a boat. The visitors would be serviced by a megaresort at the top, and a restaurant, gift shop, and amphitheater at the bottom. Fortunately, the Navajo Nation, on whose land this would occur, considers the Little Colorado a sacred site and has stopped the development for the time being. In a similar vein, the park is threatened just two miles from the South Rim entrance by Tusayan—another huge resort development that would include thousands of homes, hotels, and commercial businesses. If enacted, the big question is, where will all the water come from to supply these developments? The only apparent options are the aquifer or the Colorado River, which are already being siphoned off at a heavy rate. Increased water use plus contamination threaten the Grand Canyon's delicate springs, crucial oases in the health and diversity of the ecosystem. Powell would be rolling in his grave.

JOURNEYING BY BOAT through the Grand Canyon is the only reasonable way to experience its entire length. More than that, we become immersed in a profound experience where we are enveloped by and within nature. We see earth not only for its monumentality, but also its complexity. Traveling one of the longest canyons in the world dislocates our sense of time and distance. Millions of visitors see the Canyon from the rim, yet only 20,000 per year have the privilege of connecting with the river within. The Colorado's average gradient of eight feet per mile makes it steeper than any US river outside Alaska. The rapids are so big that it even has its own rating system, because that of other rivers is inadequate.

Basically, everything about the Grand Canyon is off the charts. As a photographer, I'm deeply inspired yet always aware that any resulting imagery woefully fails to depict the true Canyon. The fact that a place so big and powerful is so little understood adds to its mystique and wonderment. How could these towering spires and buttes once have been at the bottom of the sea? Like many of the greatest things on earth—be they music, art, or architecture—the Grand Canyon defies explanation but provides an intrinsically rich, profound, and potentially transcendent experience. Contrasting with an official report in 1858 that described the Canyon as "altogether valueless," its depth of 6,000 feet from rim to river encompasses five of our seven life zones, the most of any US national park.

We might add a personal life zone for what we discover and take away within ourselves. The Grand Canyon and its river make us glad to be and feel alive. As an intricate world apart, it expands our inner world with humility and reverence. But the Canyon just is, just there, and as we open to its embrace, we must do so knowing that this sacred cathedral of rock and ages has become a house of cards. We float the river at its mercy, but its fate is up to us.

Night view from camp at Pancho's Kitchen

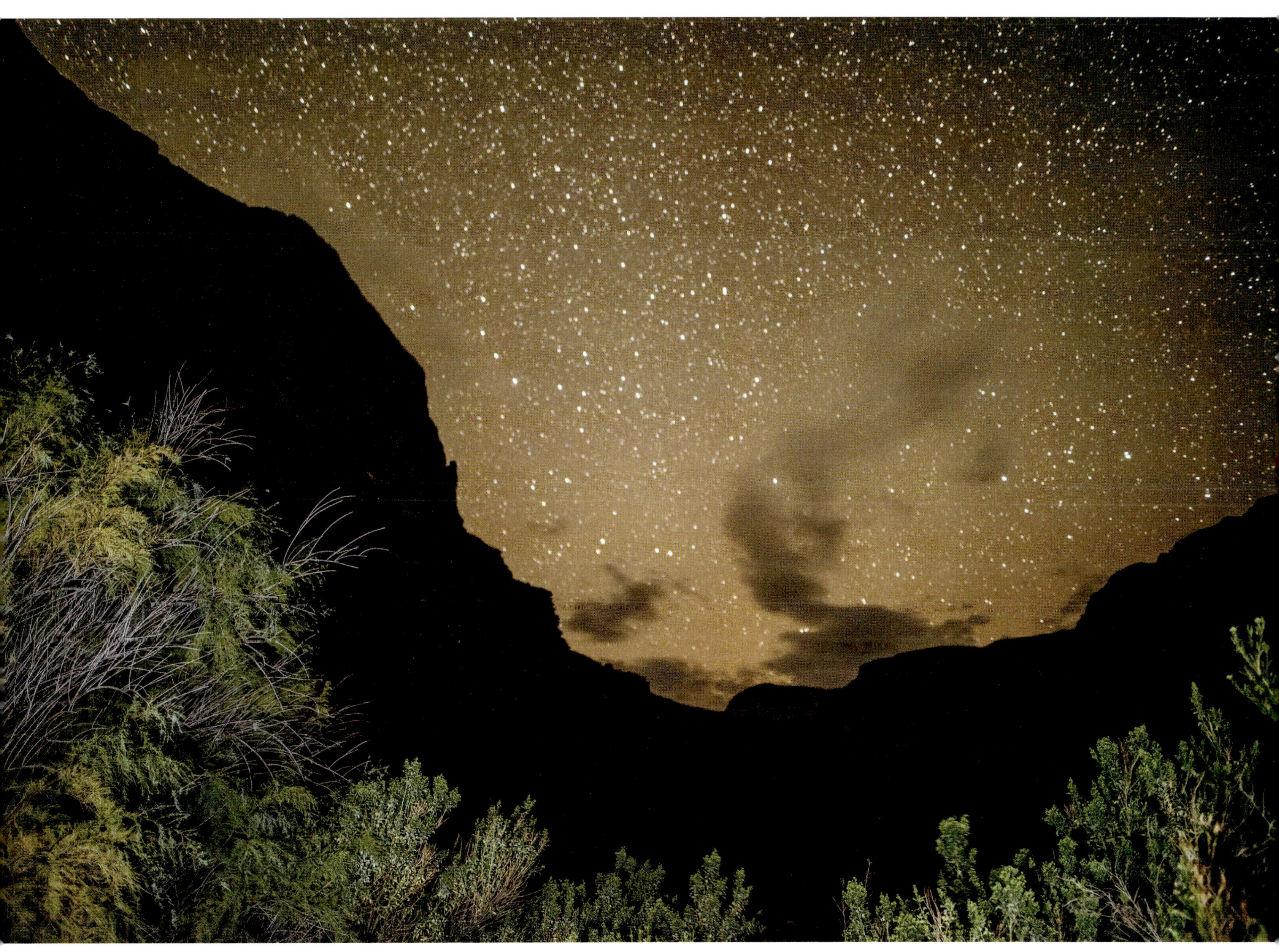

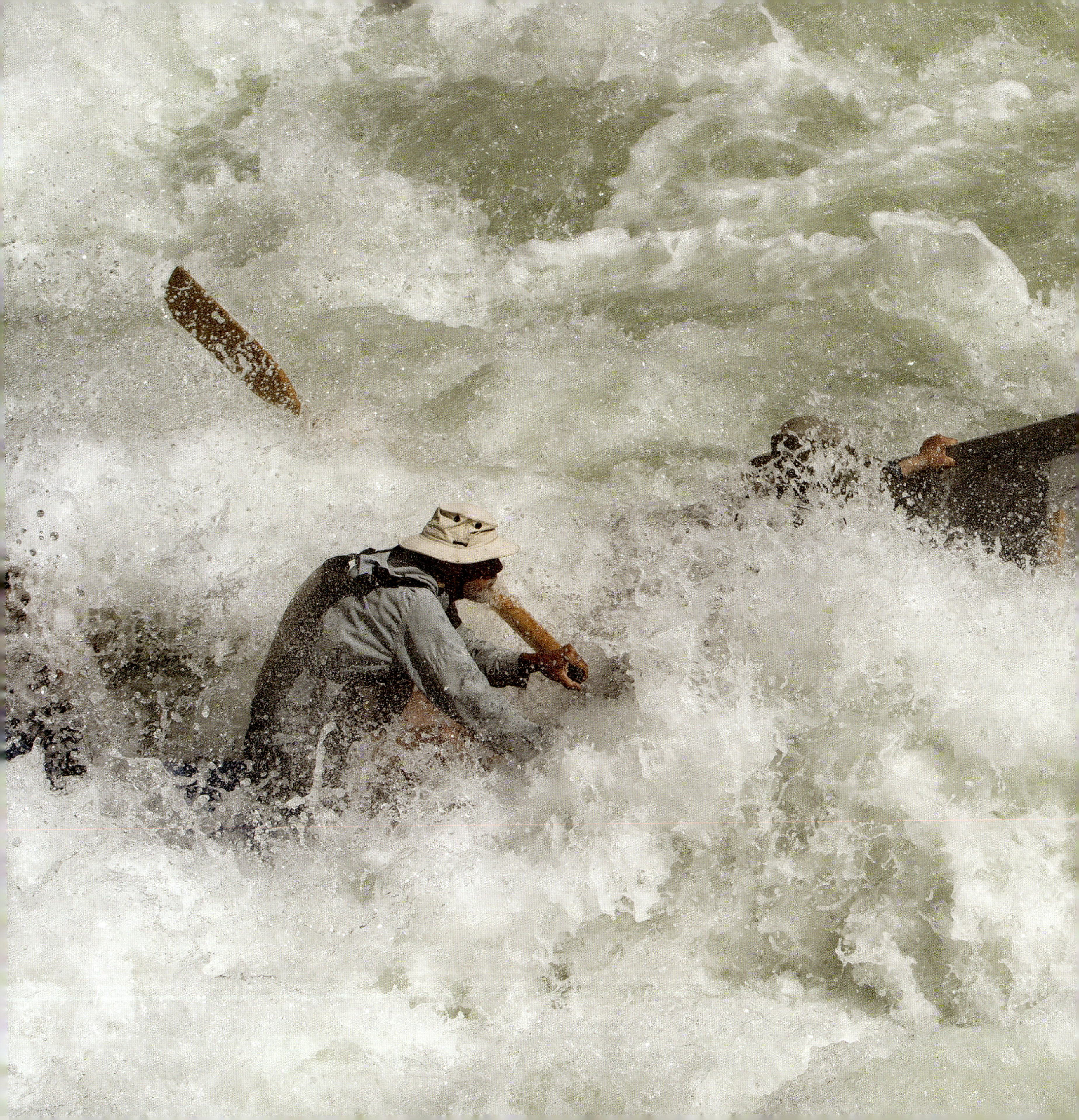

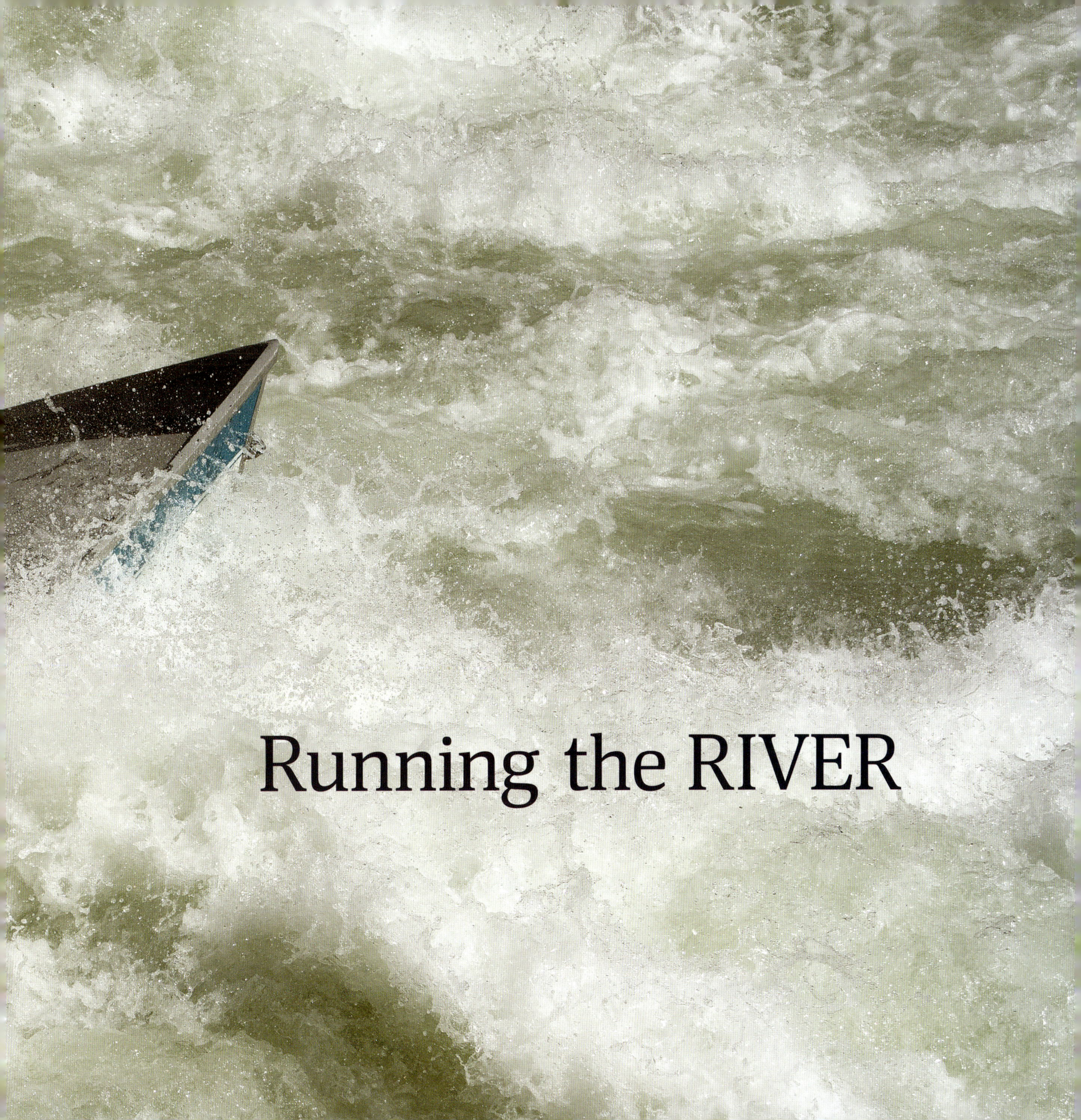

Running the RIVER

▲ Dory navigating Lava Falls Rapid

▶ 13 Mile Rapid

▼ Great blue heron (left) and prince's-plume (right)

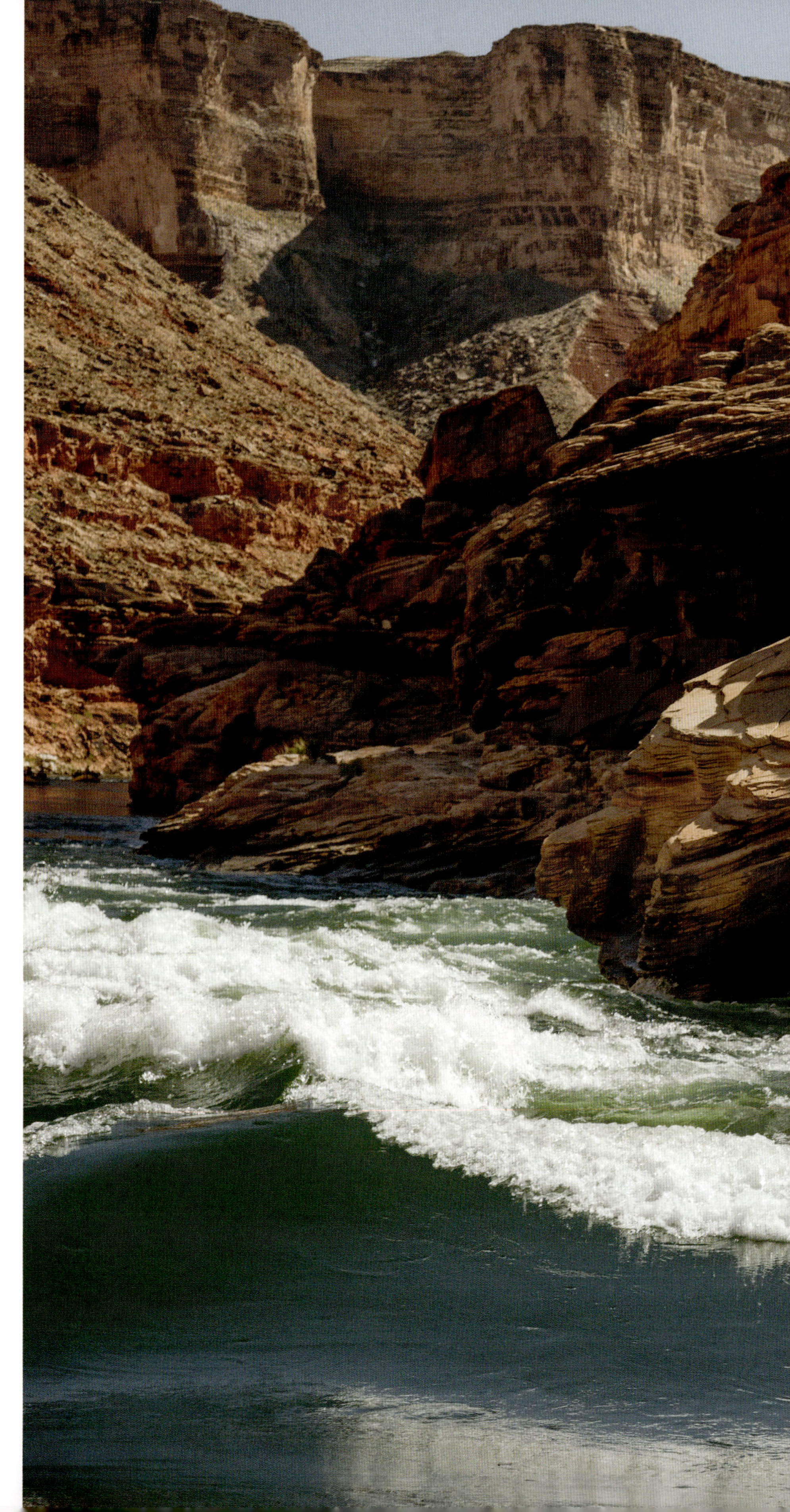

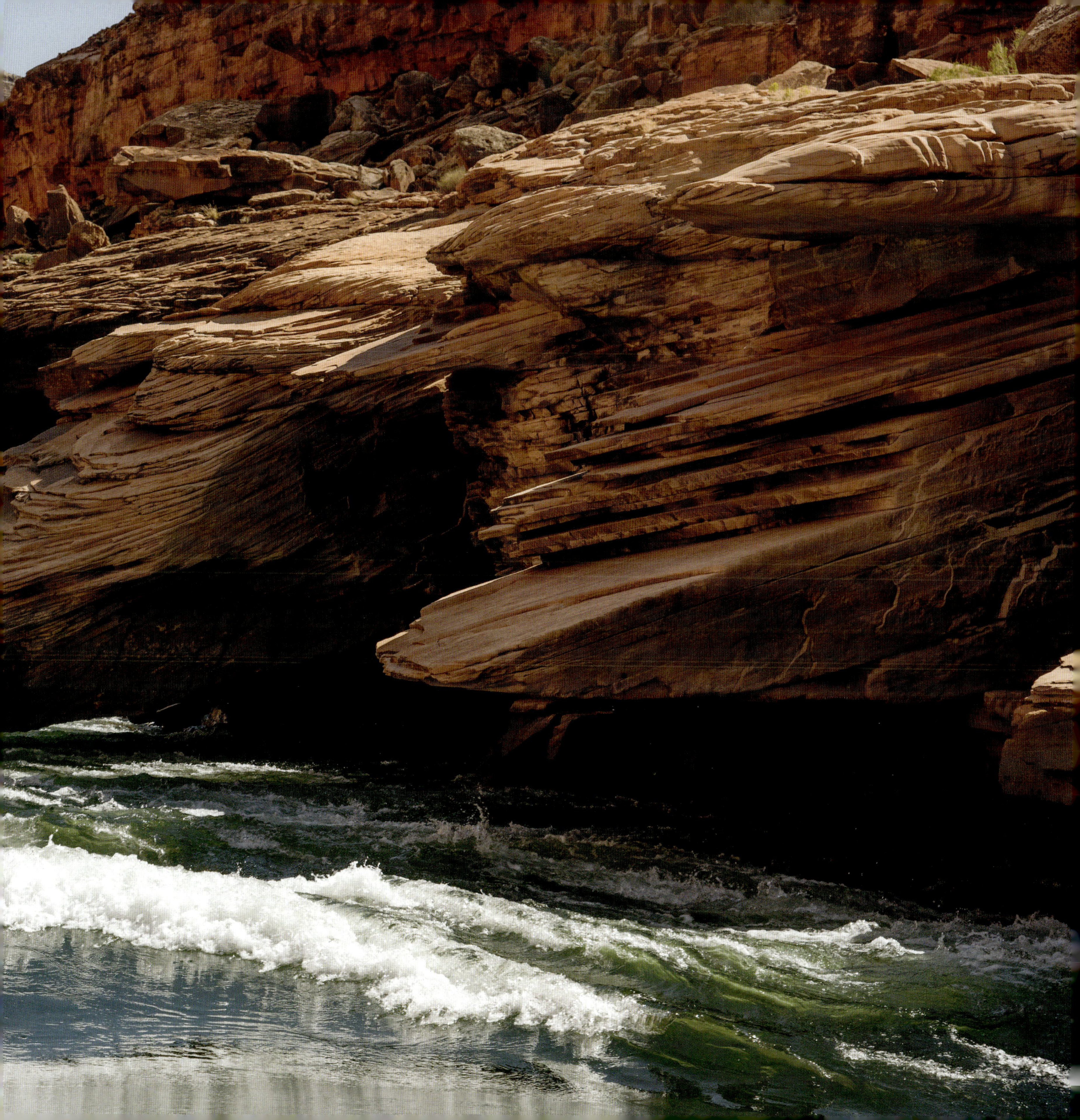

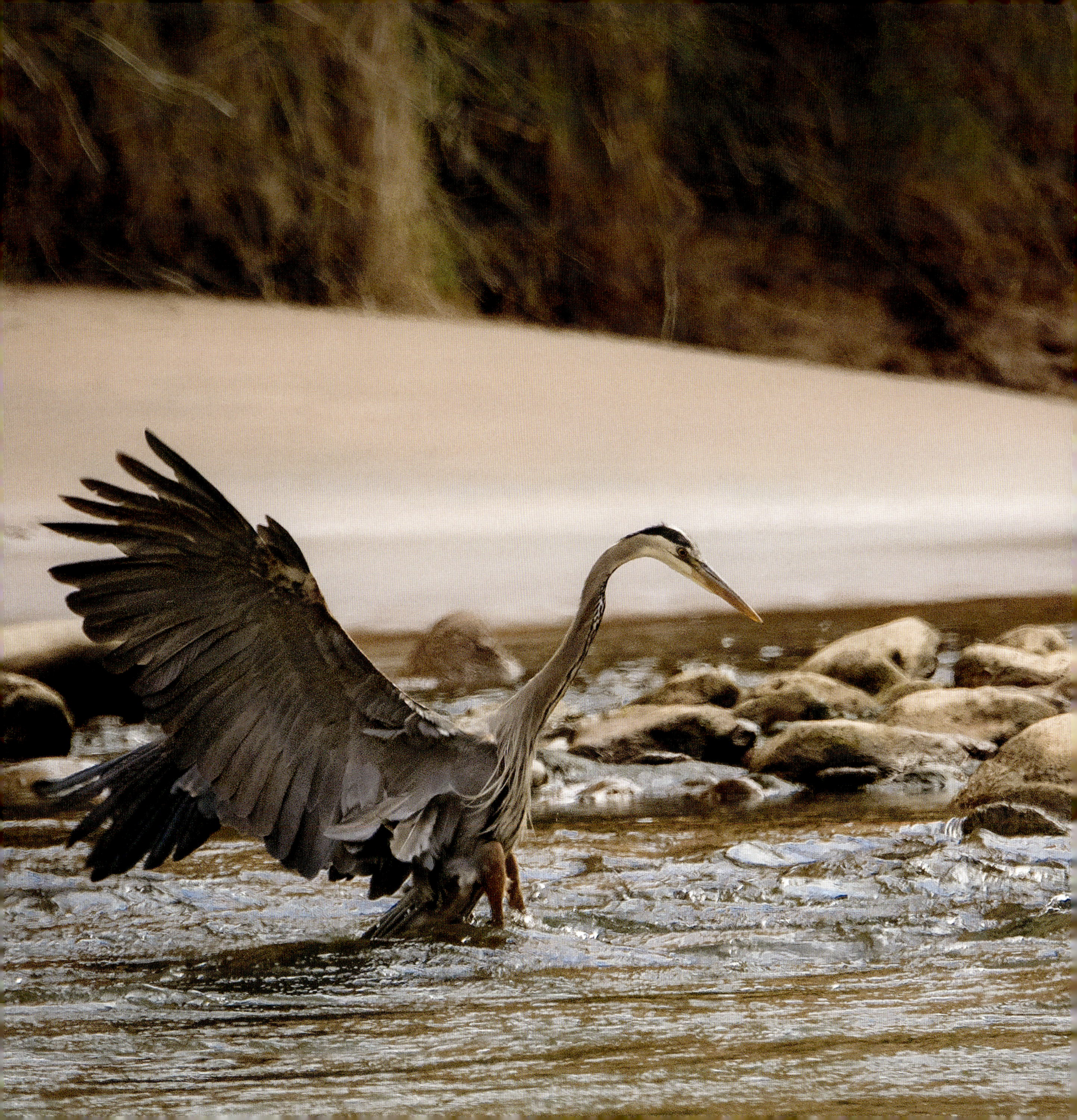

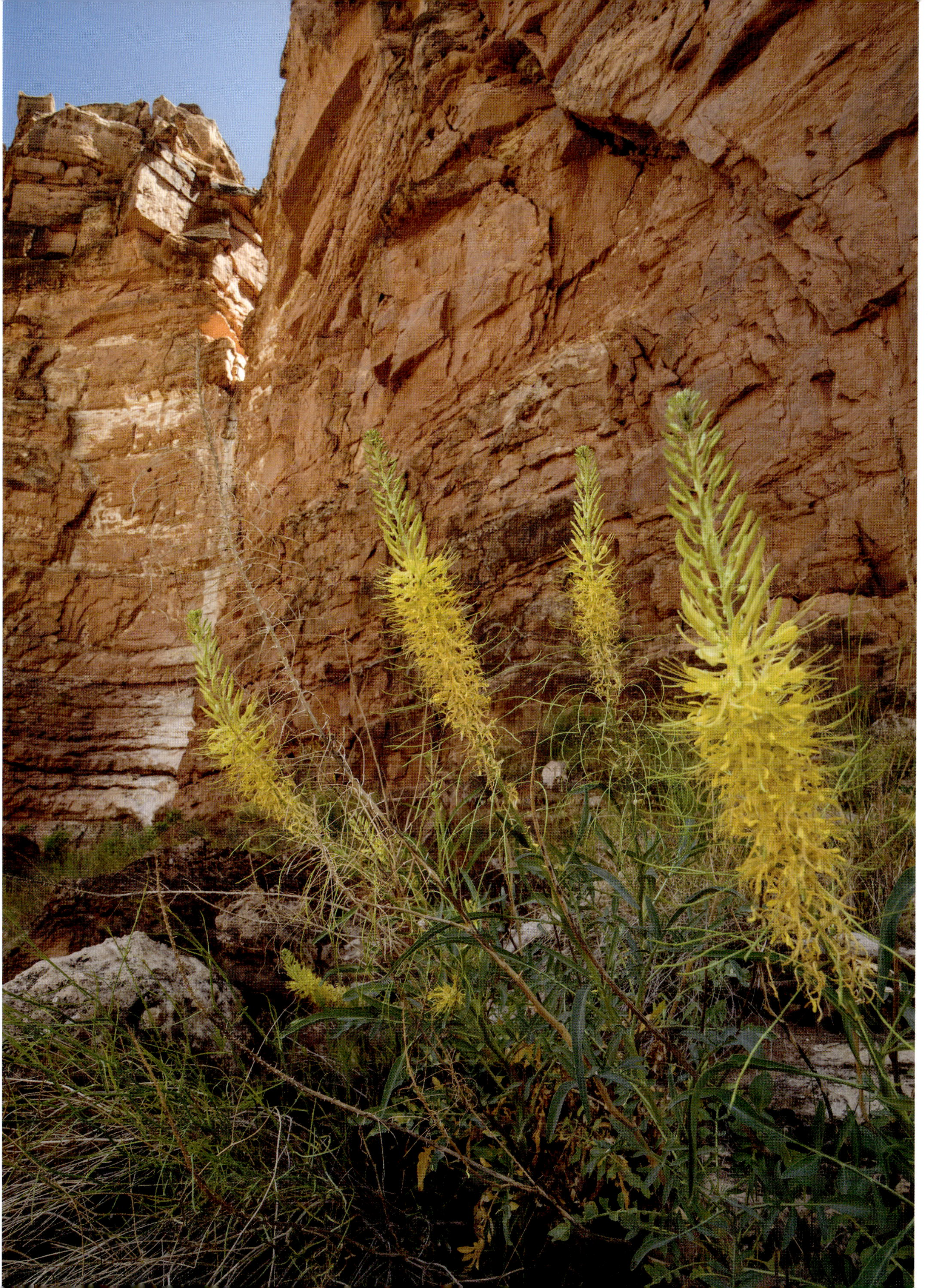

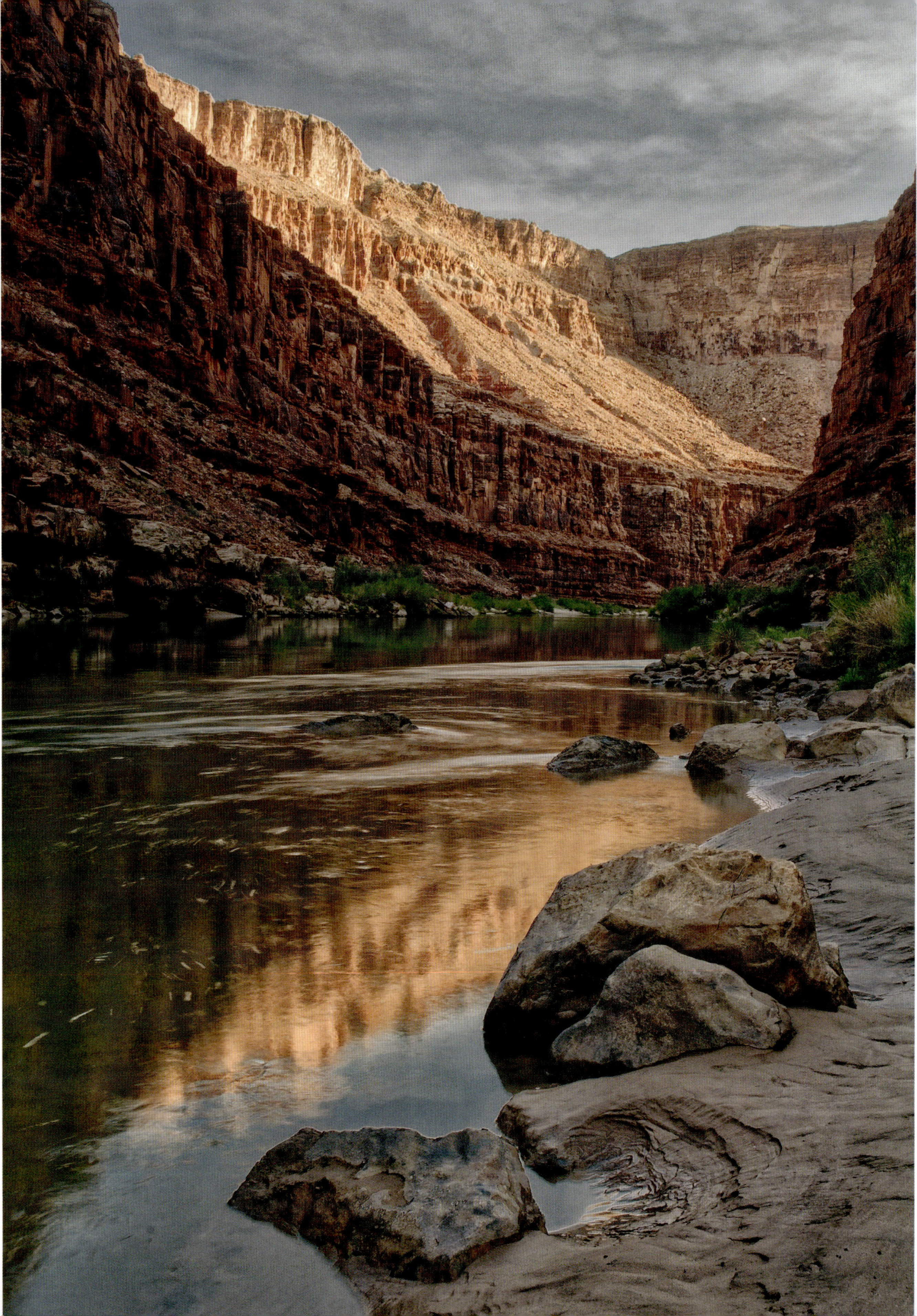

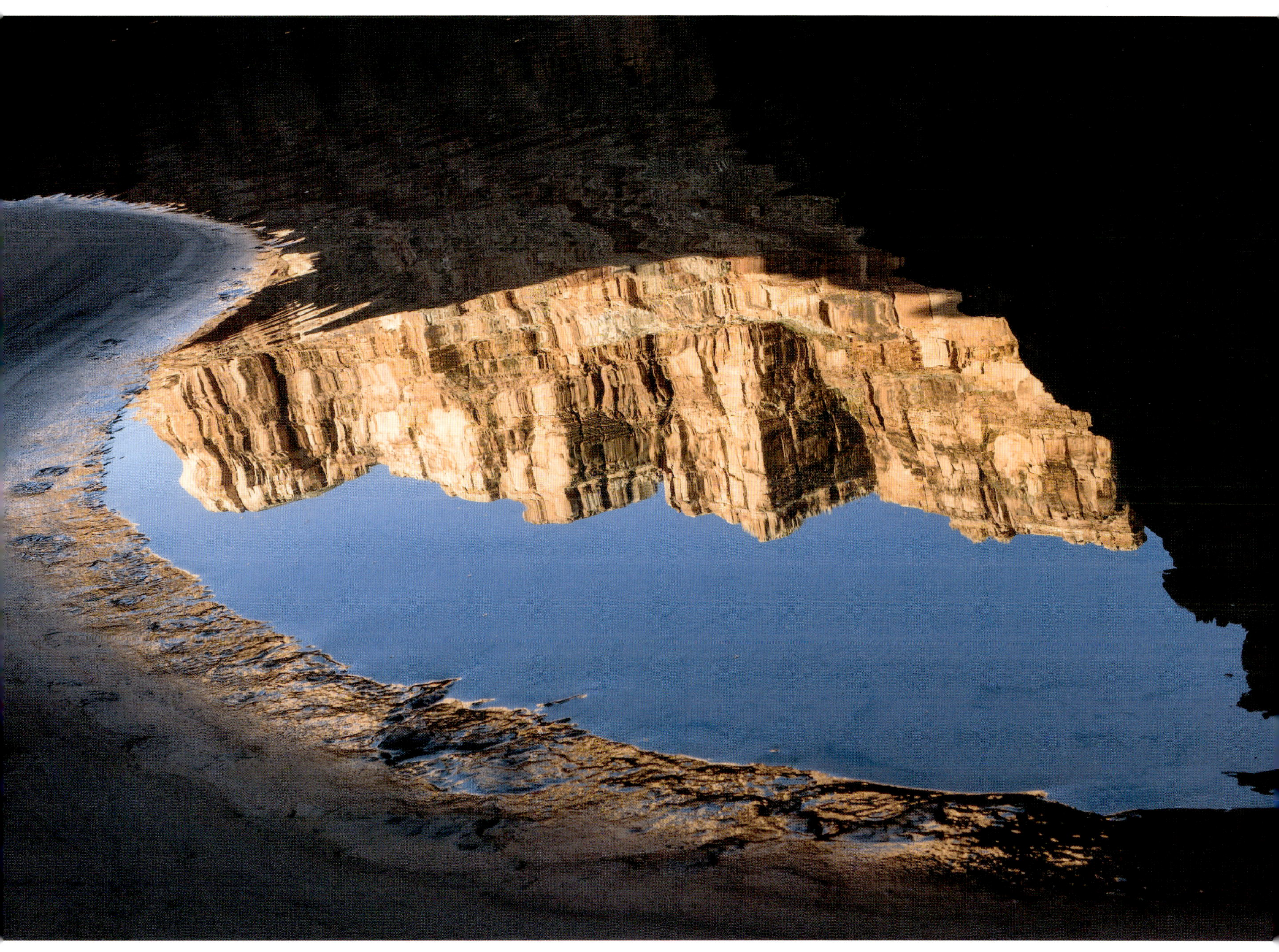

◀ View upriver from 19.5 Mile Camp ▲ River's edge and reflections, 19.5 Mile Camp

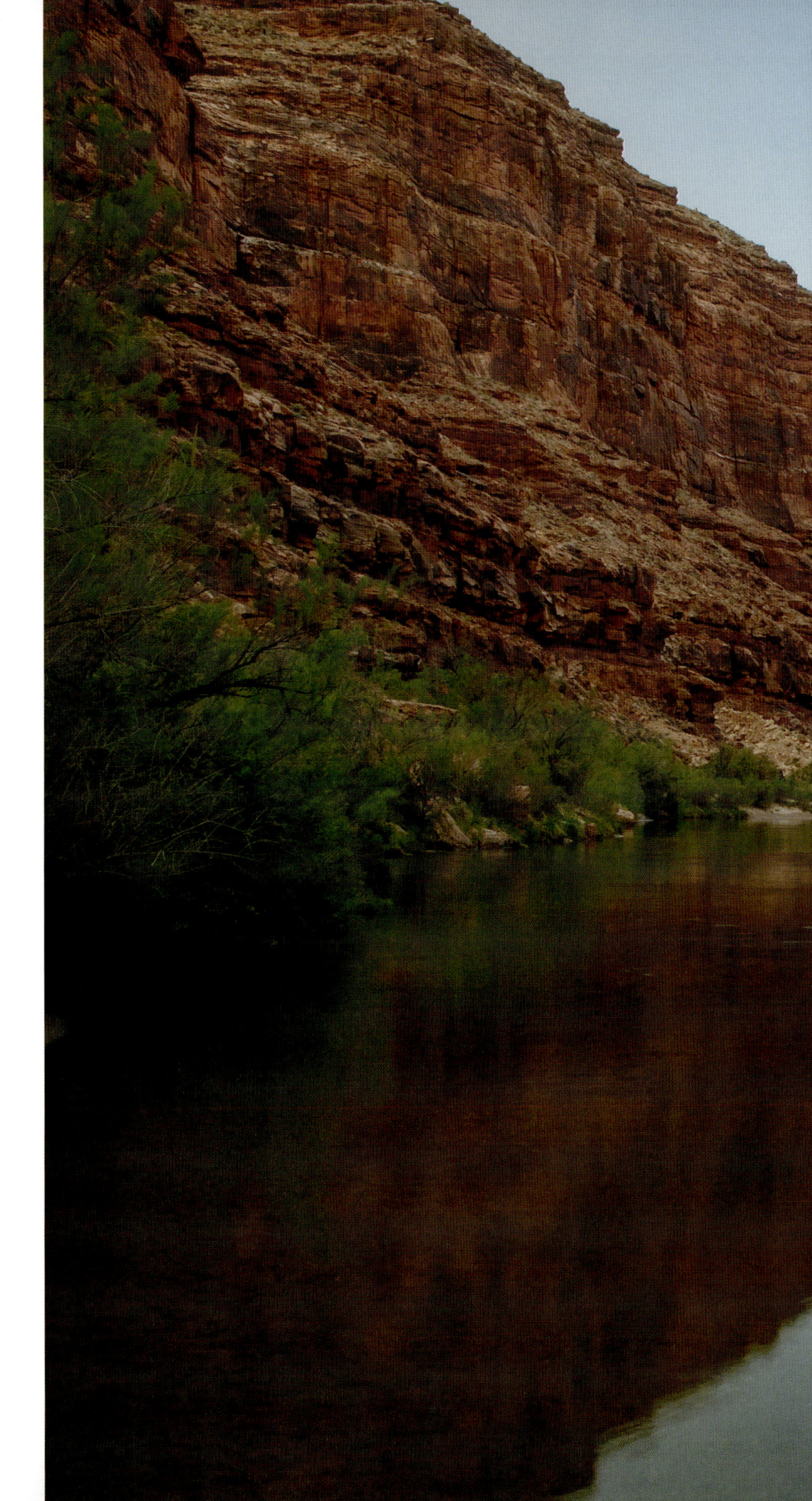

Early morning view downriver
with moon from 19.5 Mile Camp

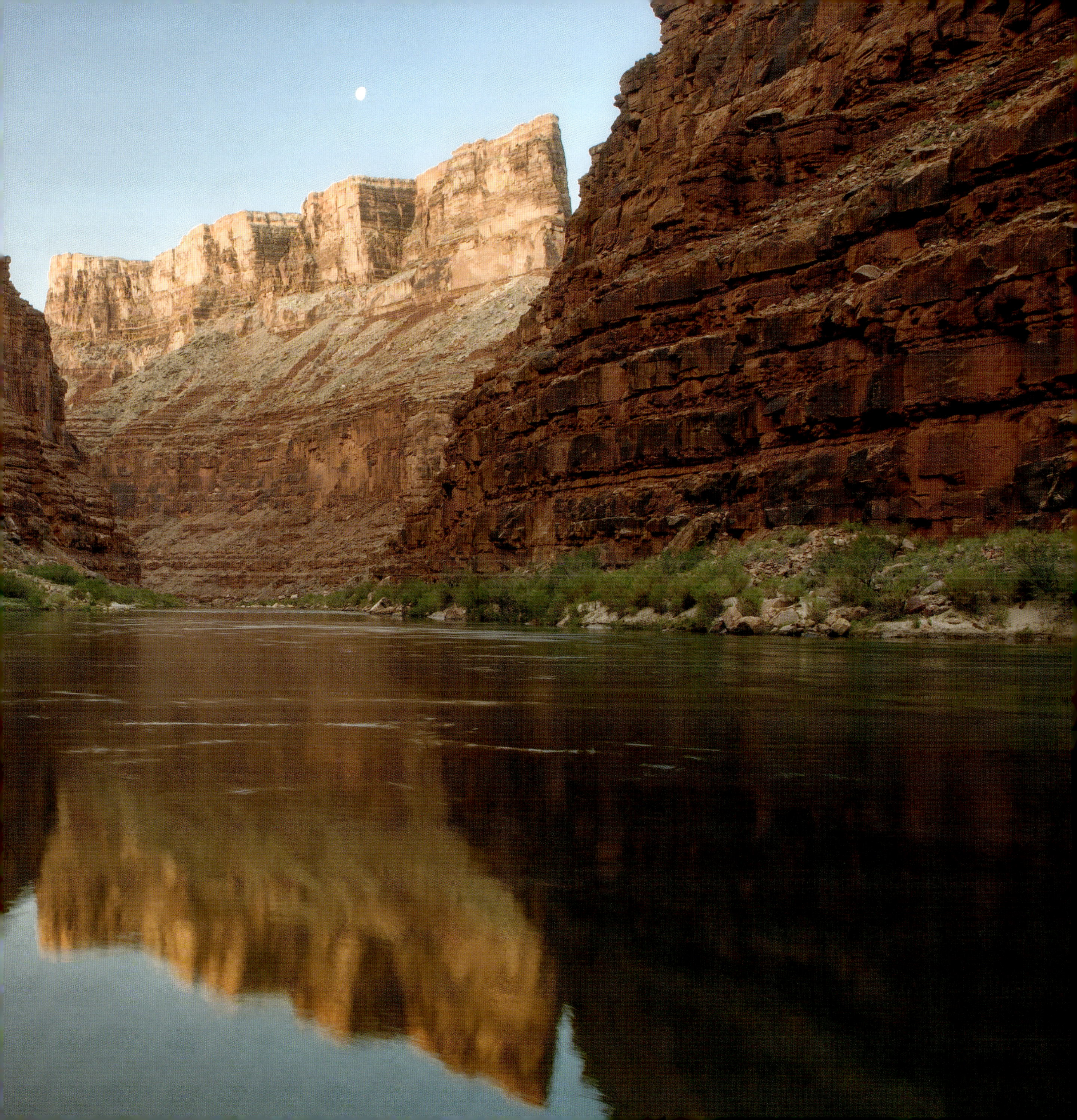

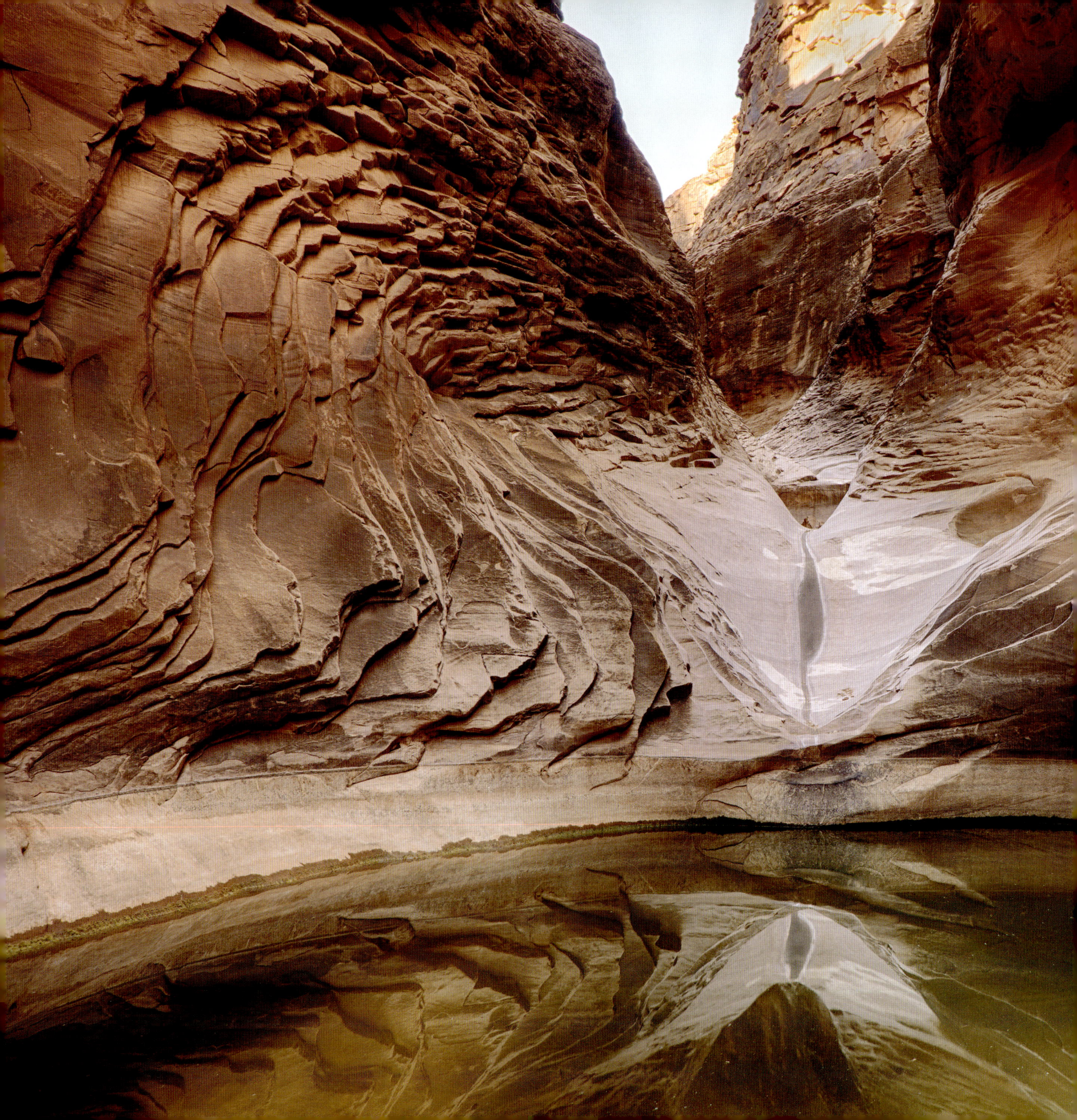

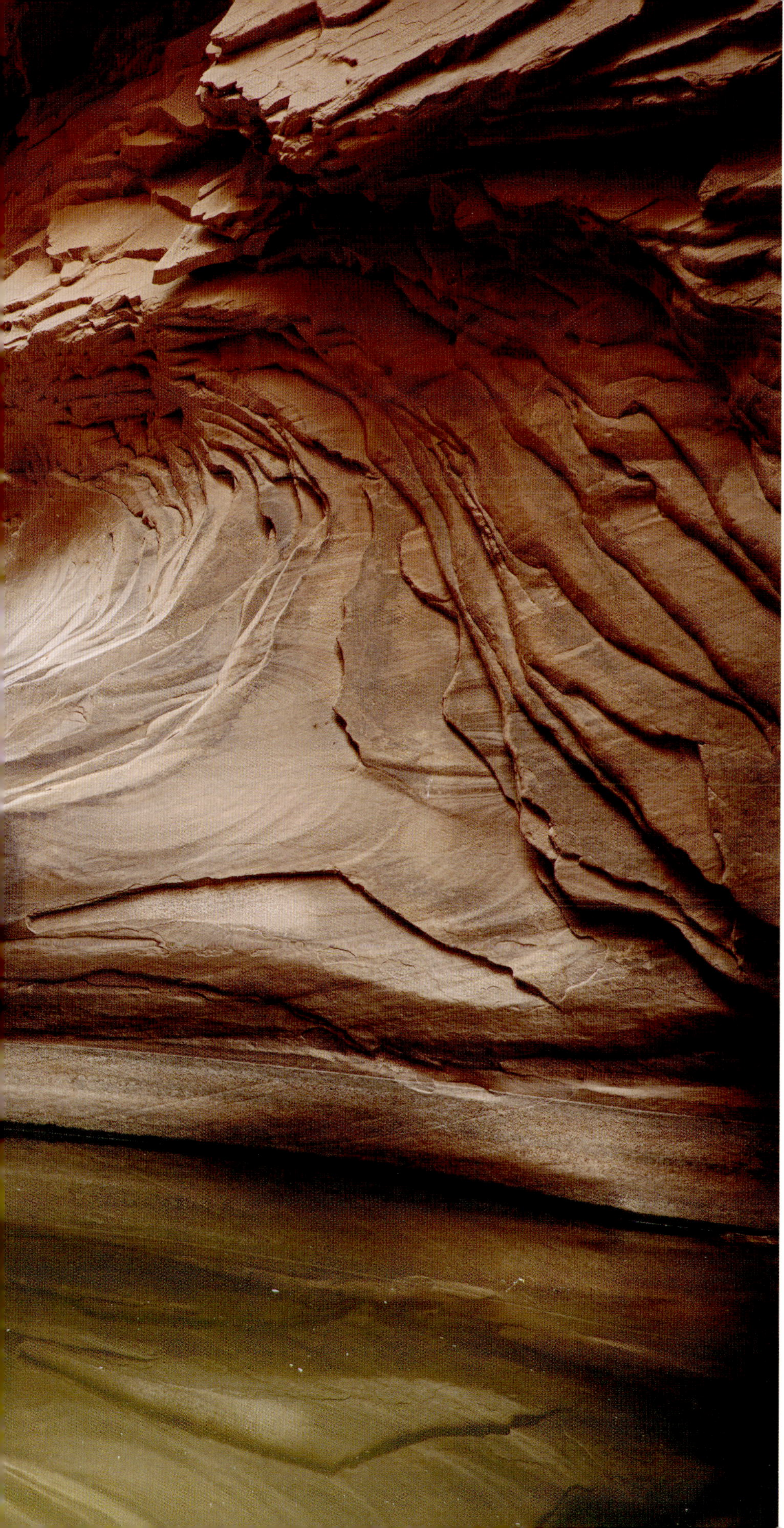

North Canyon

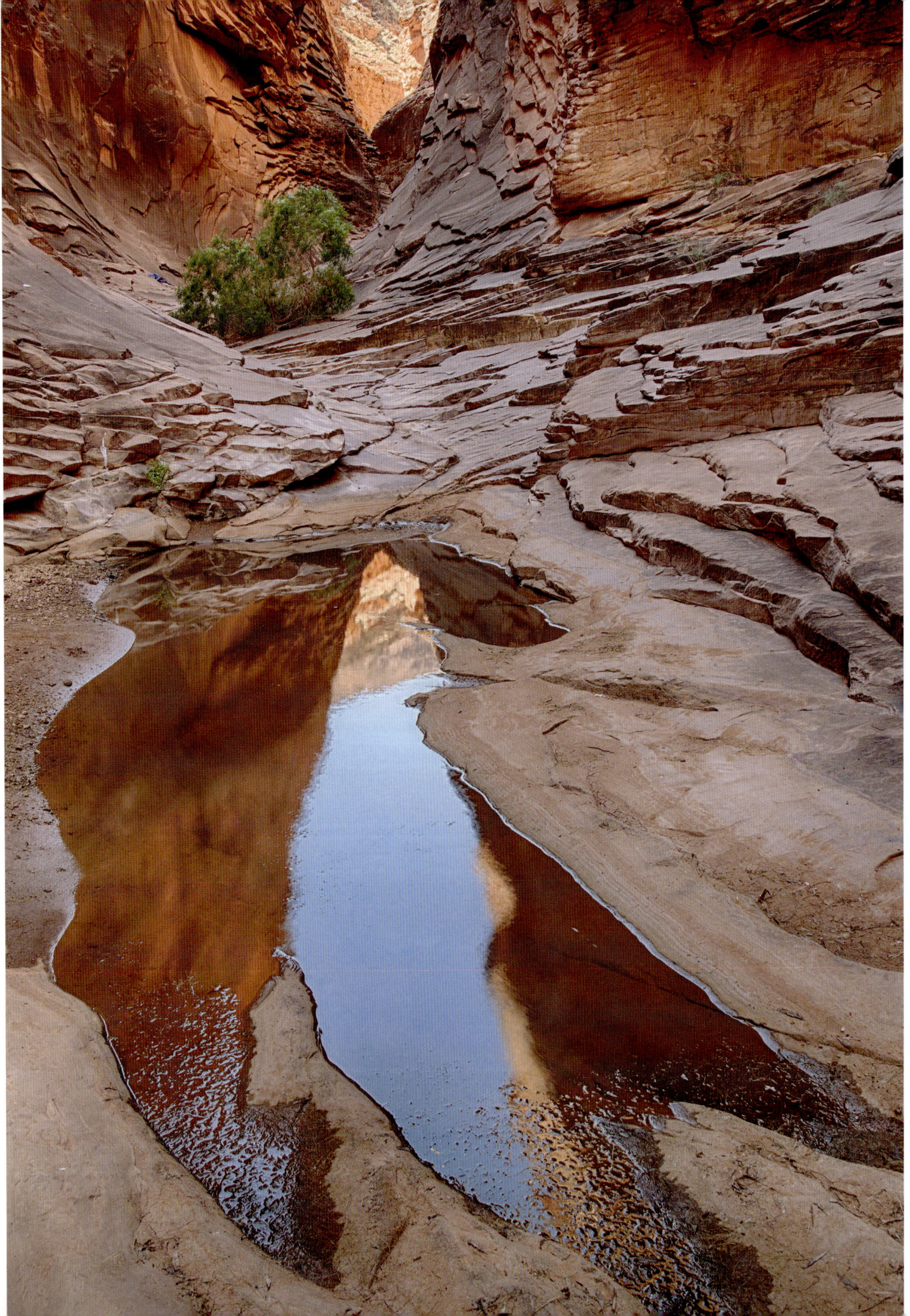

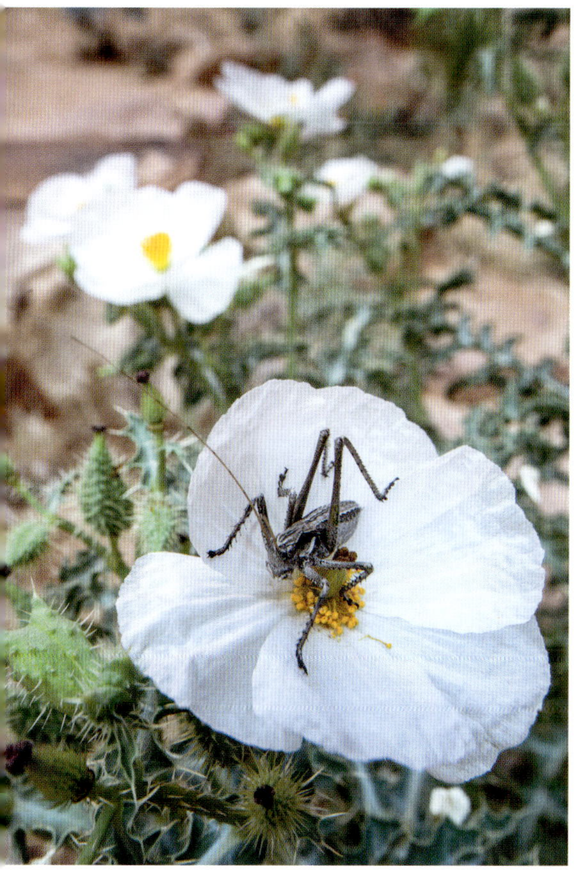

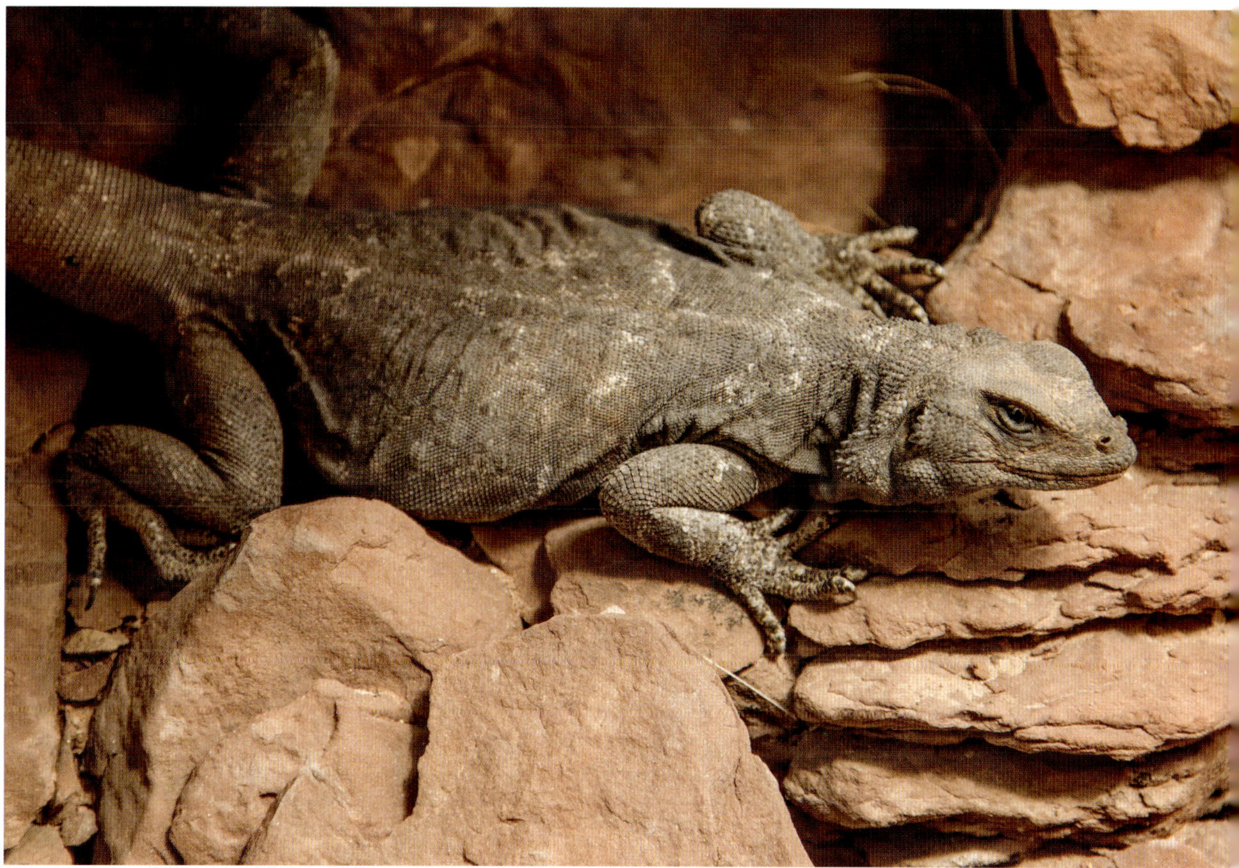

◀ Pool, North Canyon ▲ Grasshopper on prickly-poppy (left) and chuckwalla (right), North Canyon

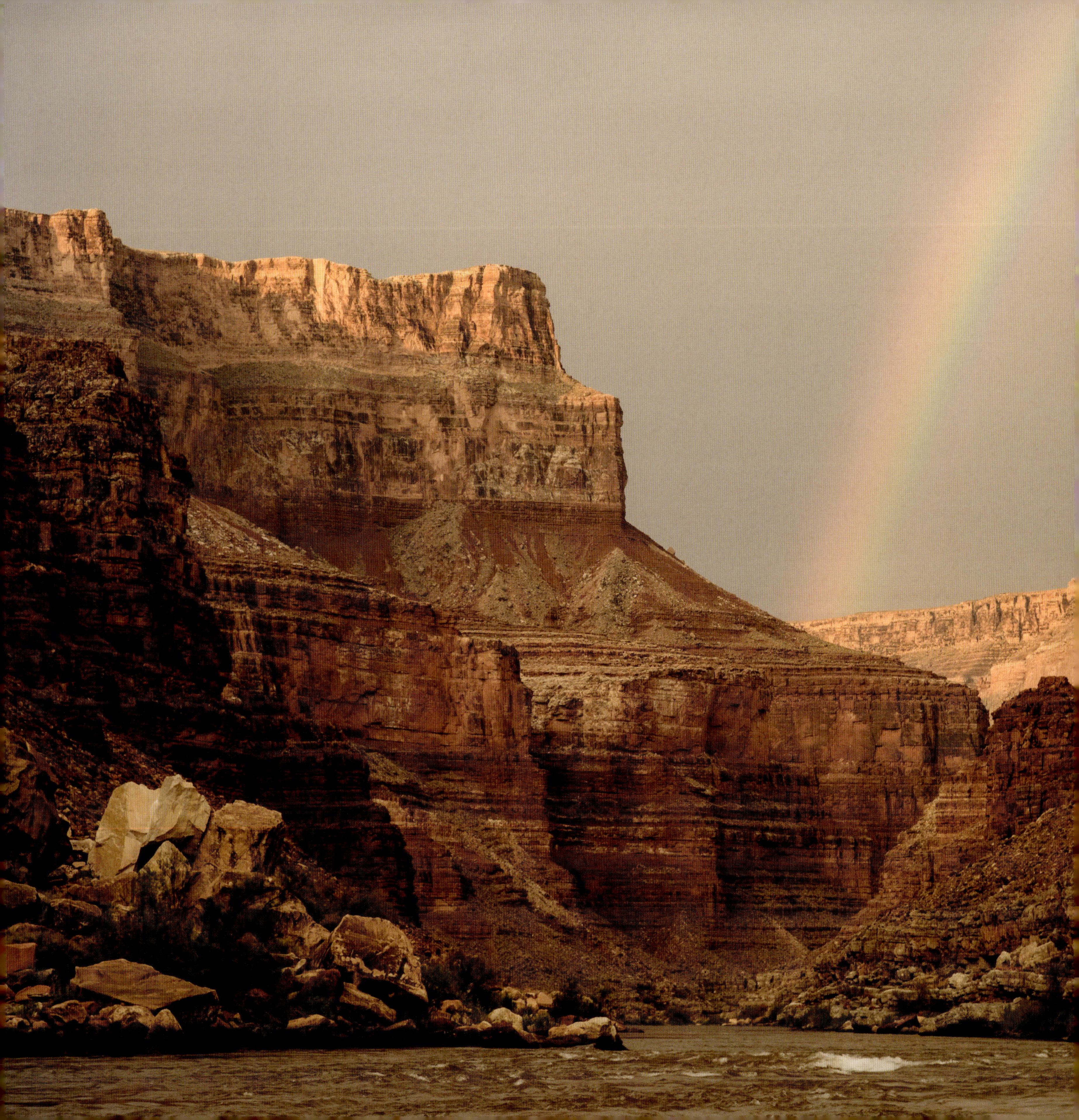

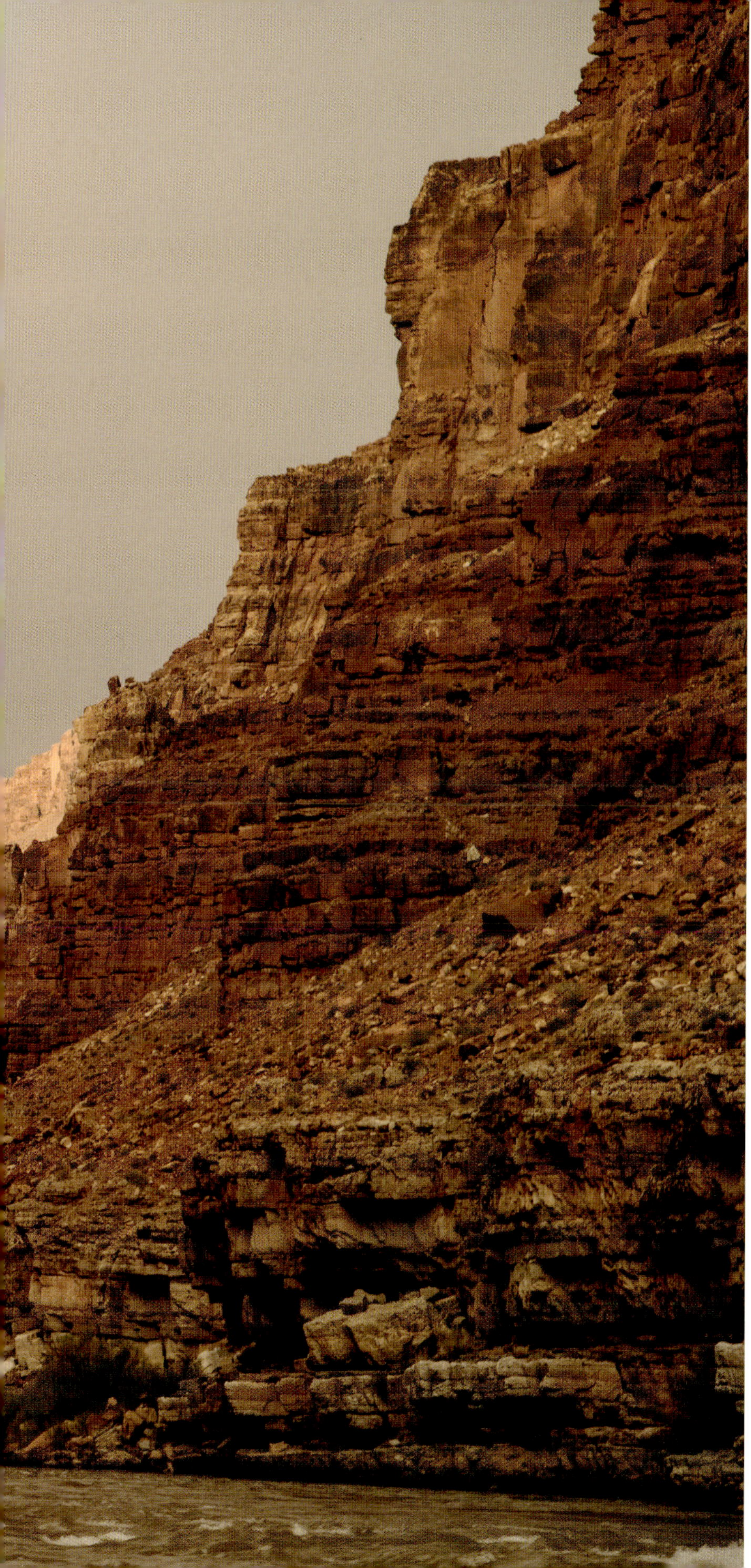

View downriver from 23 Mile Camp

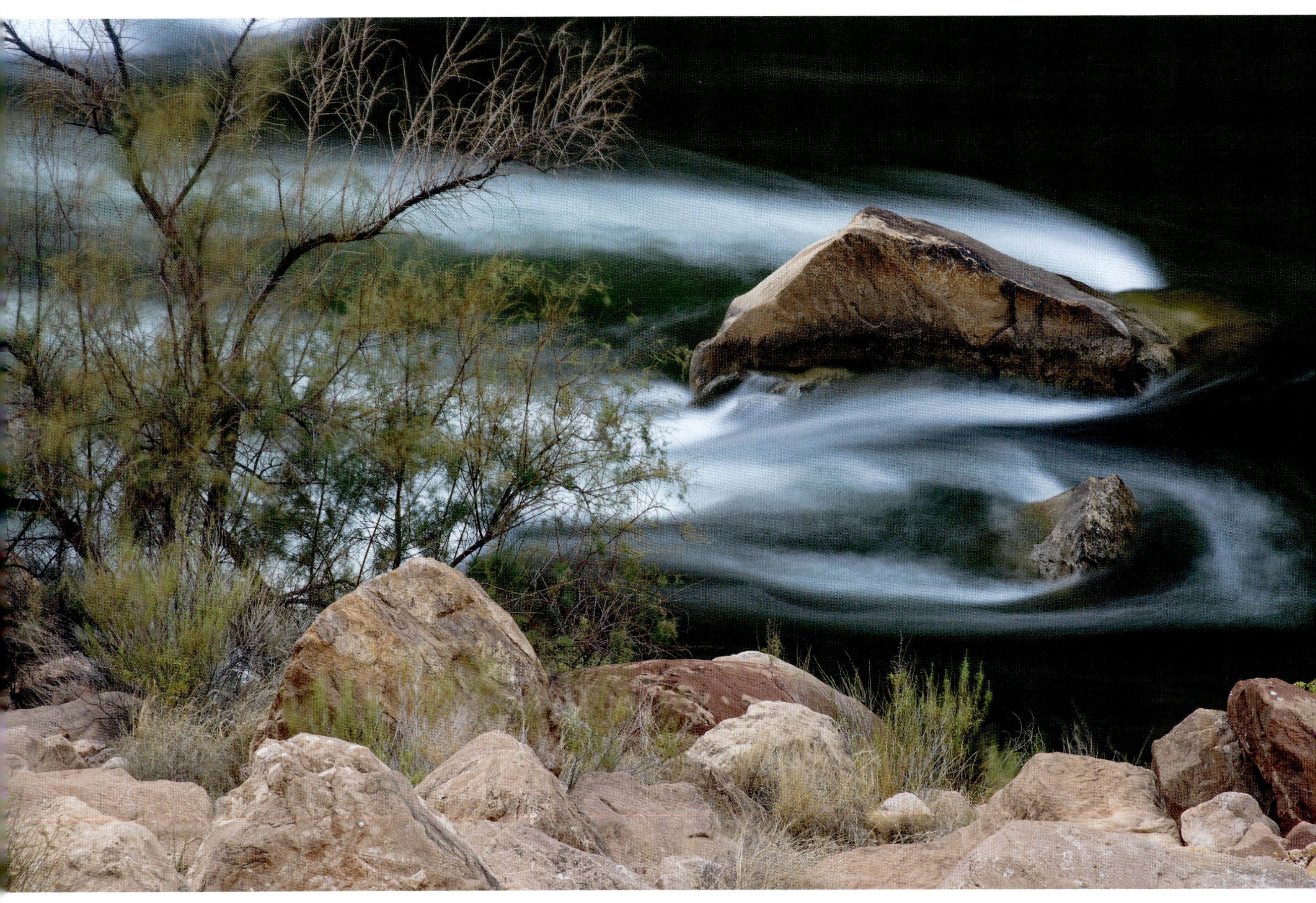

Rocks and rapid, 23 Mile Camp

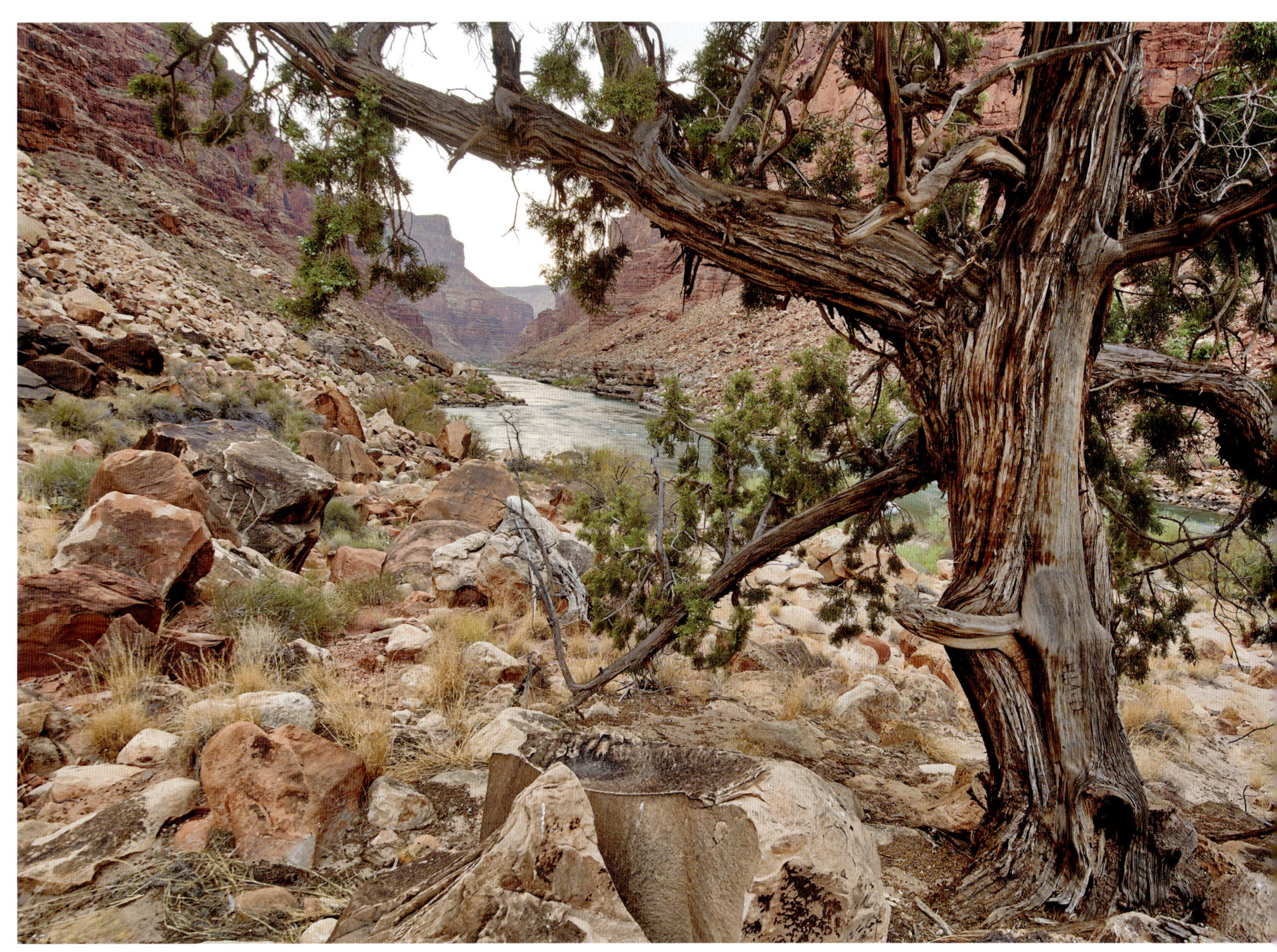

Utah juniper tree bearing an inscription more than 100 years old, 23 Mile Camp

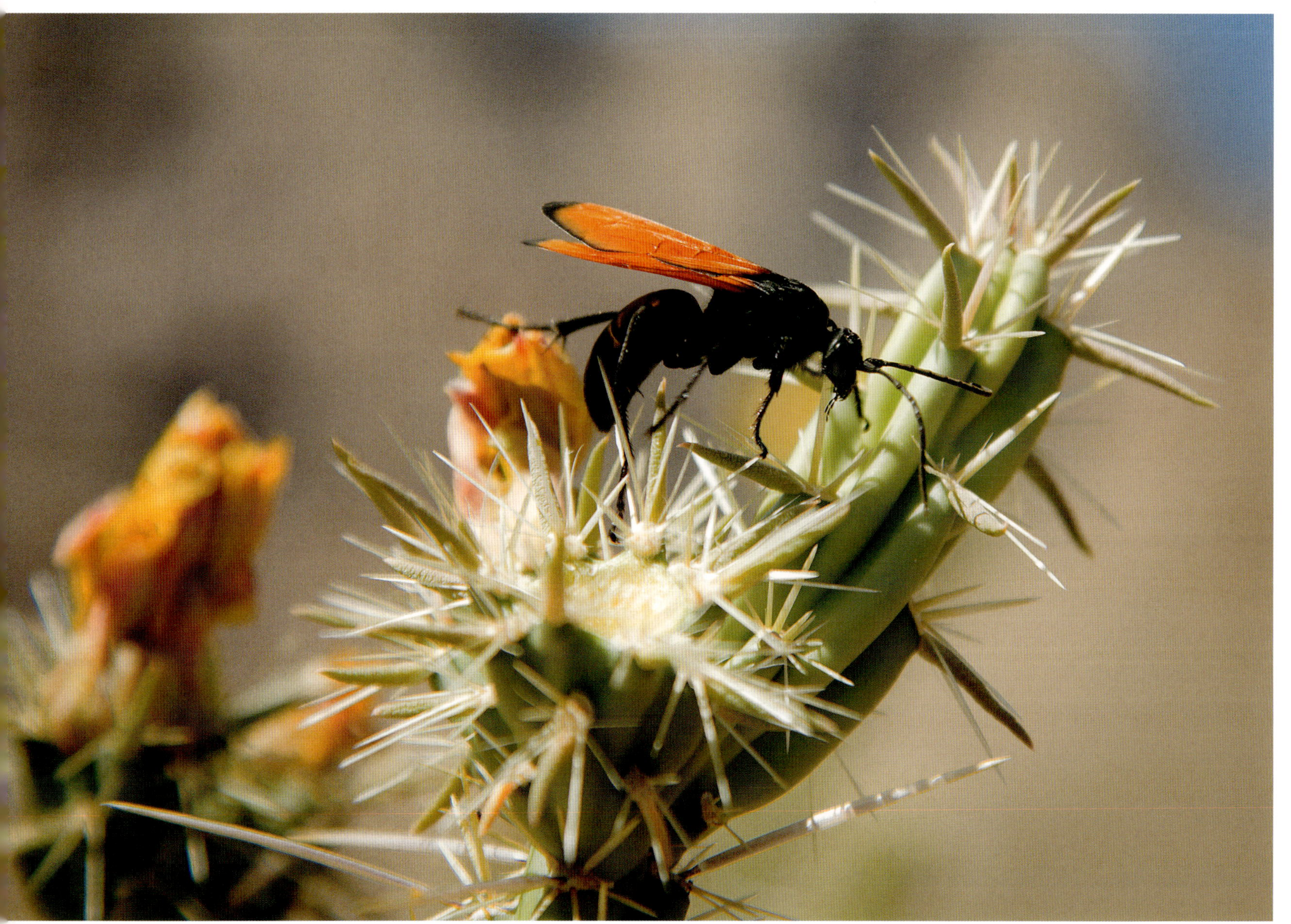

▲ Tarantula hawk on Buckhorn cholla cactus ▶ Golden columbine

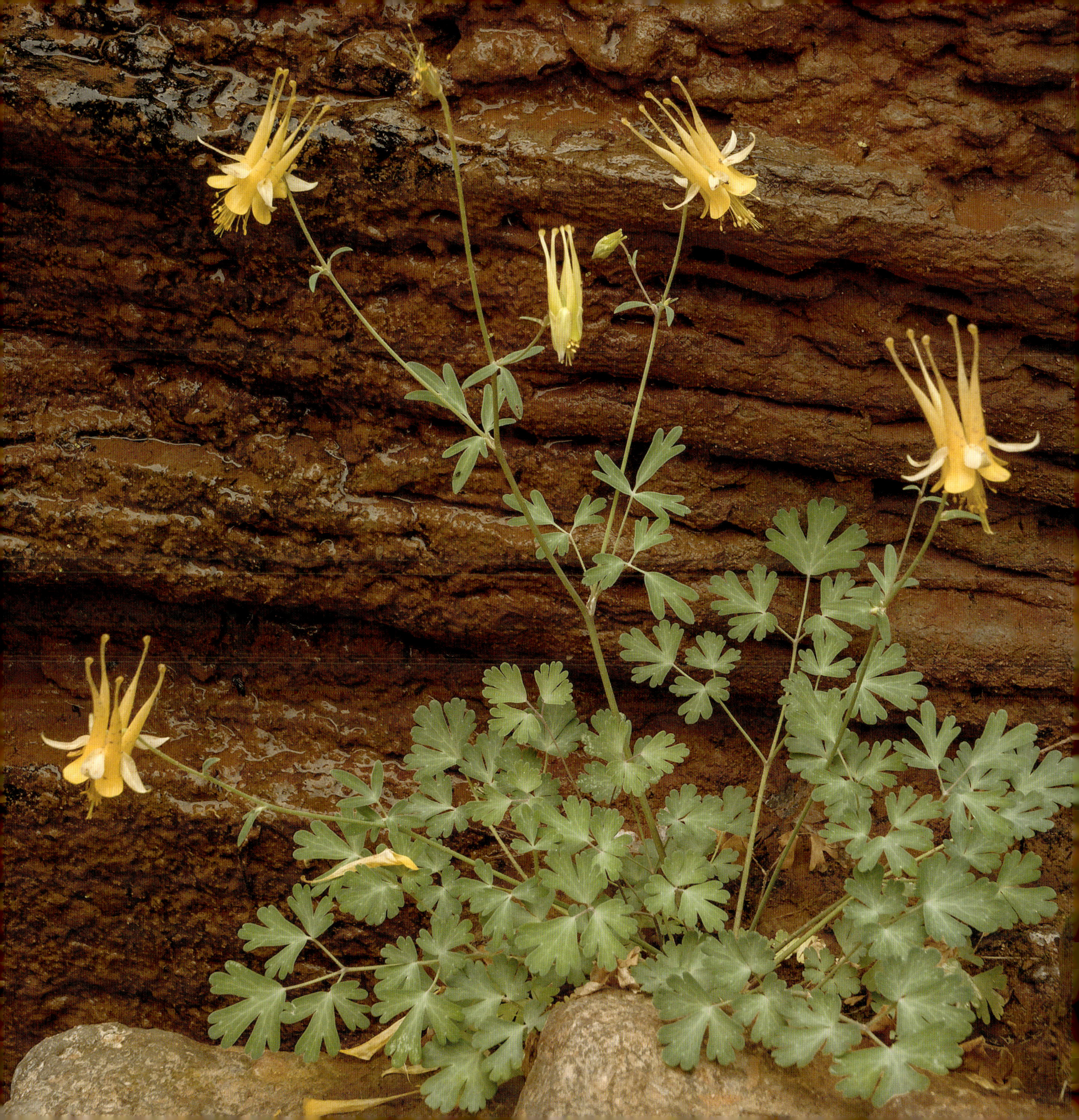

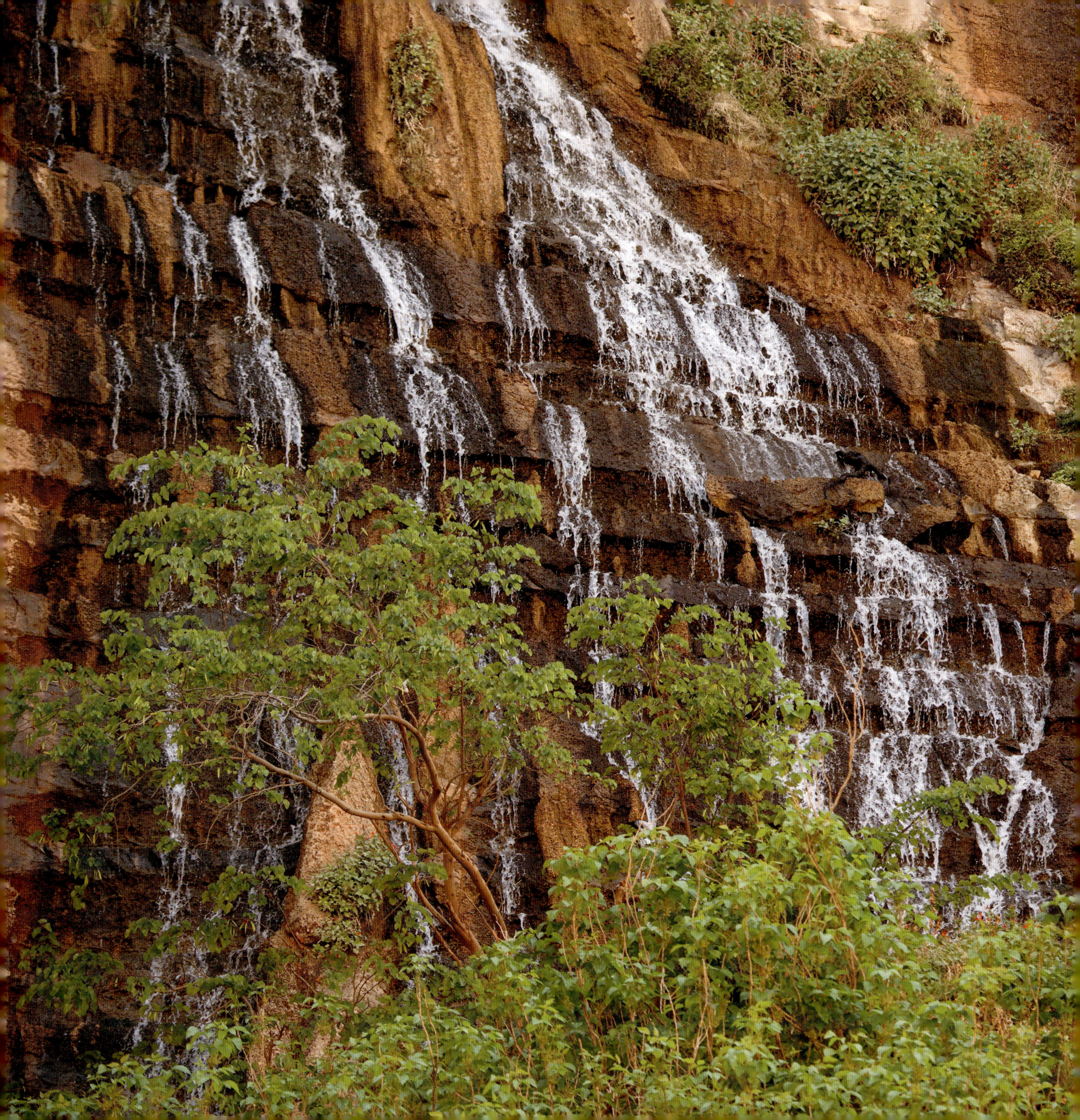

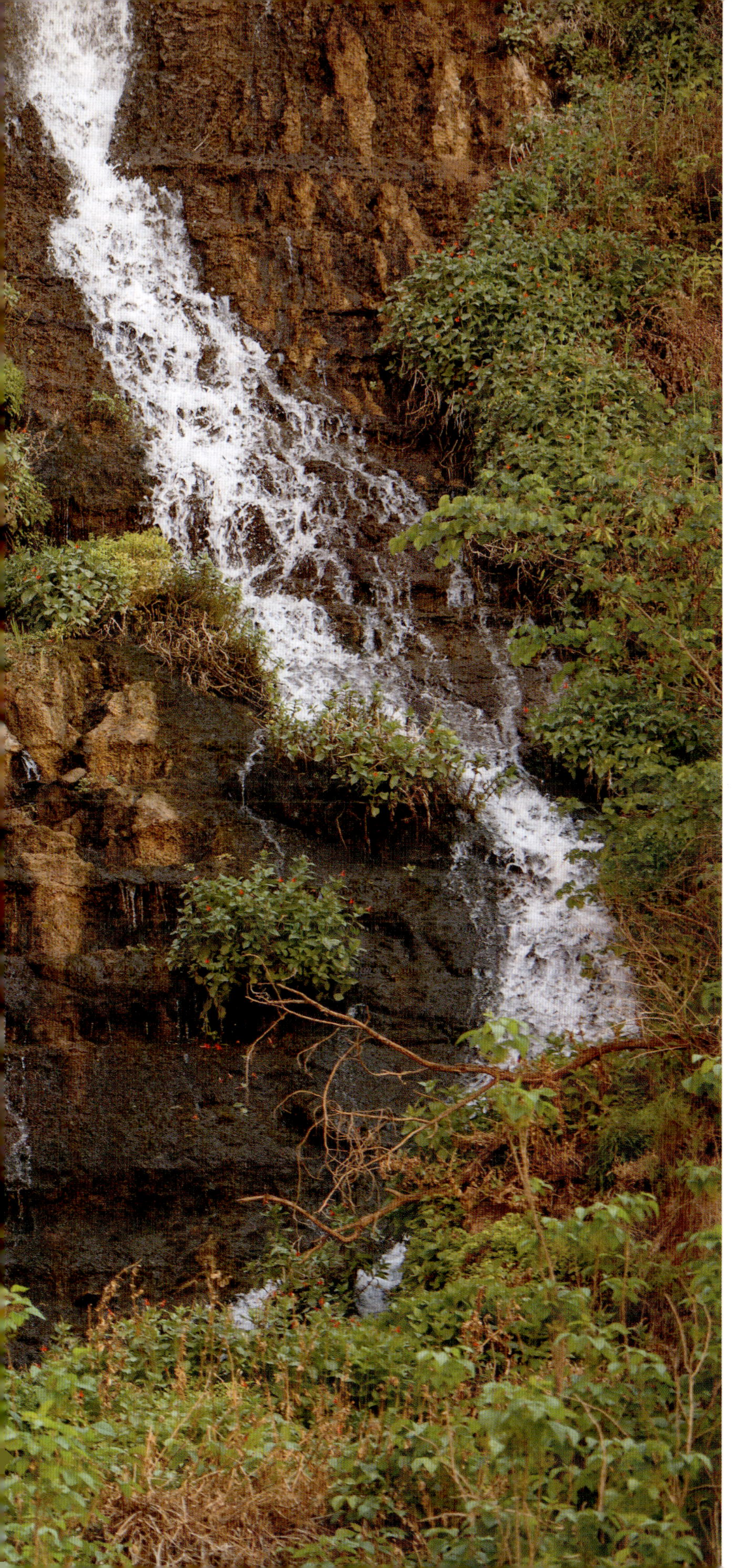

Vasey's Paradise

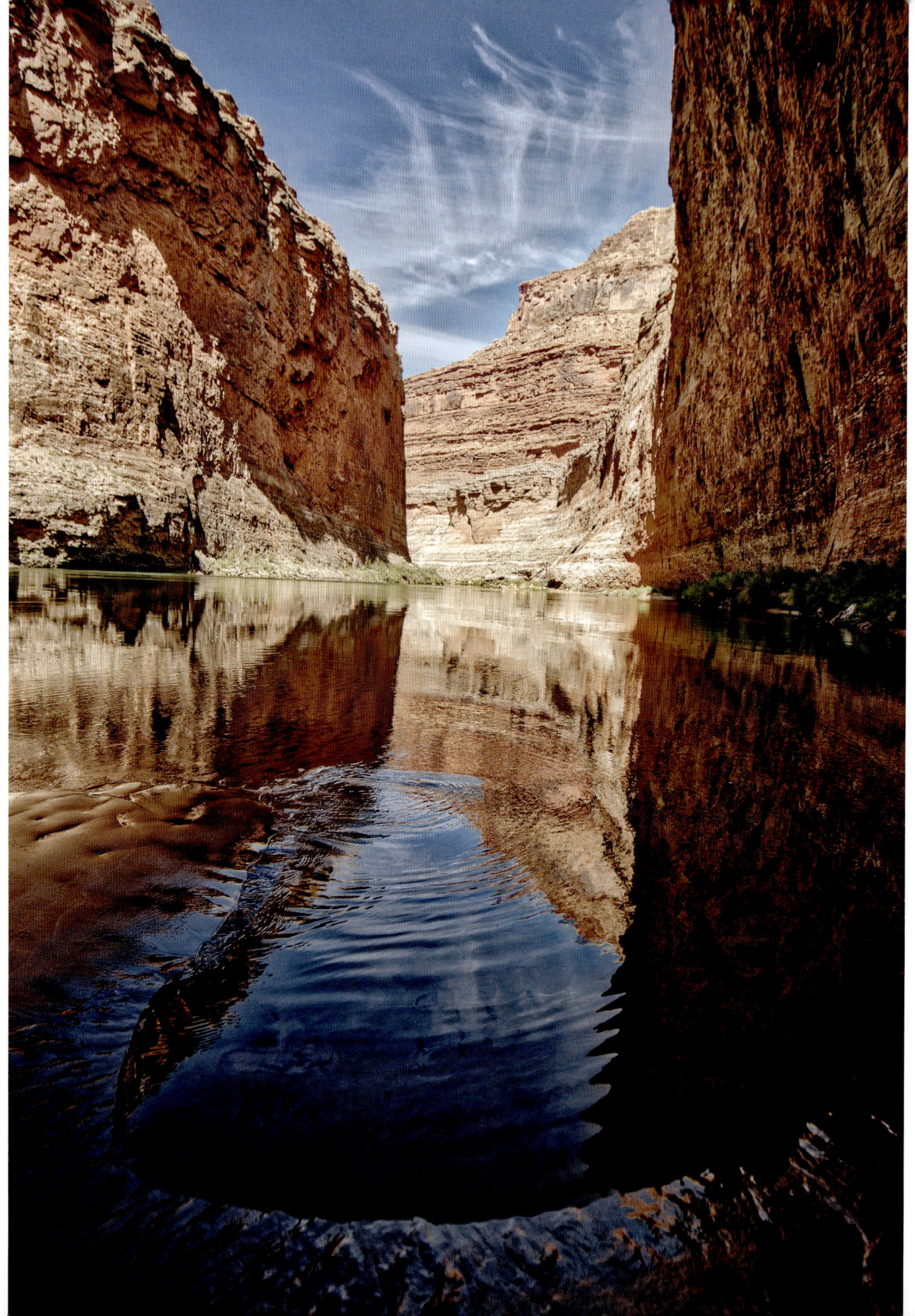

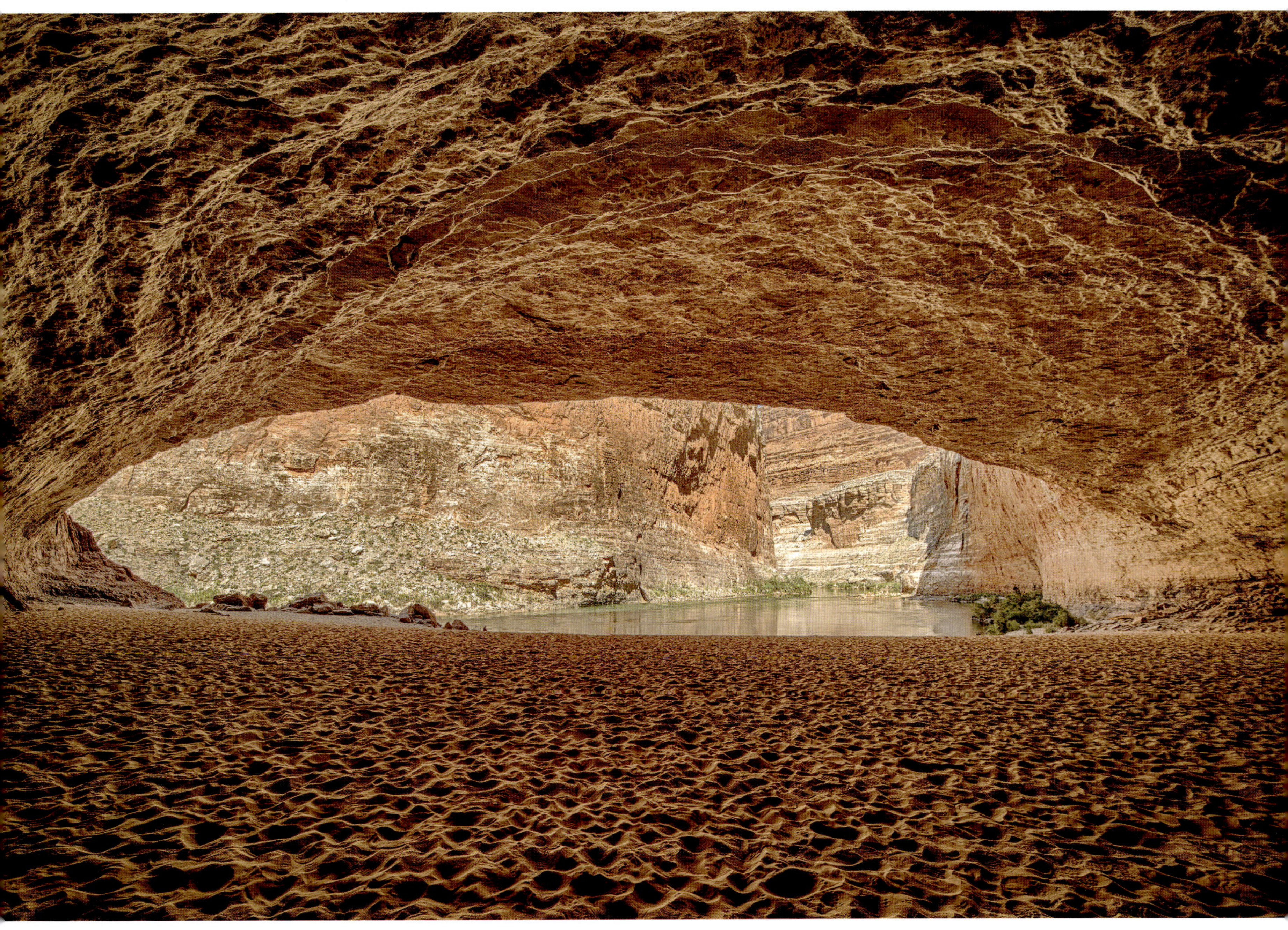

◀ View upriver from Redwall Cavern ▲ Redwall Cavern

“Robbie’s Rainbow” (see page 24), Eminence Camp

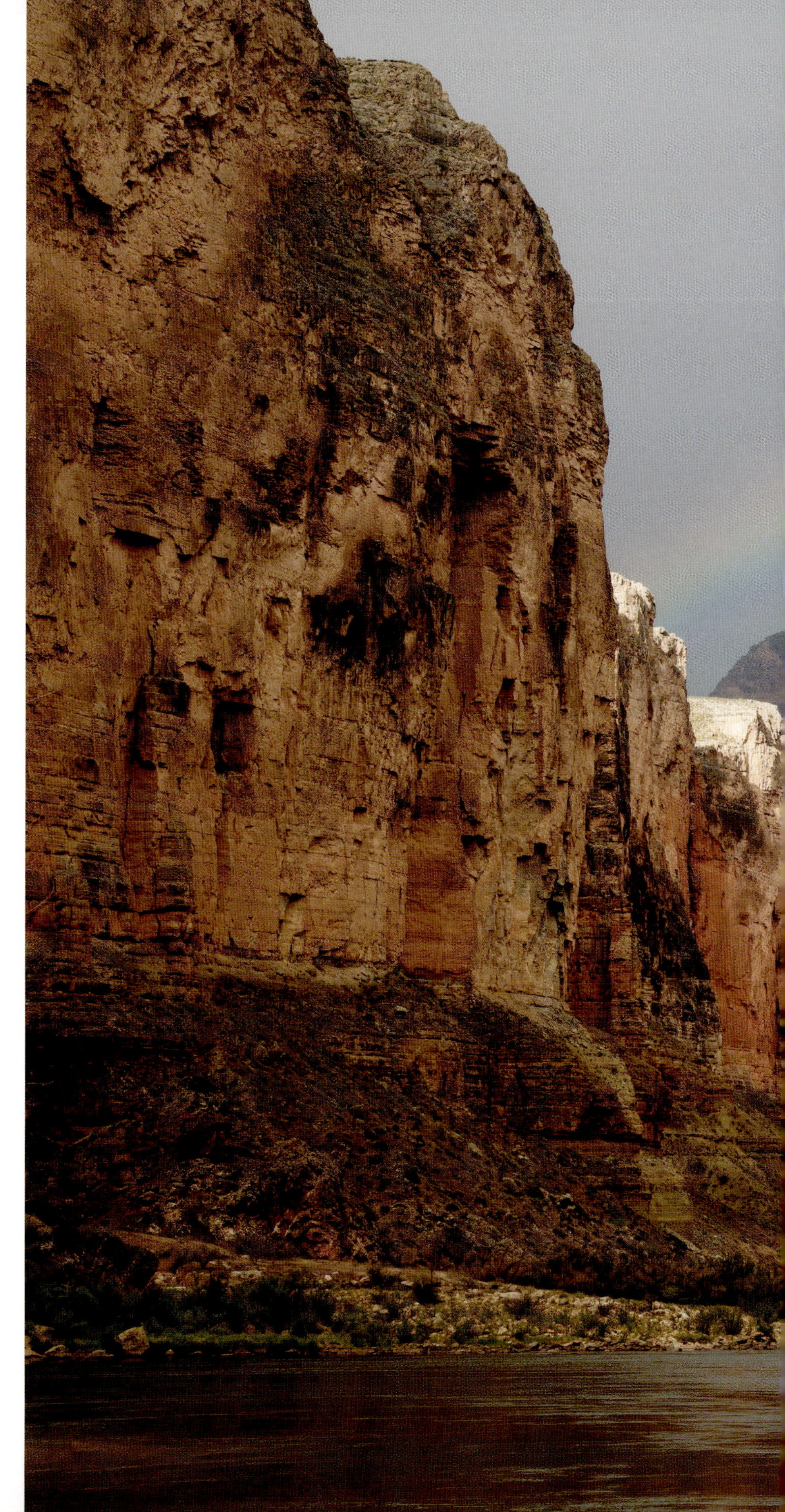

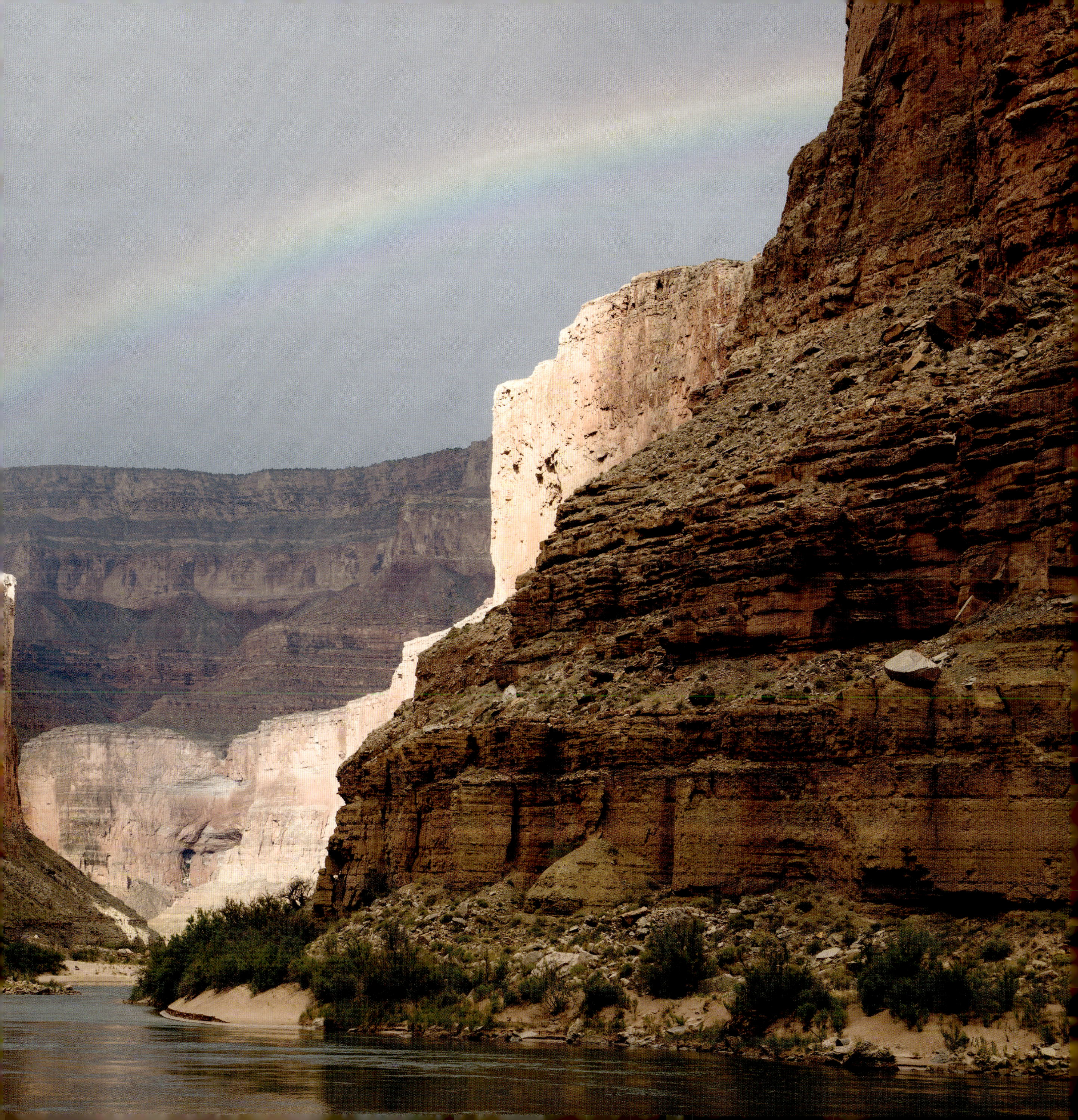

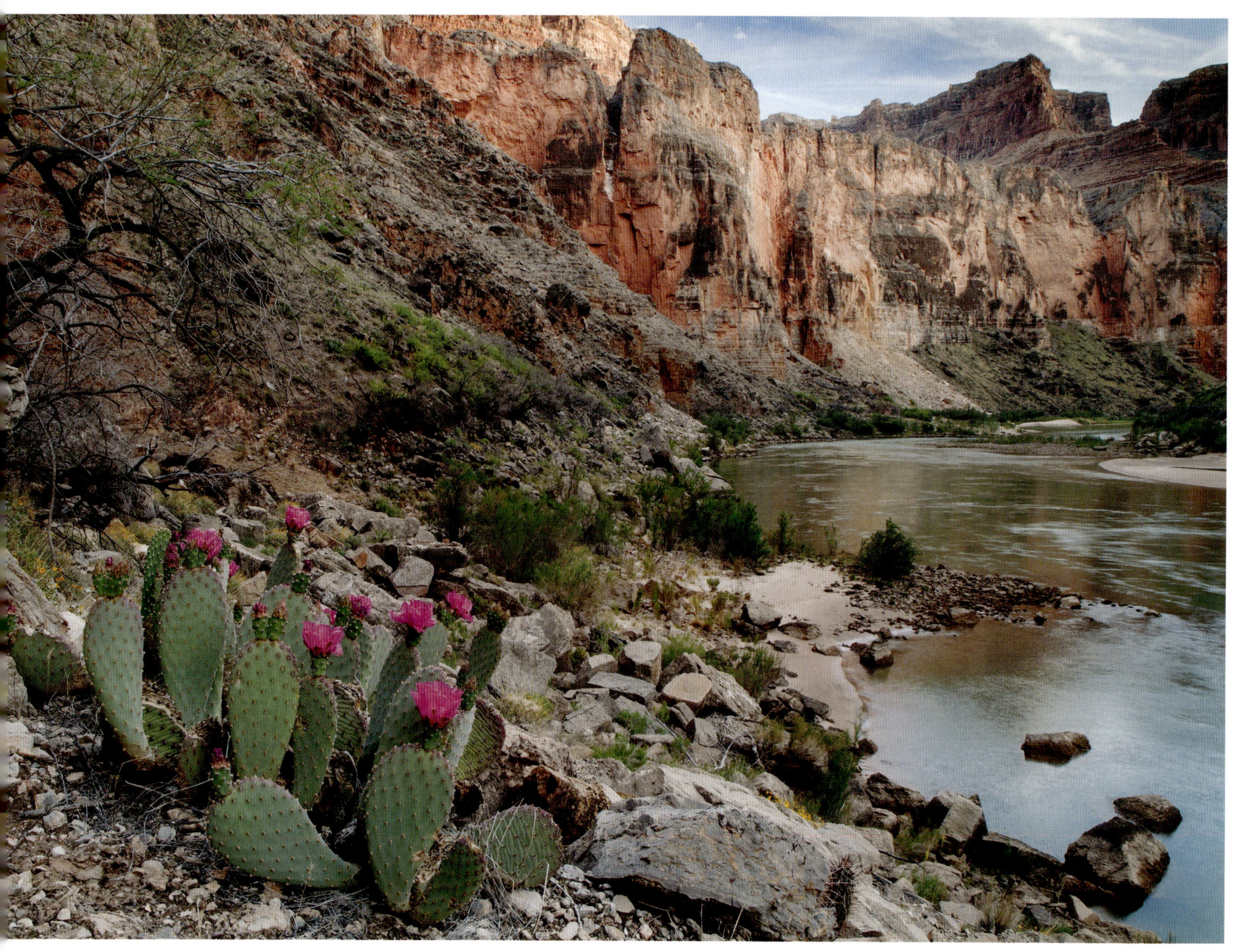

Grand Canyon beavertail cactus, Eminence Camp

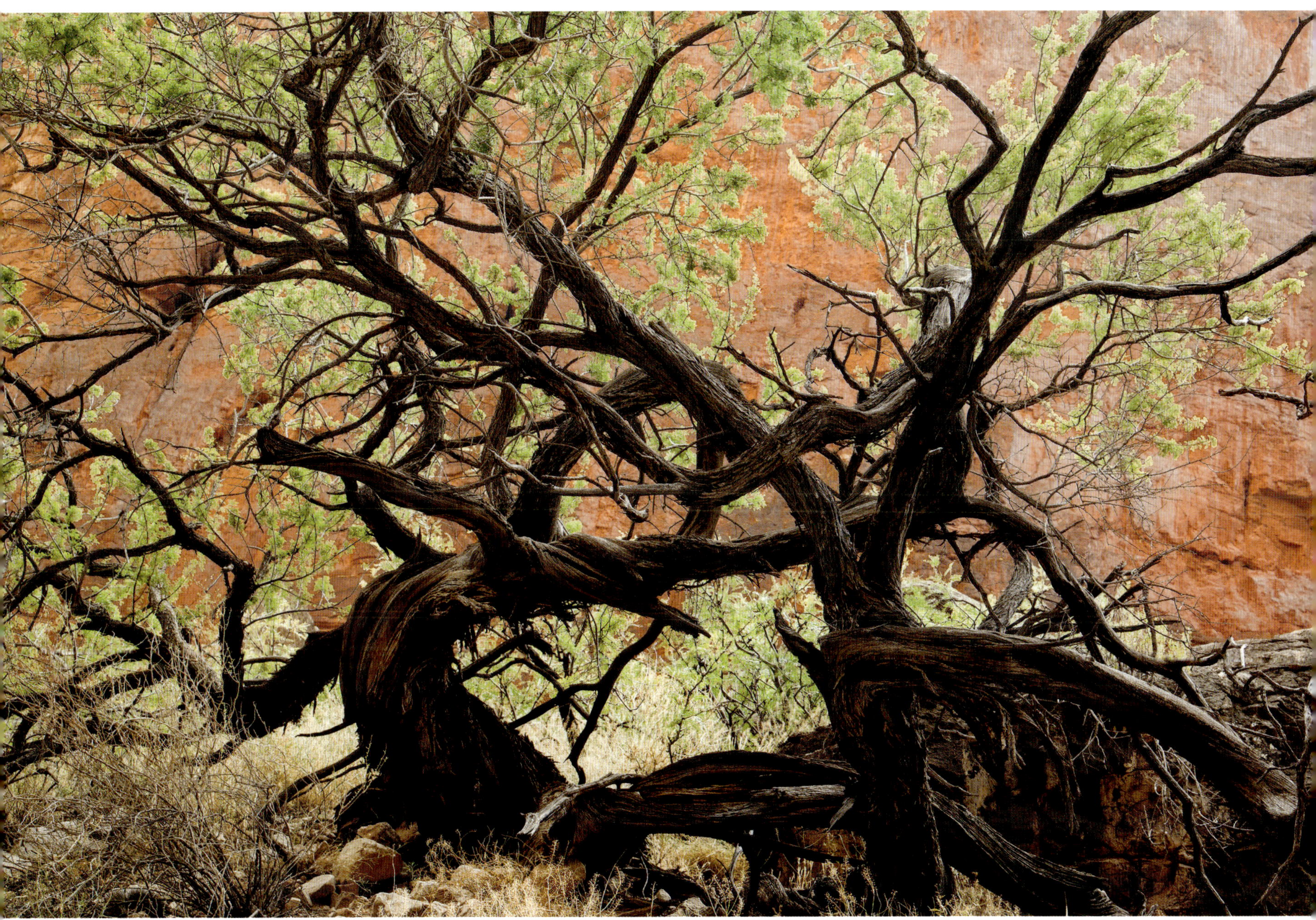

▲ Mesquite tree, Eminence Camp ▼ View upriver from Lower Saddle Camp

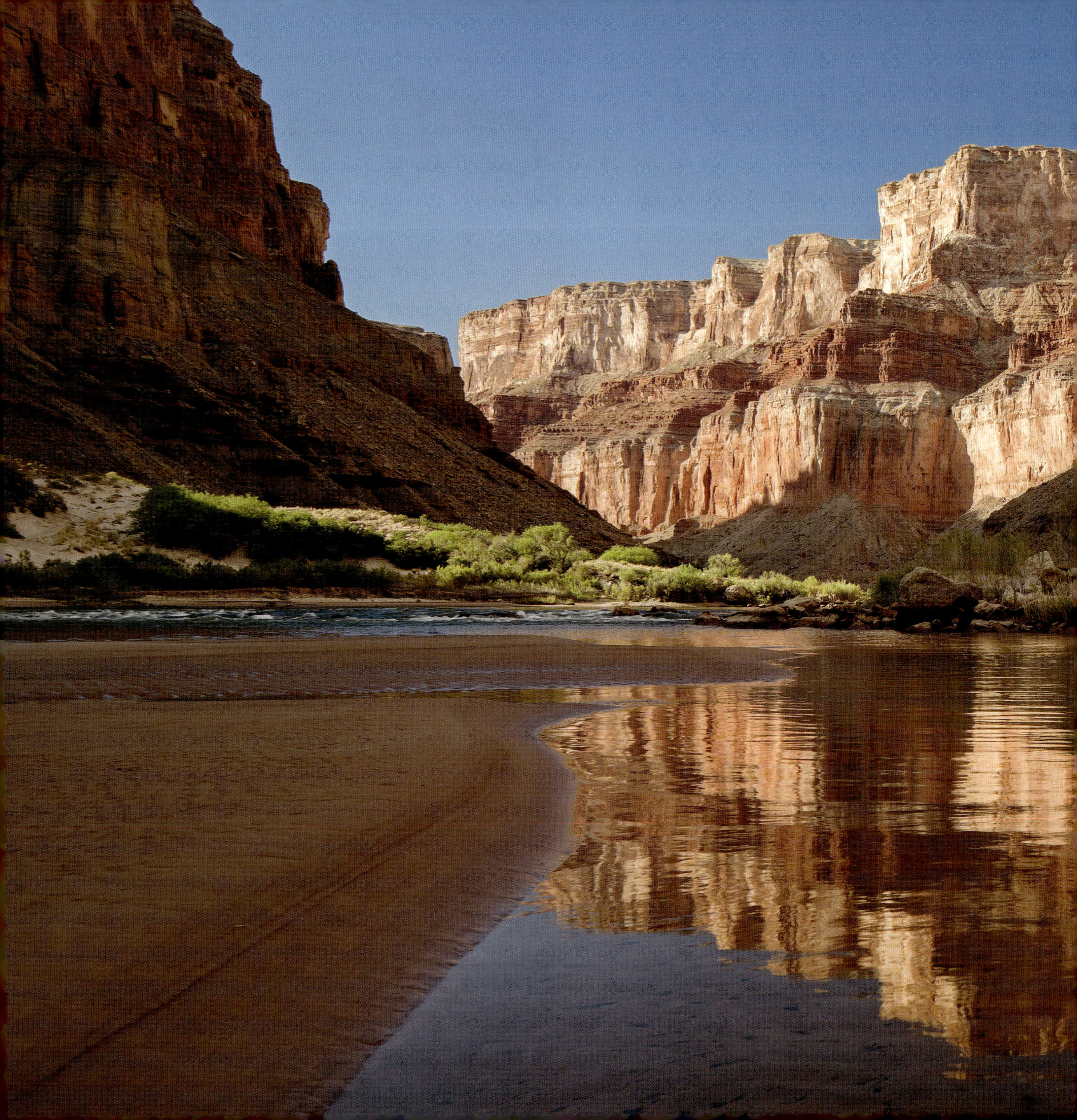

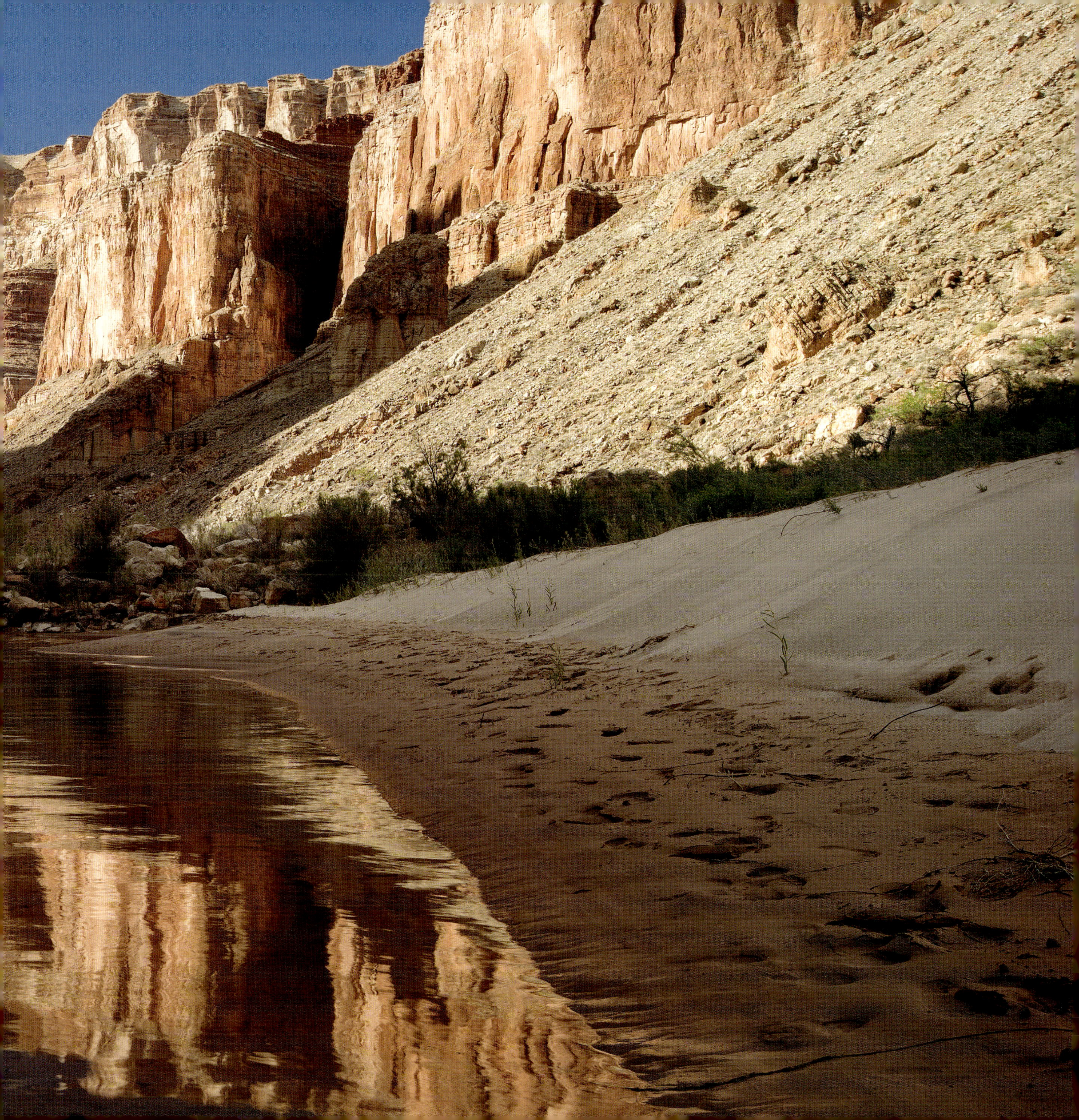

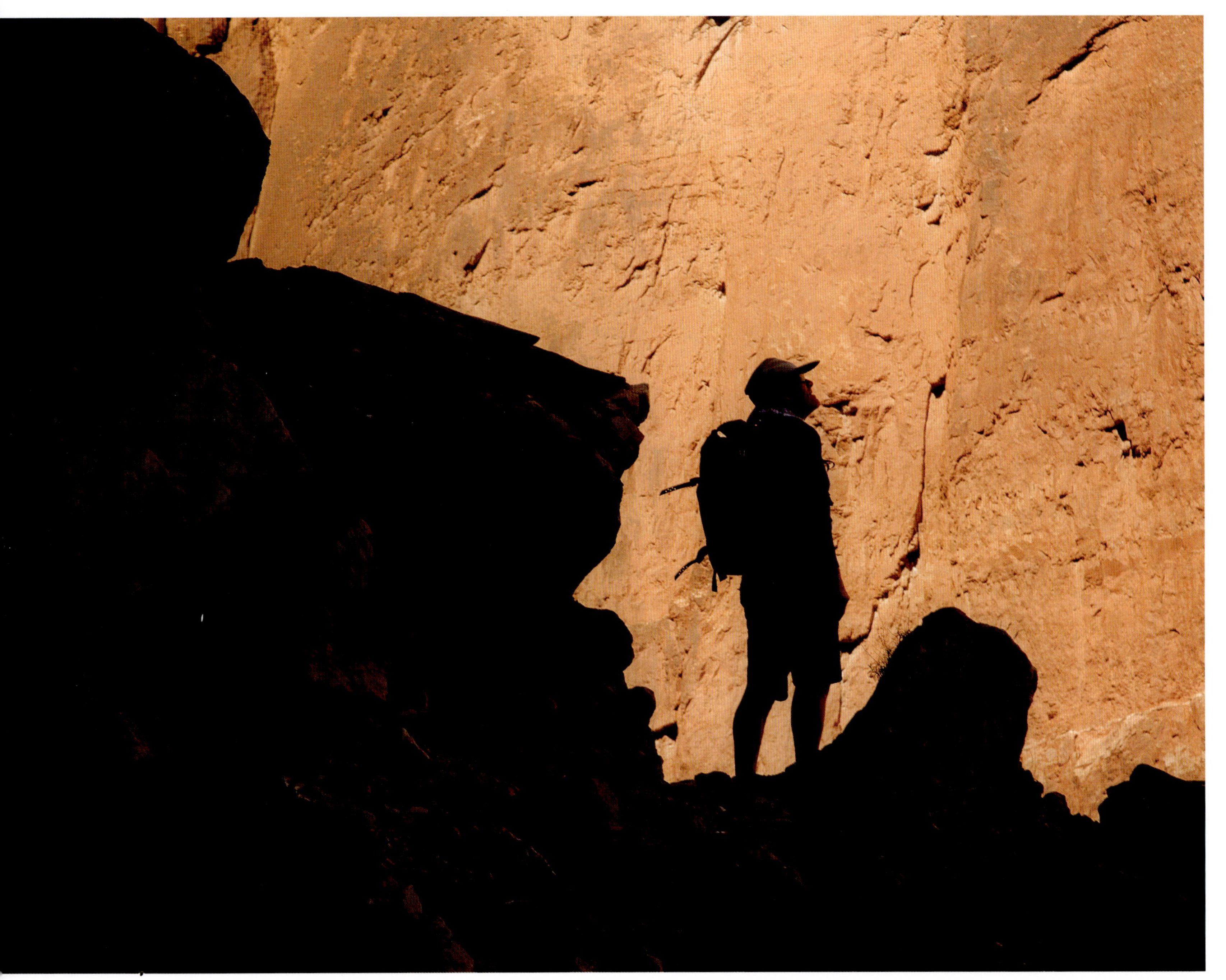

Hiker in Saddle Canyon

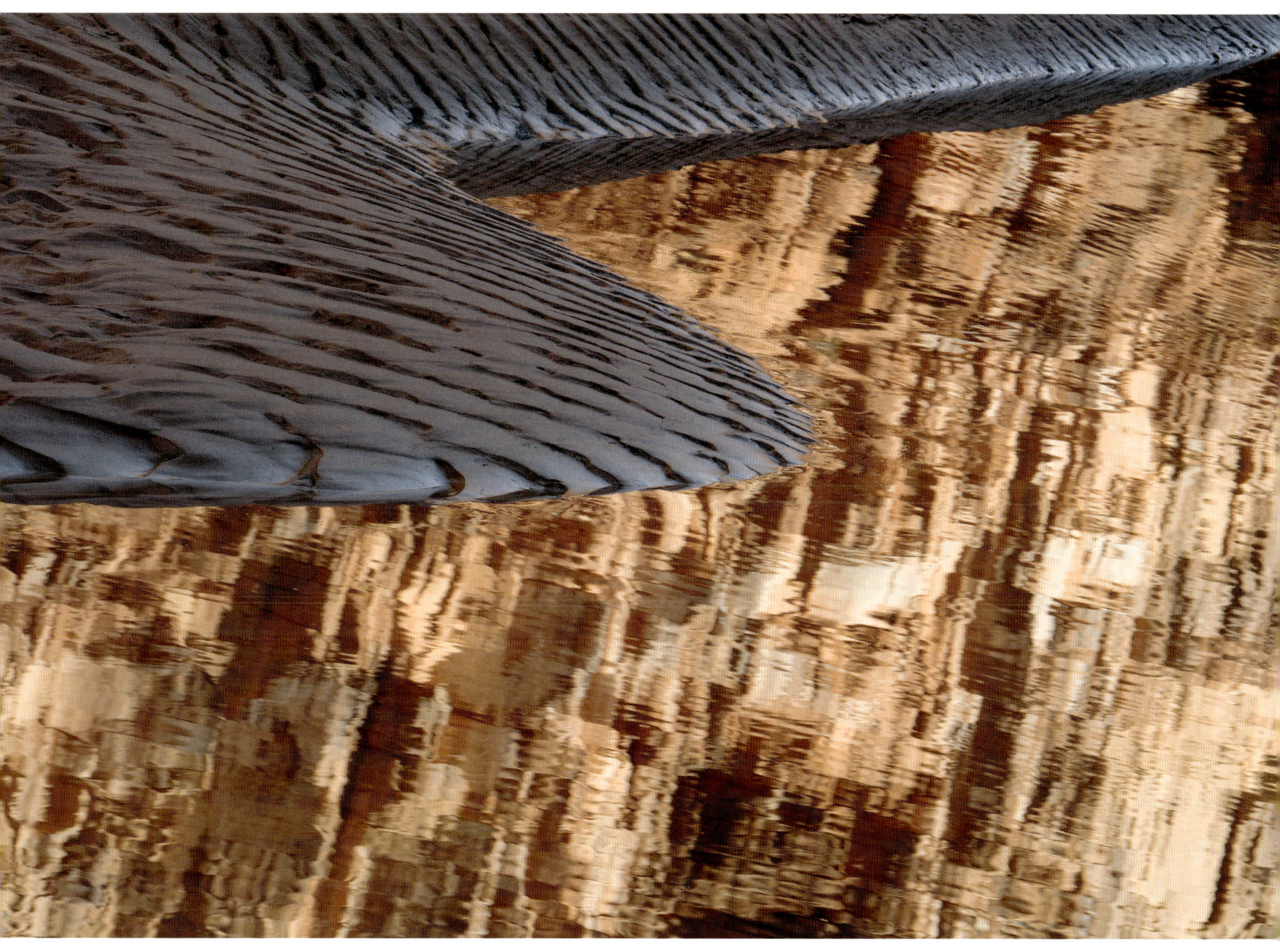

Sandbar and reflections, Lower Saddle Camp

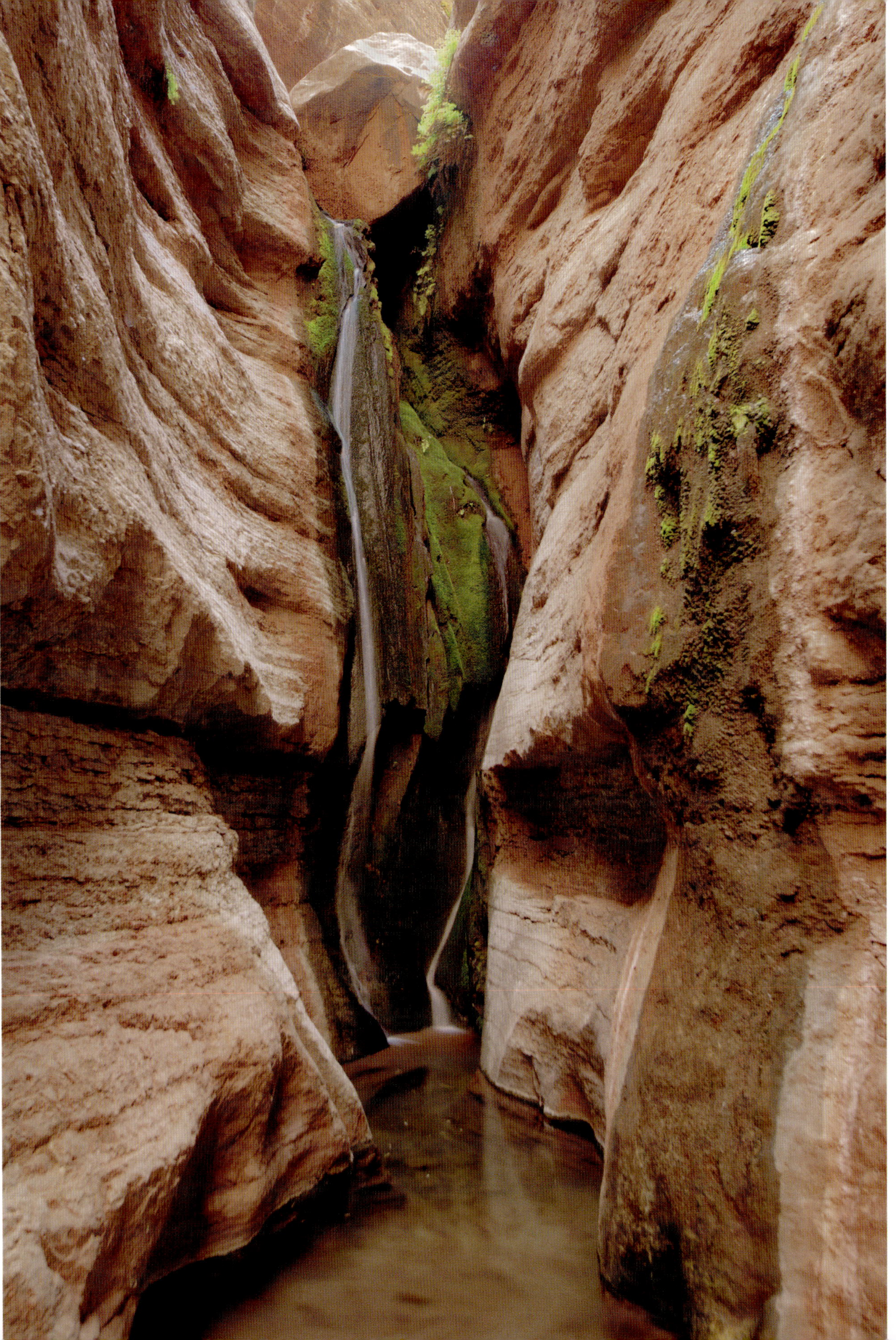

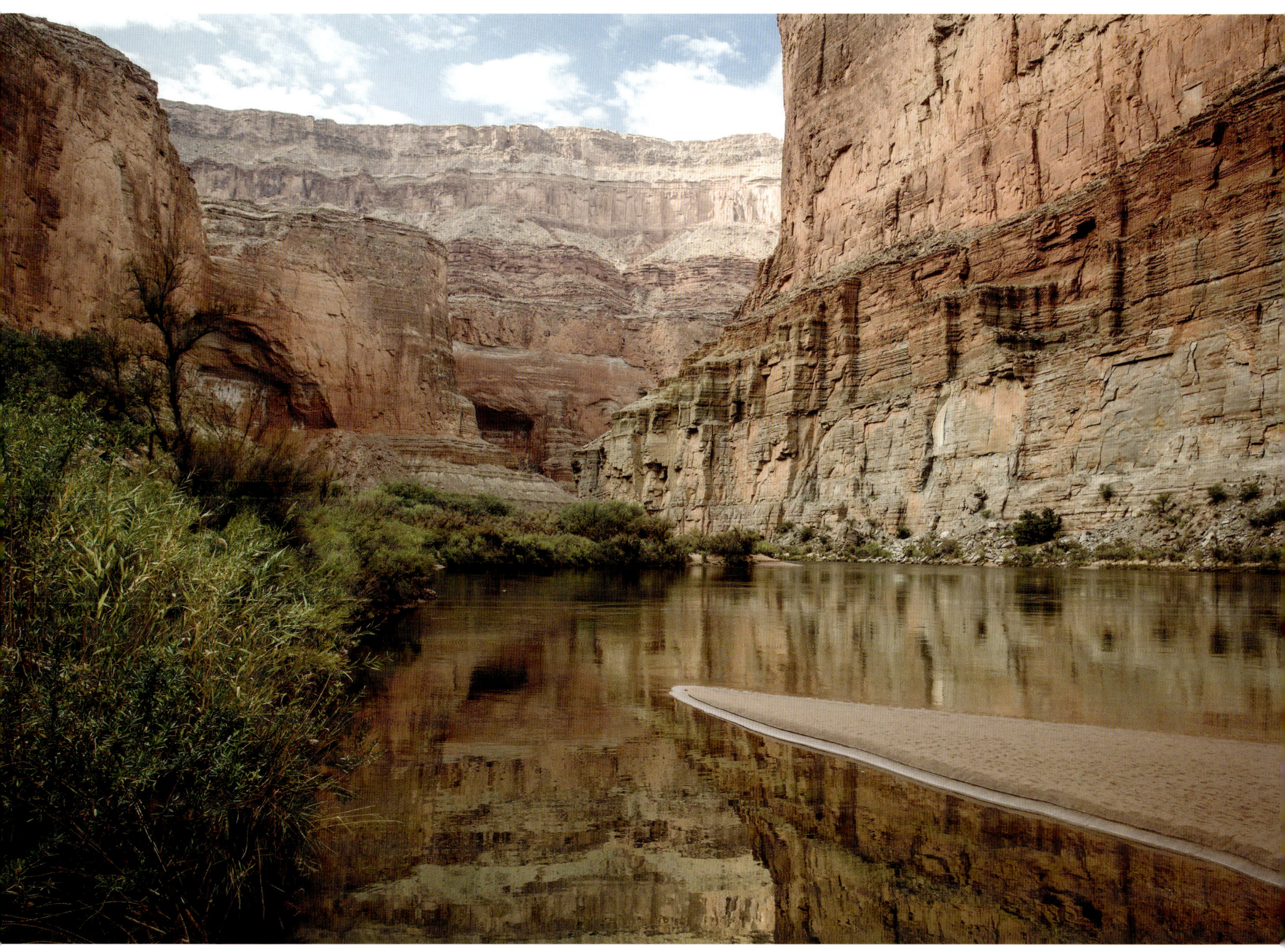

◀ Saddle Canyon ▲ Saddle Canyon Camp

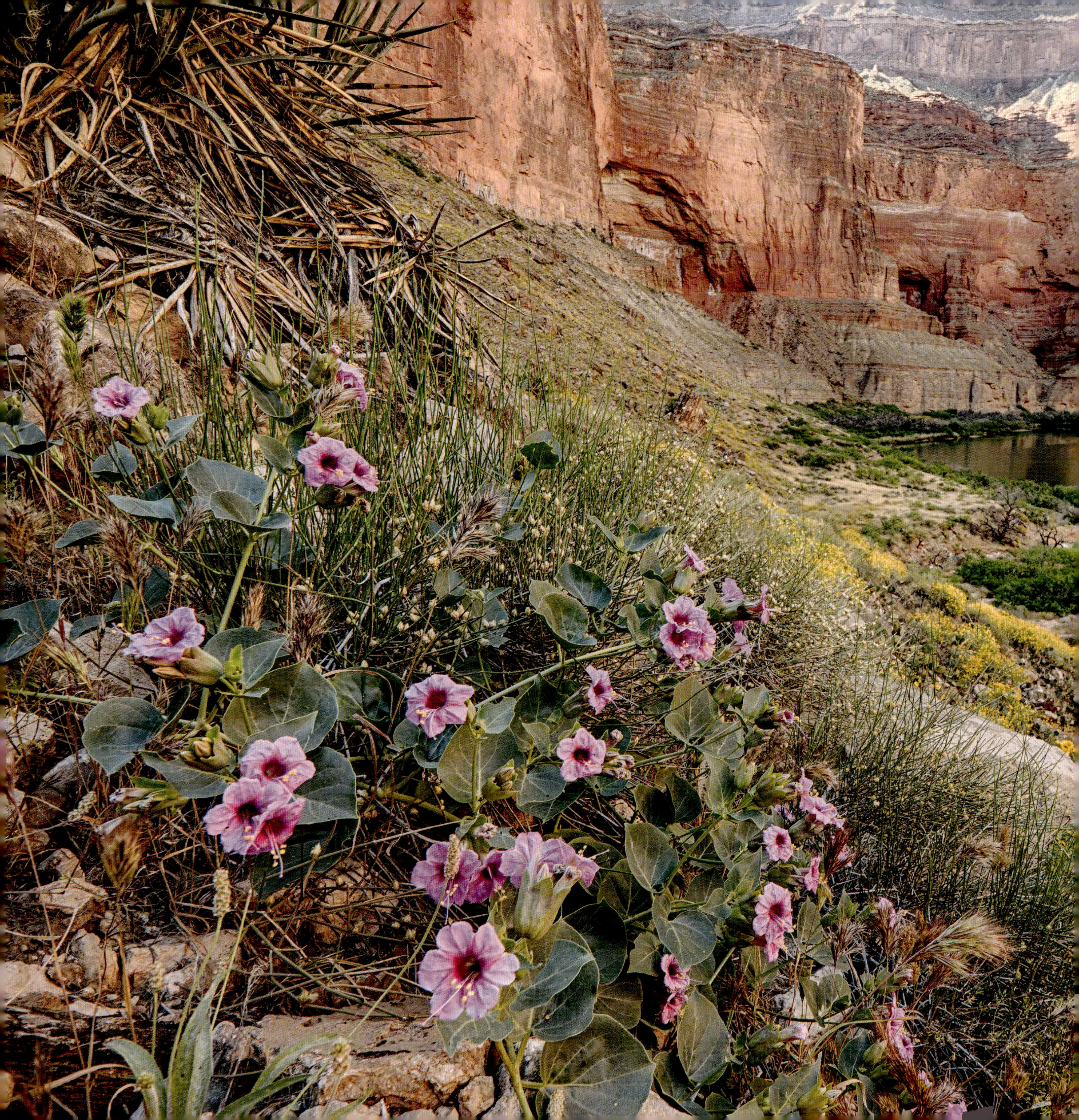

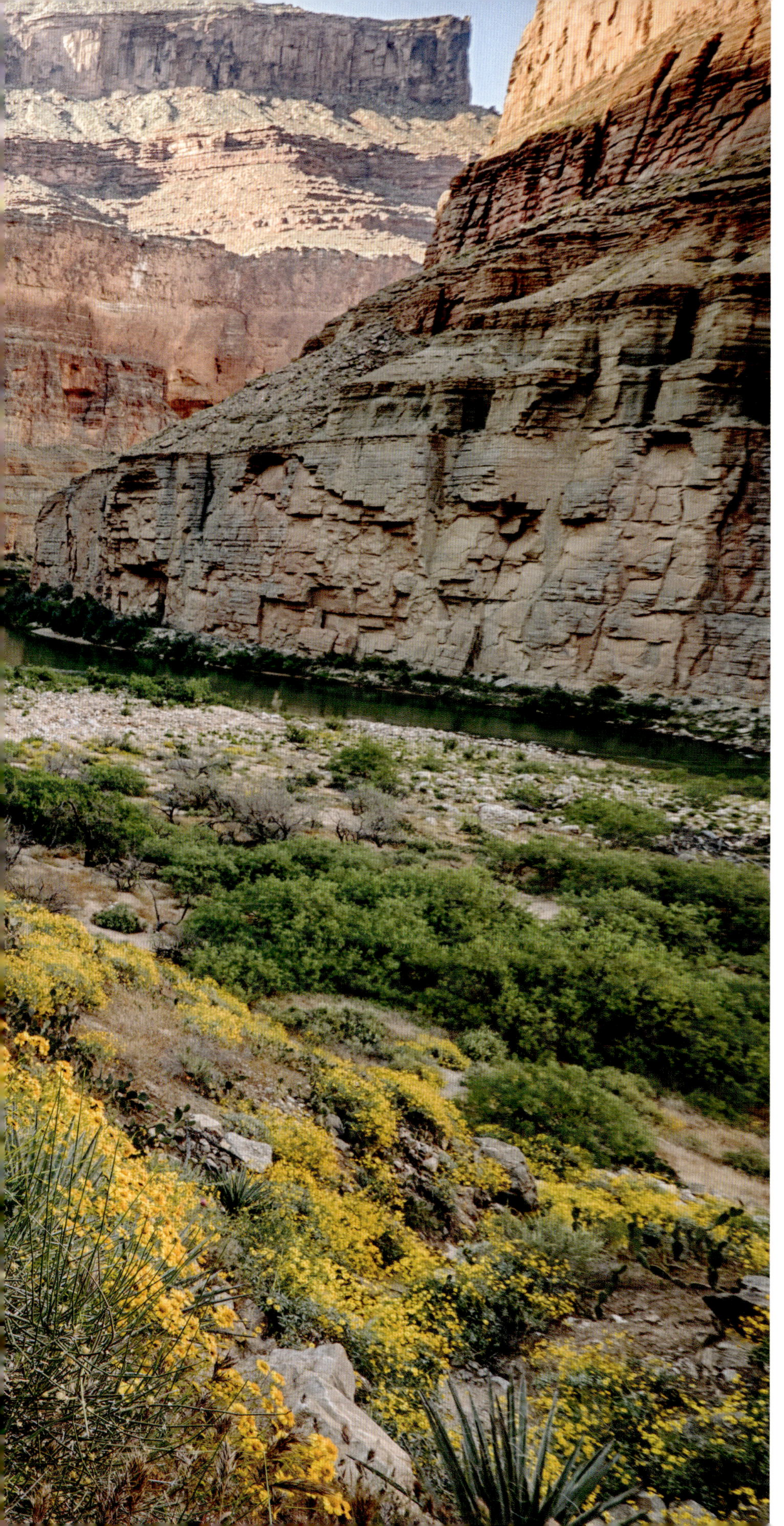

◀ Desert four o'clock flowers, Saddle Canyon

▼ Brittlebush flowers (left), canyon tree frog (right, top), and swallowtail butterfly on scarlet lobelia (right, bottom), Saddle Canyon

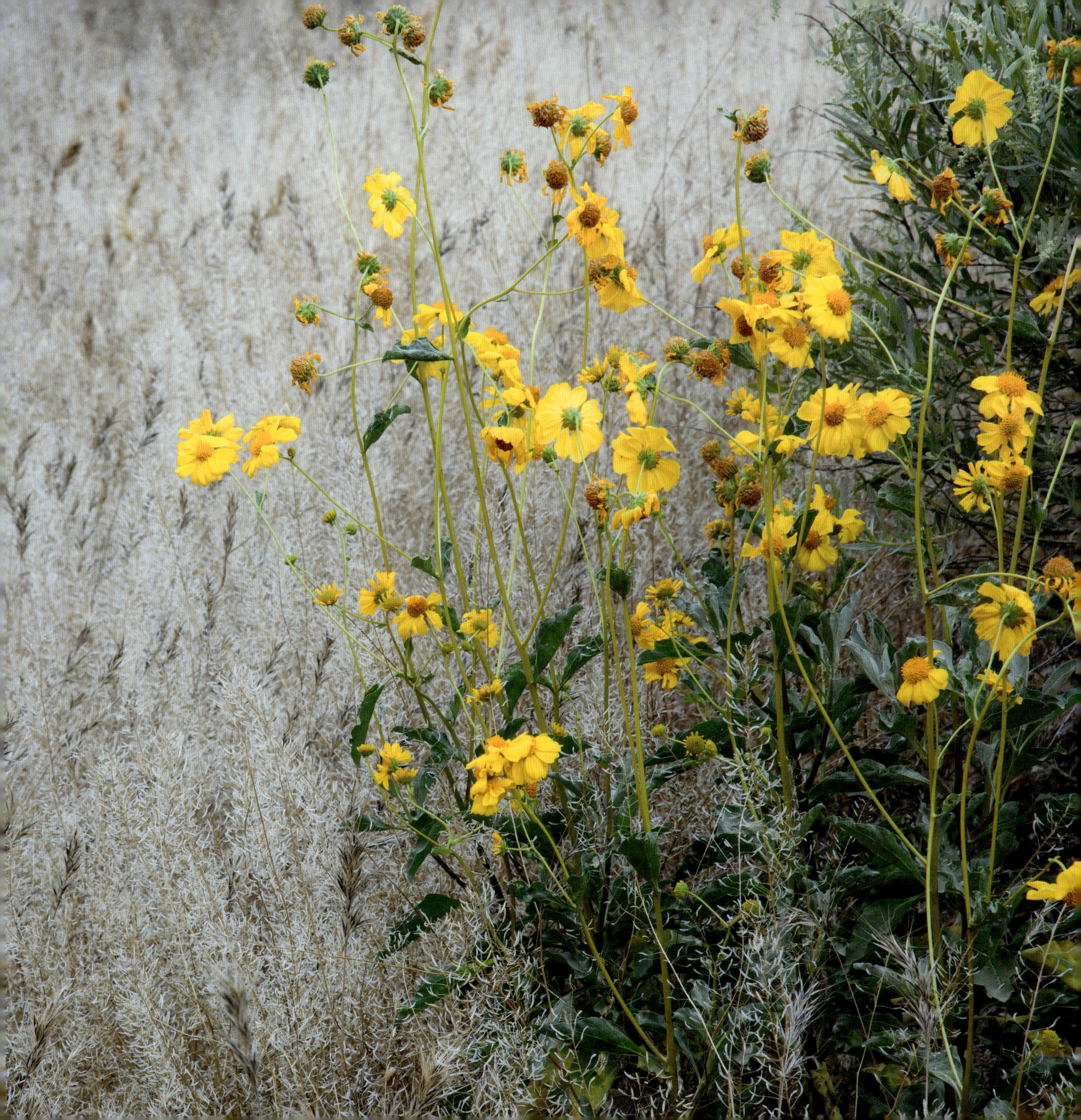

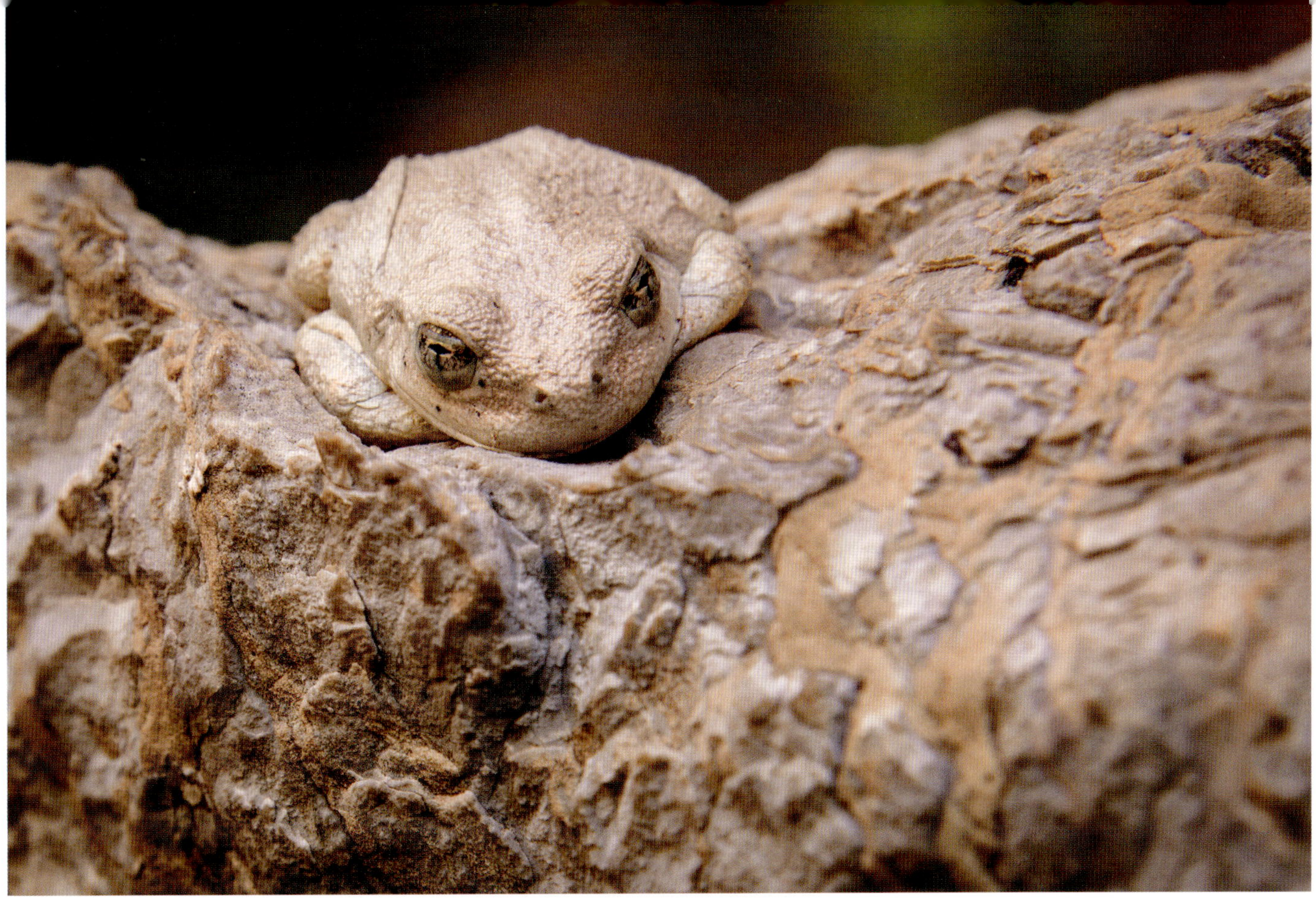

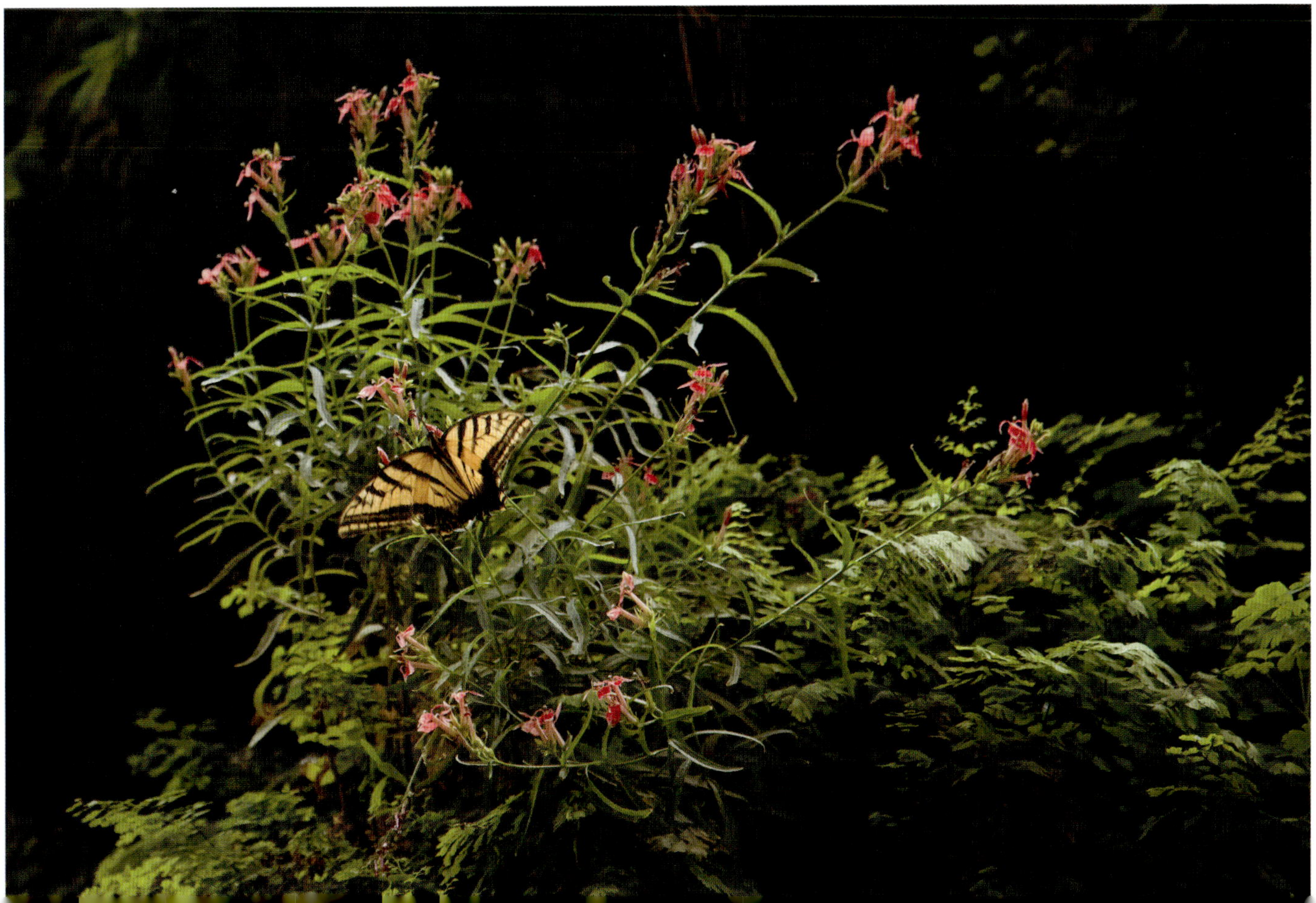

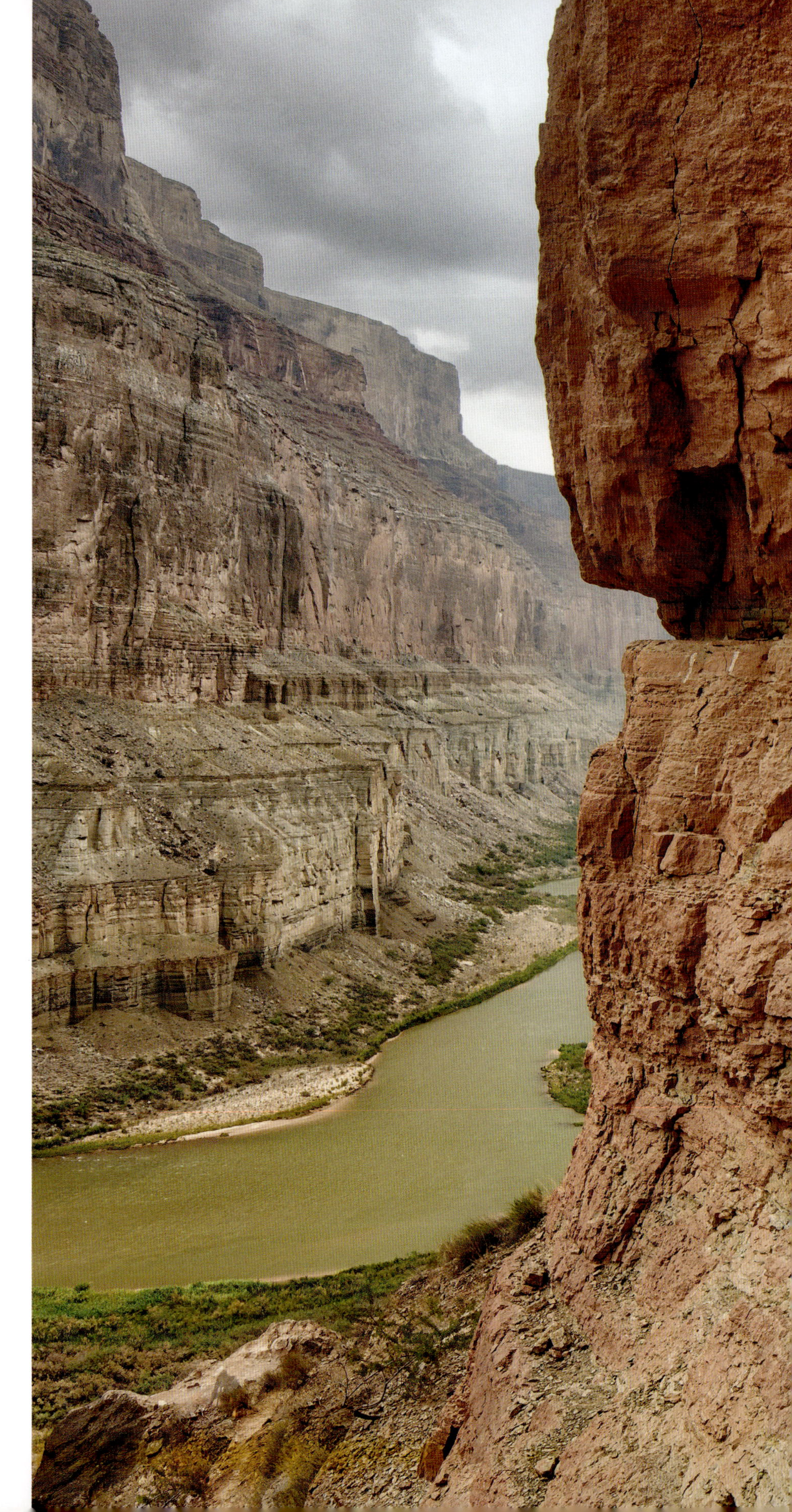

▶ Nankoweap Granaries

▼ Mesquite tree (left, top and bottom) and Colorado River (right), Nankoweap Granaries

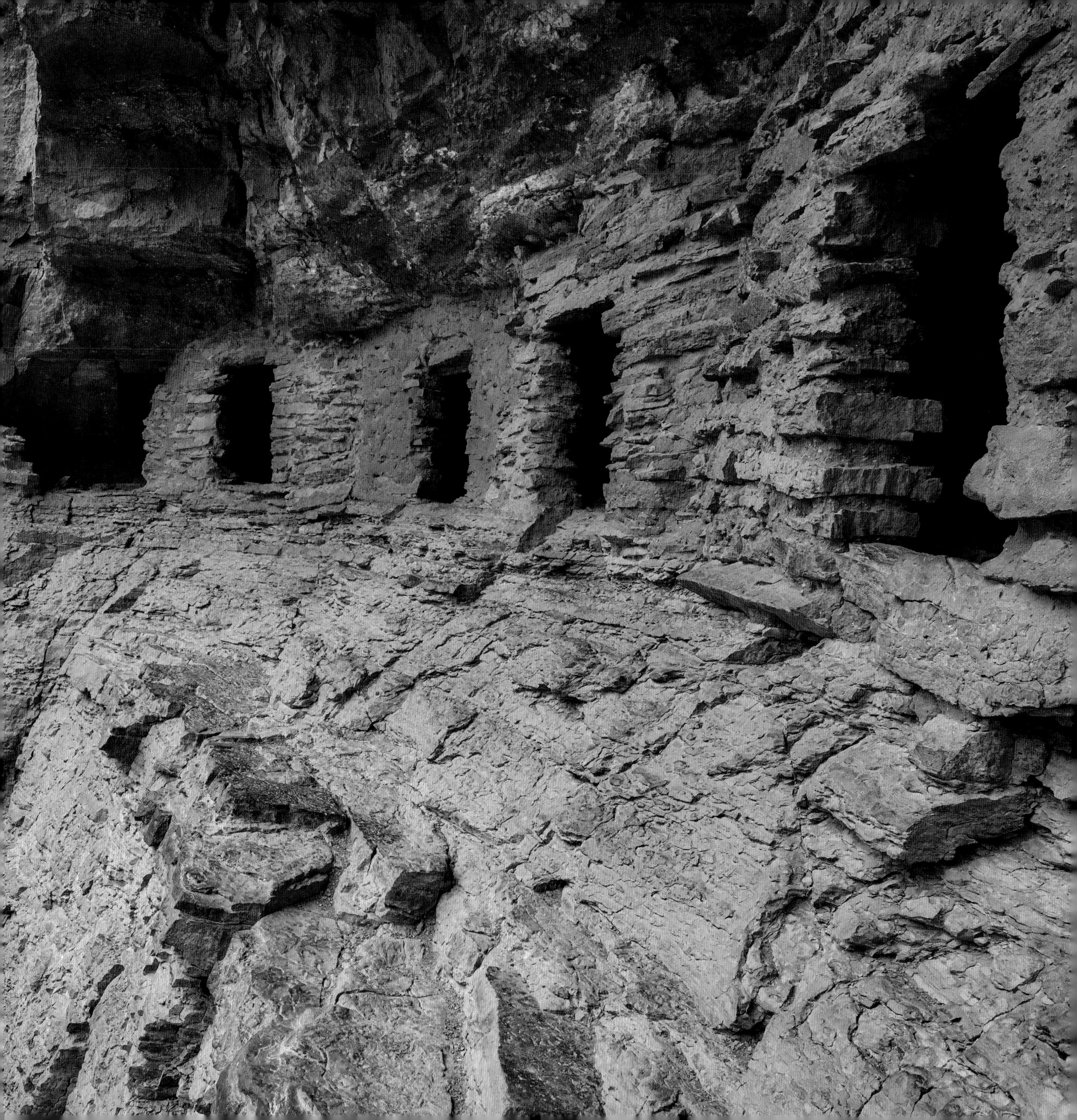

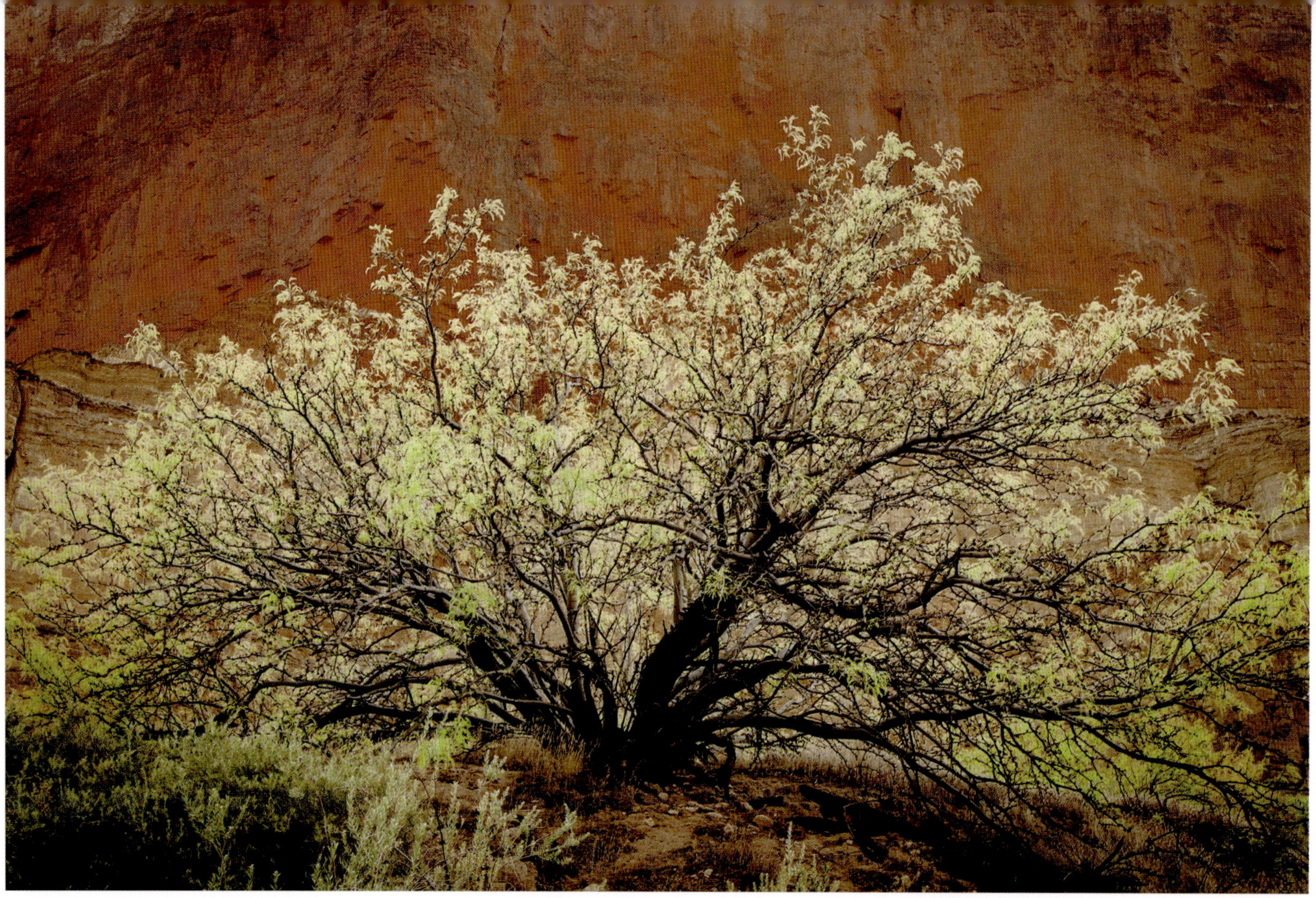

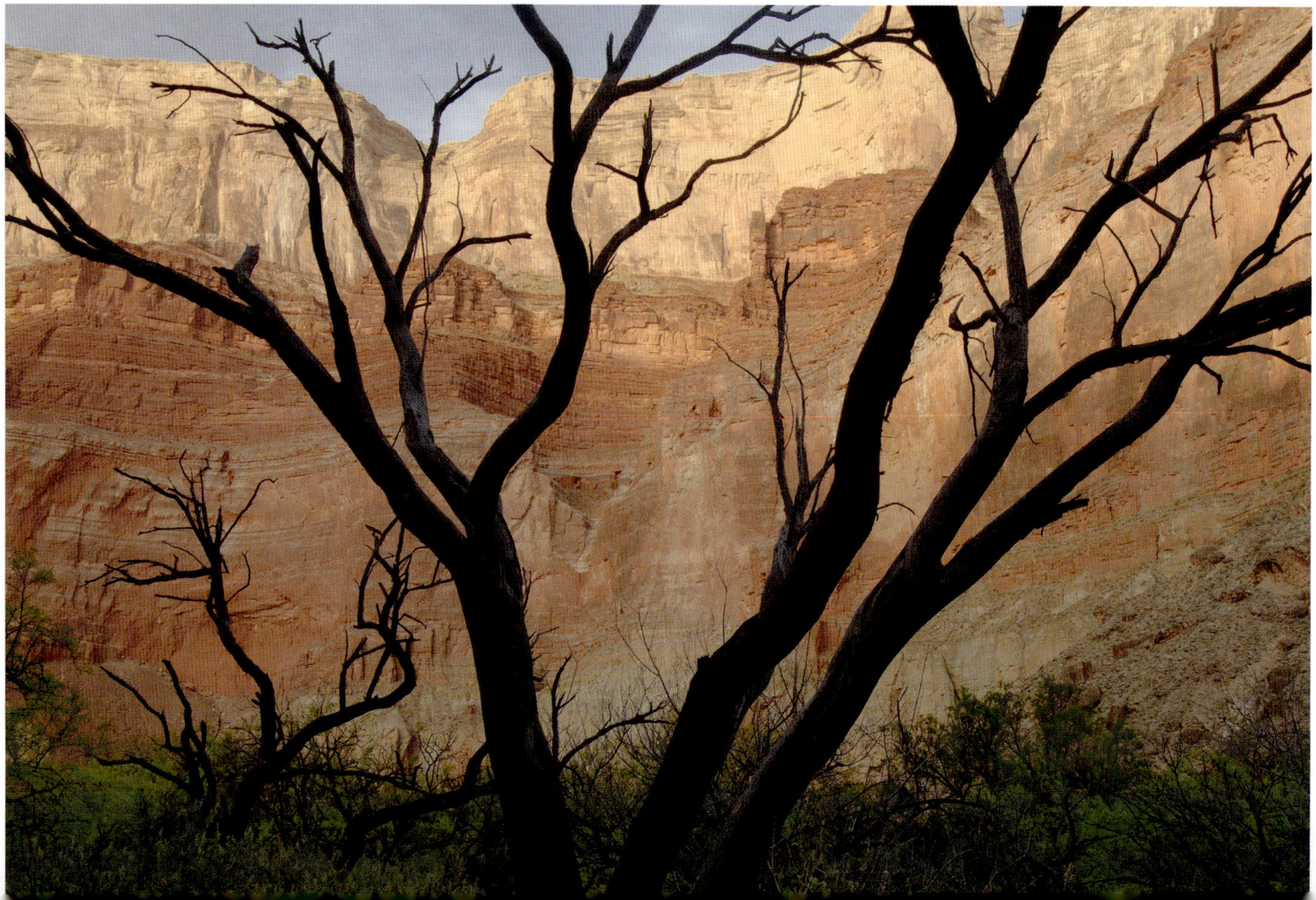

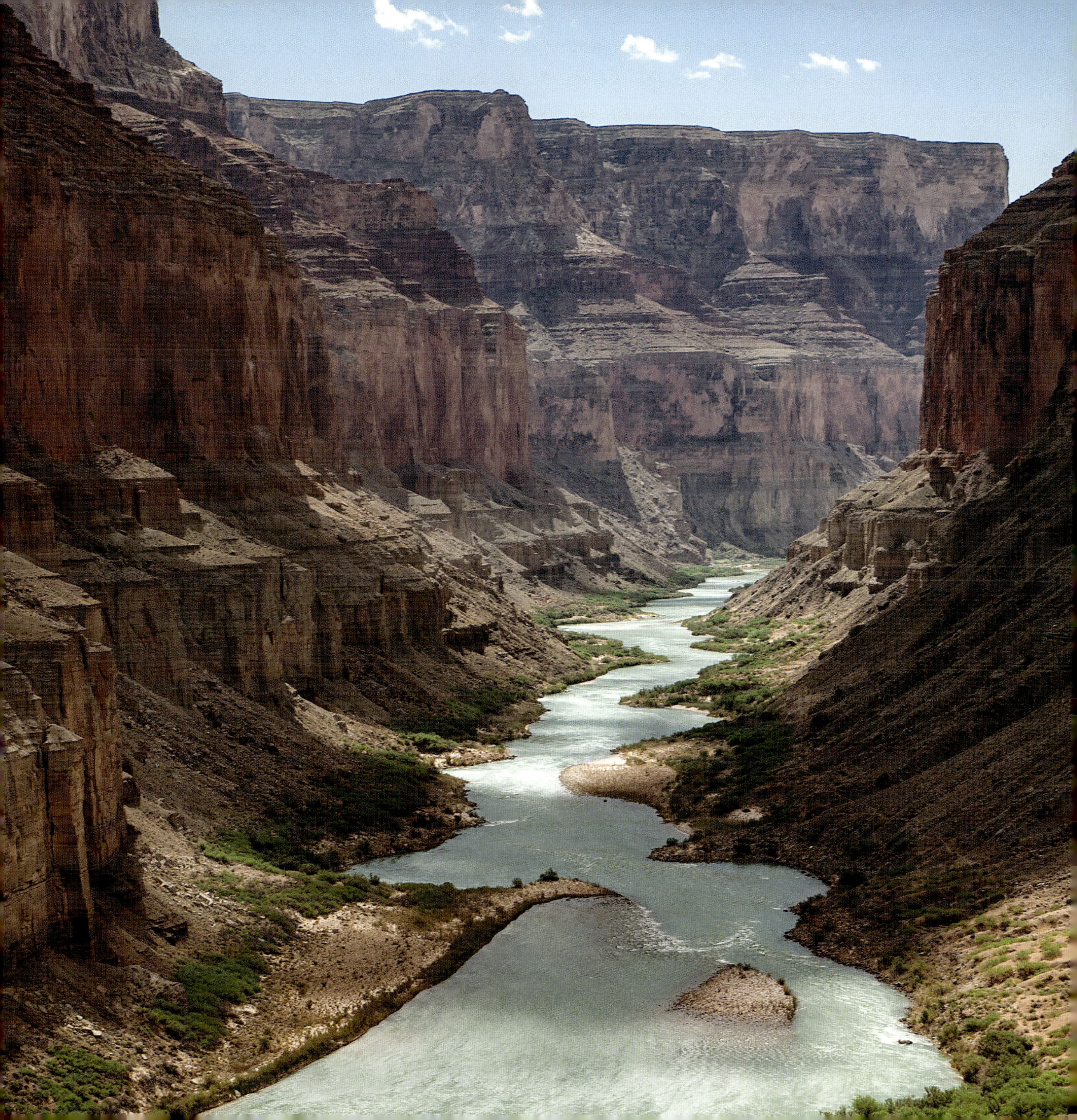

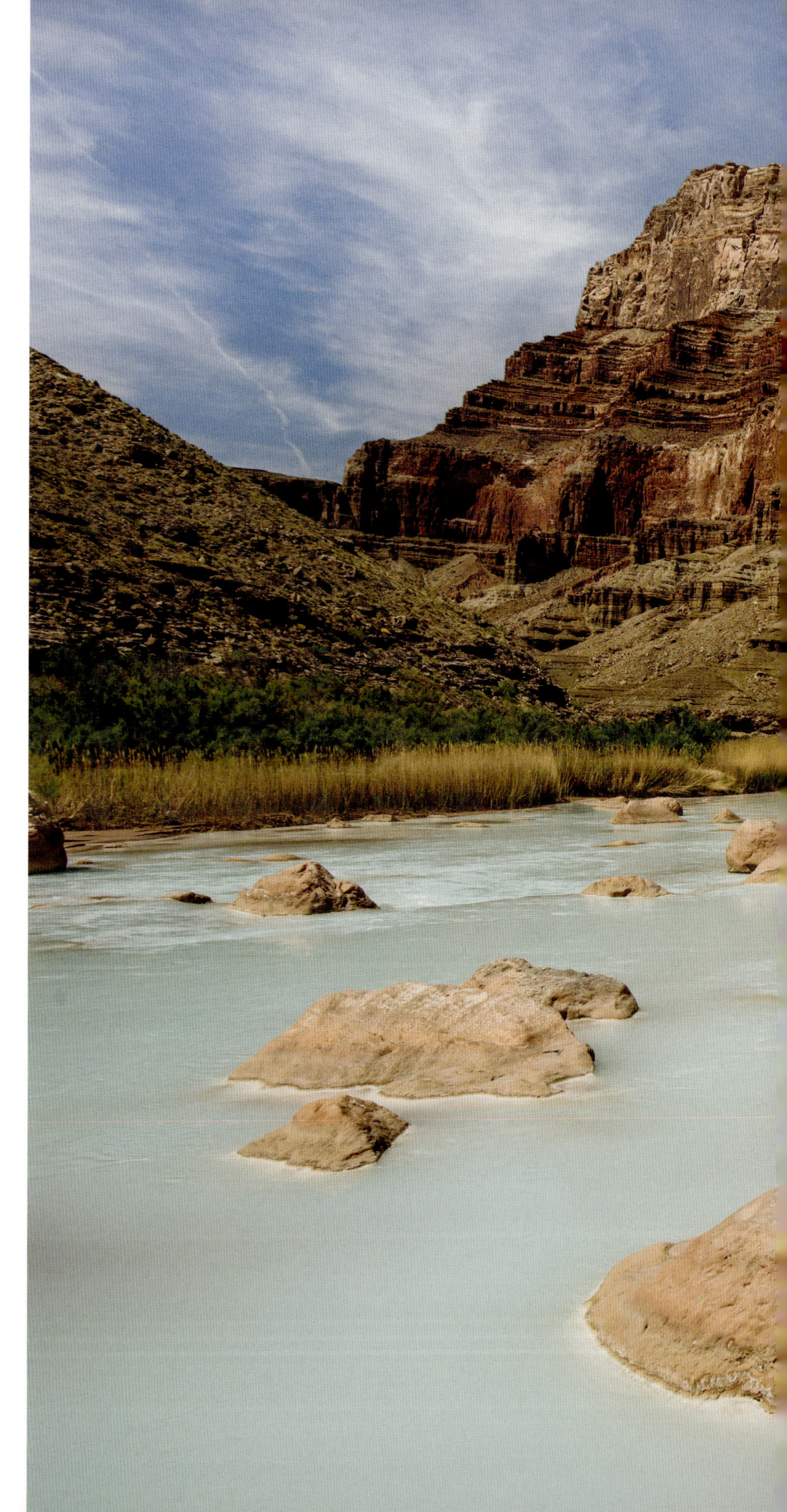

Little Colorado River

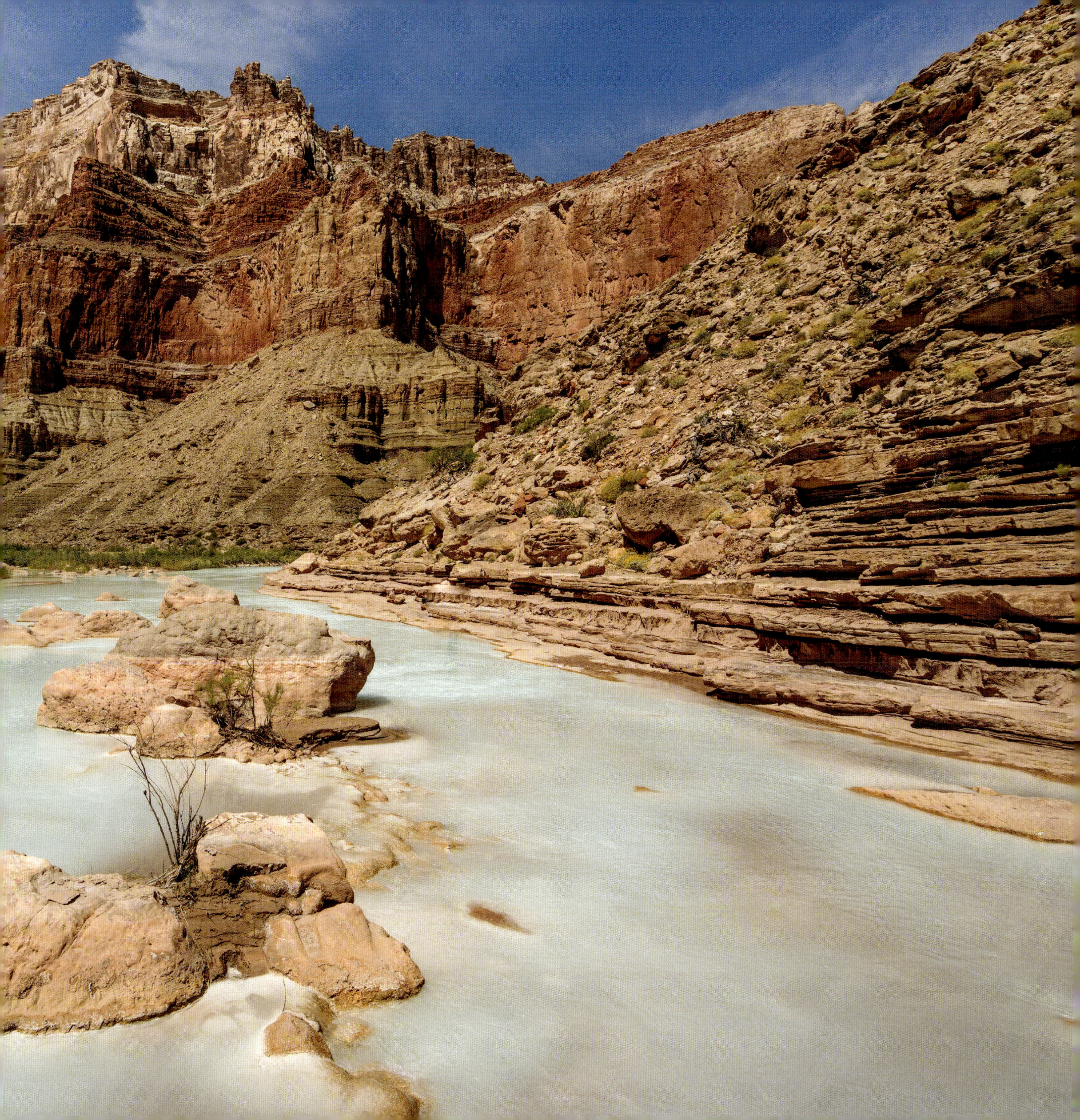

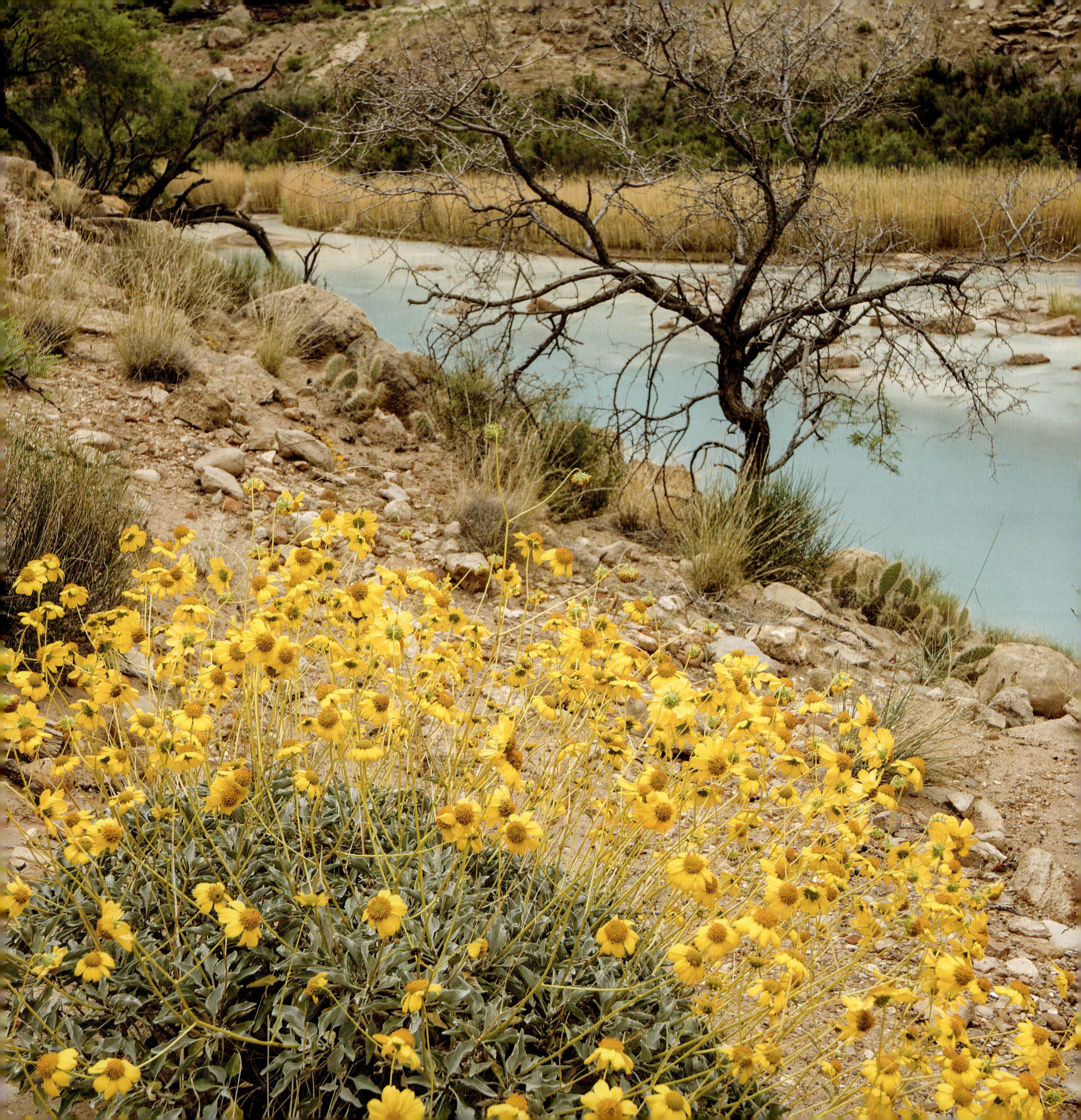

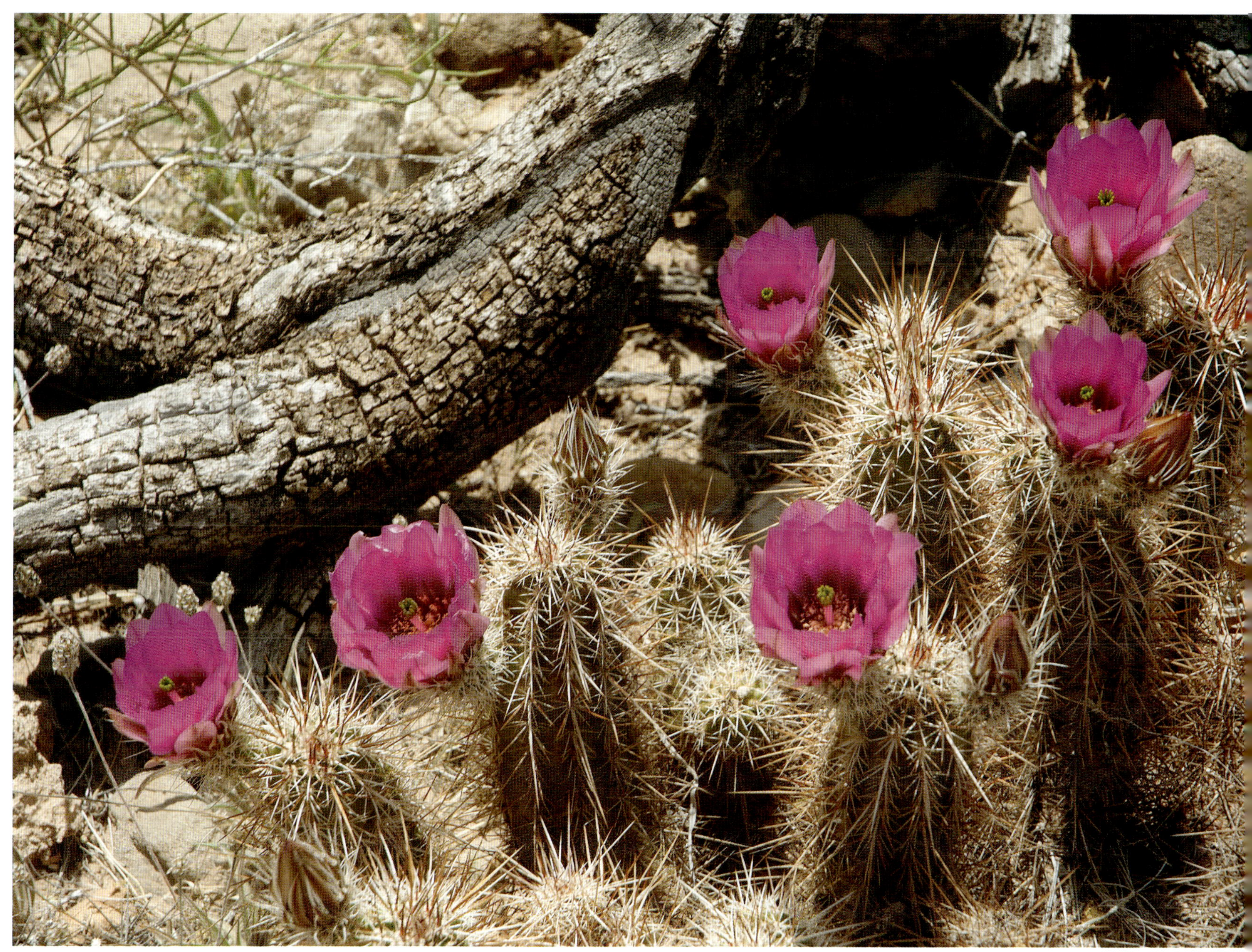

◀ Brittlebush along the Little Colorado River ▲ Engelmann hedgehog cactus, Little Colorado River

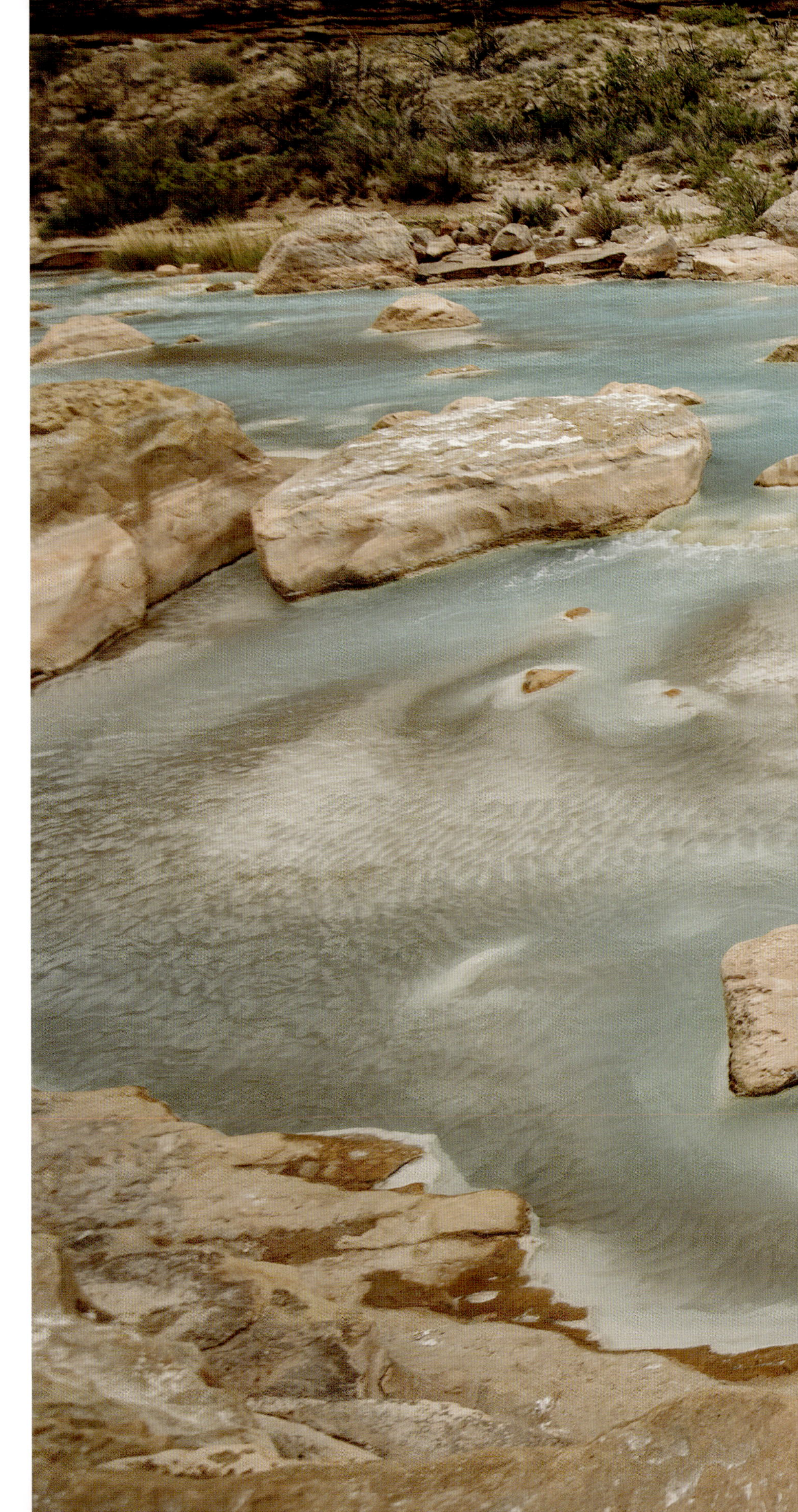

▶ Little Colorado River

▼ Silt and sand deposits (left and right, top) and dead tree stump (right, bottom), Little Colorado River

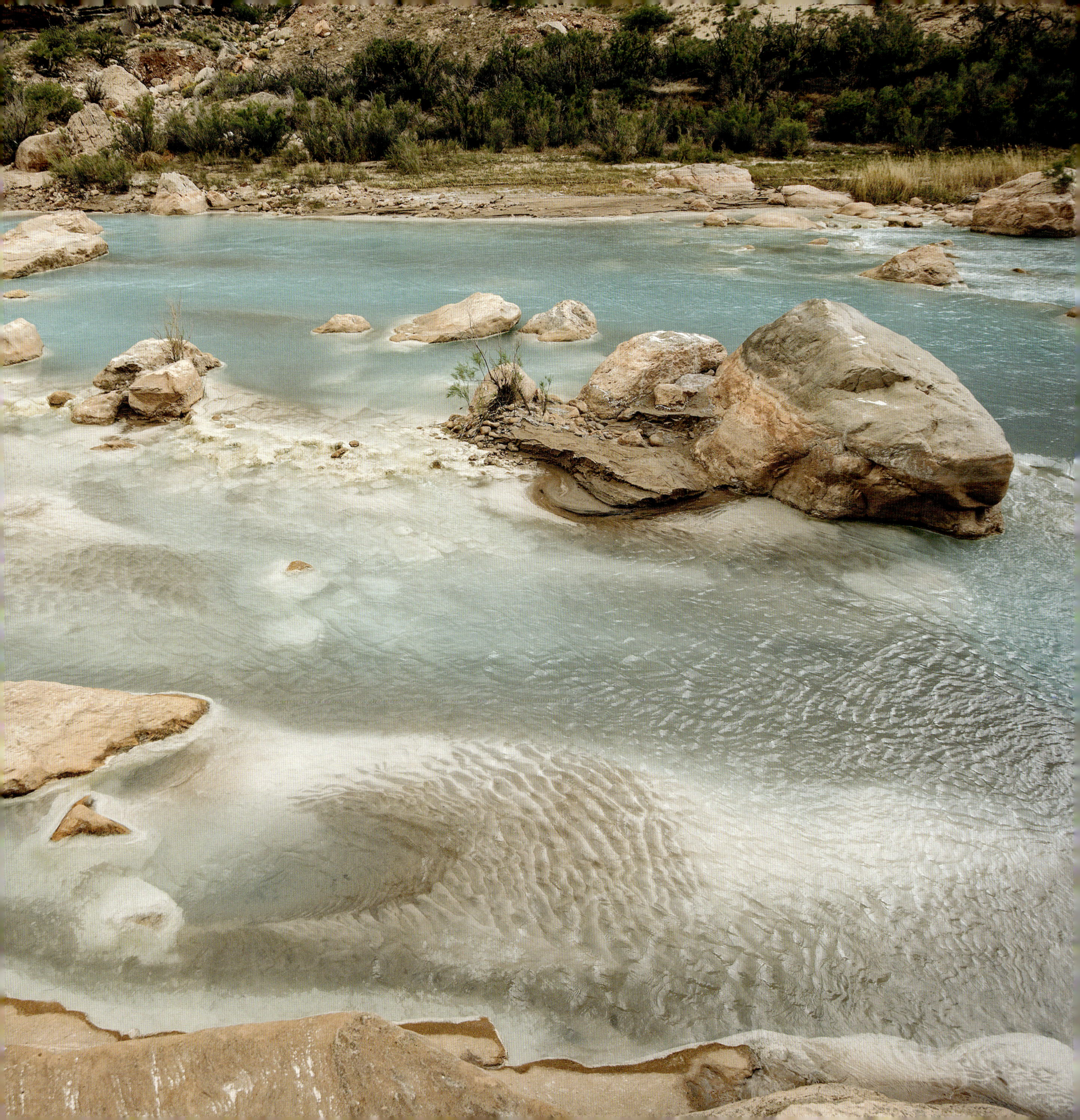

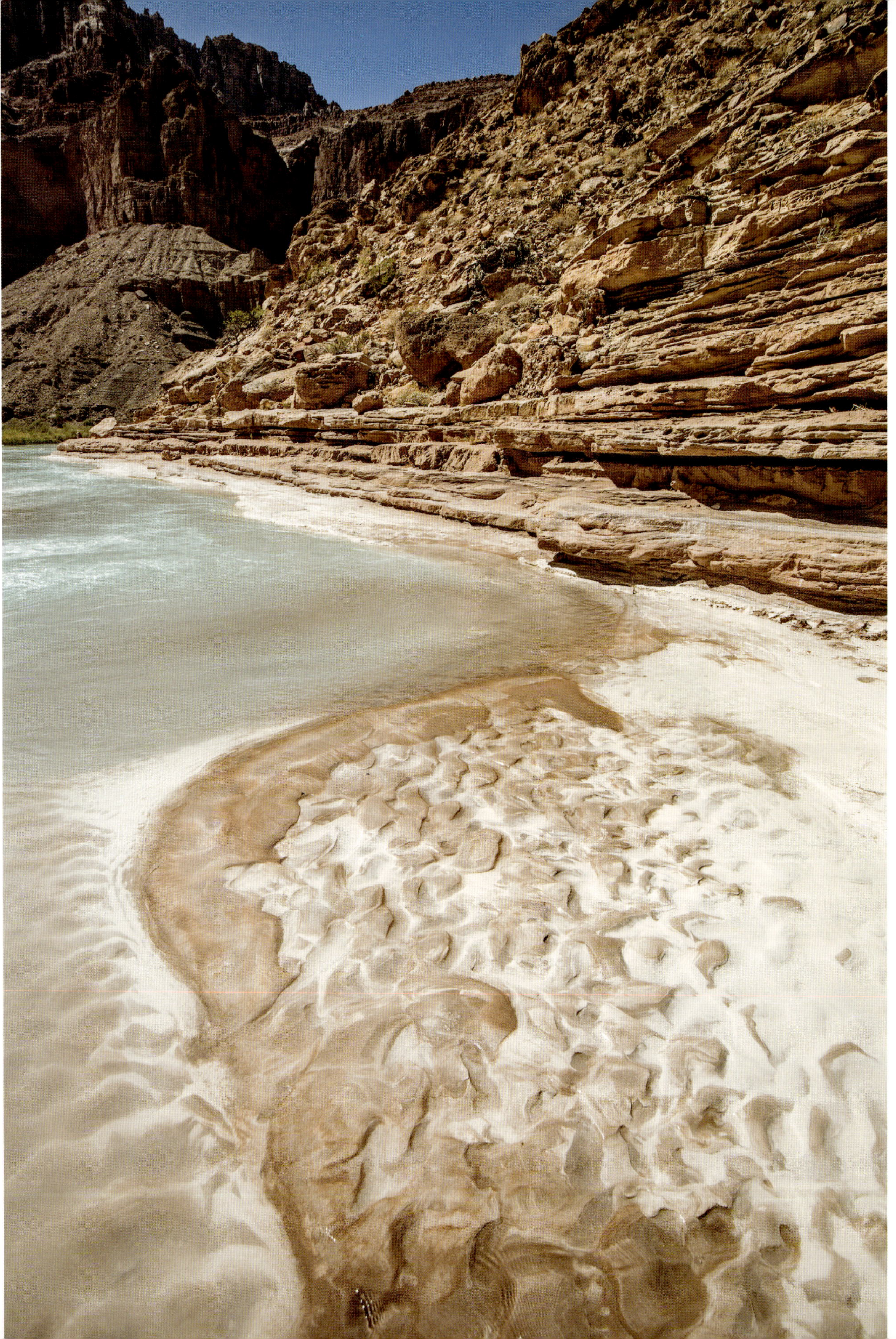

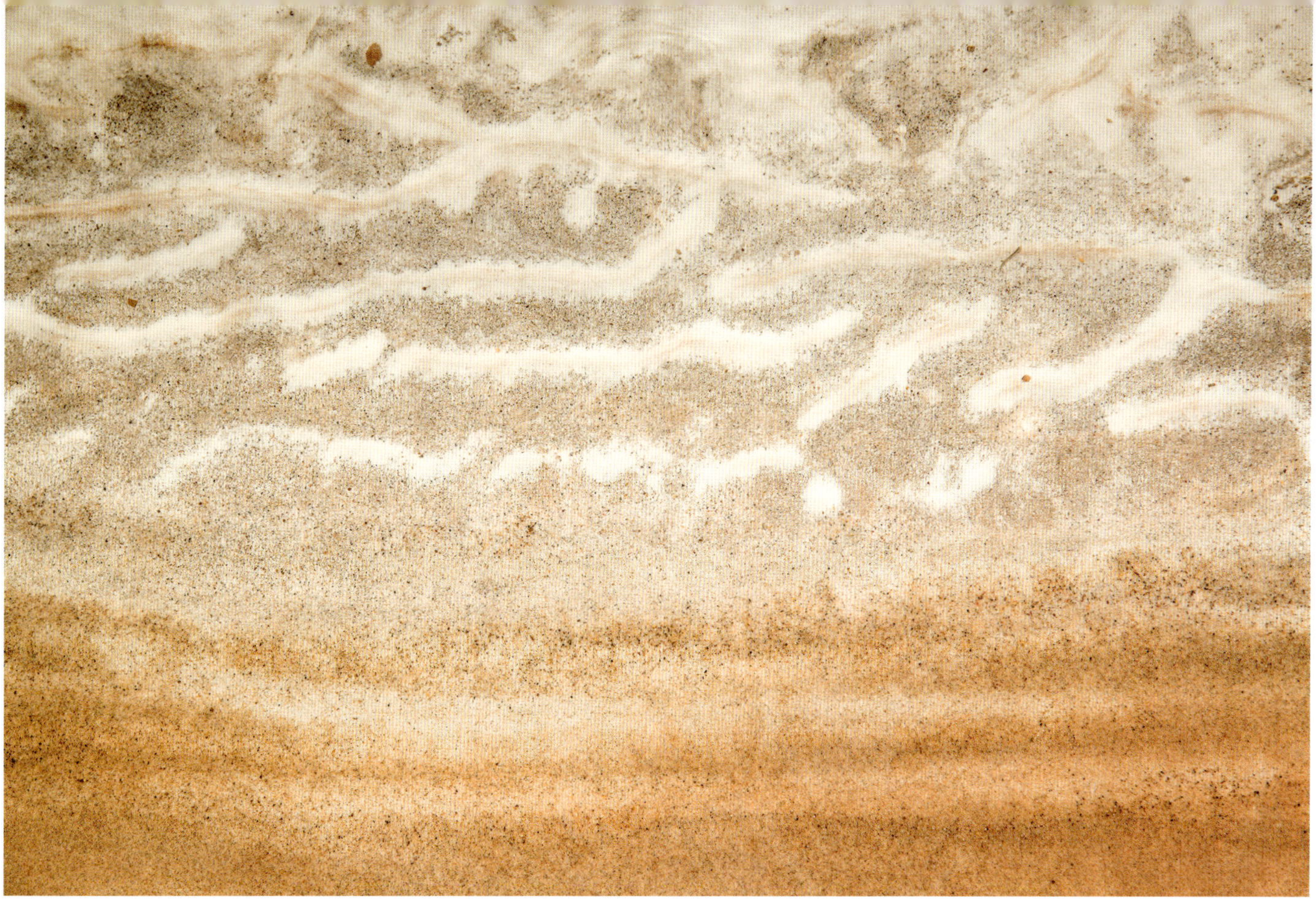

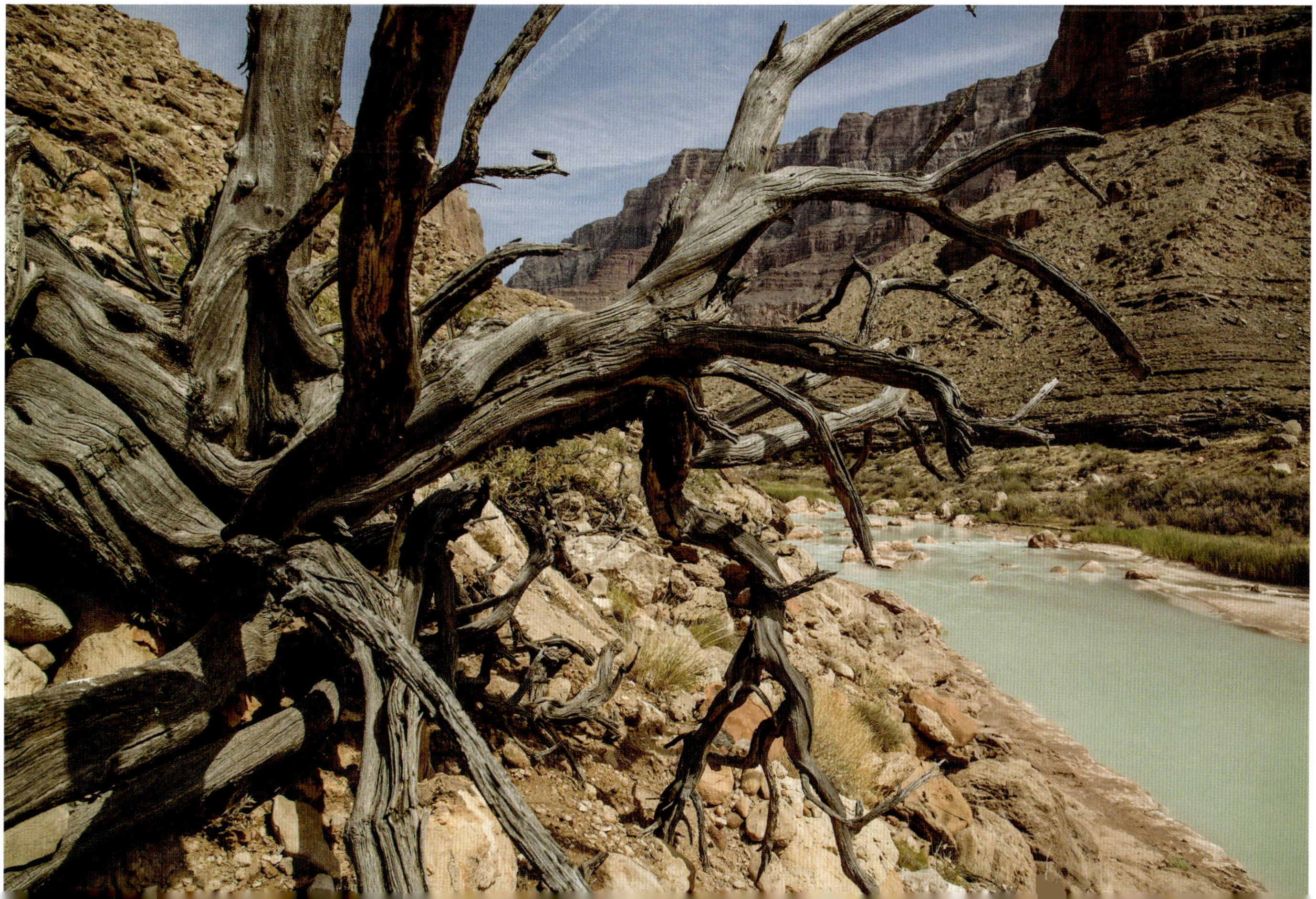

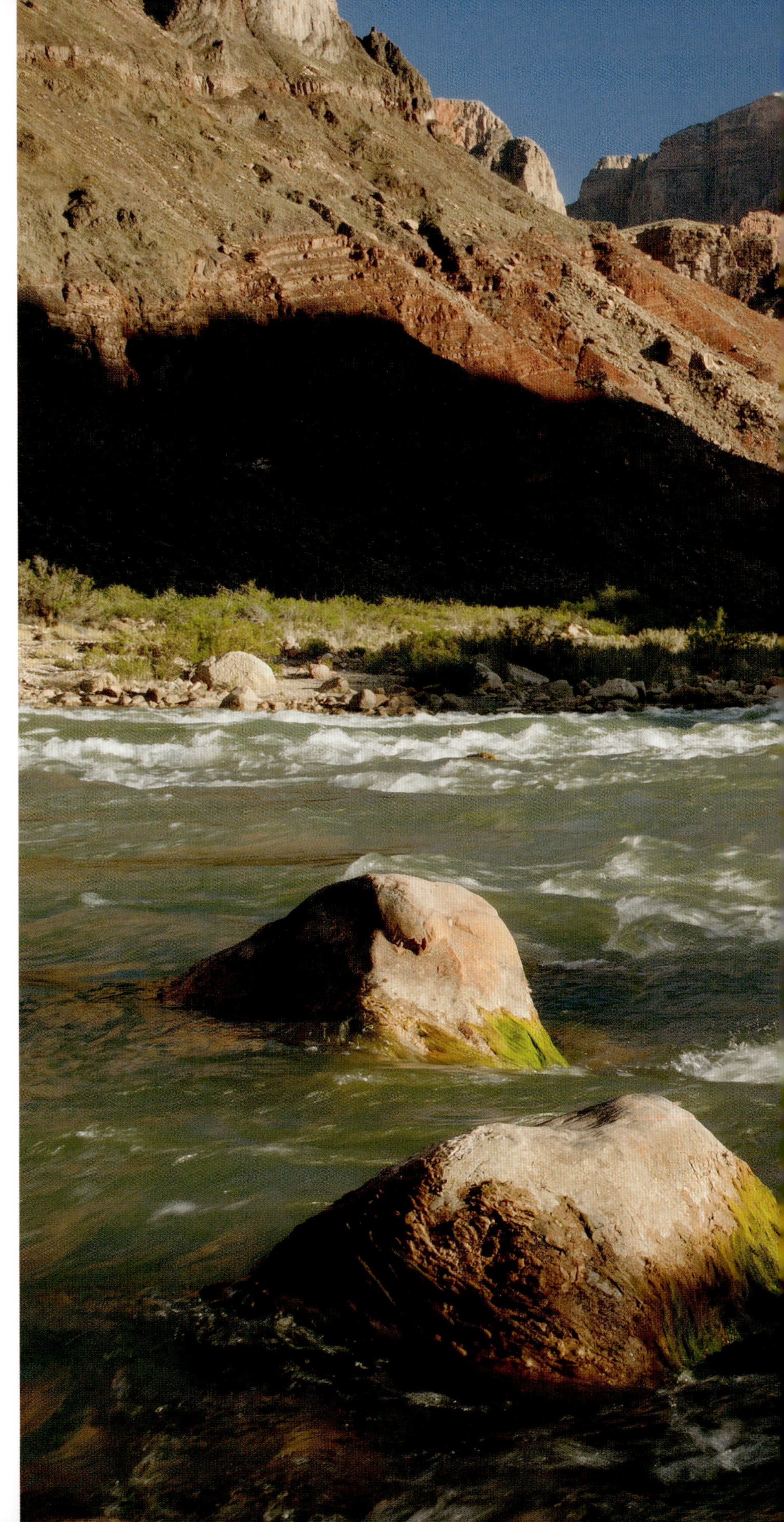

View downriver from Lava Chuar Camp

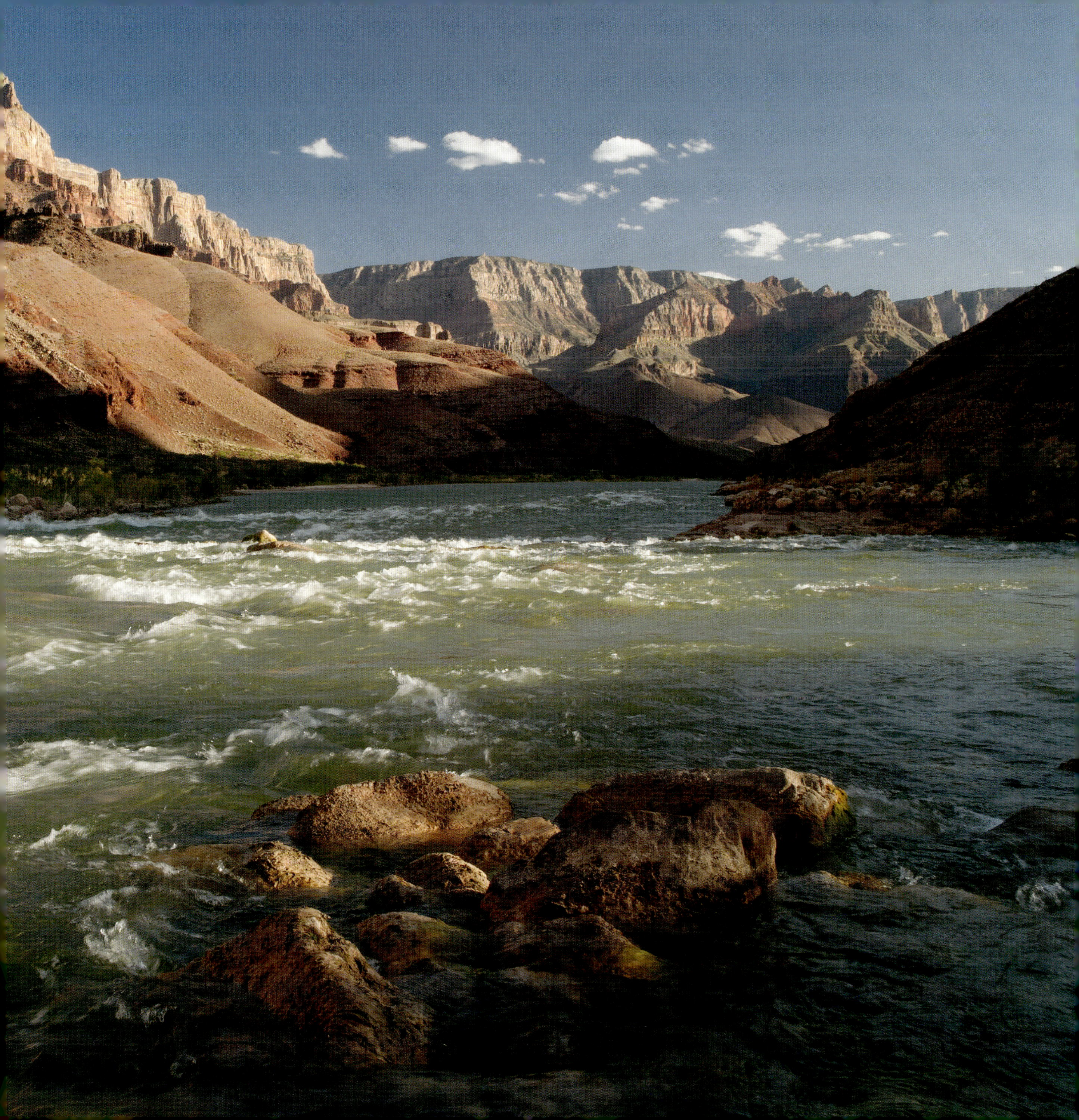

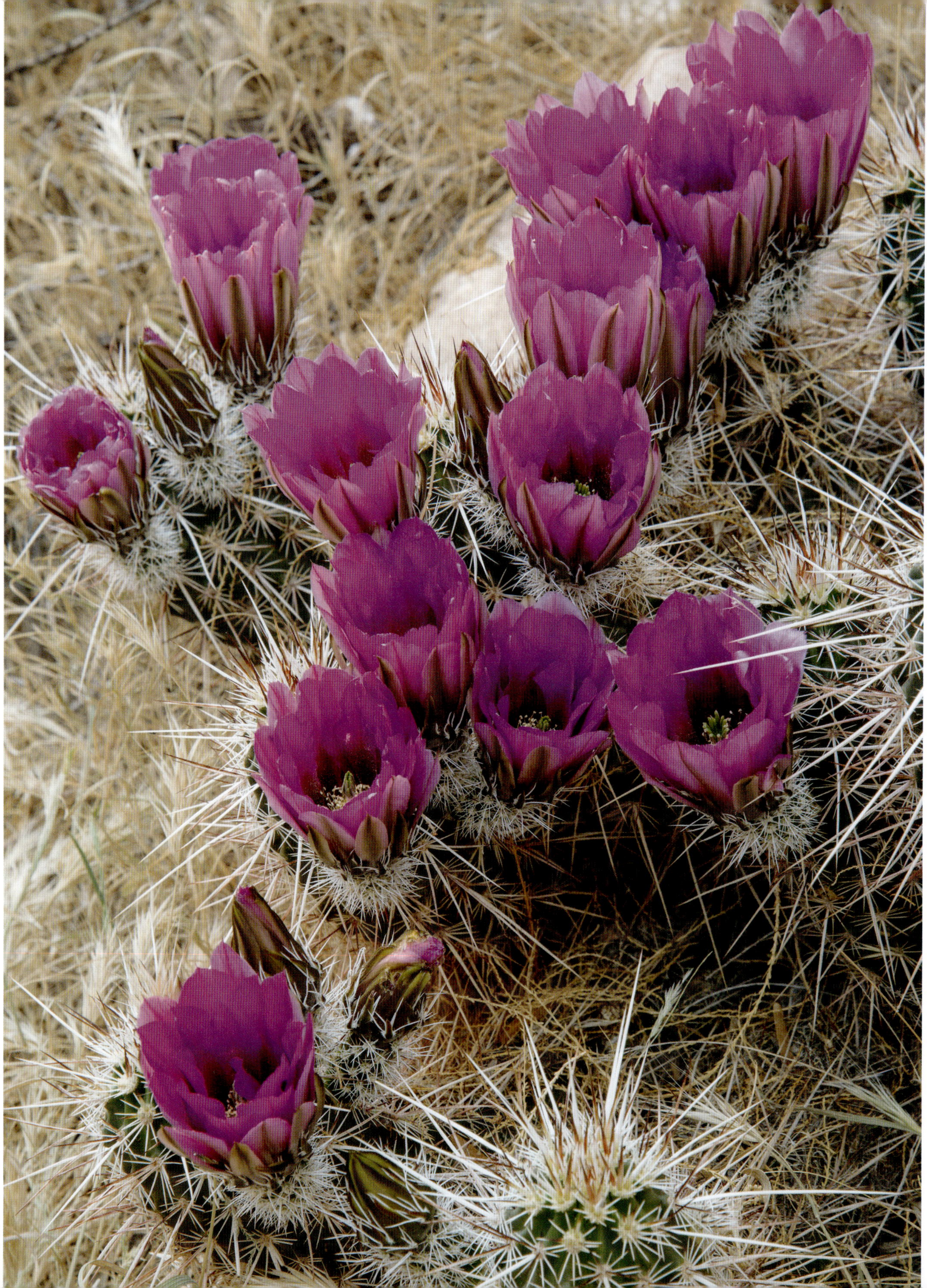

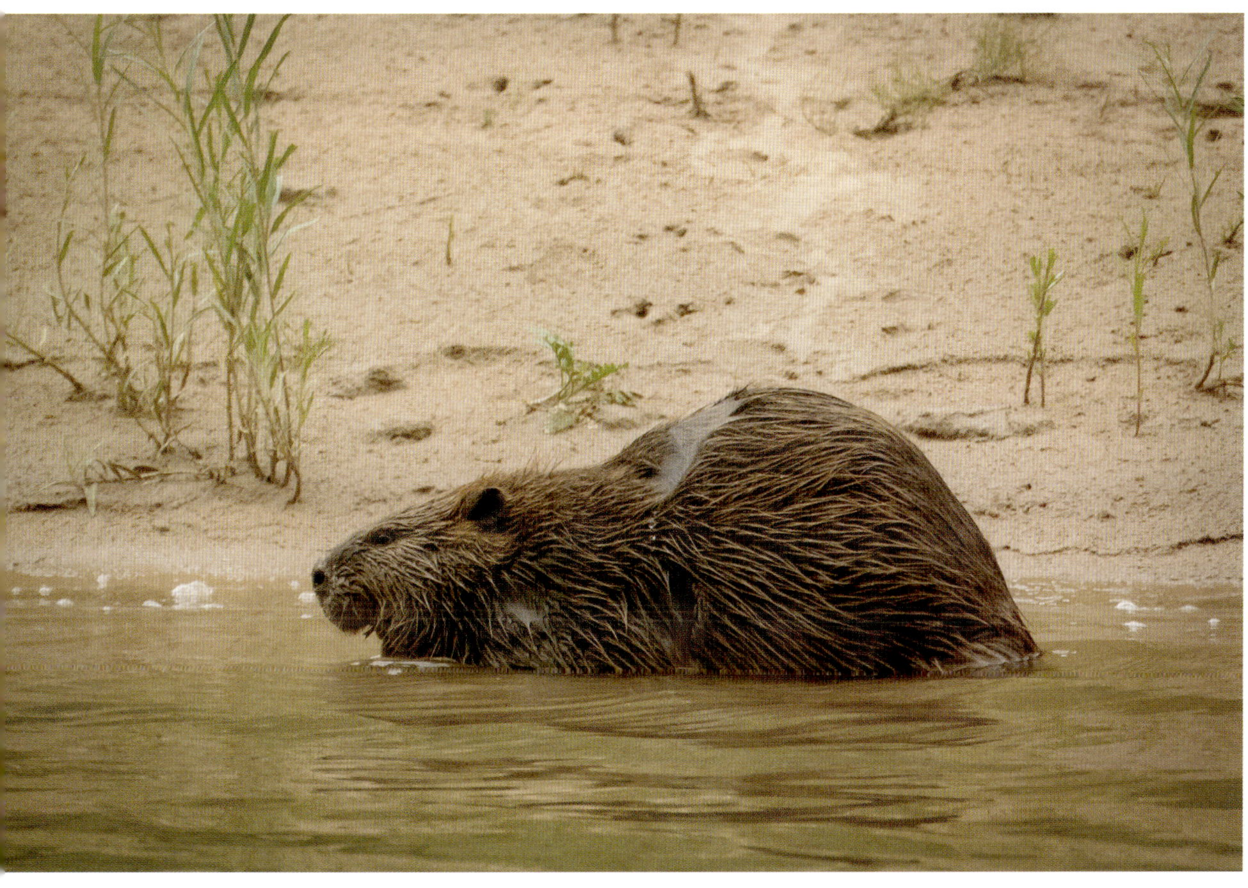

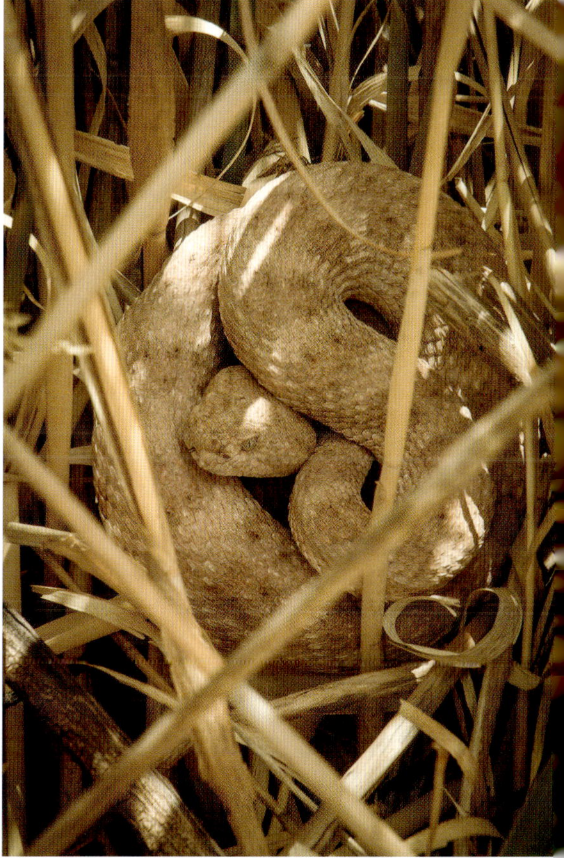

◄ Engelmann hedgehog cactus ▲ Beaver (left) and Grand Canyon rattlesnake (right)

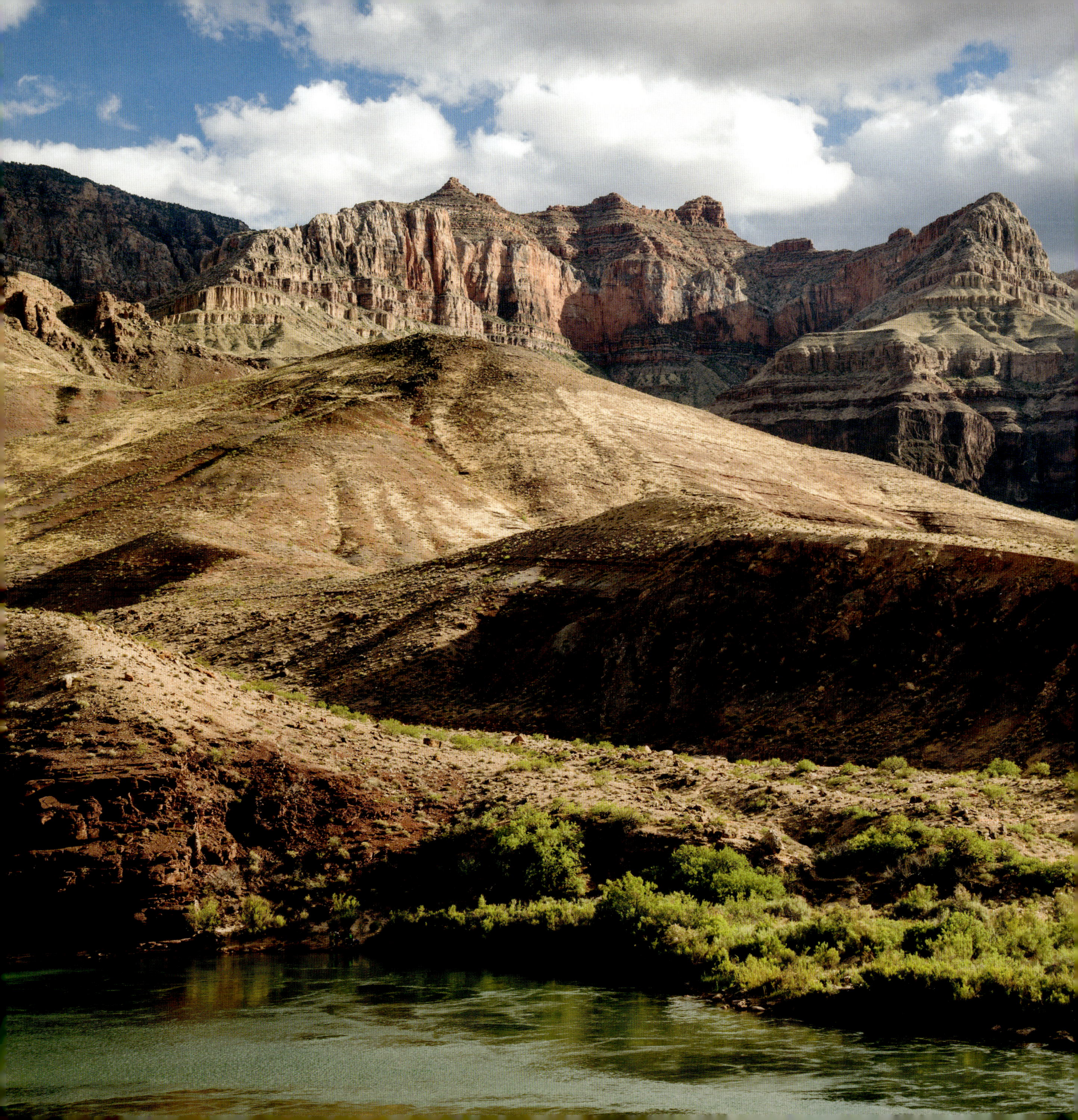

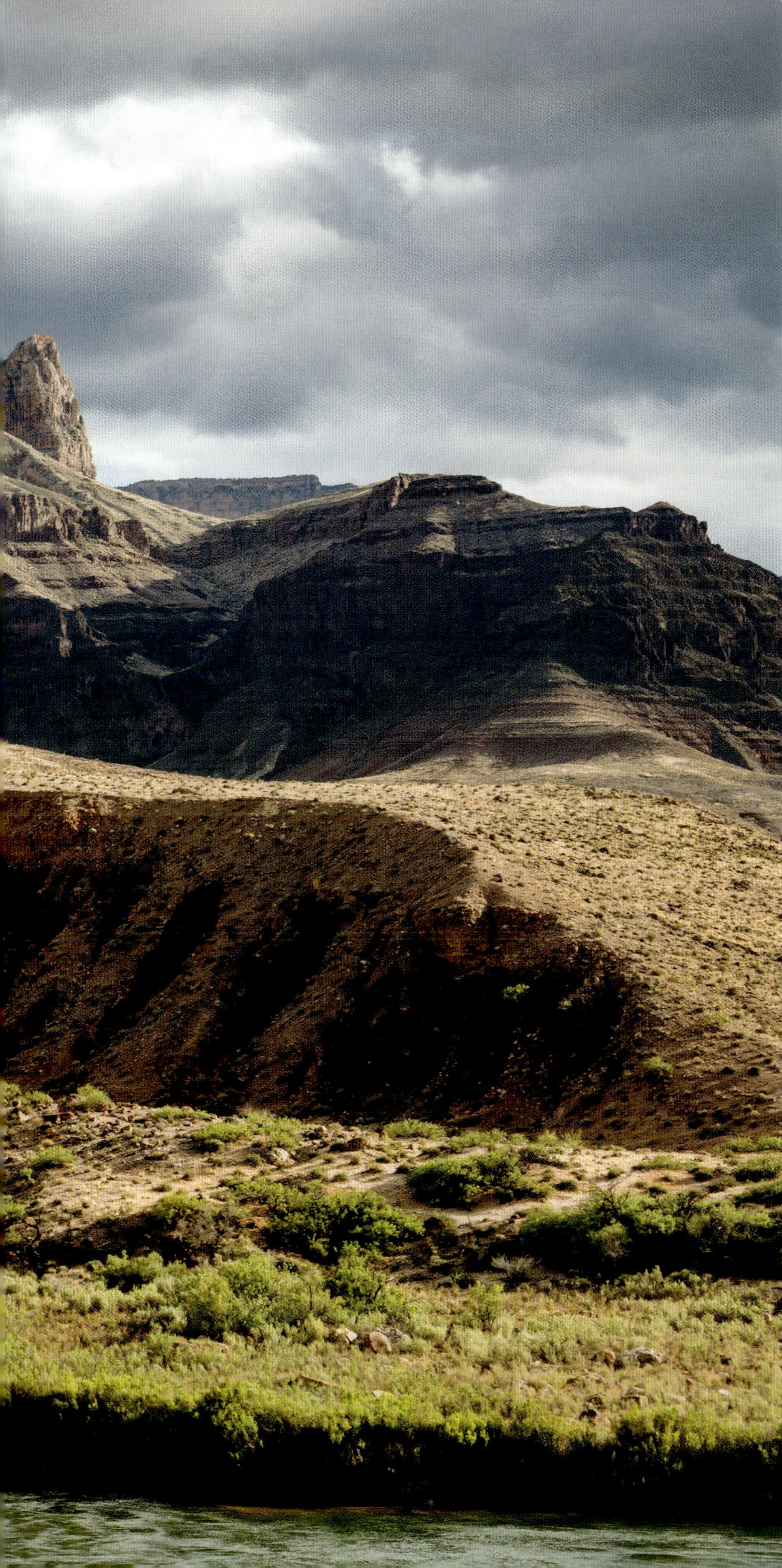

◀ Tanner Camp

▼ Sunset (left) and pale evening-primrose (right), Tanner Camp

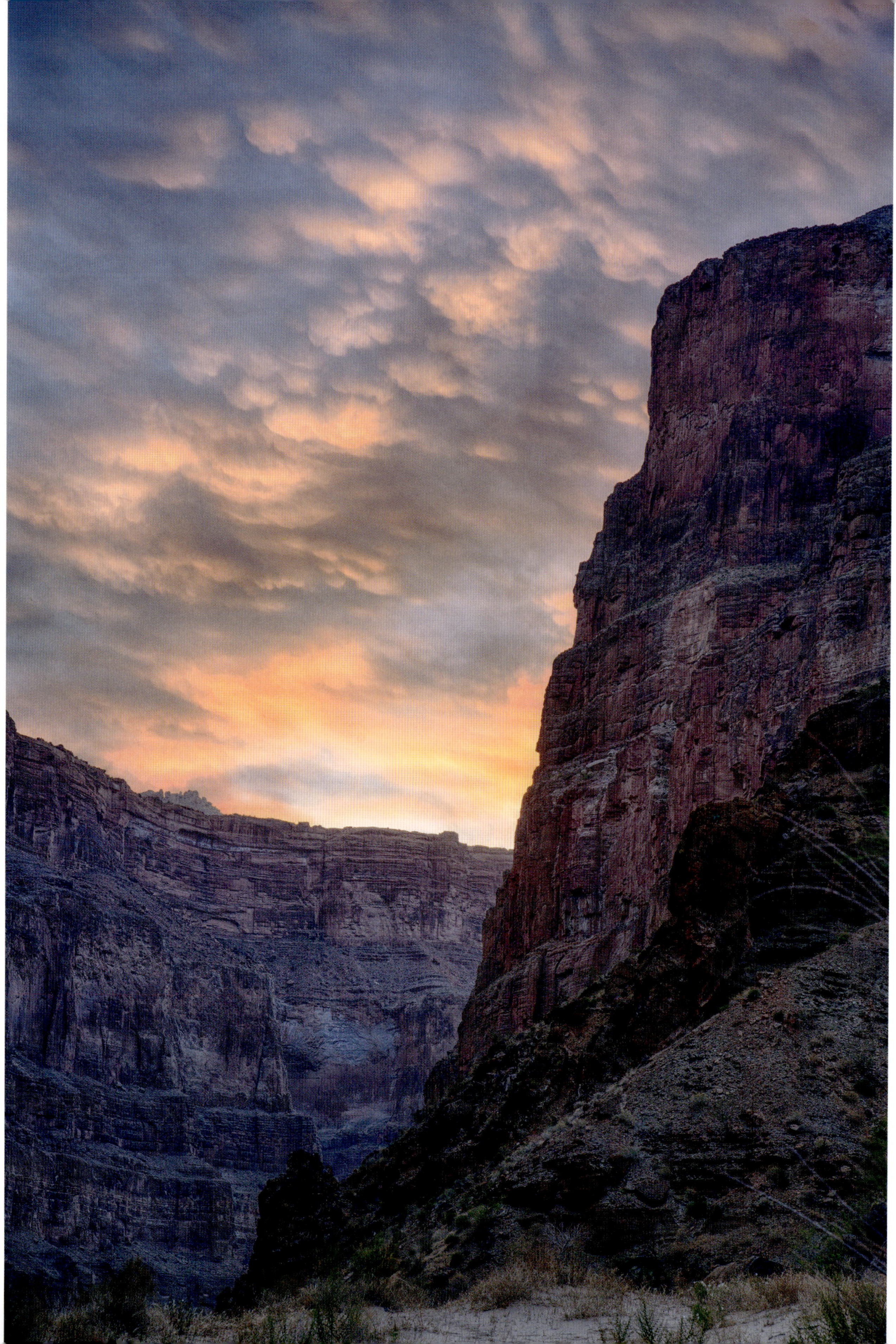

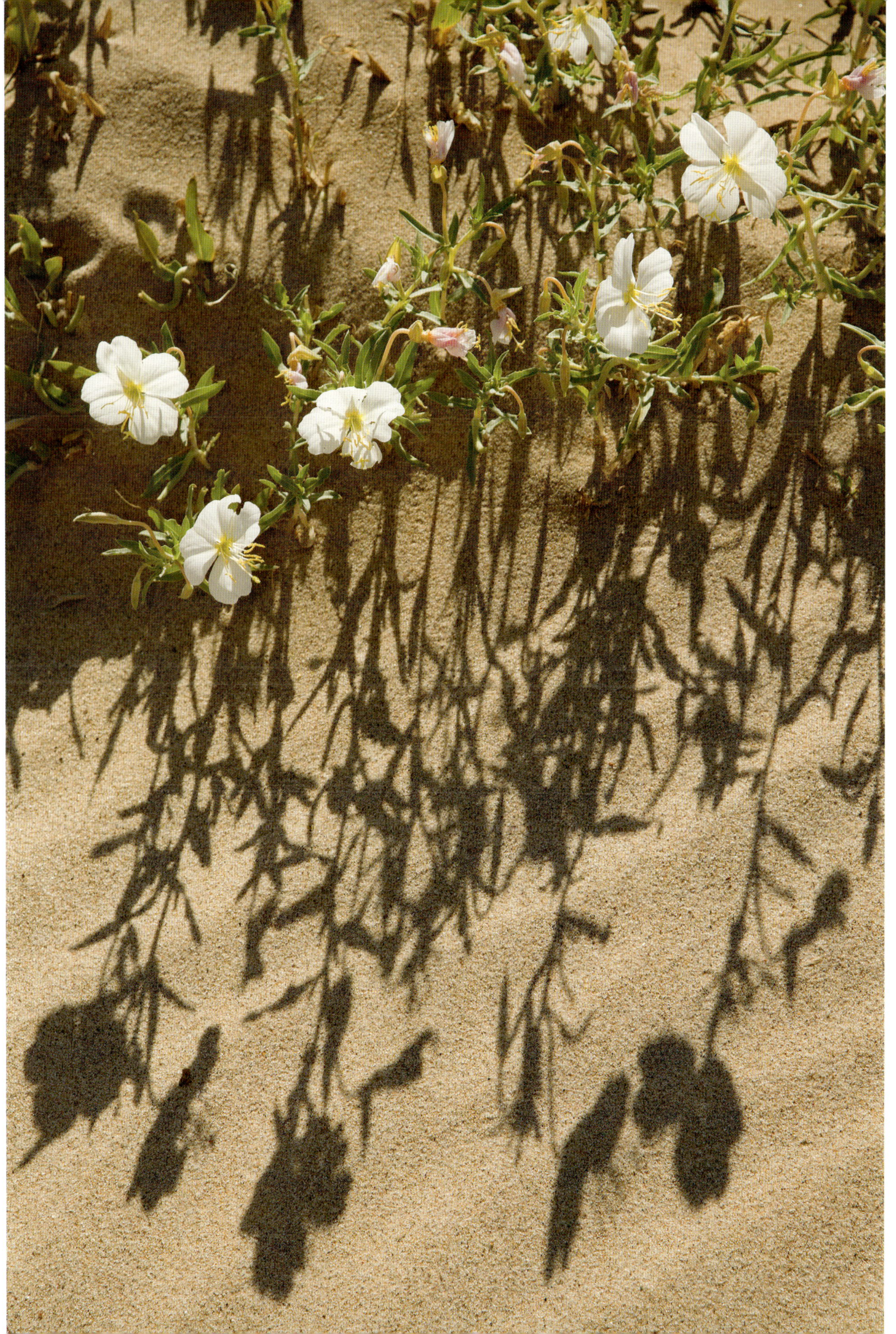

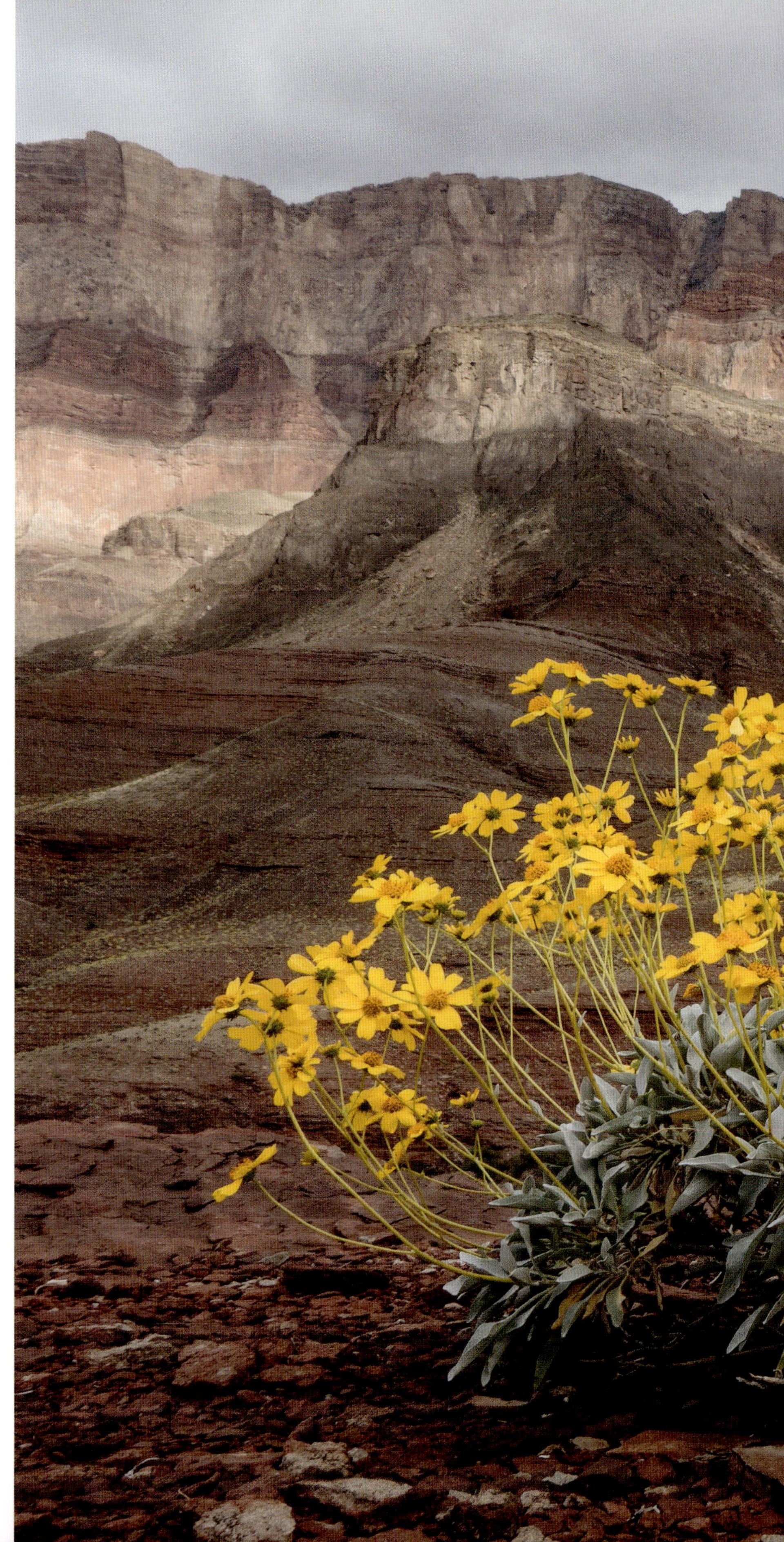

▶ Brittlebush above Tanner Camp looking across to Comanche Point

▼ Apollo Temple on the North Rim

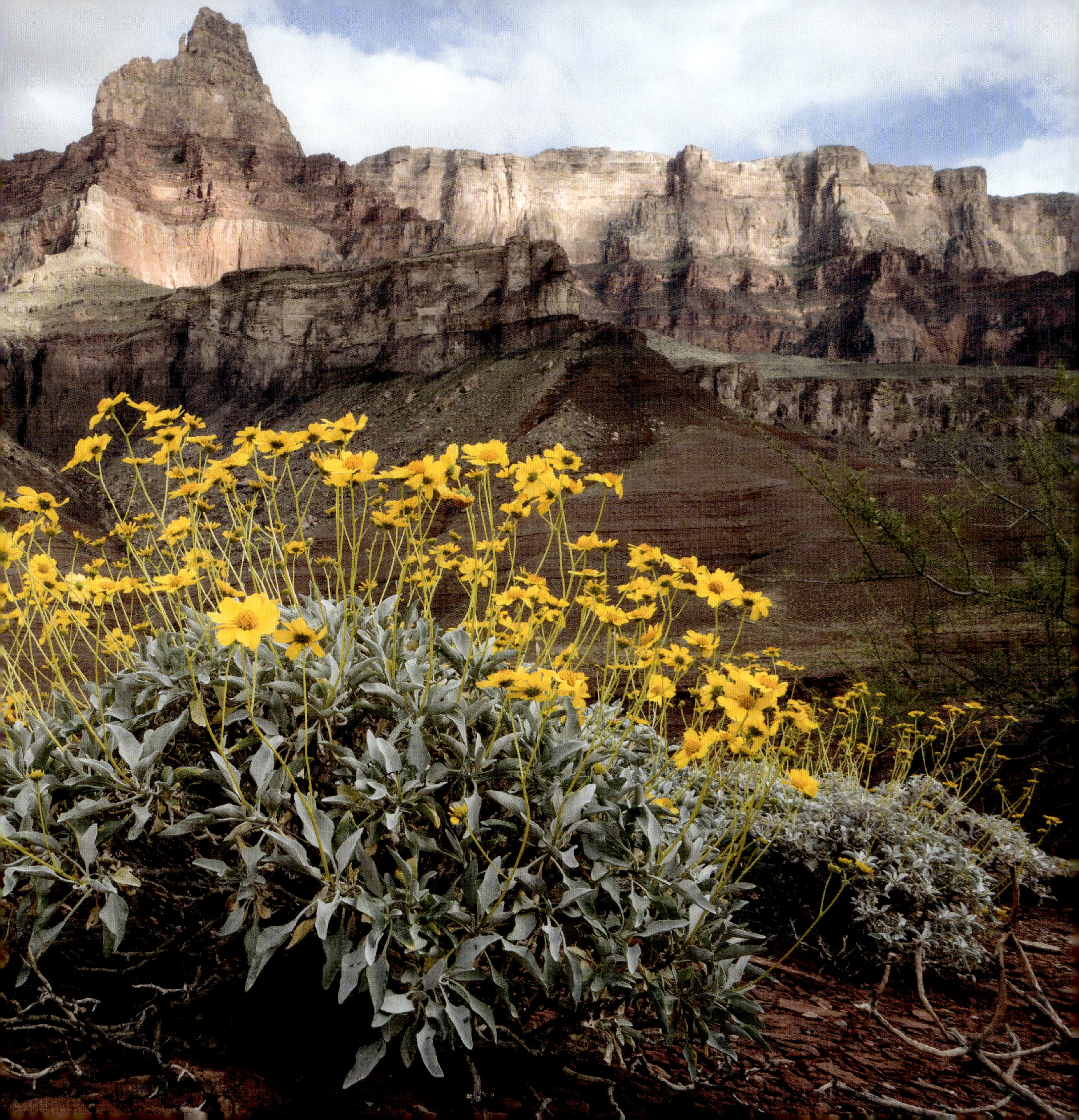

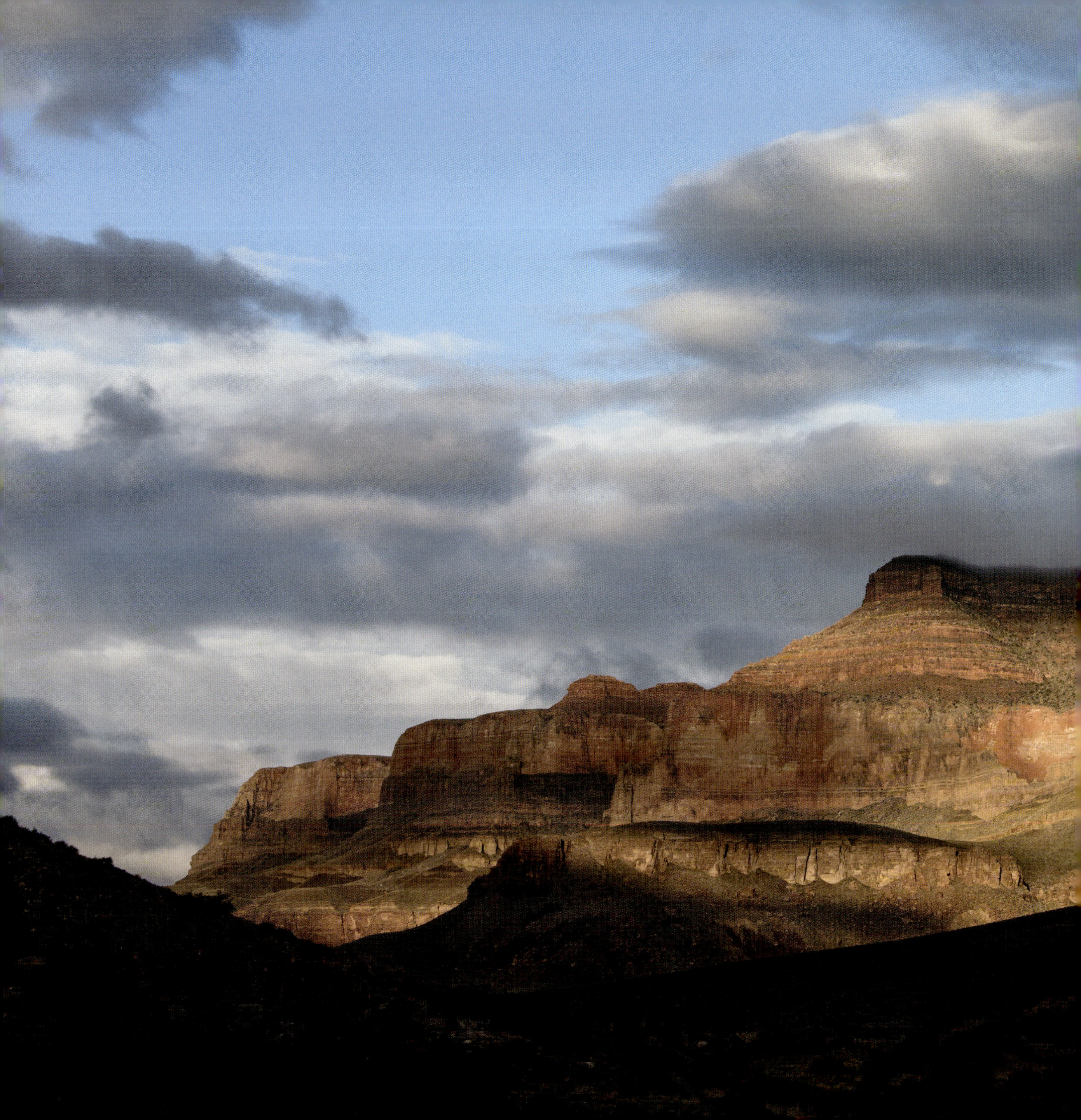

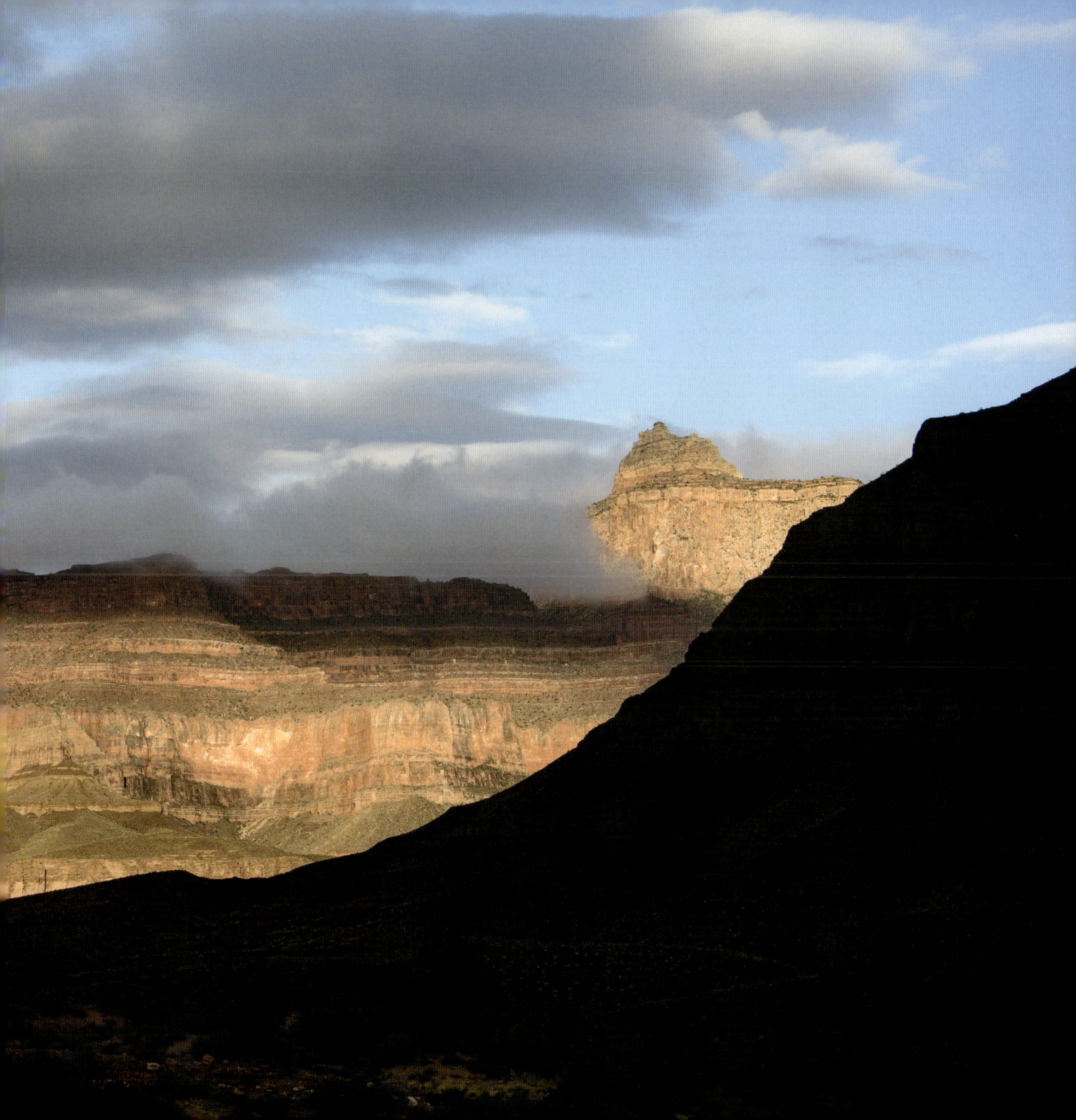

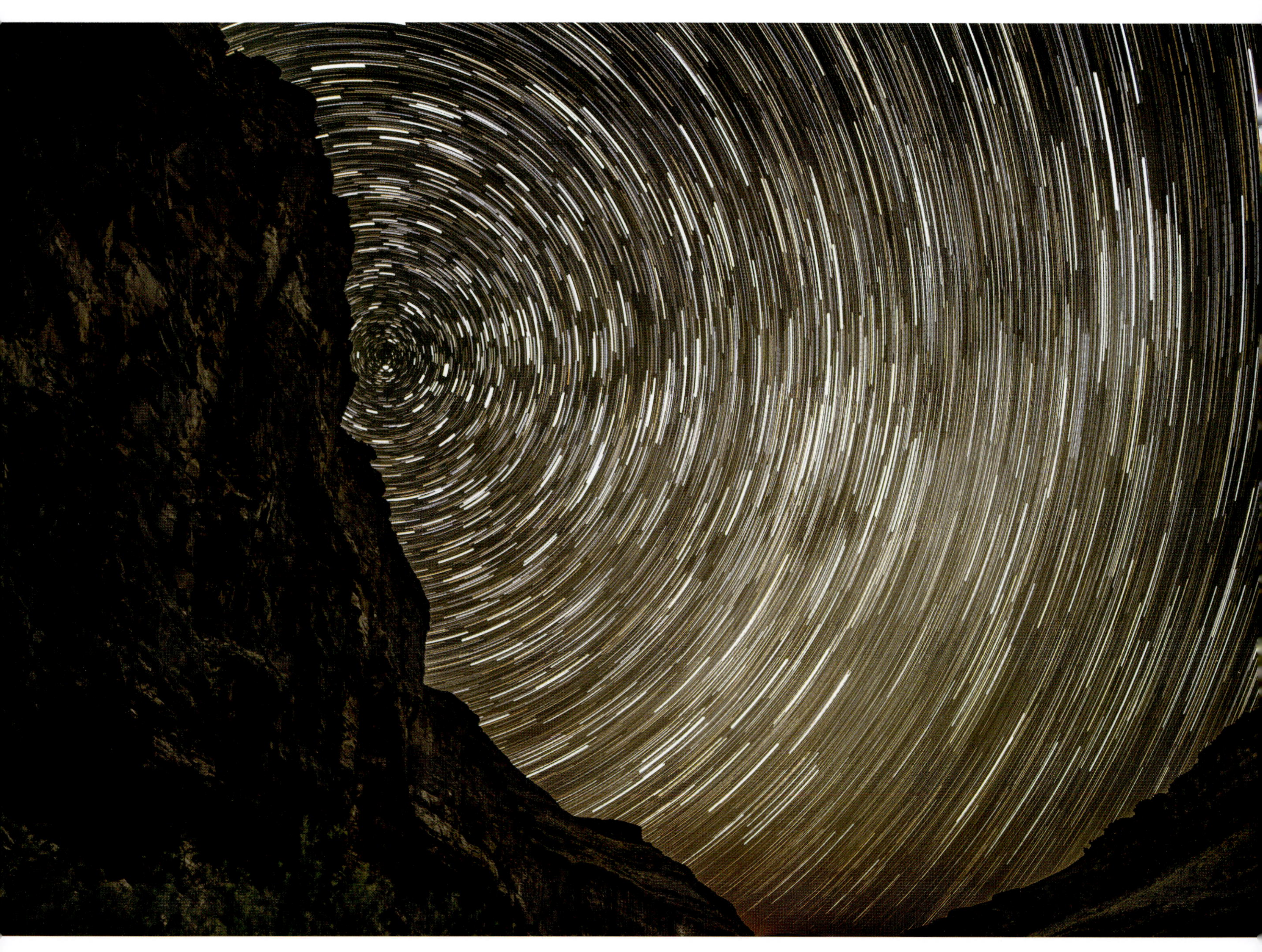

Time-lapse star trails around the North Star, Lower Neville Camp

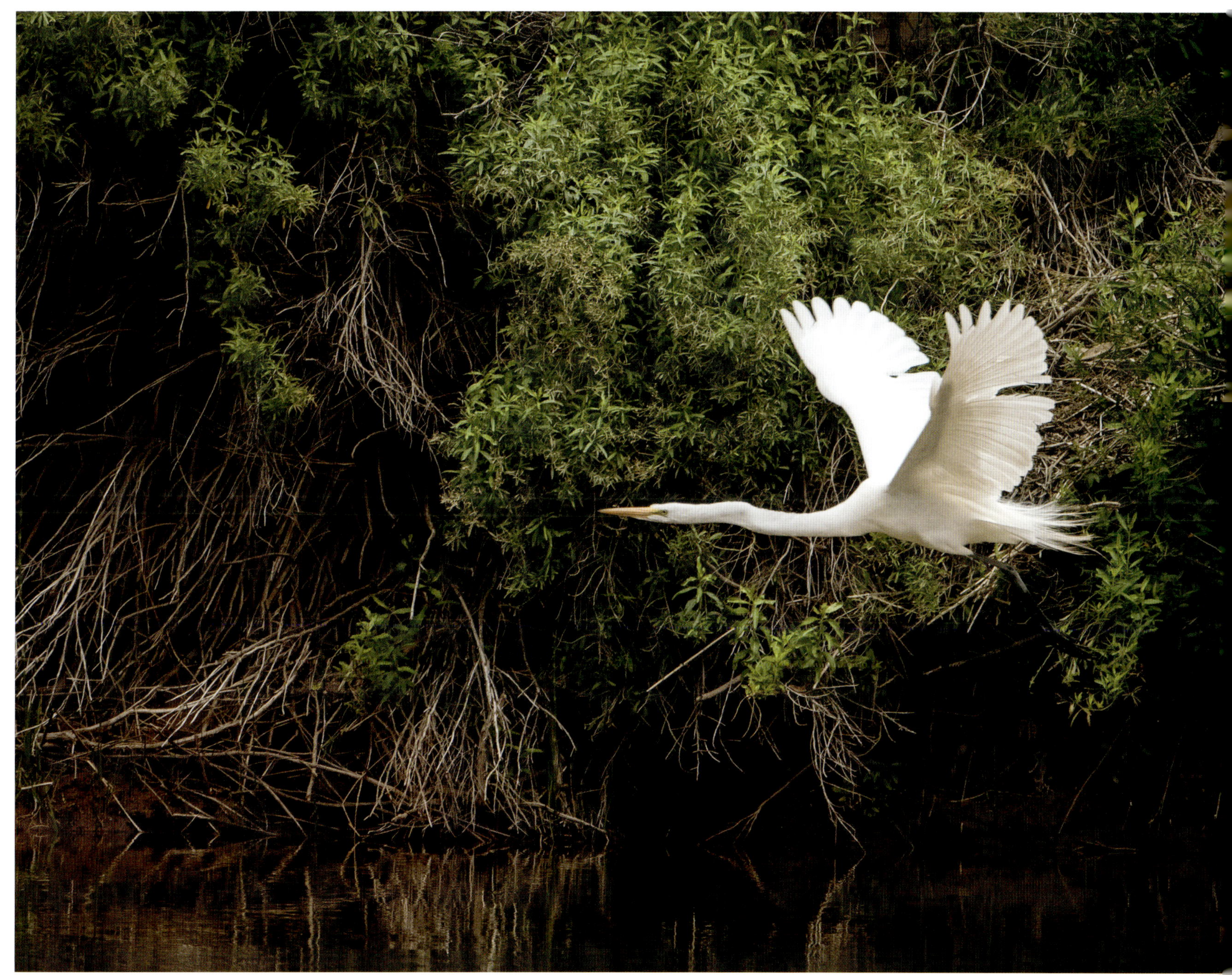

Great egret

Raft navigating Granite Rapid

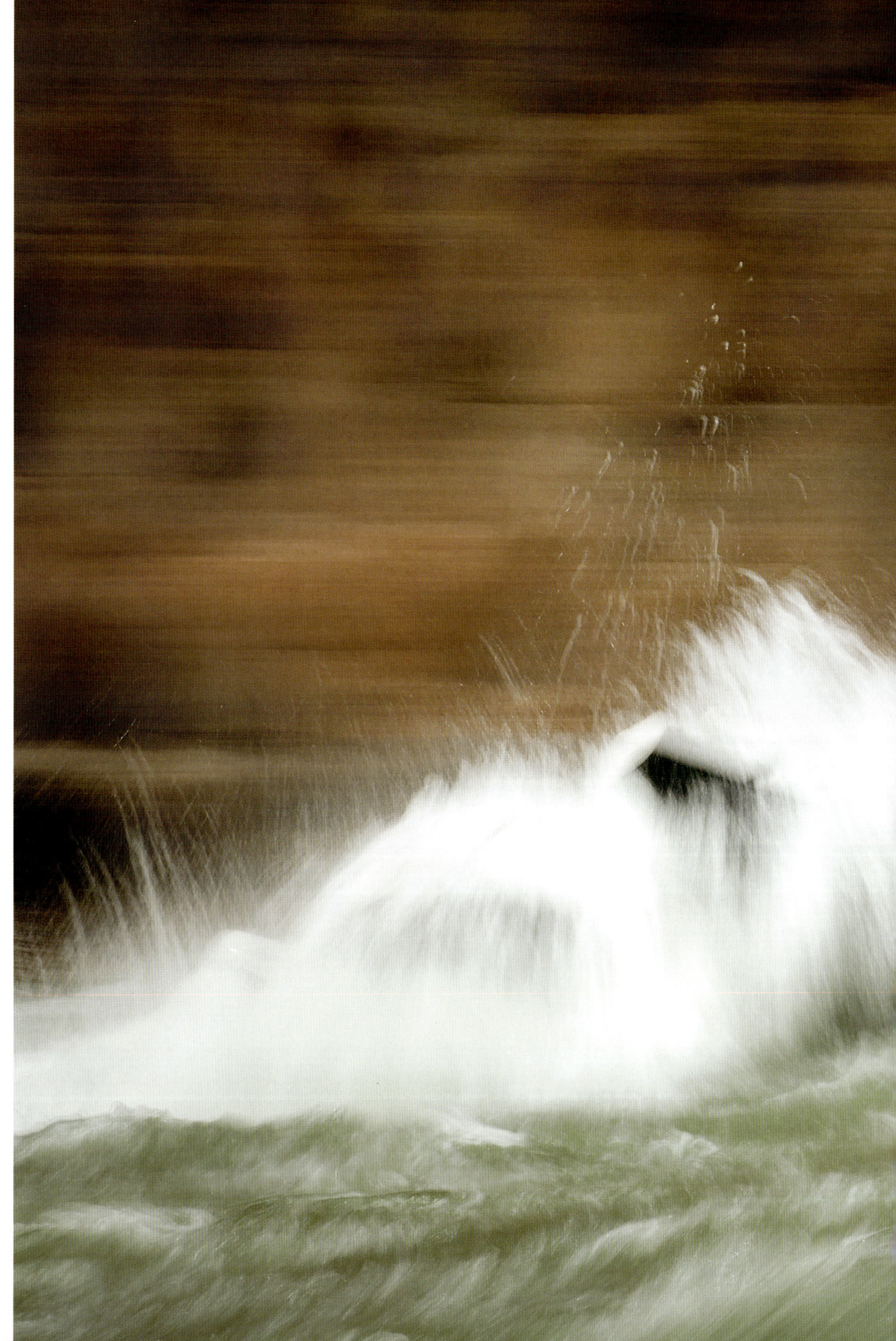

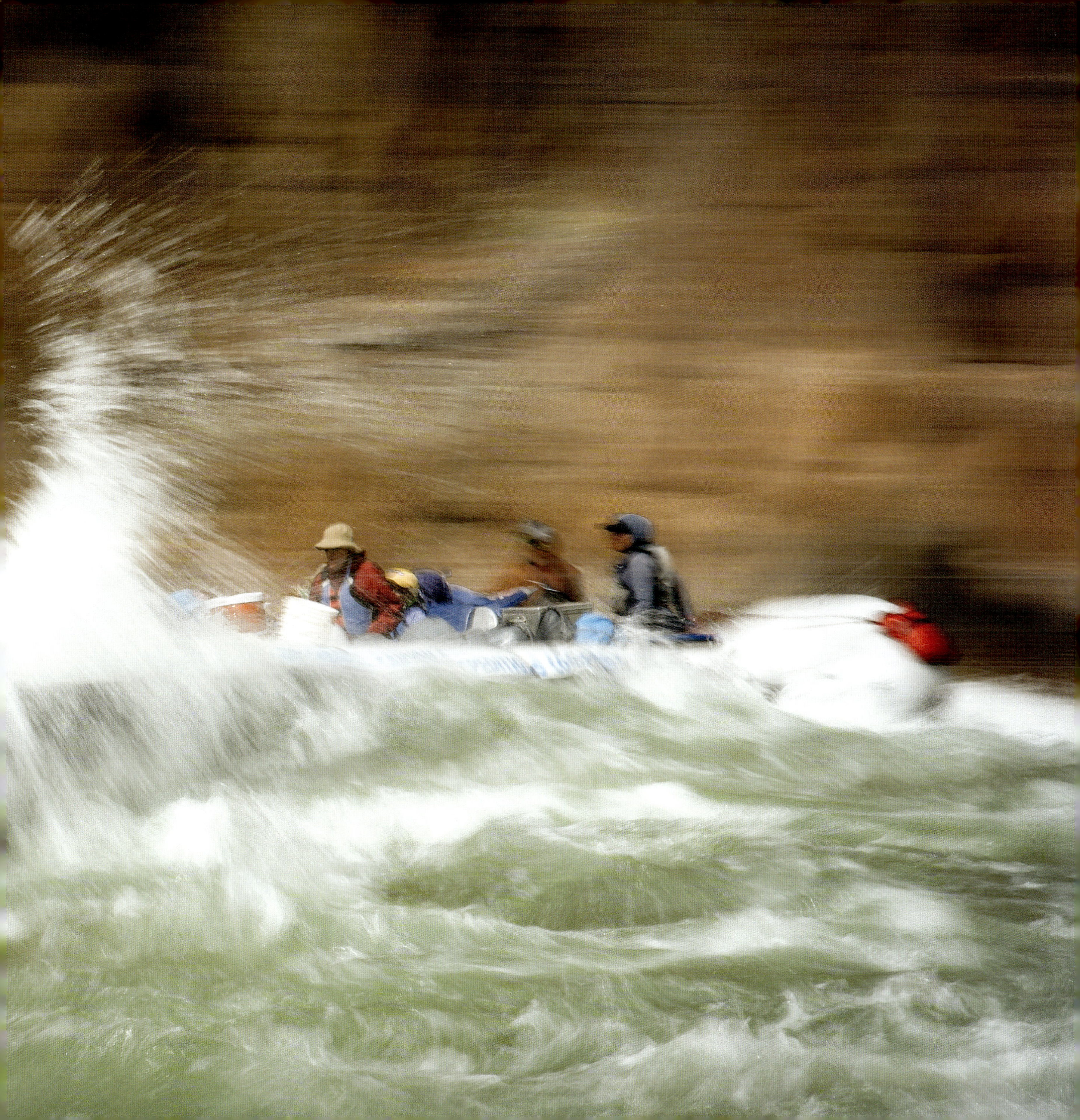

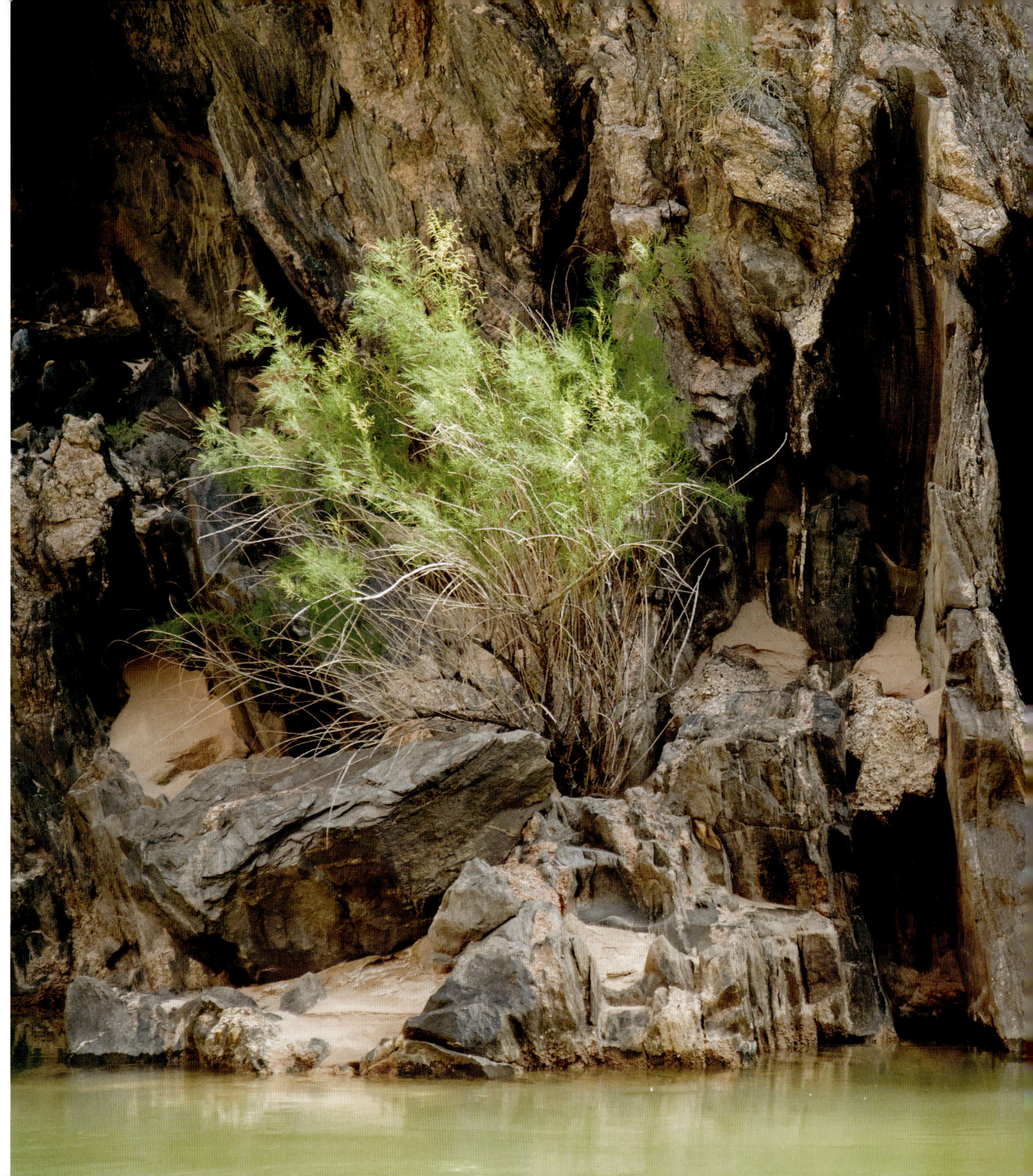

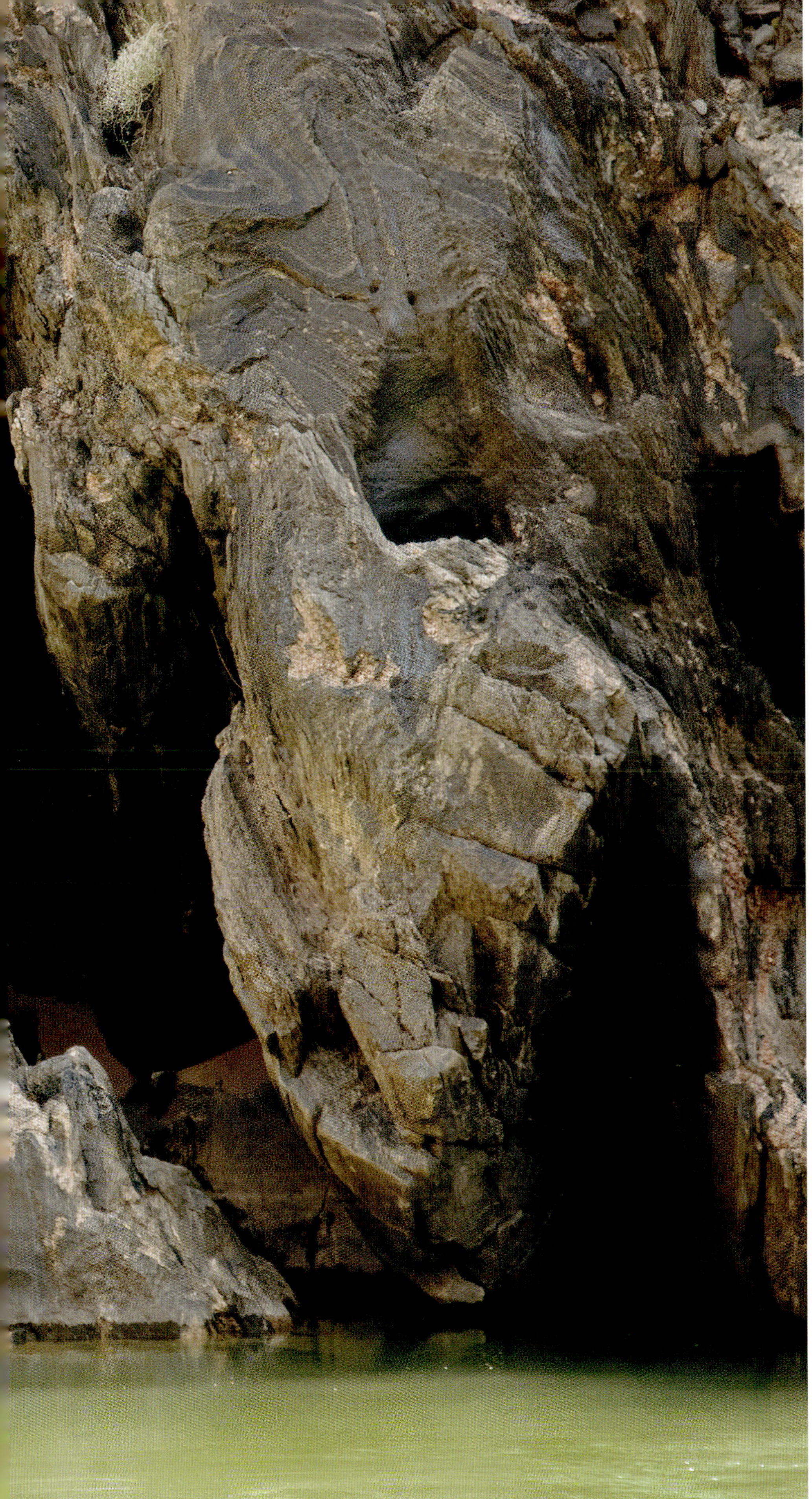

Tamarisk along the river's edge

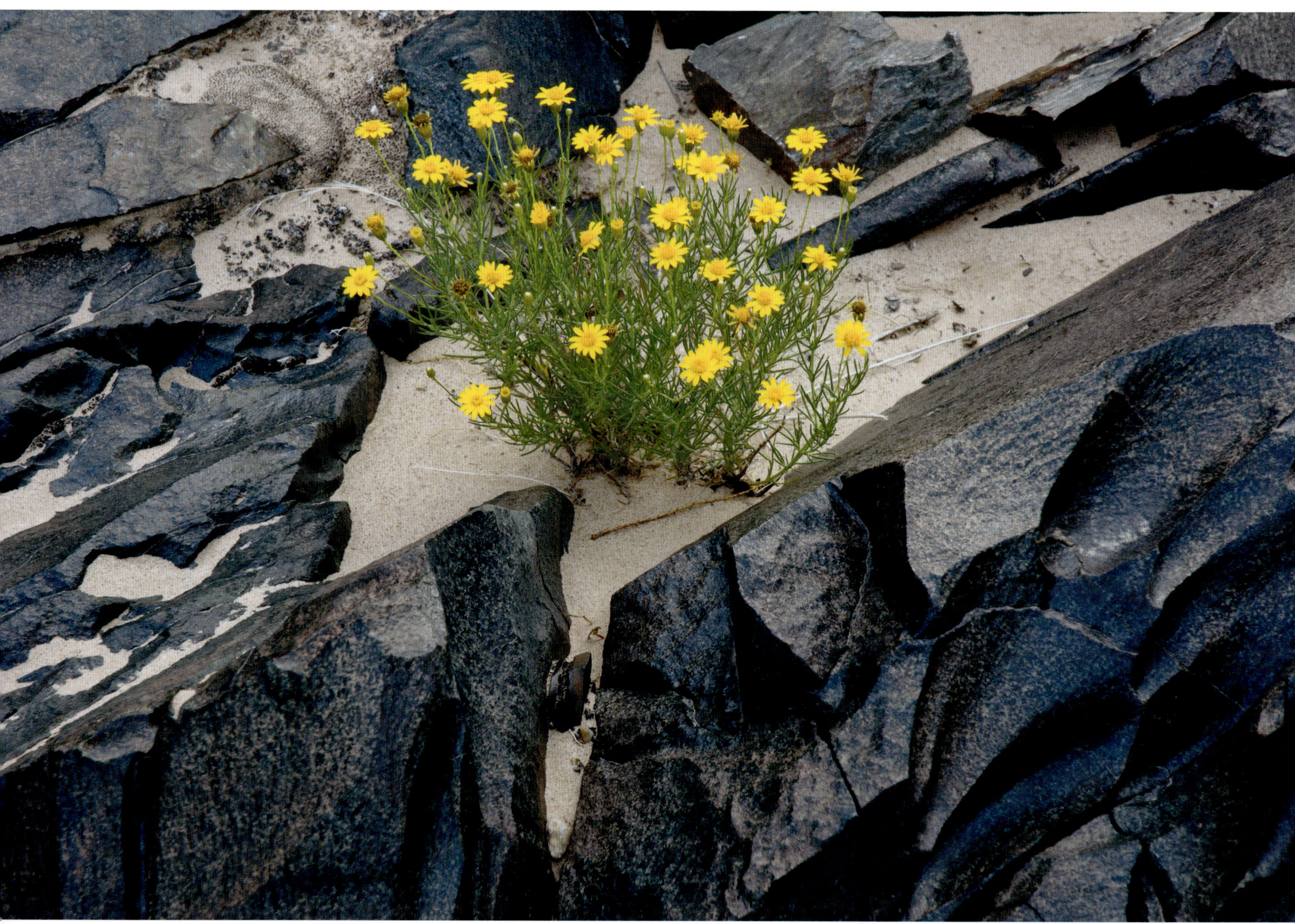

▲ Fetid-marigold, Schist Camp ▶ Utah century plant in bloom, Schist Camp ▼ View upriver (left) and Milky Way (right), Schist Camp

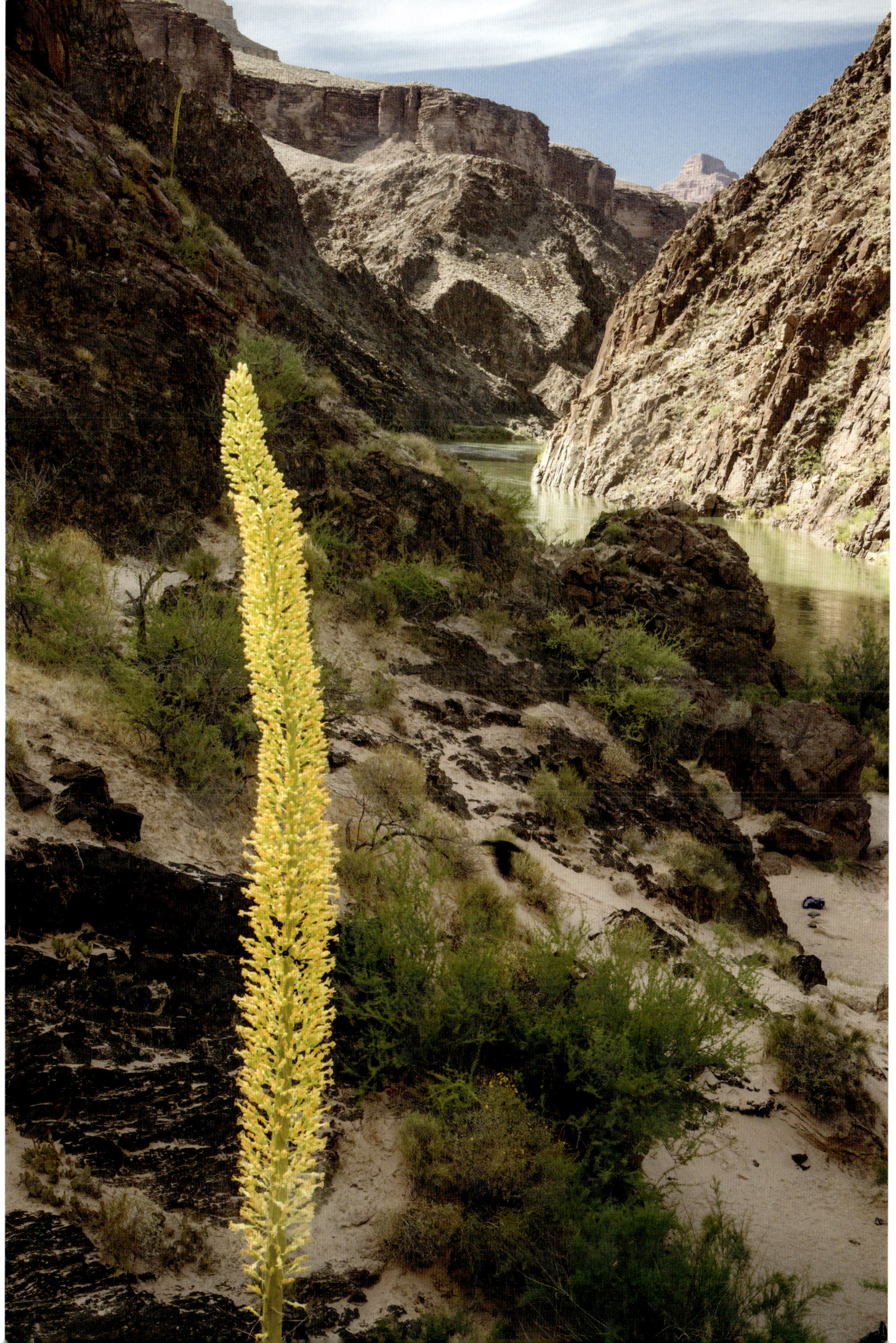

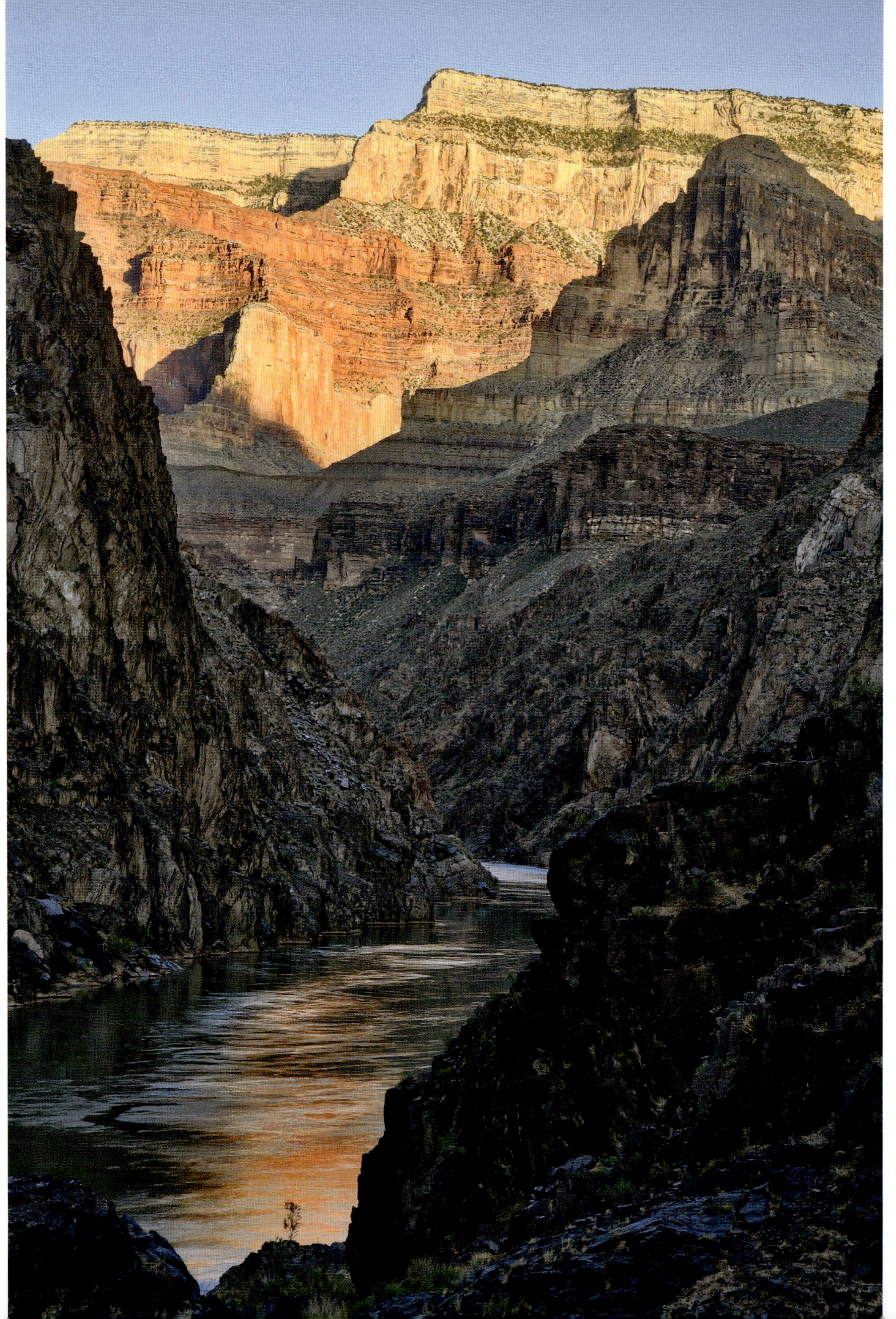

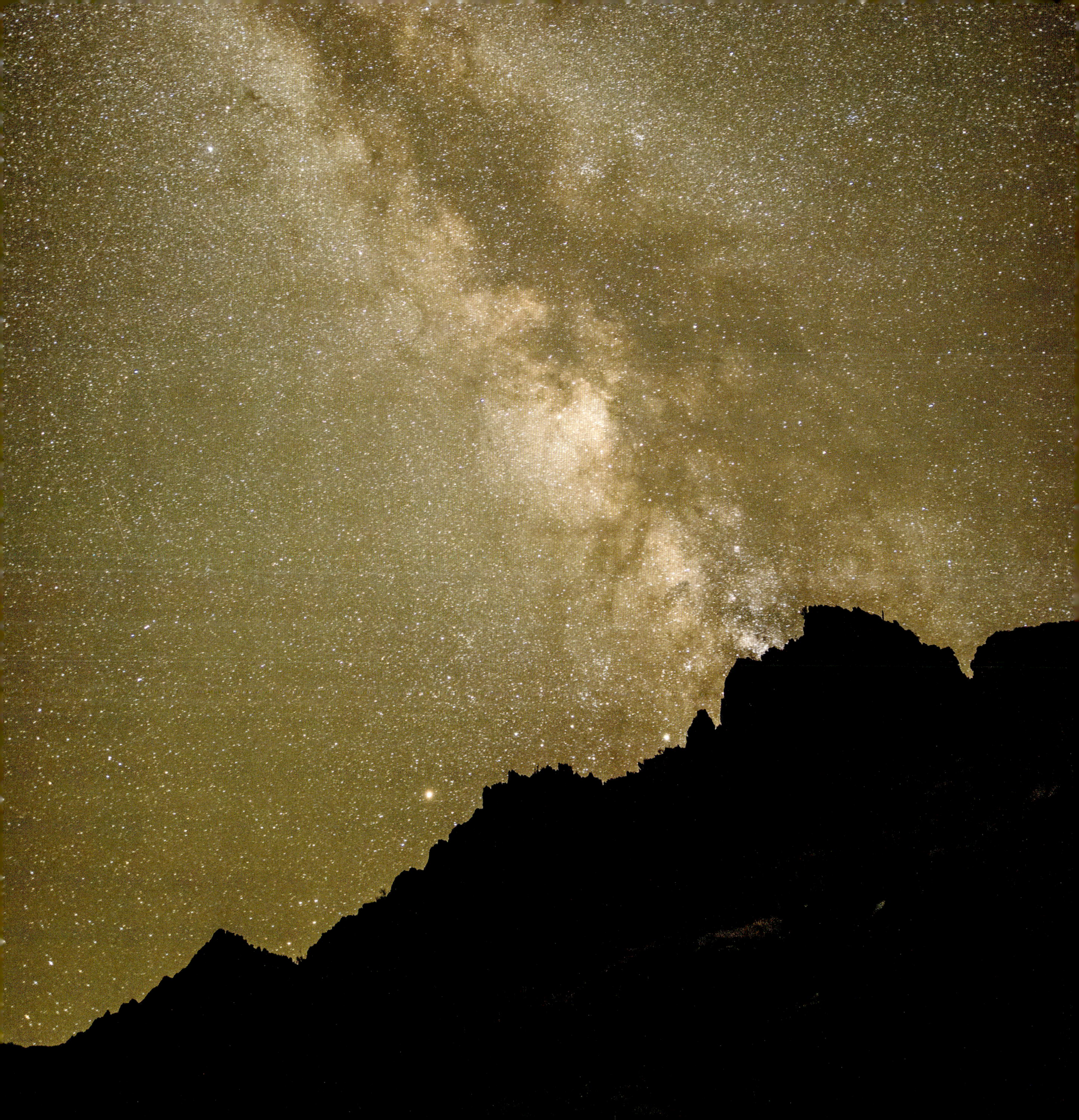

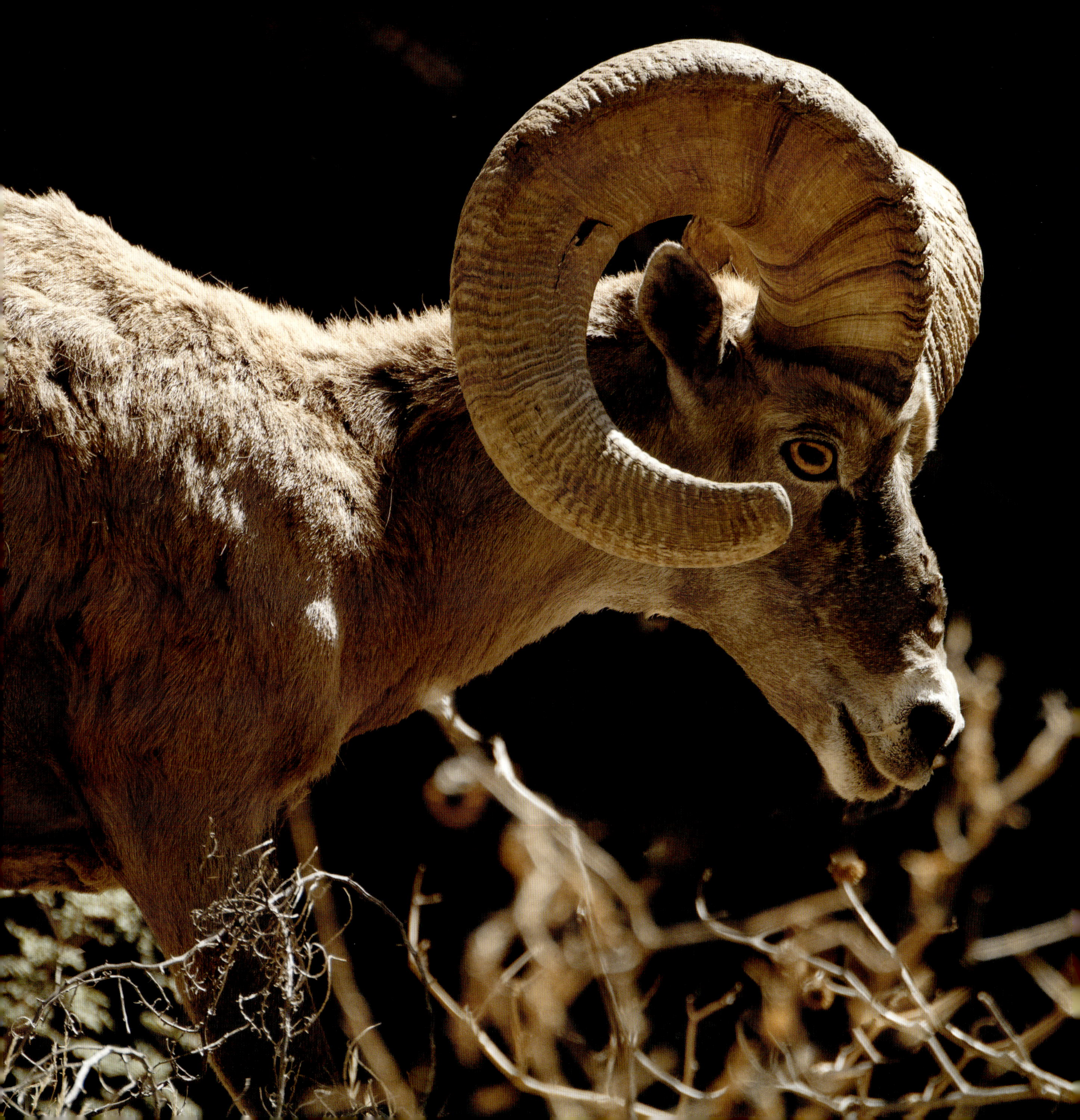

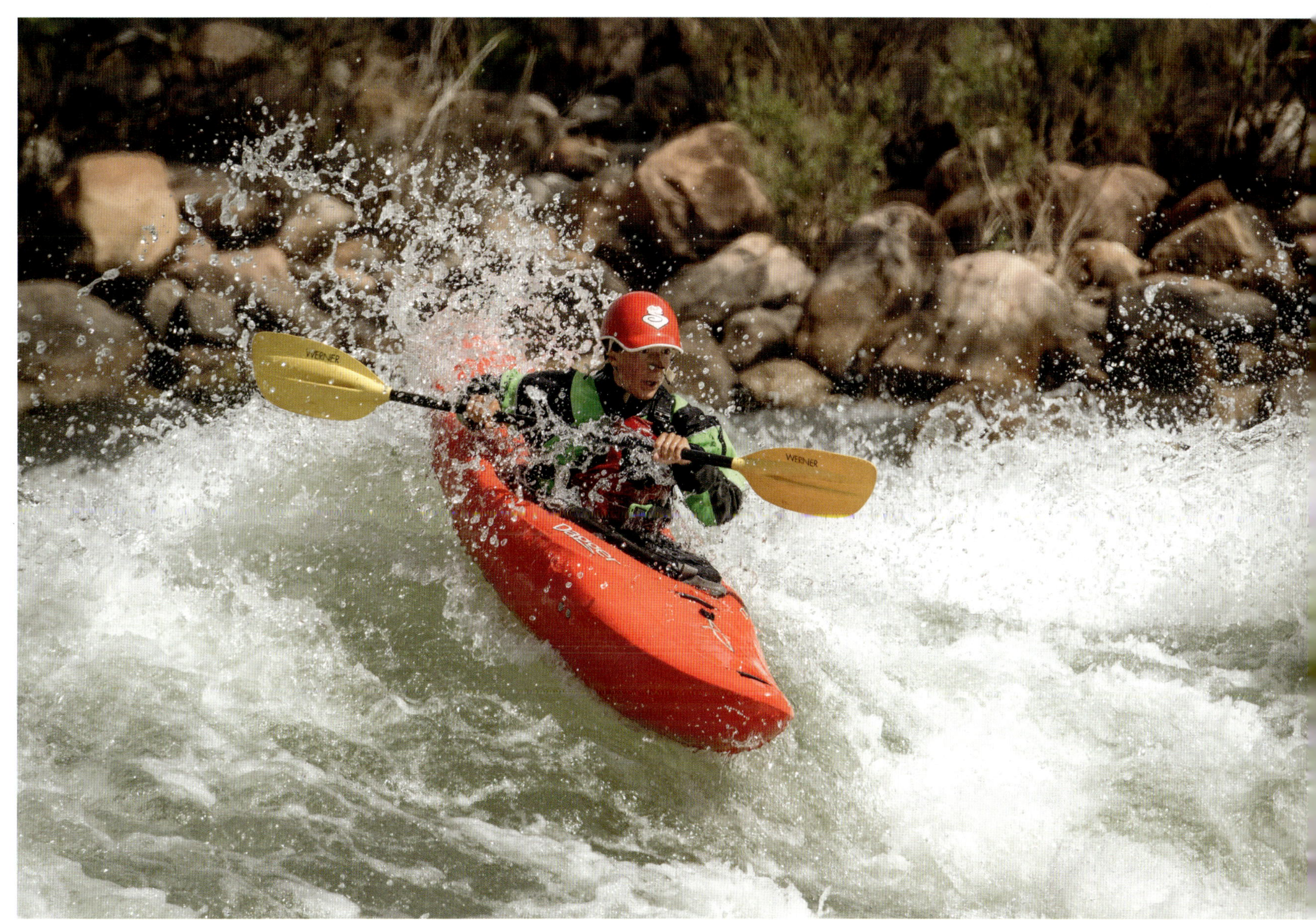

◄ Desert bighorn ram ▲ Young kayaker braving Crystal Rapid

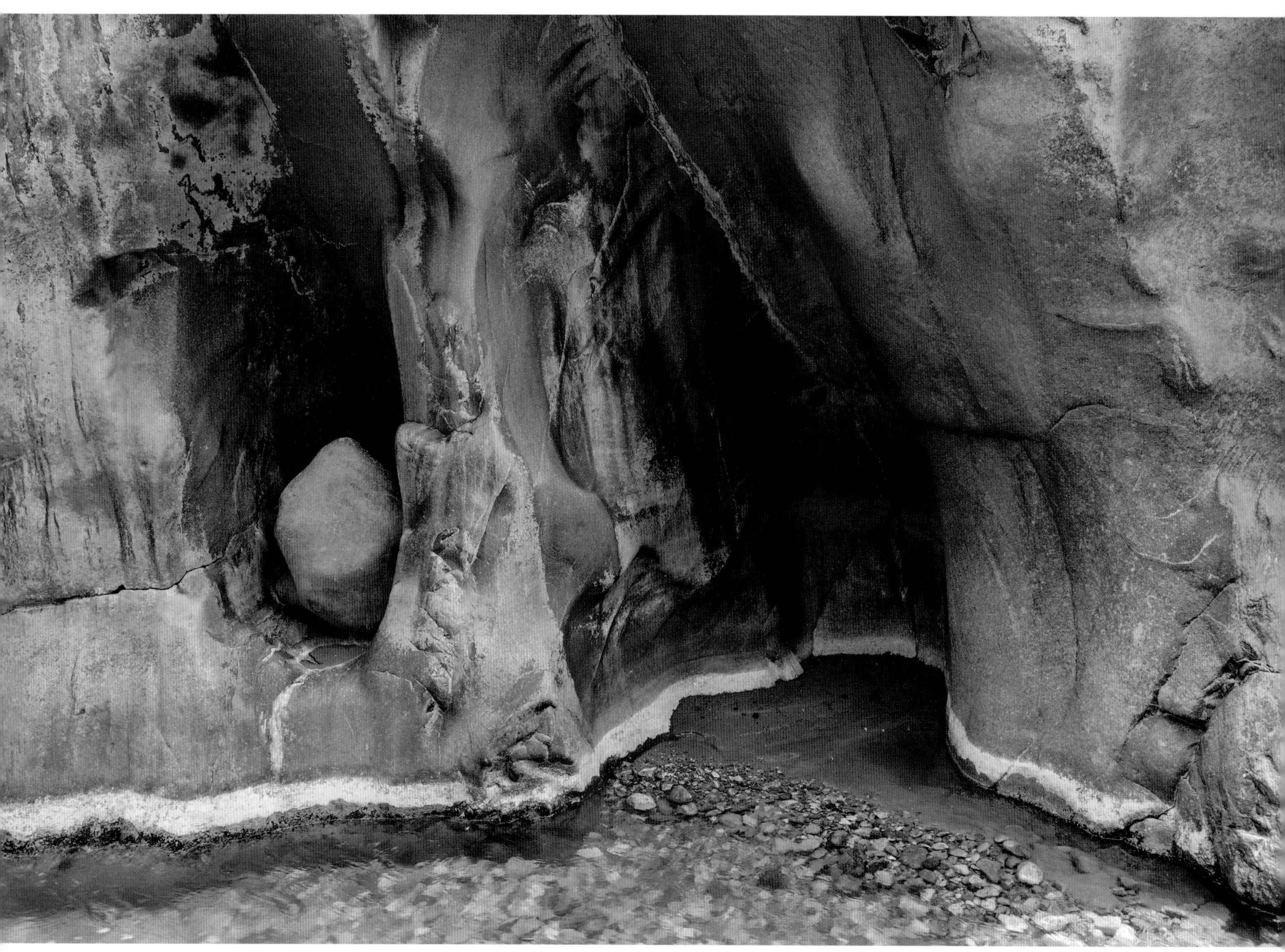

▲ Shinumo Canyon ▶ Shinumo Canyon

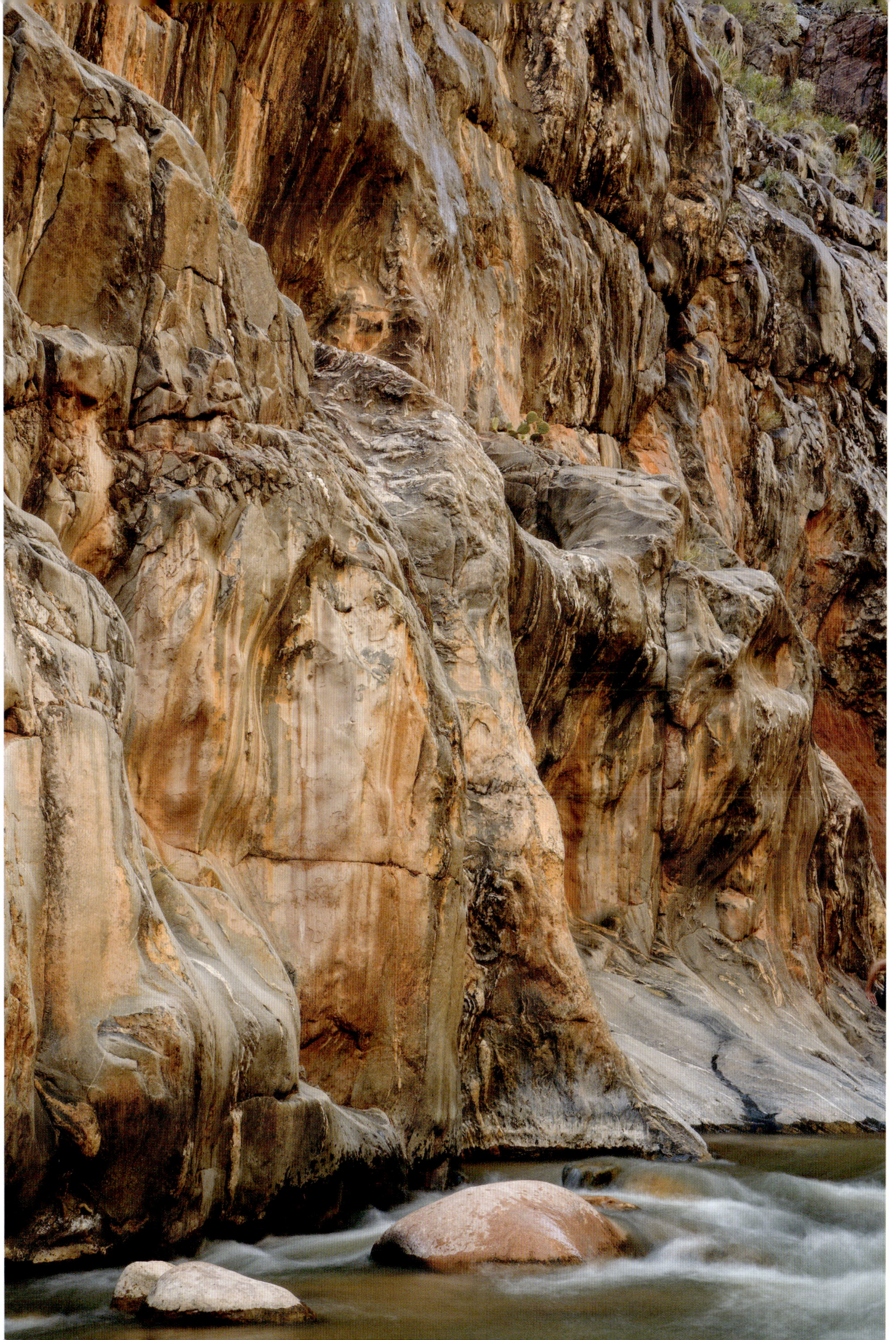

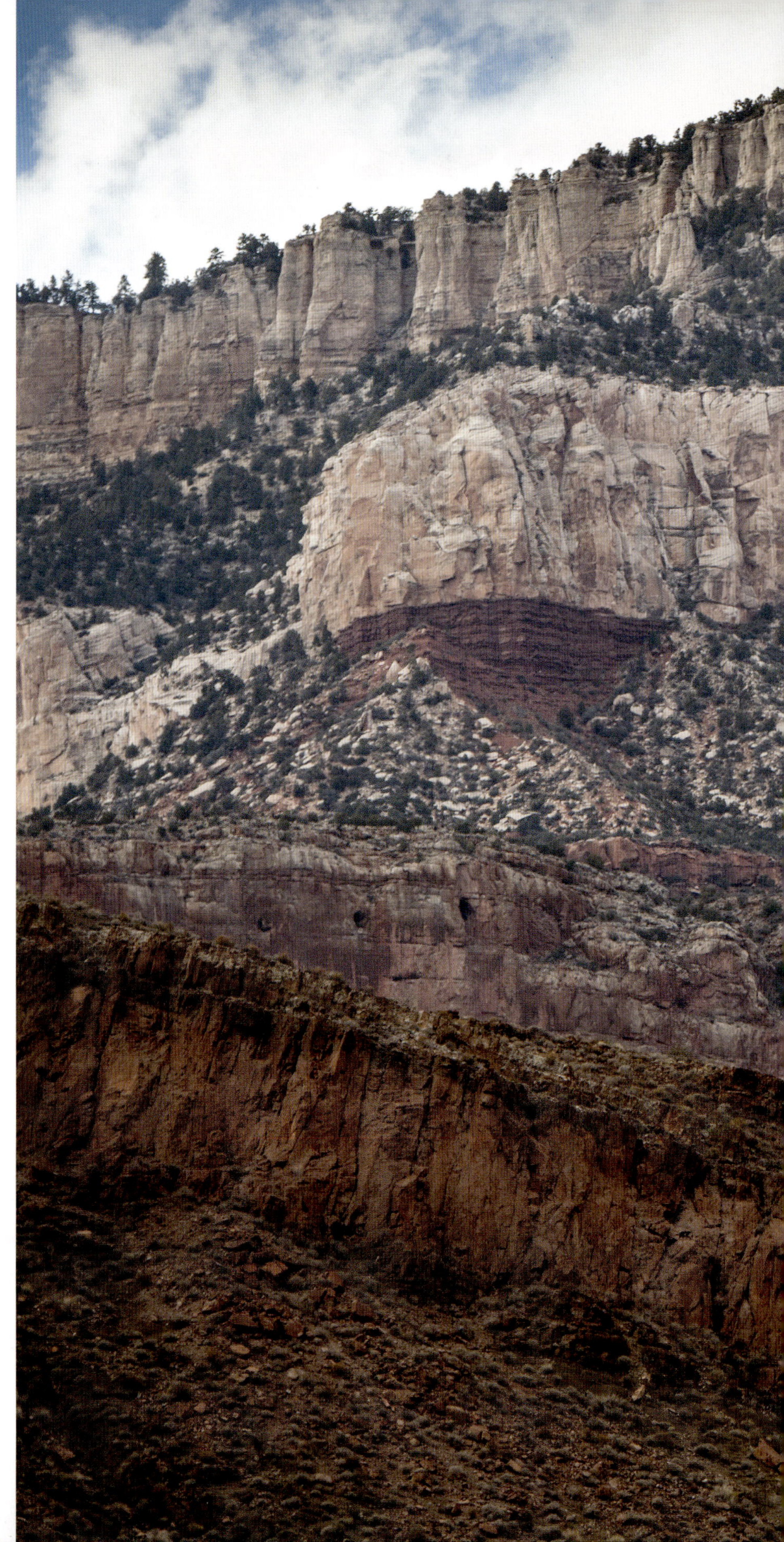

Powell Plateau from near Bass Camp

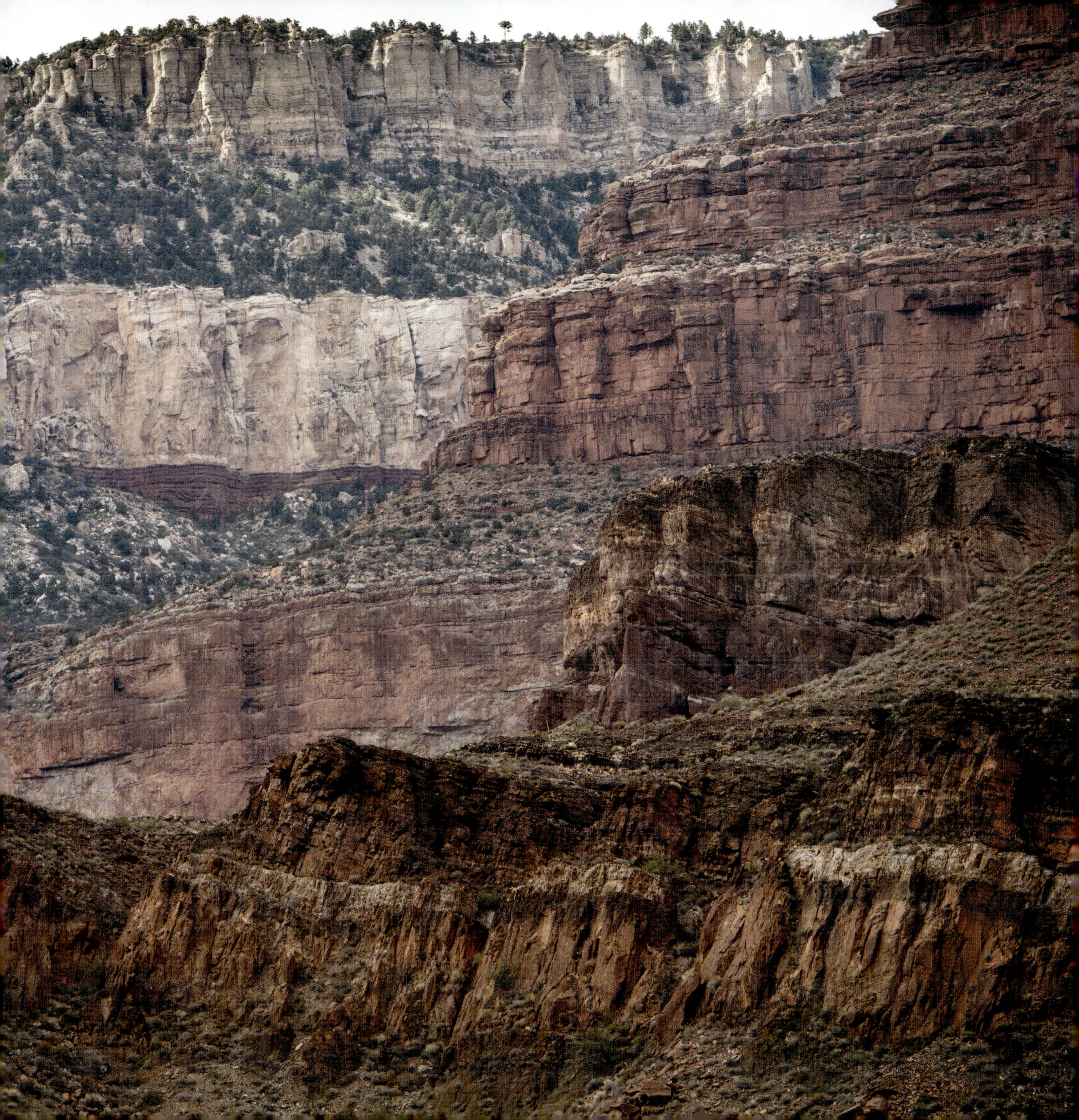

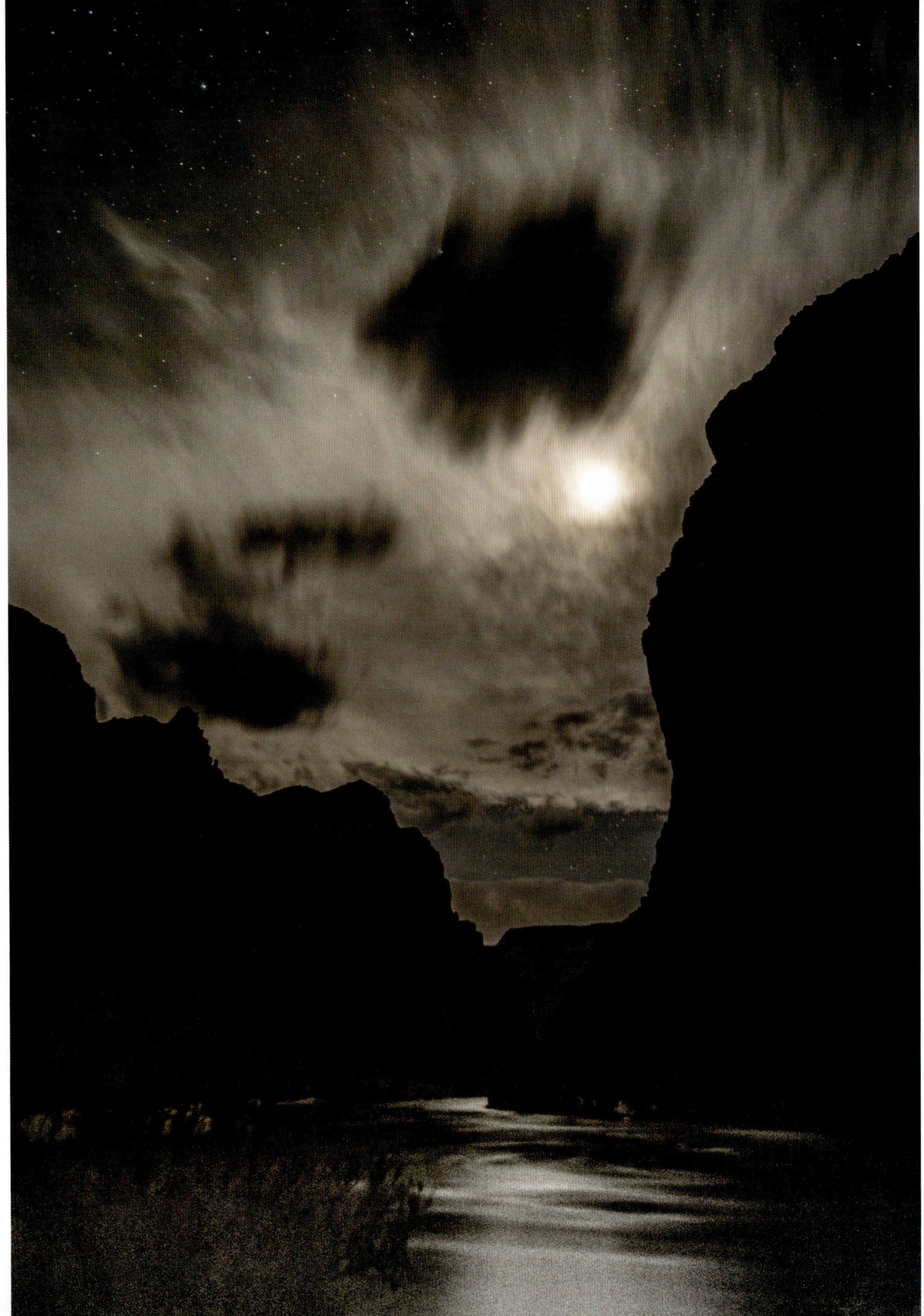

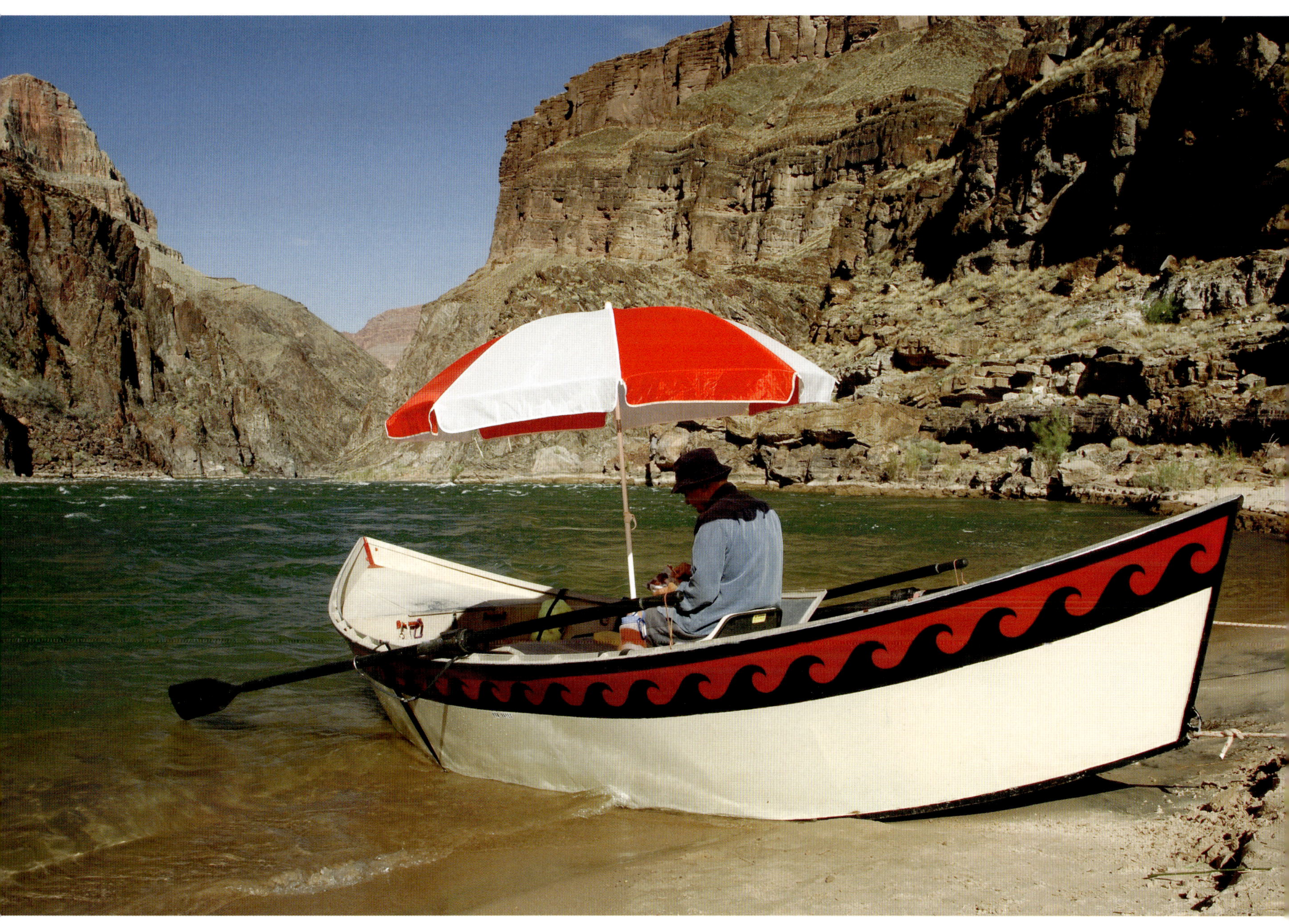

◀ View downriver with full moon from 110 Mile Camp ▲ Roderick Nash in *Canyon Dancer*, 110 Mile Camp

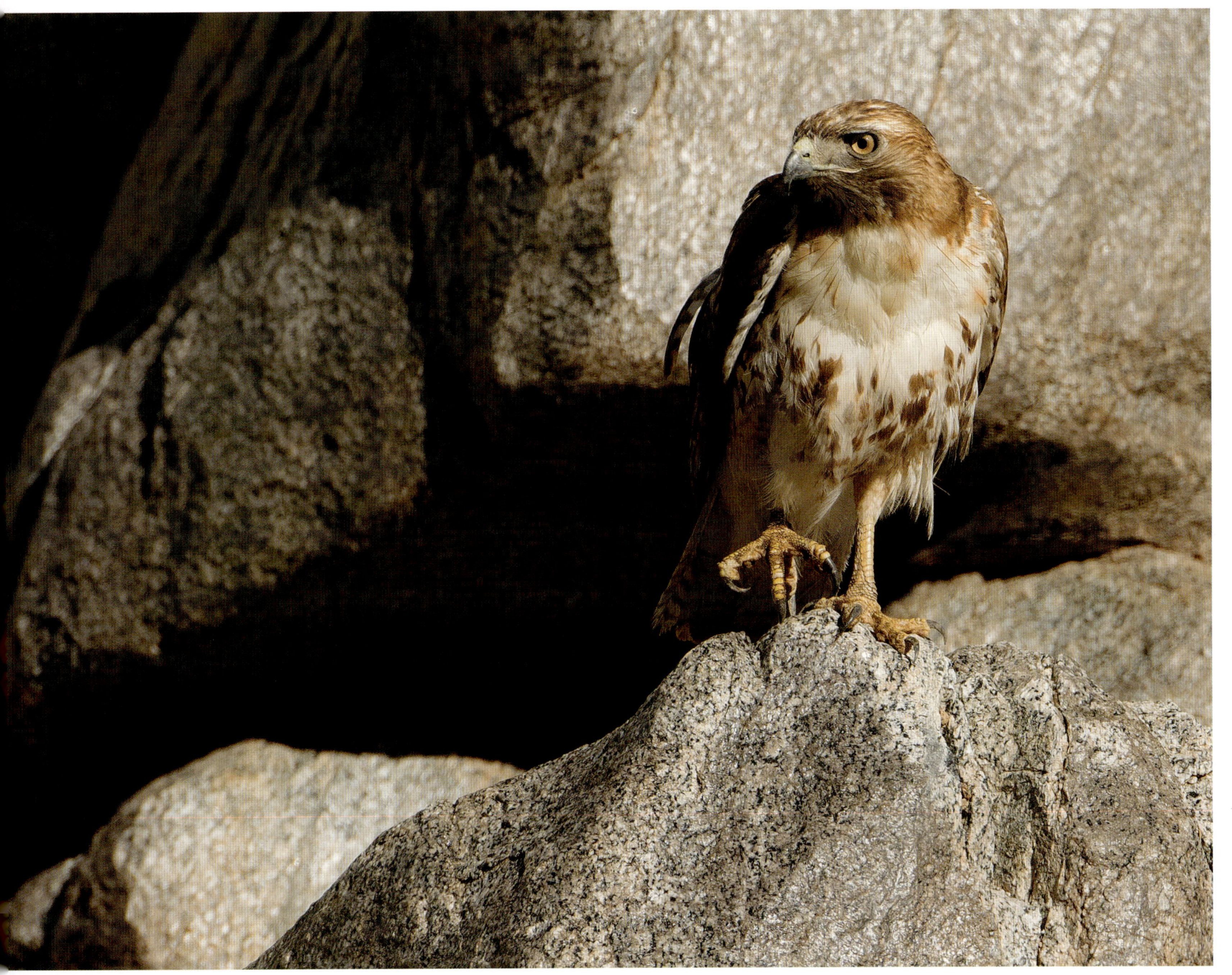

Red-tailed hawk

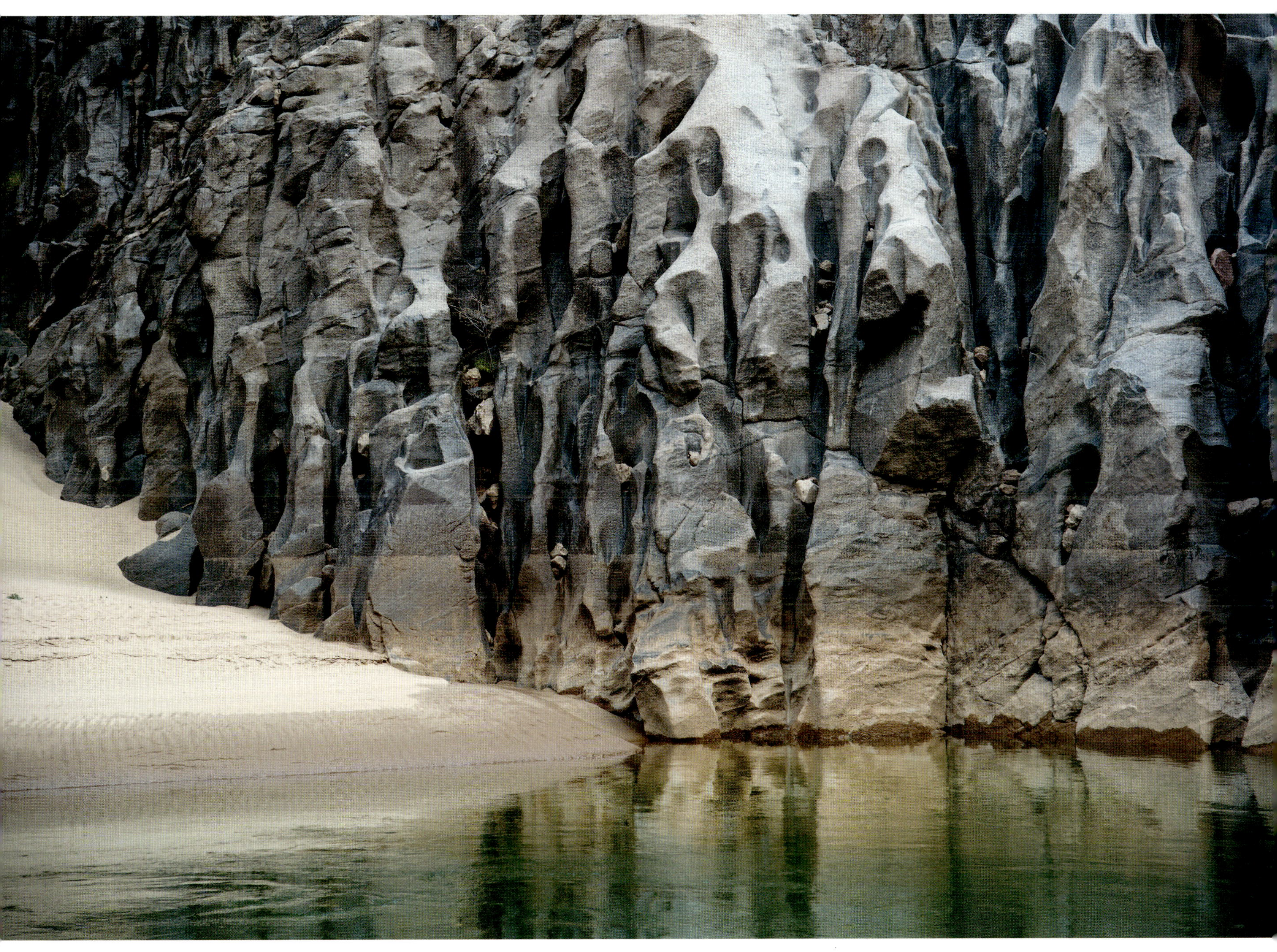

River's edge around mile 113

▶ Elves Chasm

▼ Canyon stream reflecting pool (left), ferns and waterfall (right, top), and Sphinx moths (right, bottom), Elves Chasm

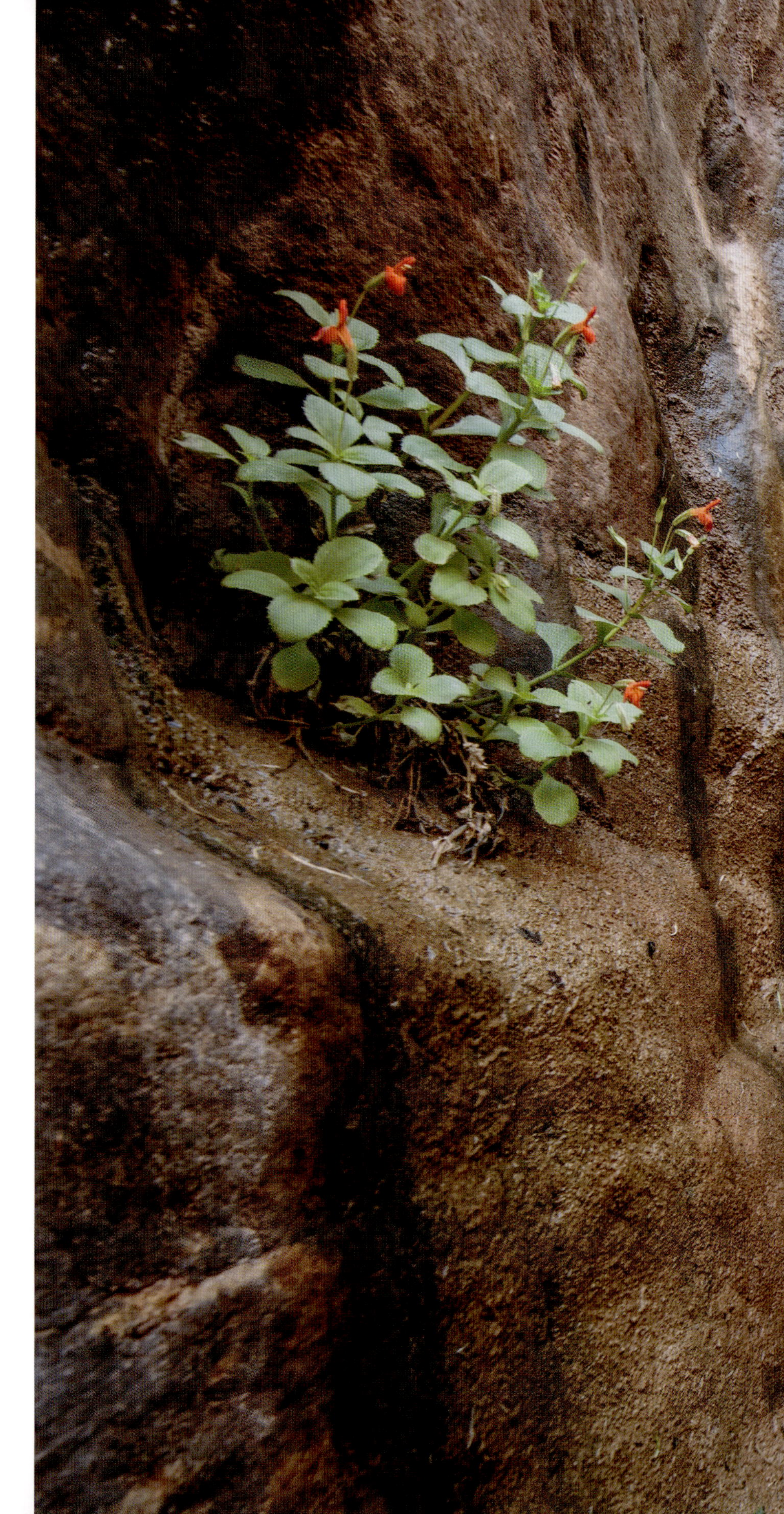

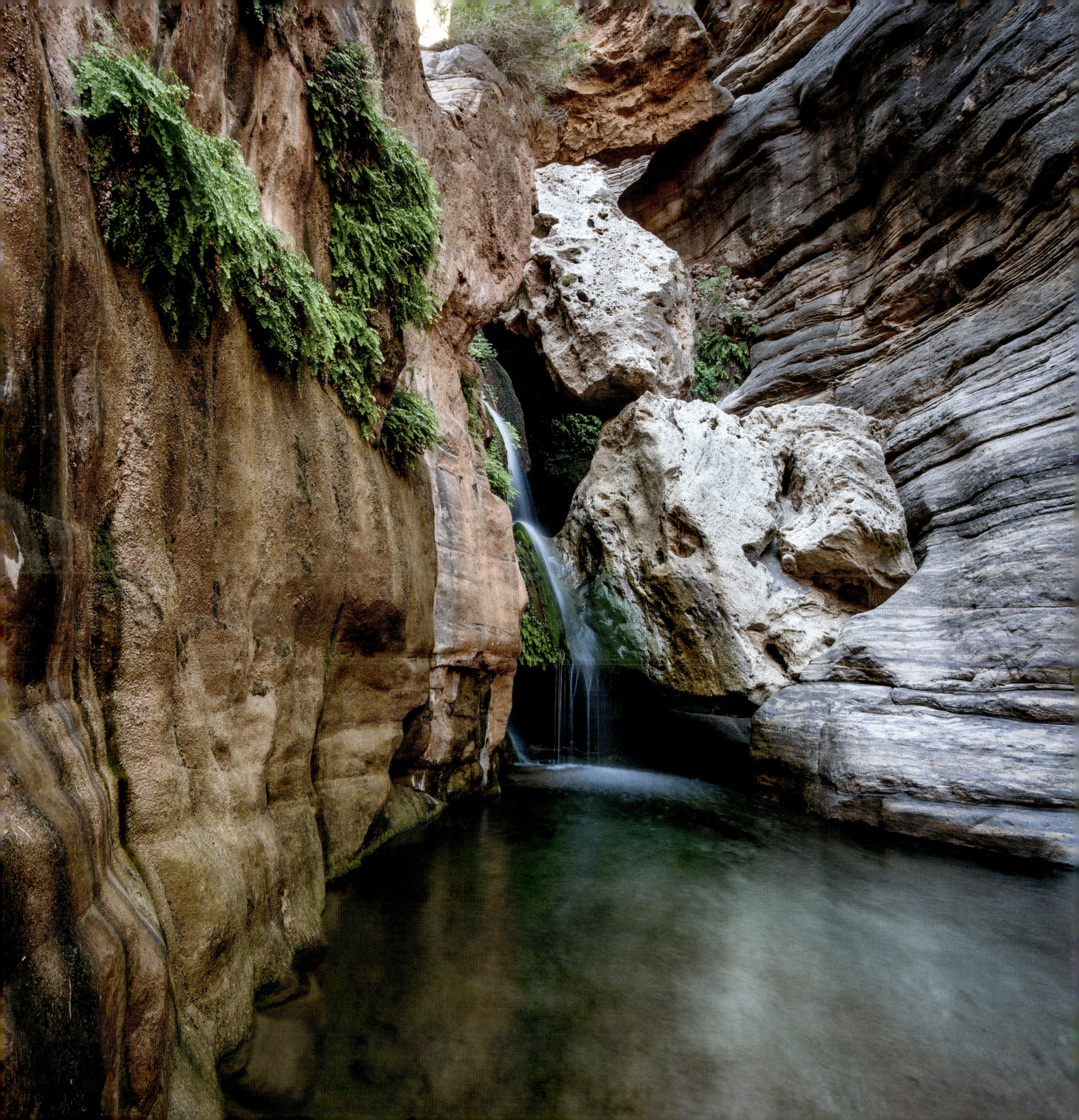

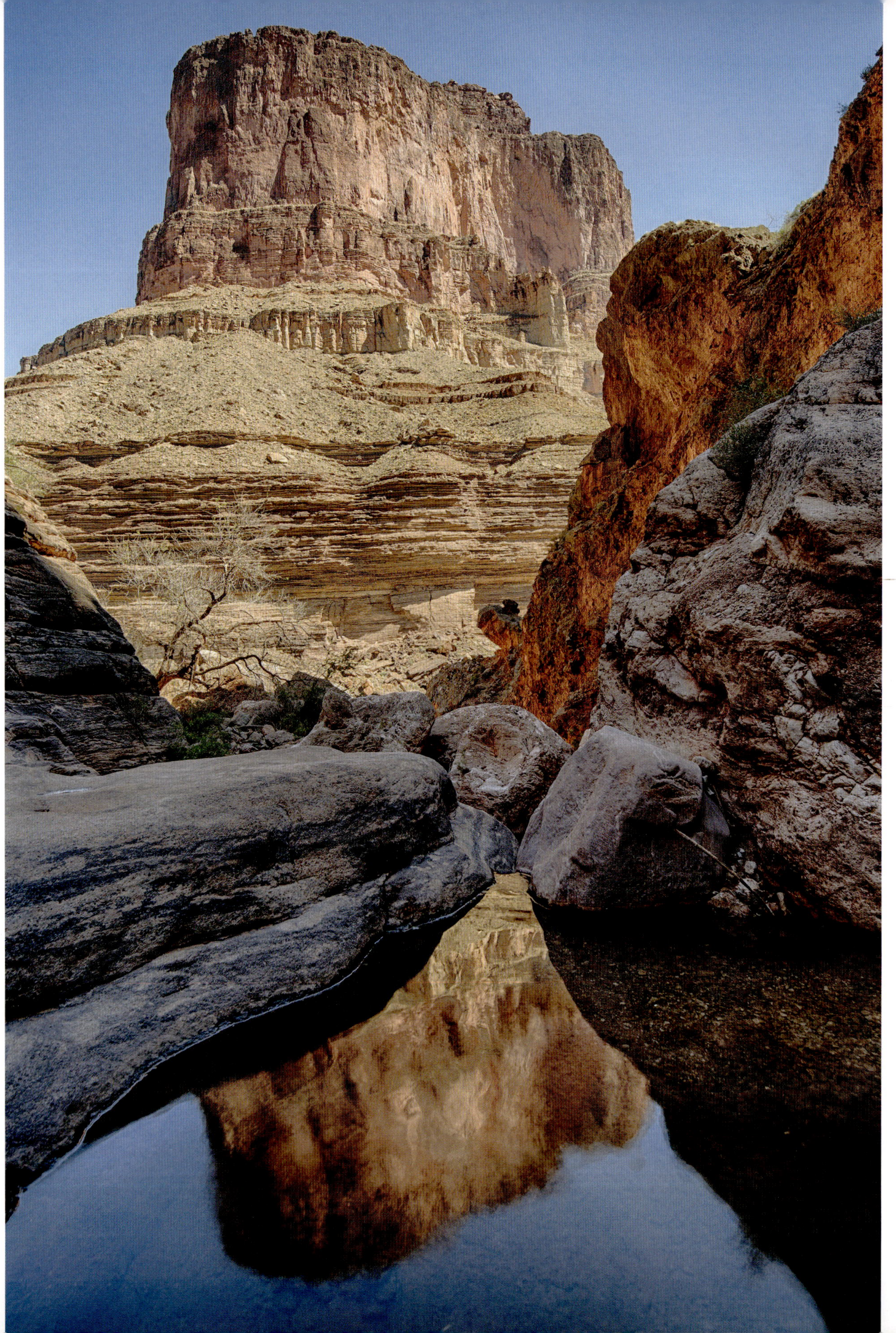

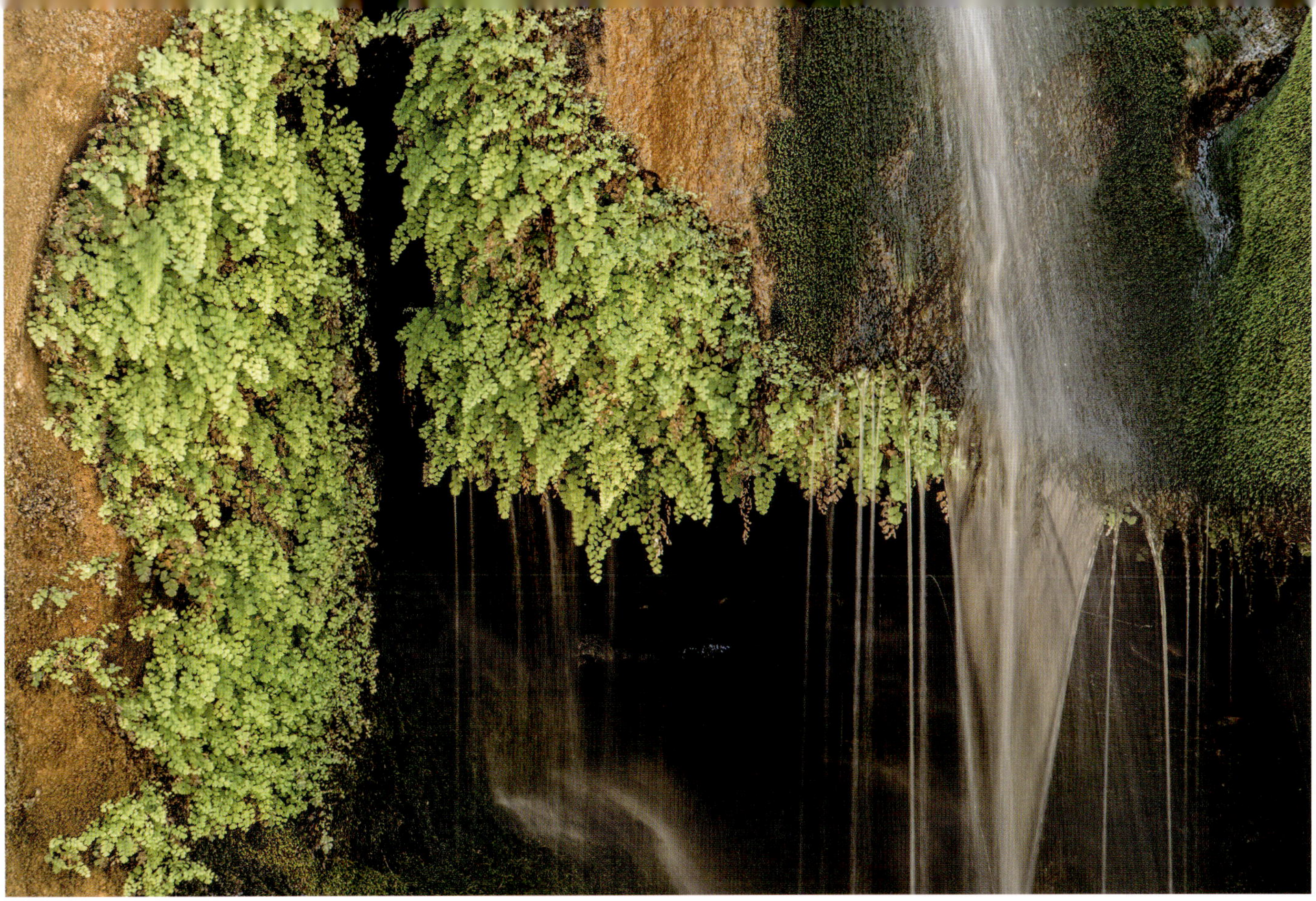

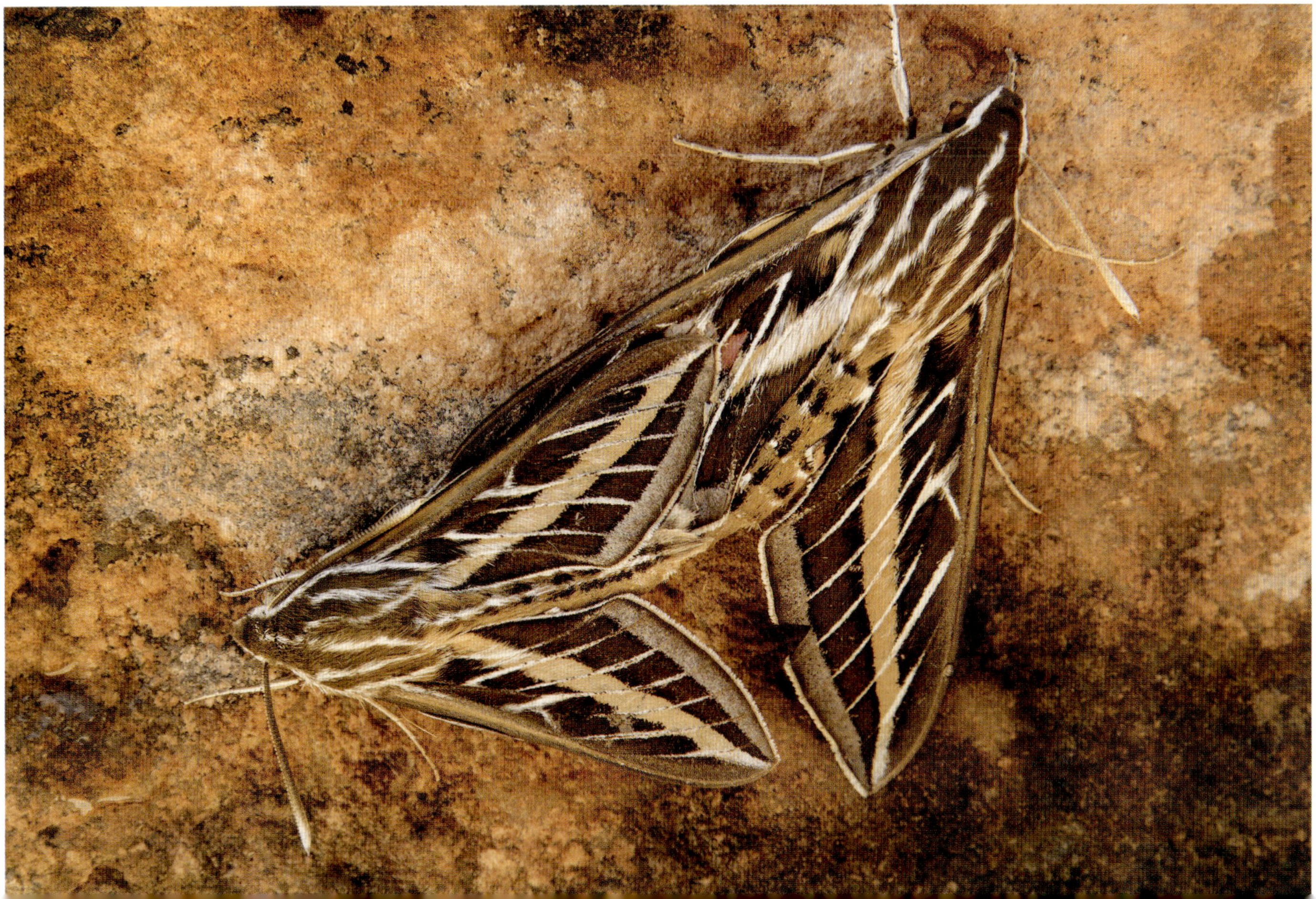

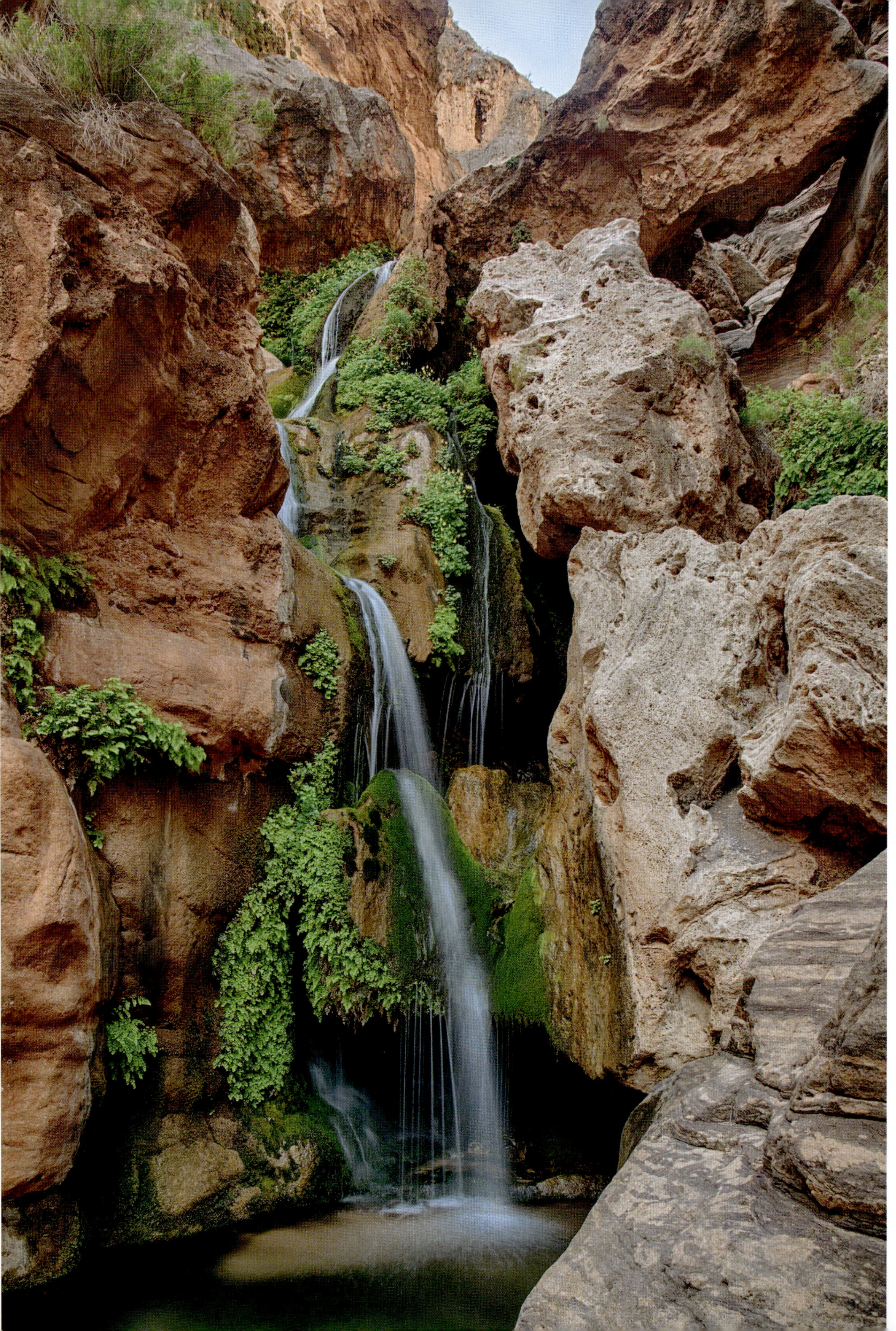

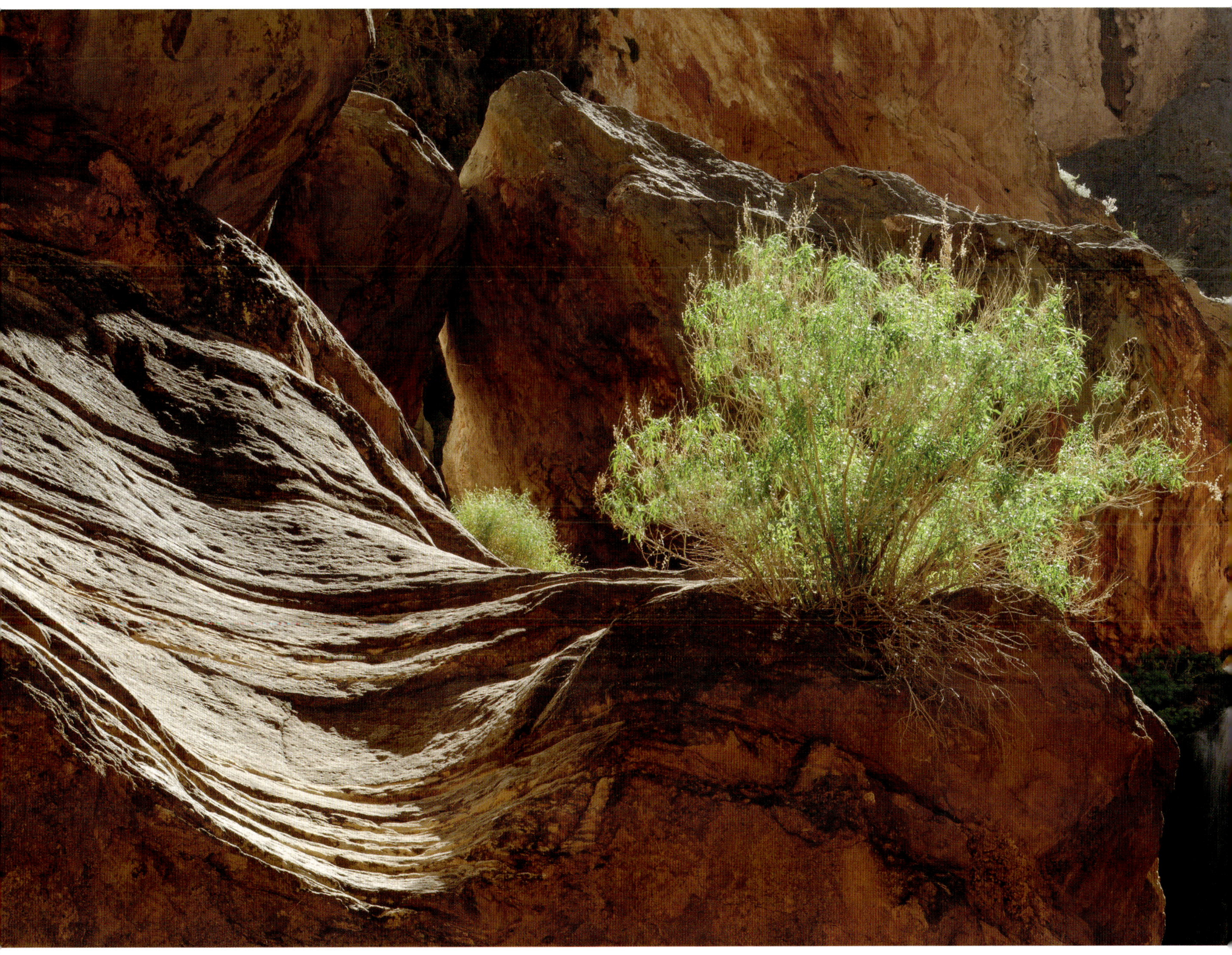

◀ Waterfall, Elves Chasm ▲ Canyon wall, Elves Chasm

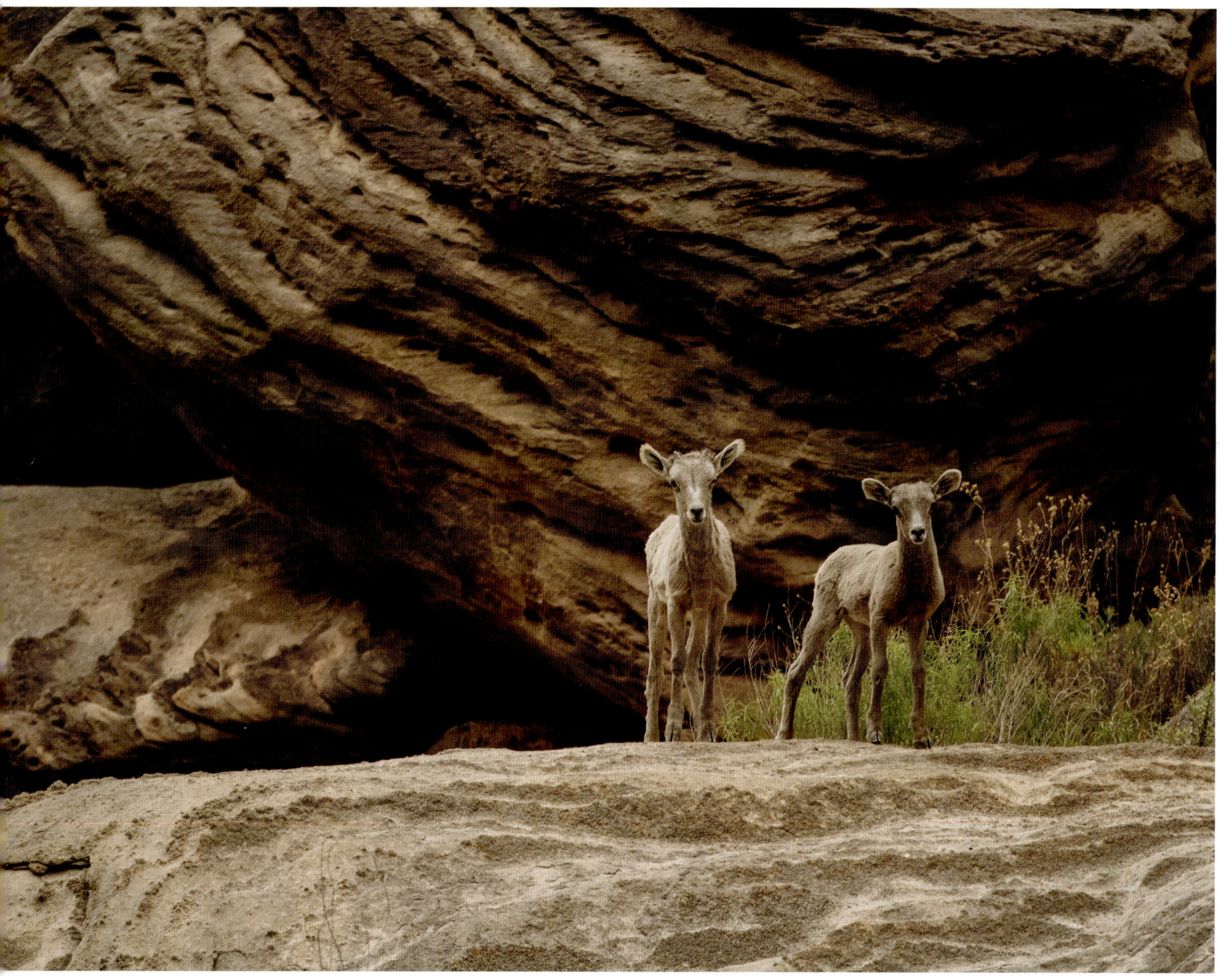

▲ Desert bighorn lambs ▶ River reflections

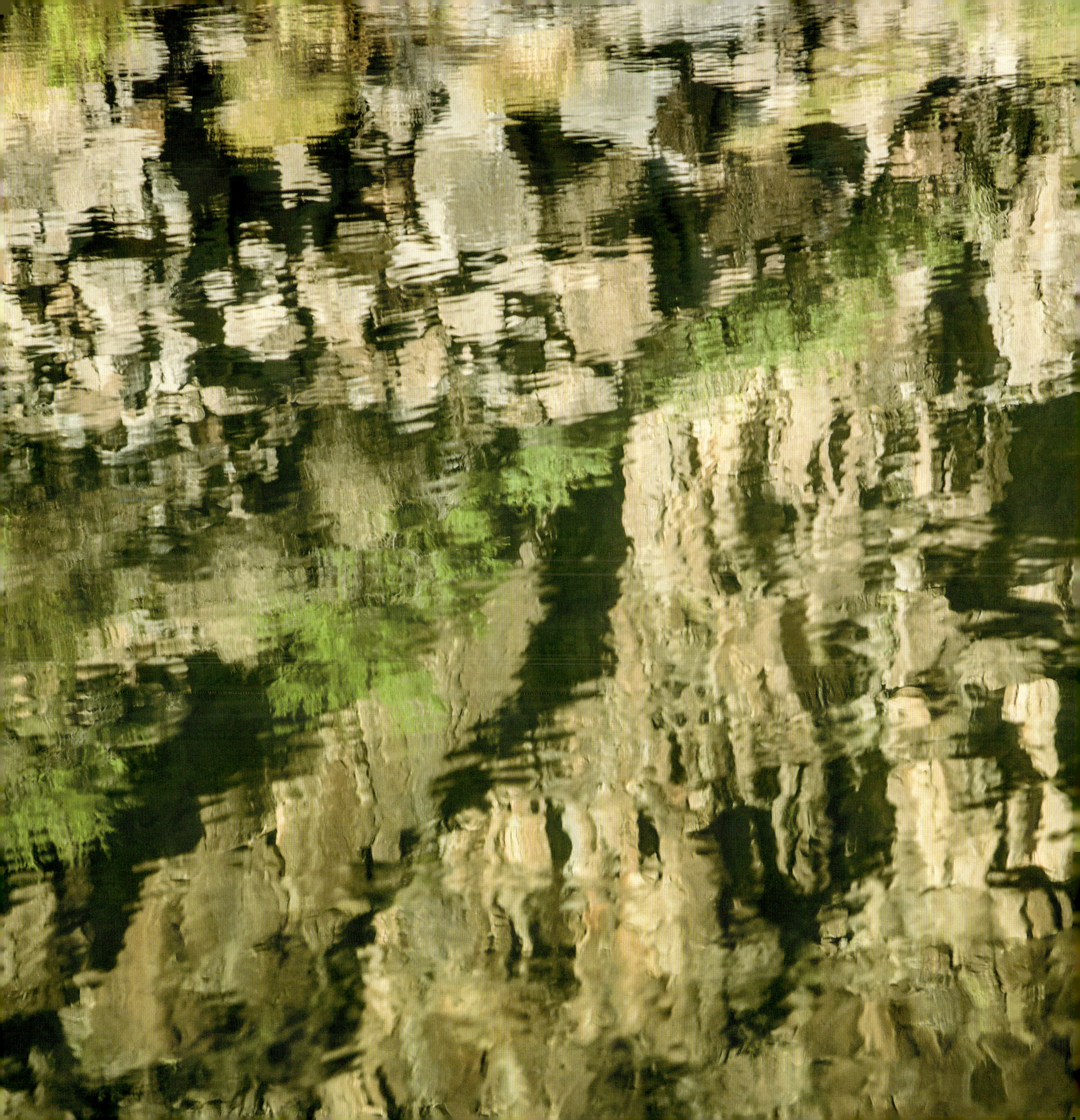

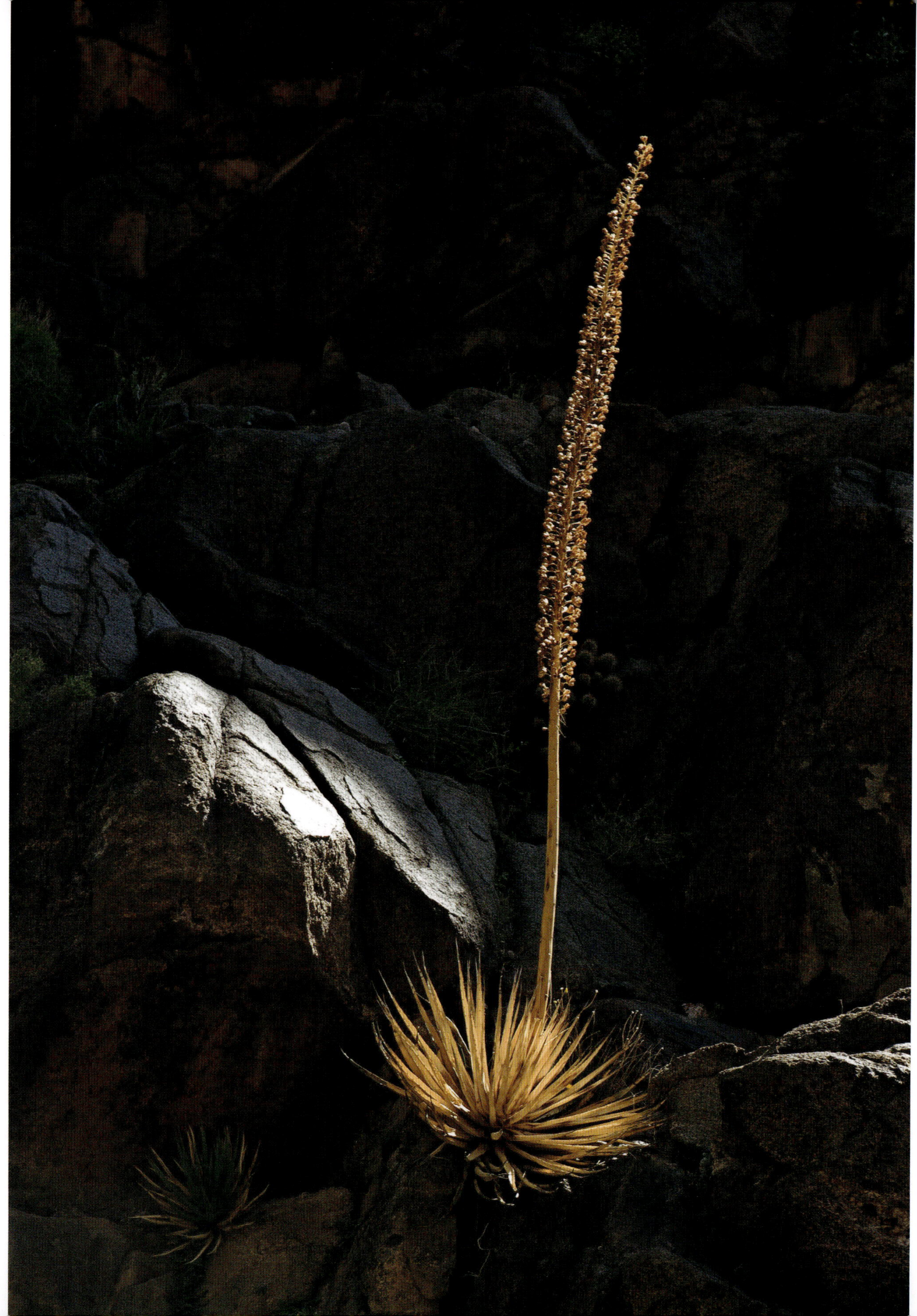

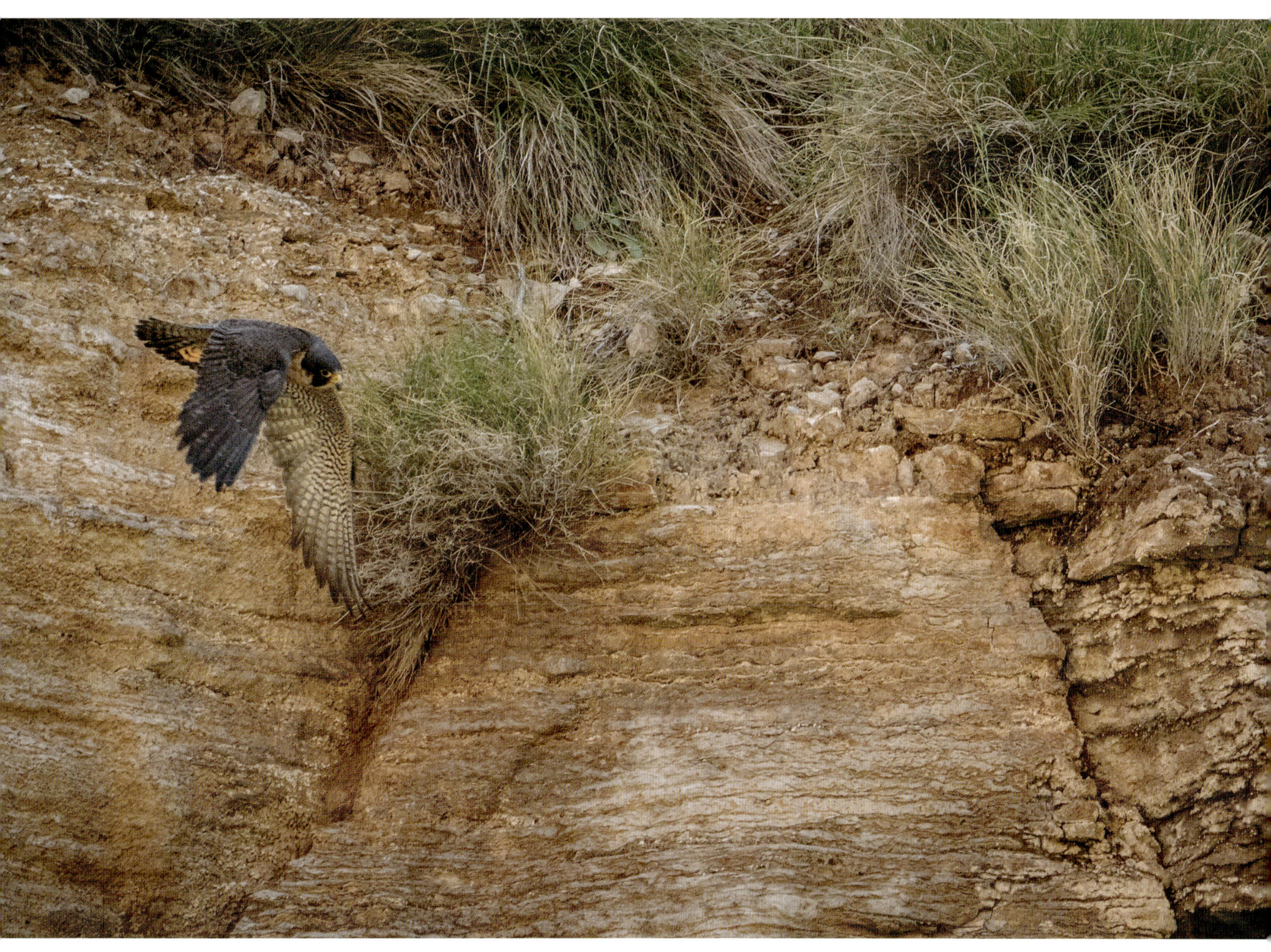

◀ Dead Utah century plant on canyon wall ▲ Peregrine falcon

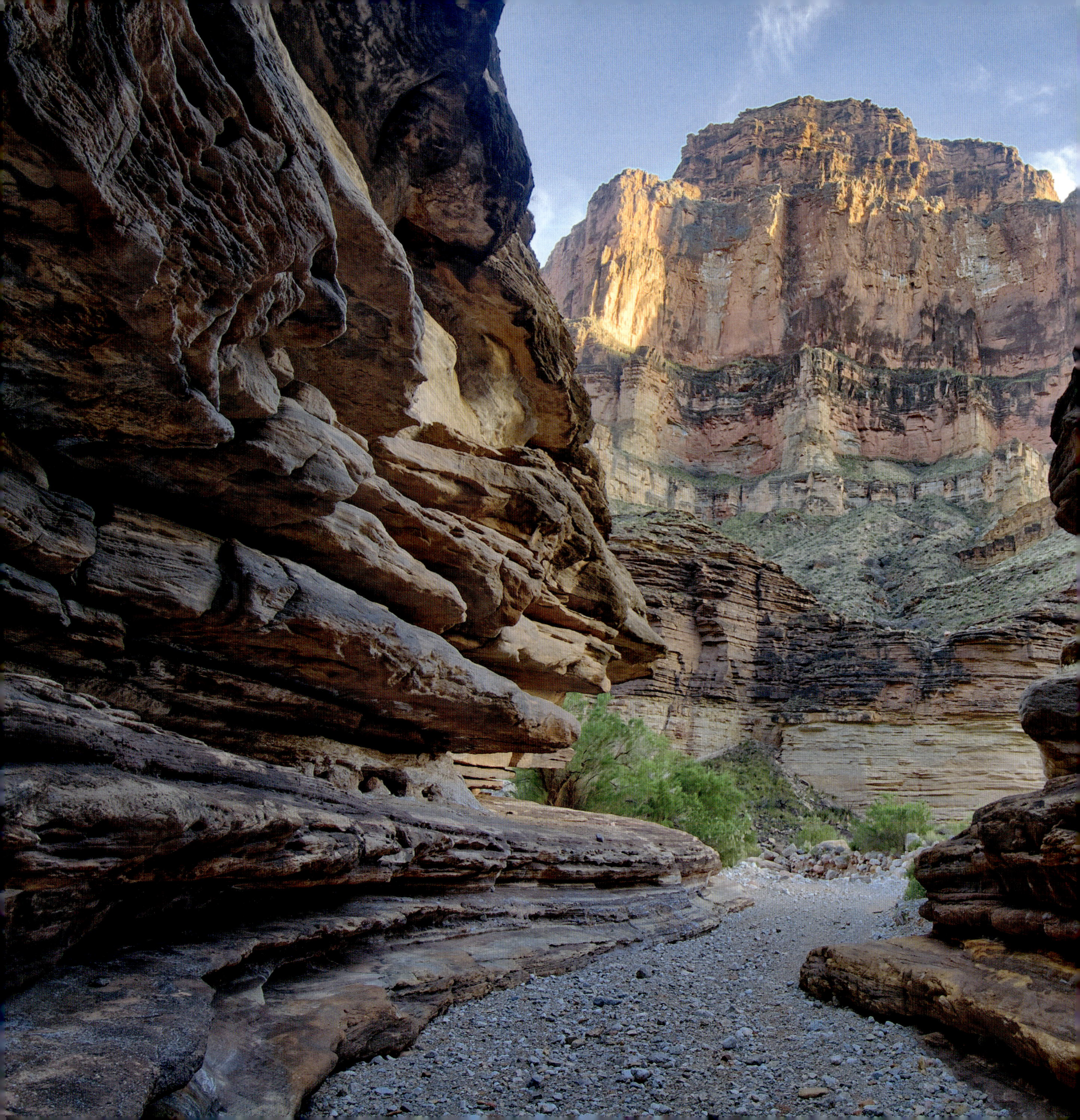

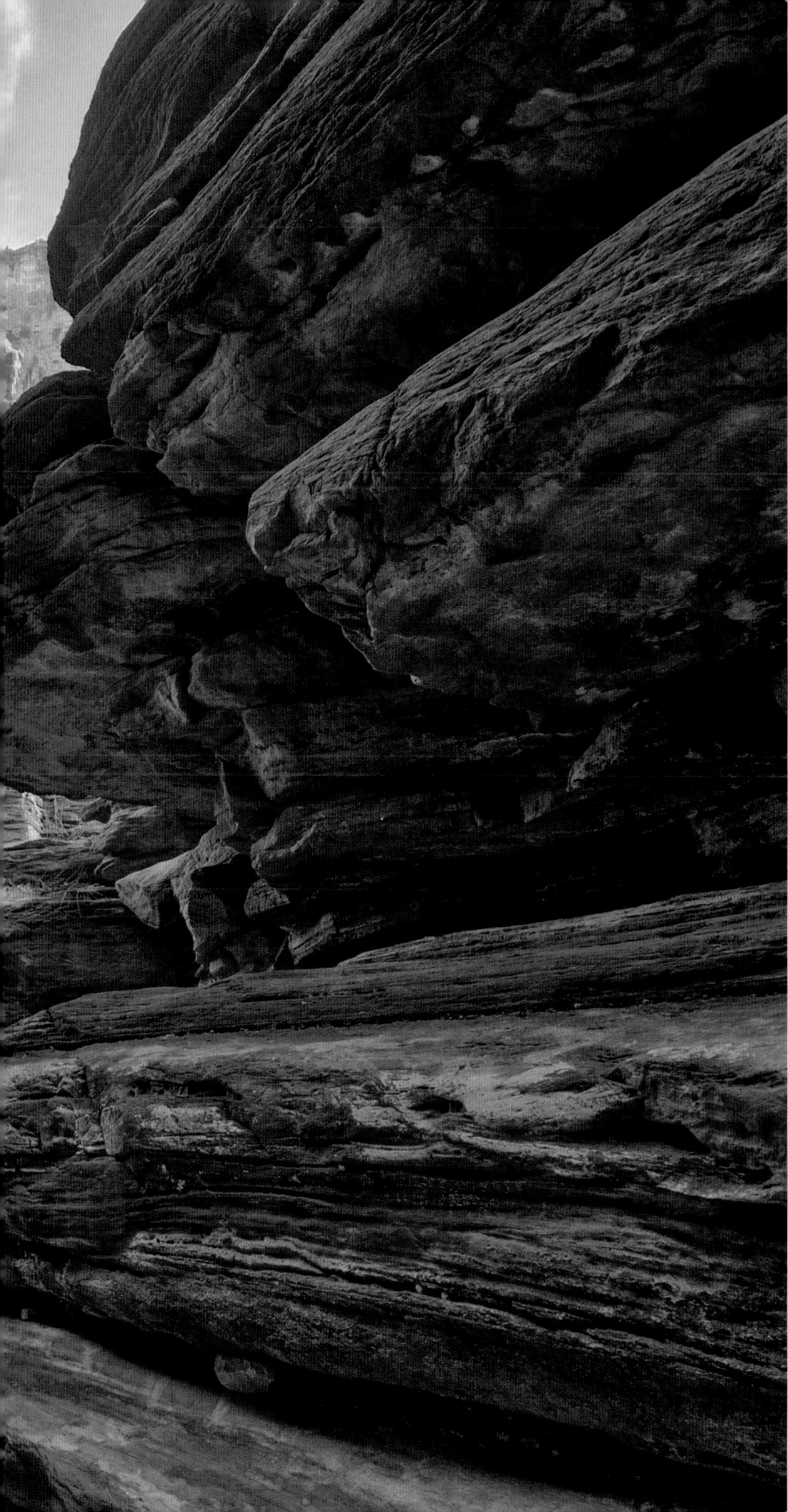

Blacktail Canyon

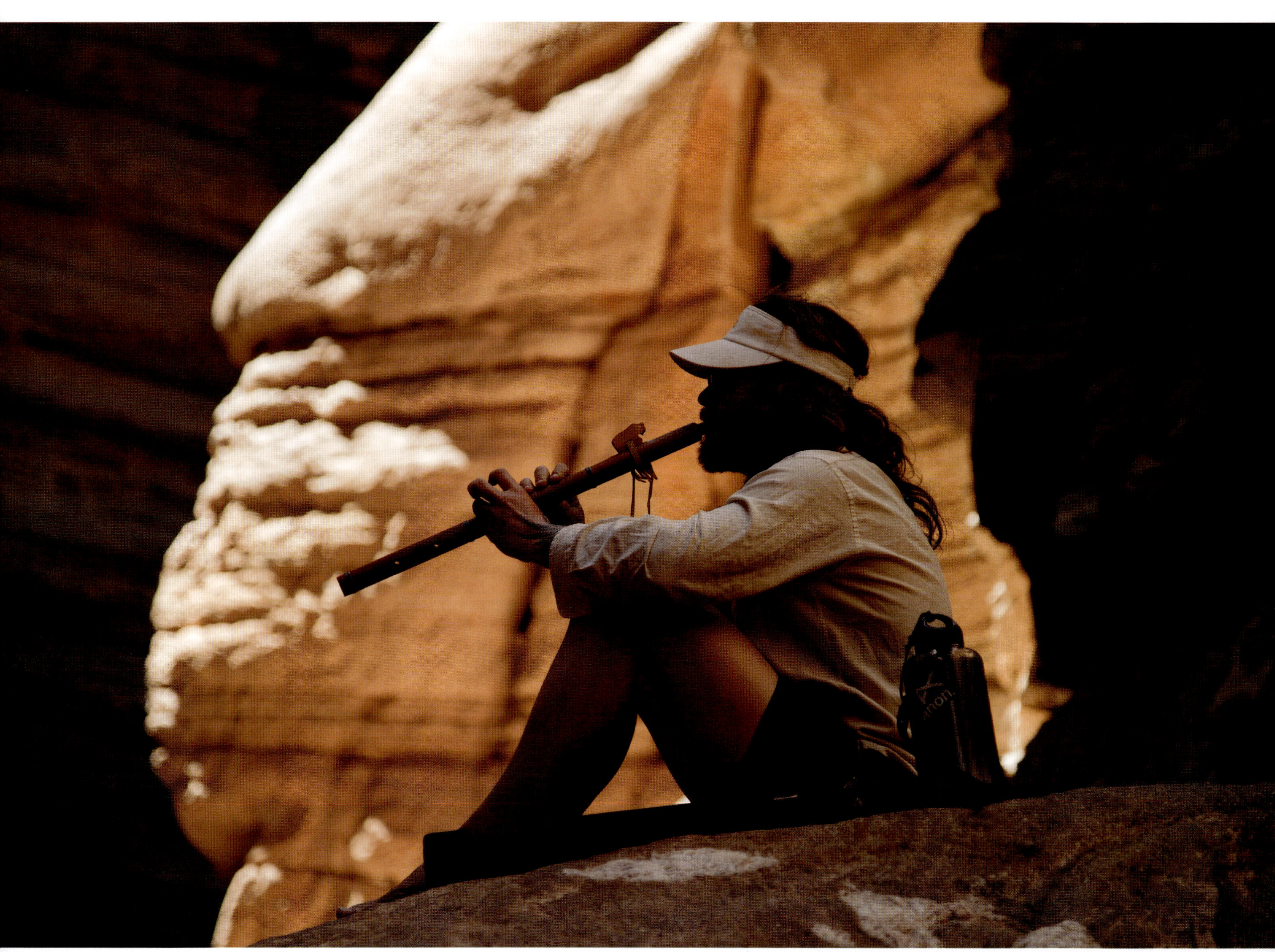

▲ Boatman Jared "Beav" Weaver playing the flute, Blacktail Canyon ▶ Skyward view from Blacktail Canyon

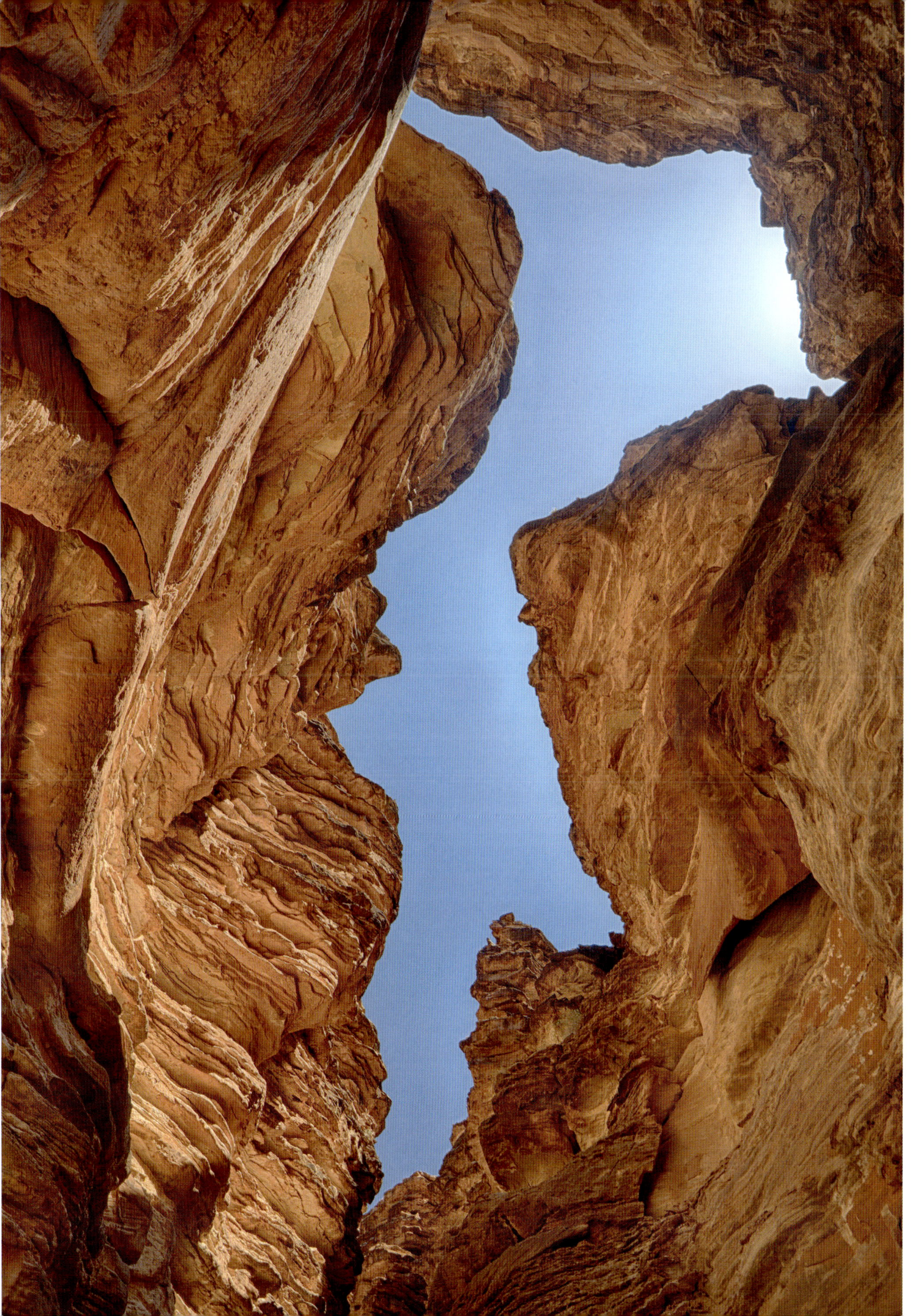

Blacktail Canyon

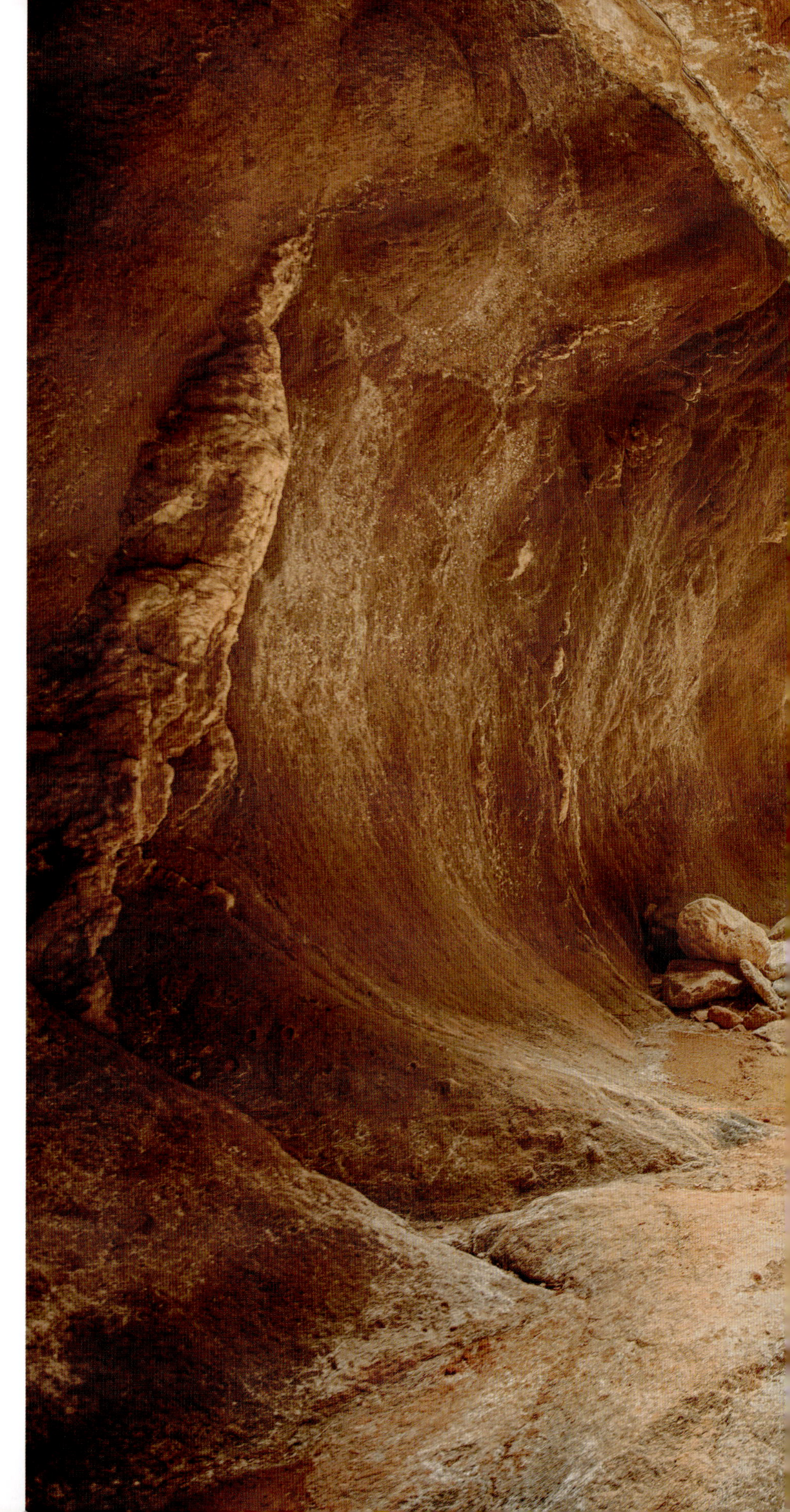

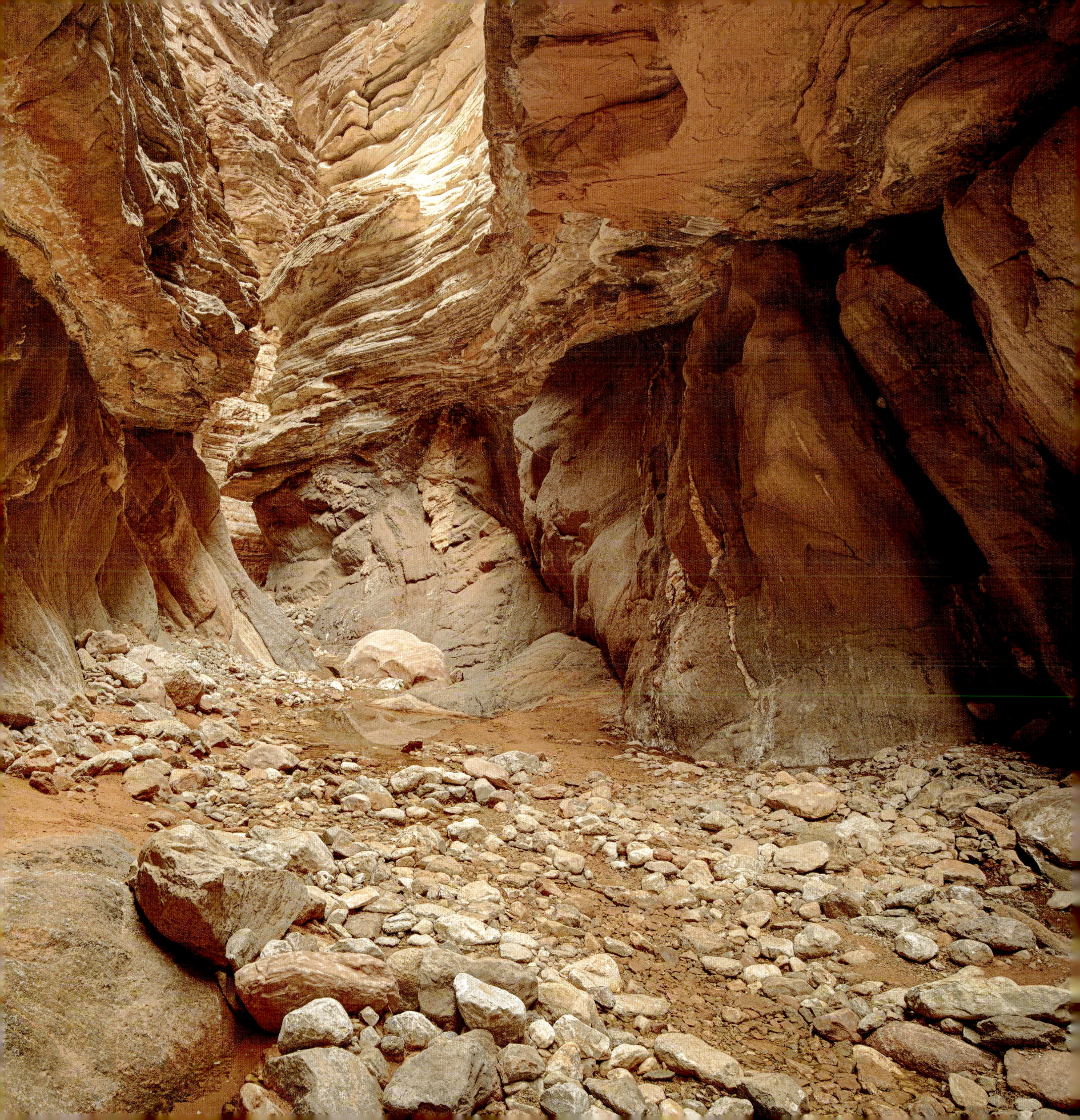

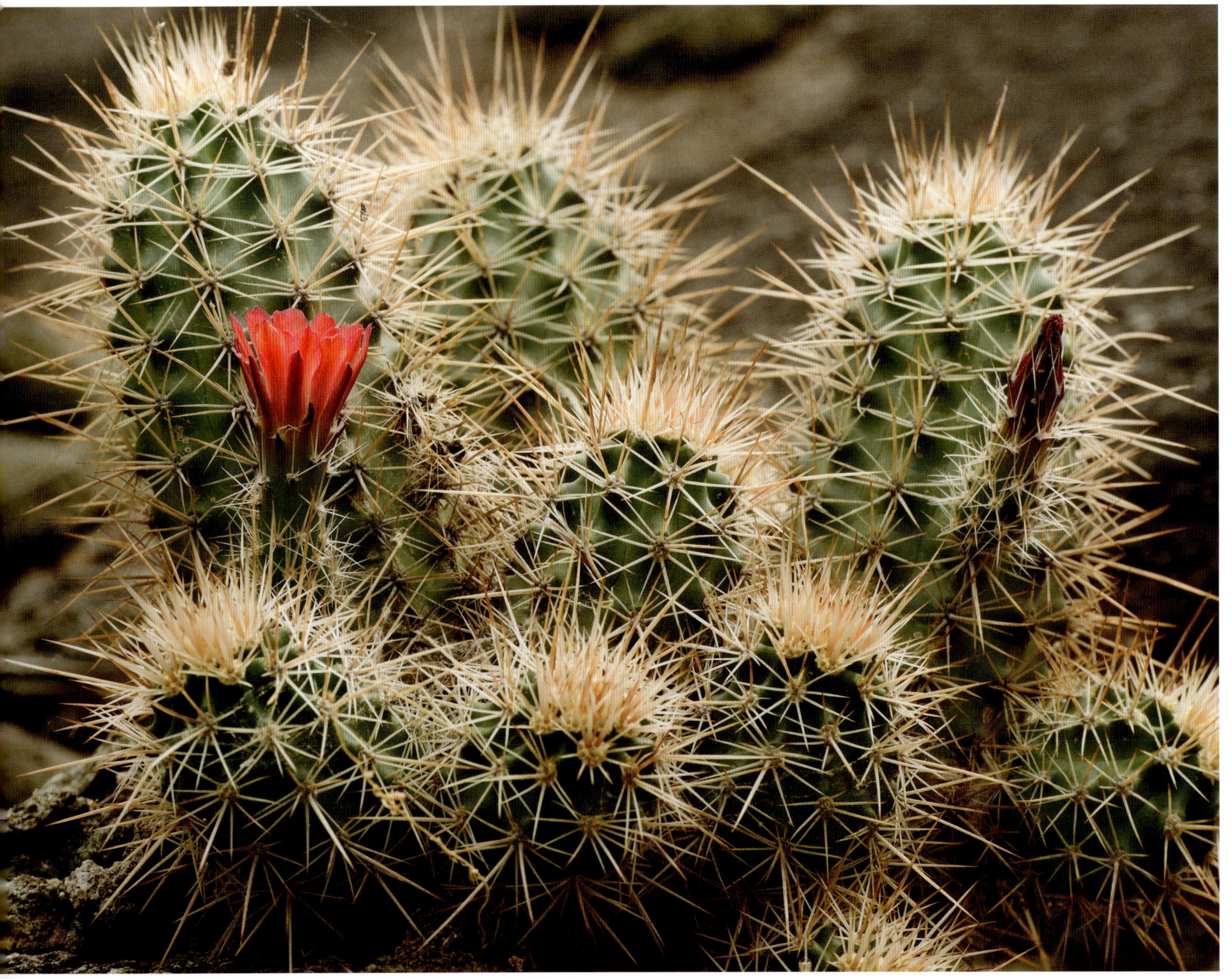

▲ Claret-cup cactus, Diabase Camp below Bedrock ▶ River and canyon wall, Upper Granite Gorge ▼ Middle Granite Gorge

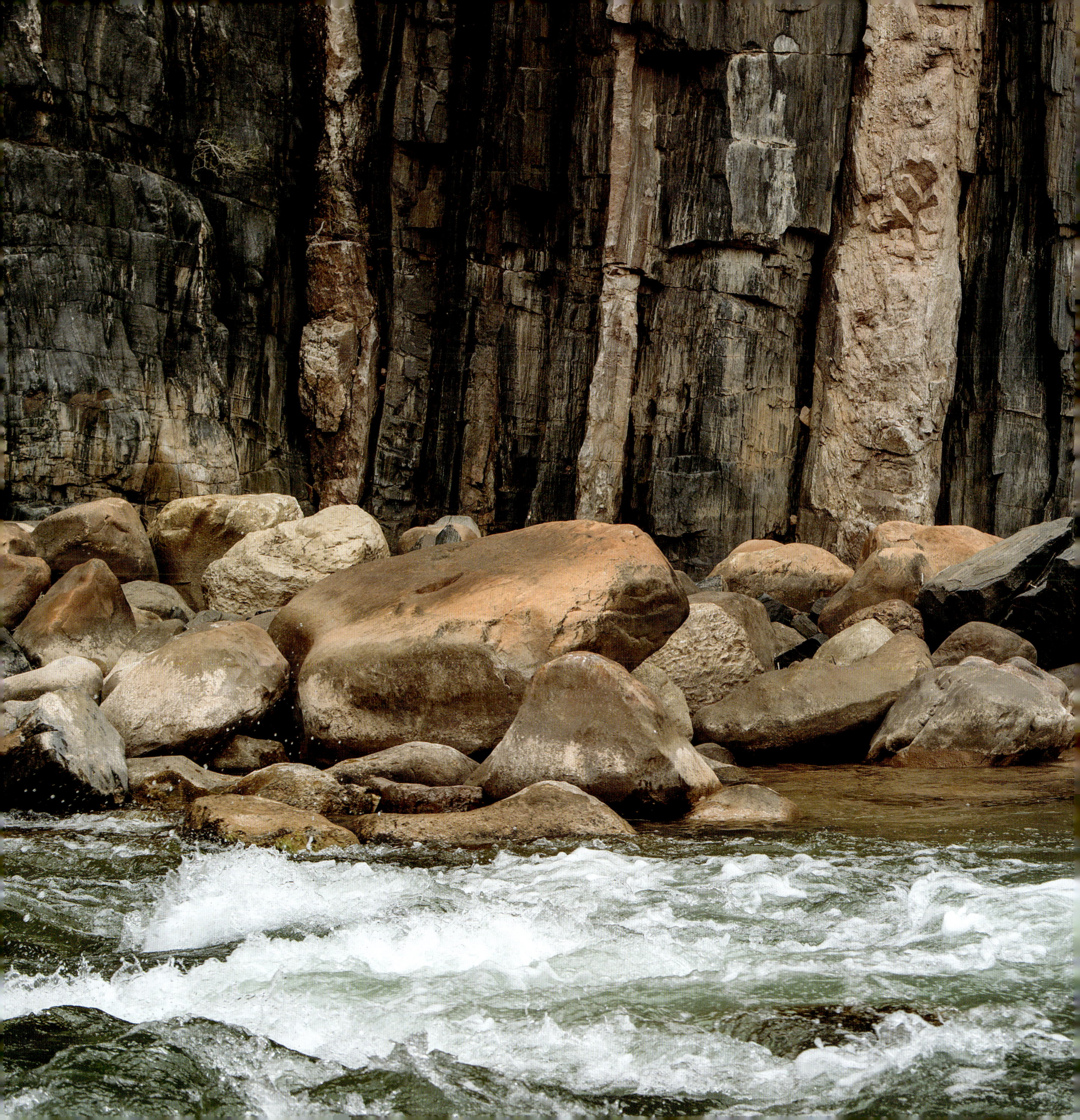

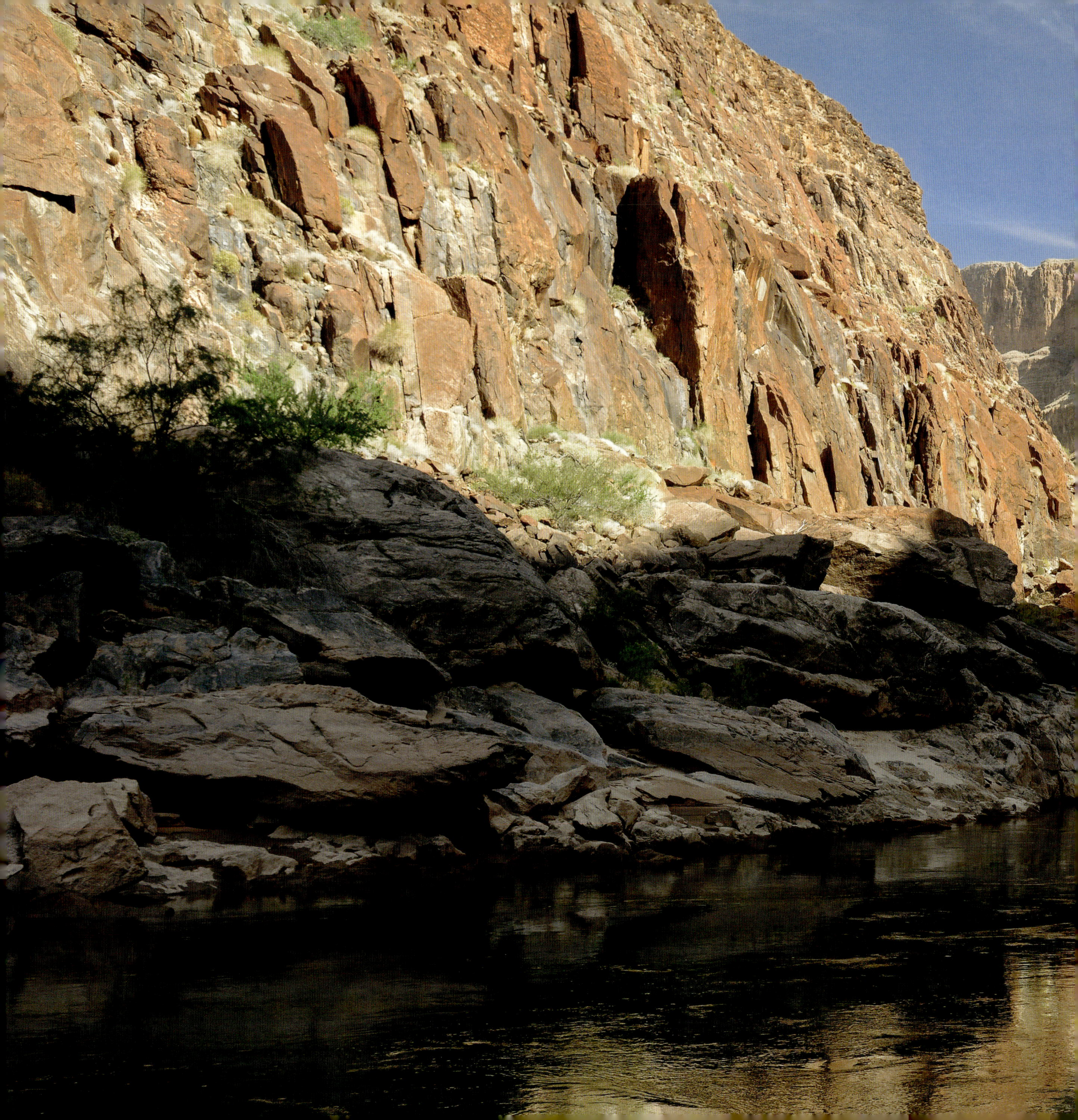

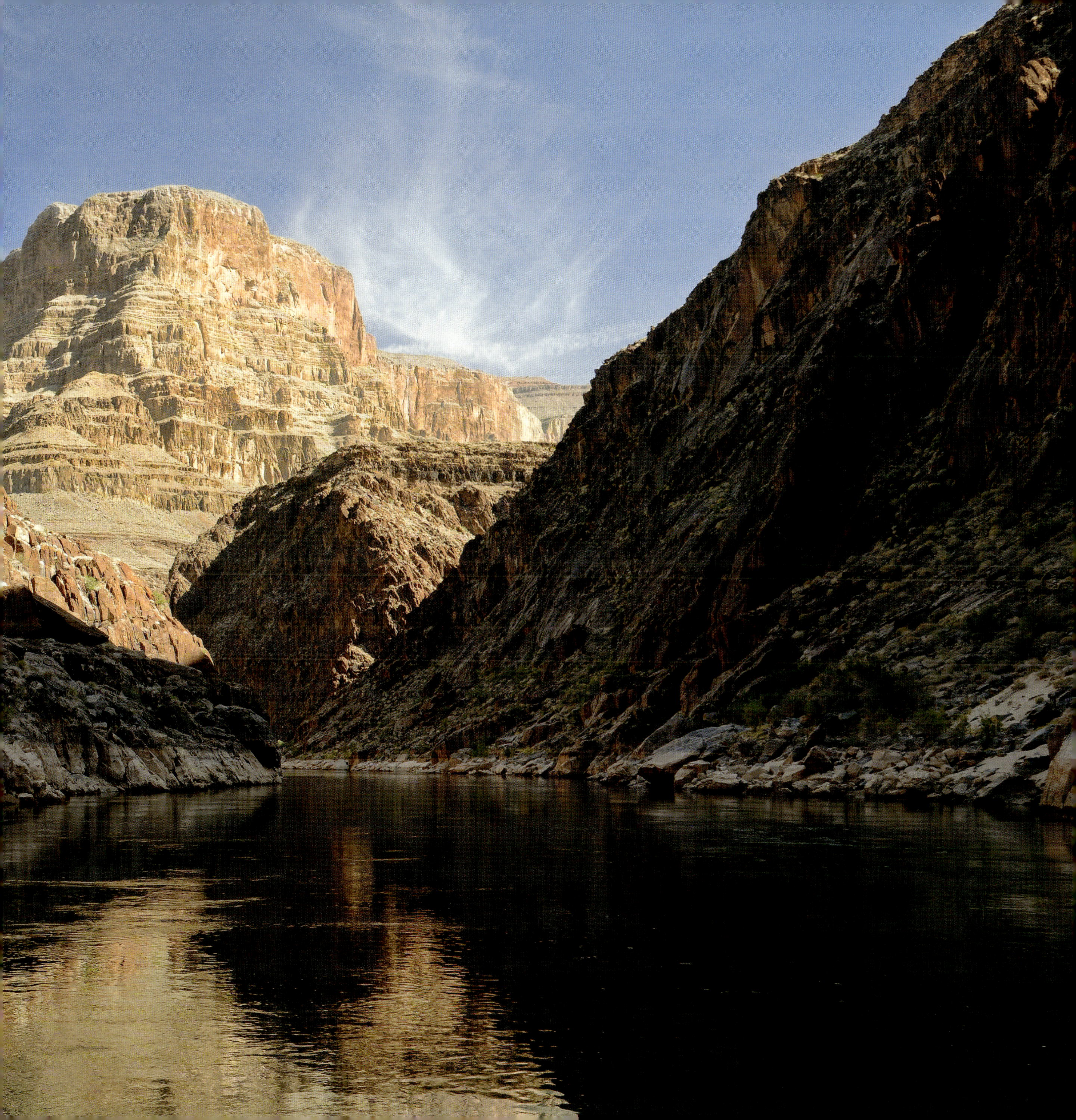

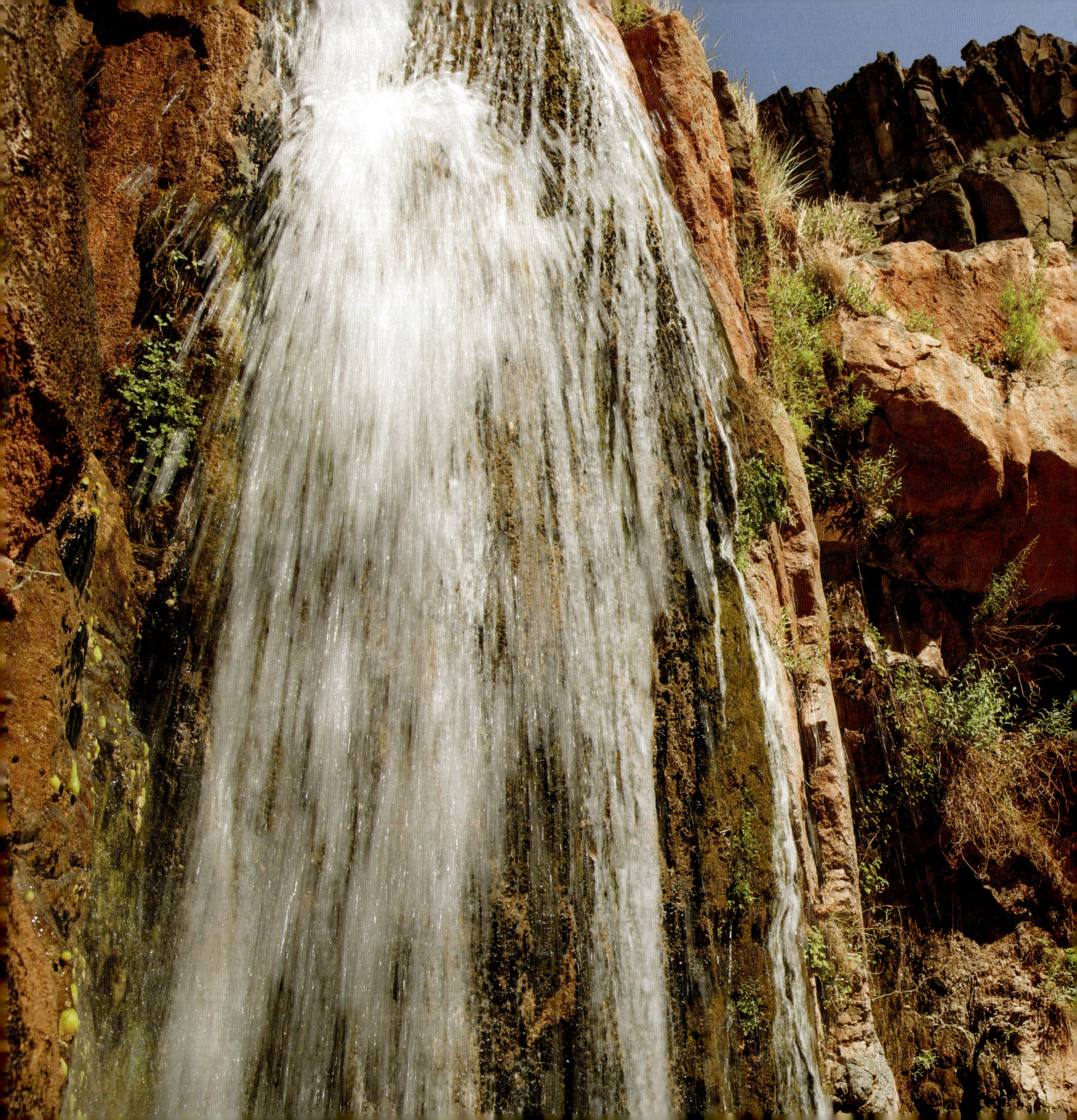

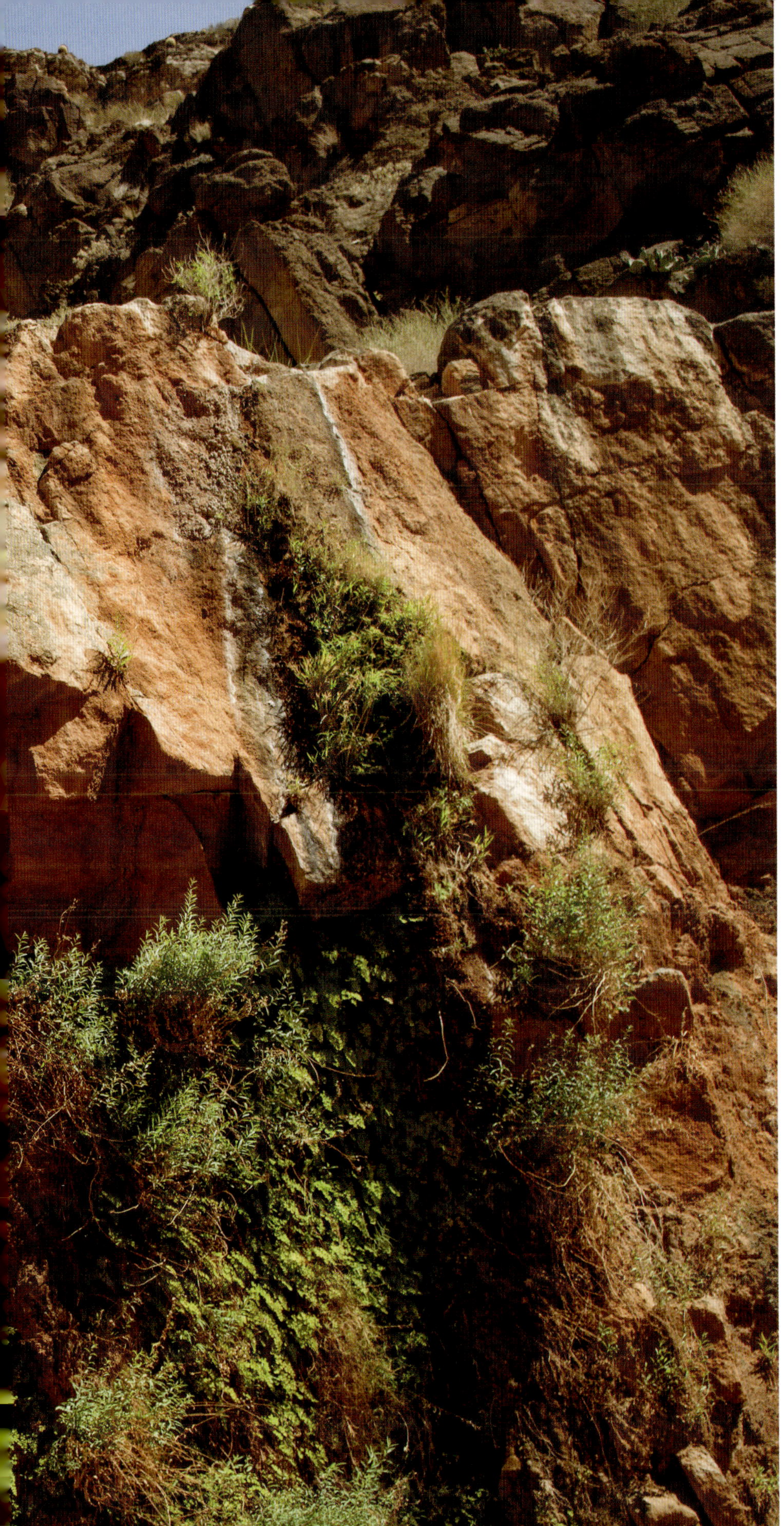

Stone Creek waterfall

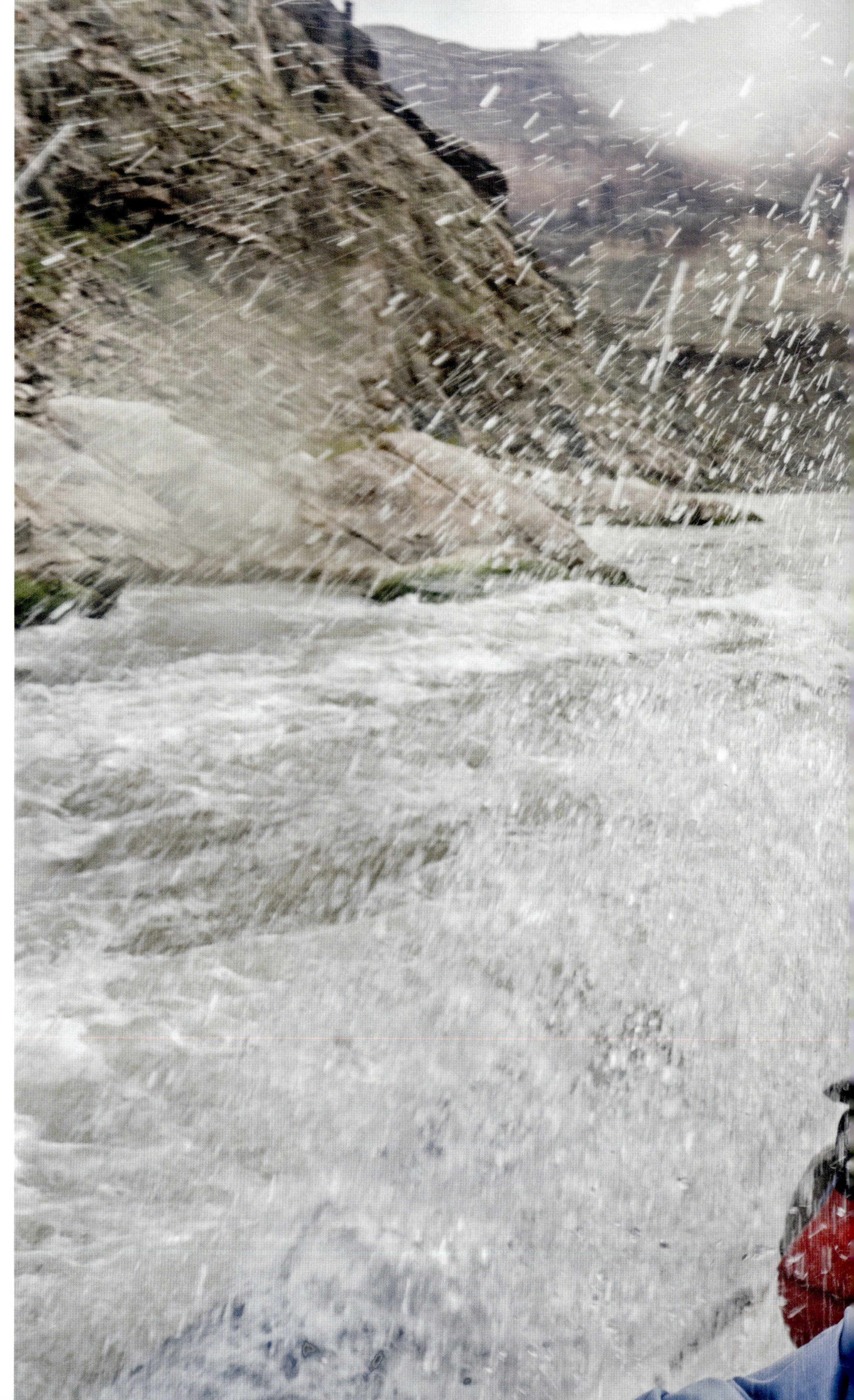

Taking Waltenberg Rapid head-on

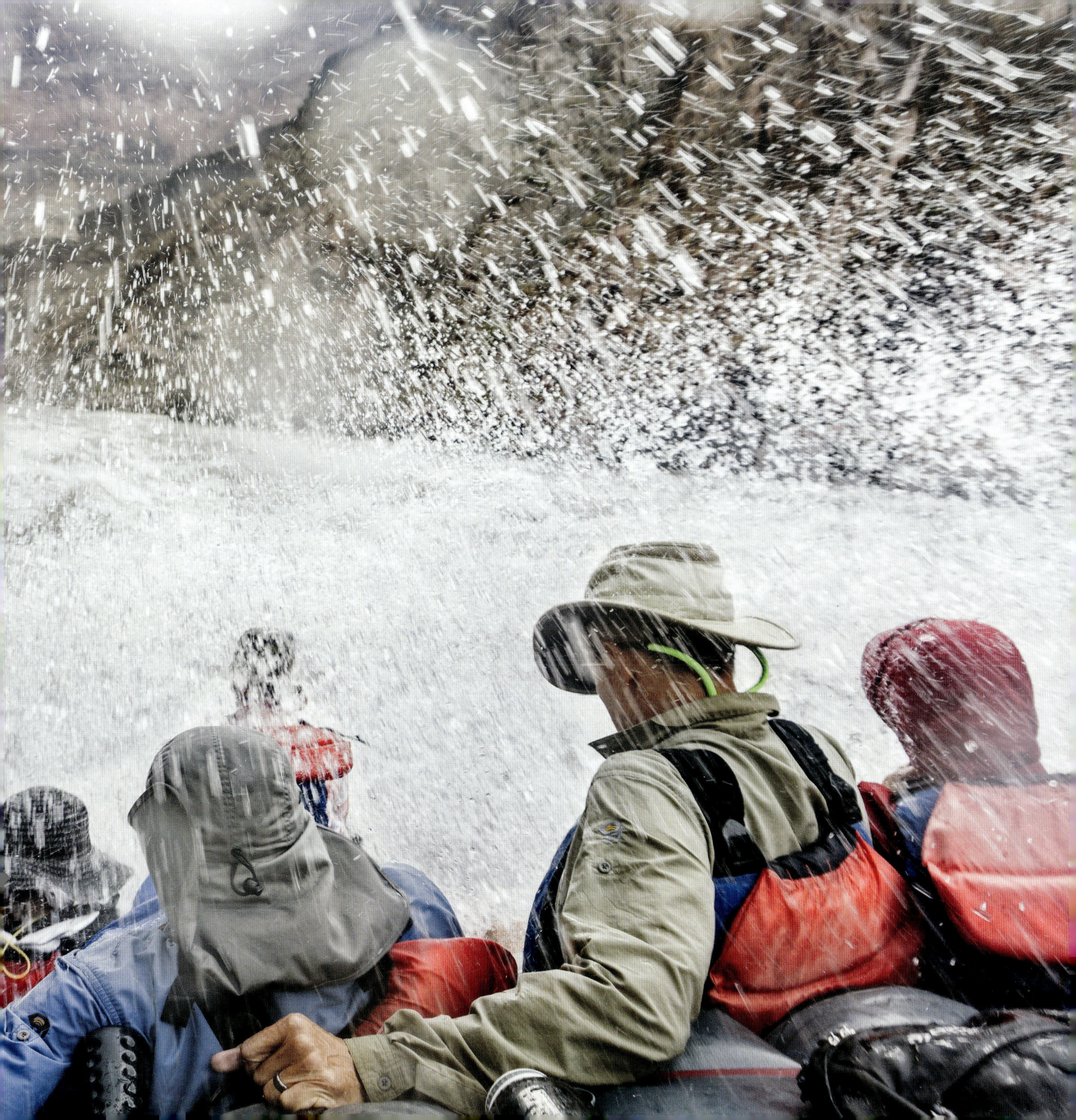

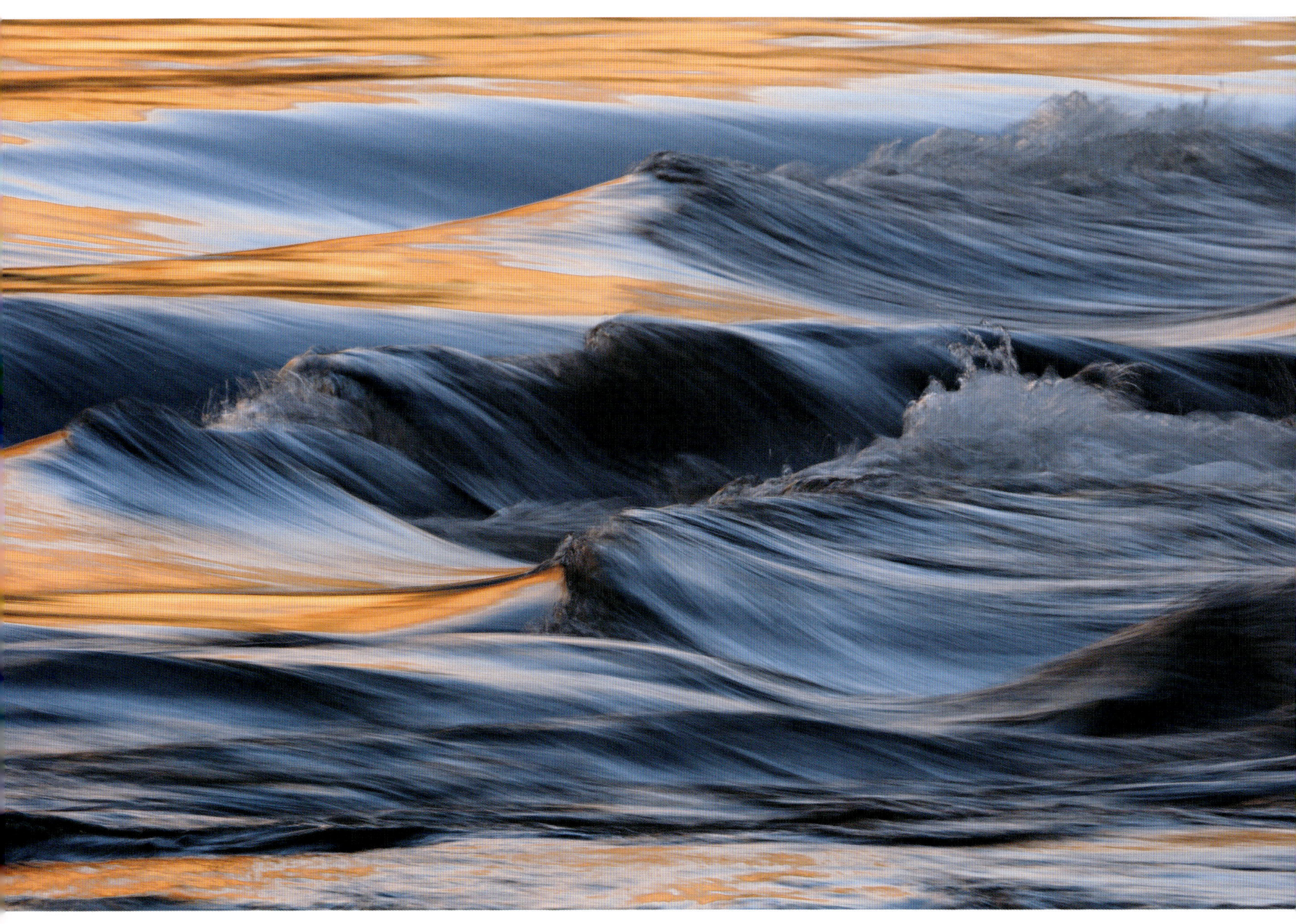

▲ River reflections ▶ Deer Creek Canyon

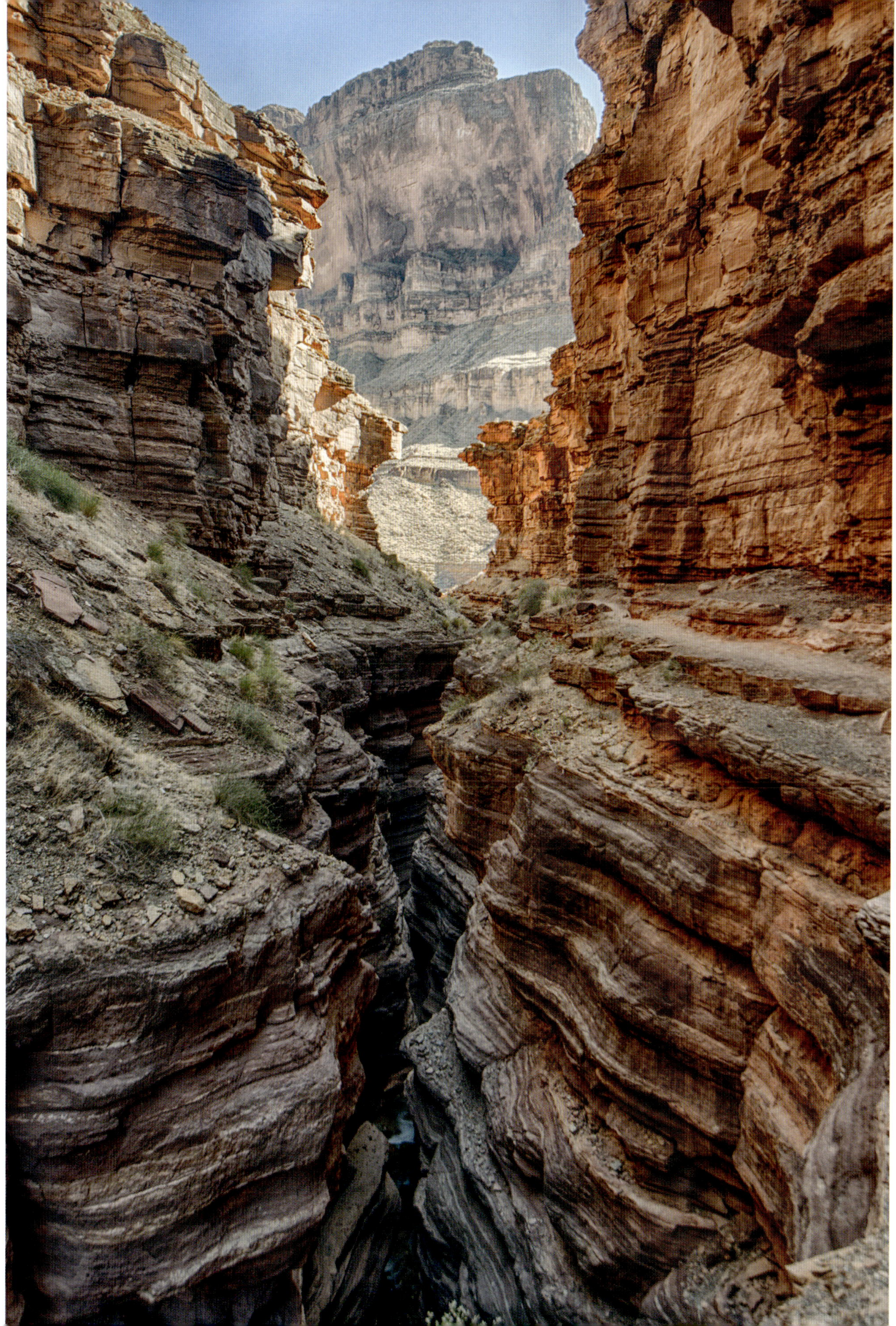

Engelmann prickly-pear cactus
opposite Deer Creek waterfall

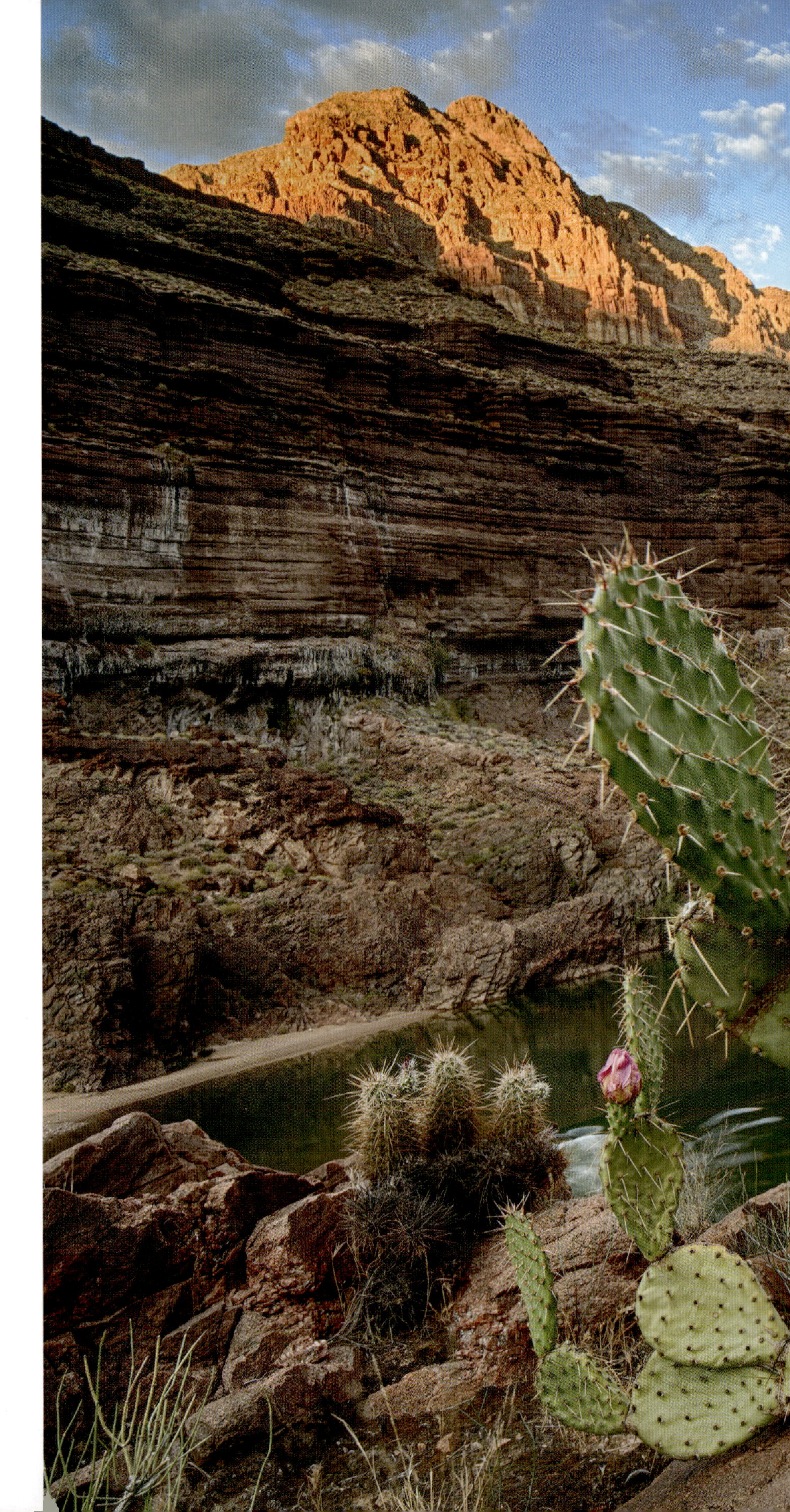

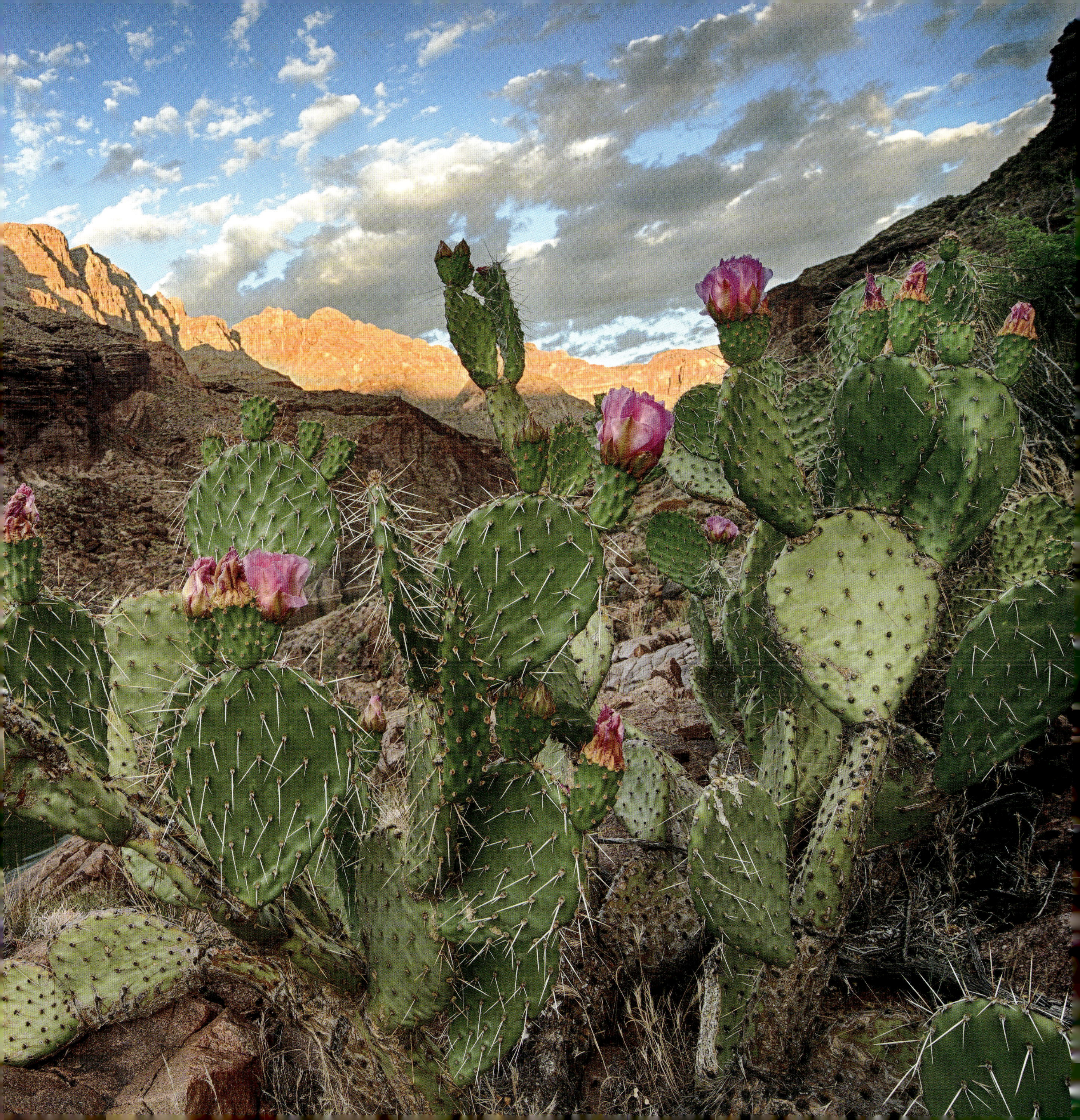

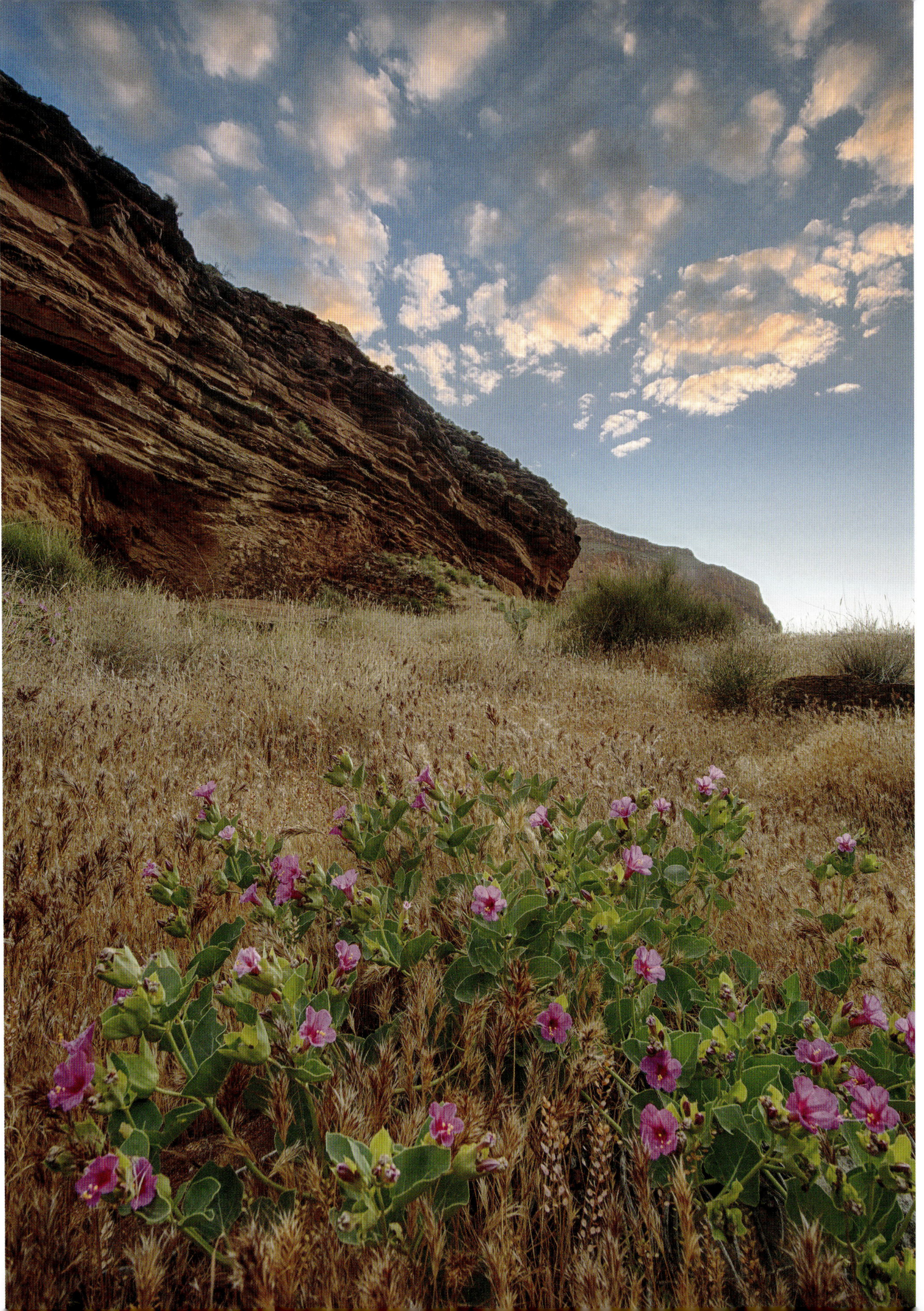

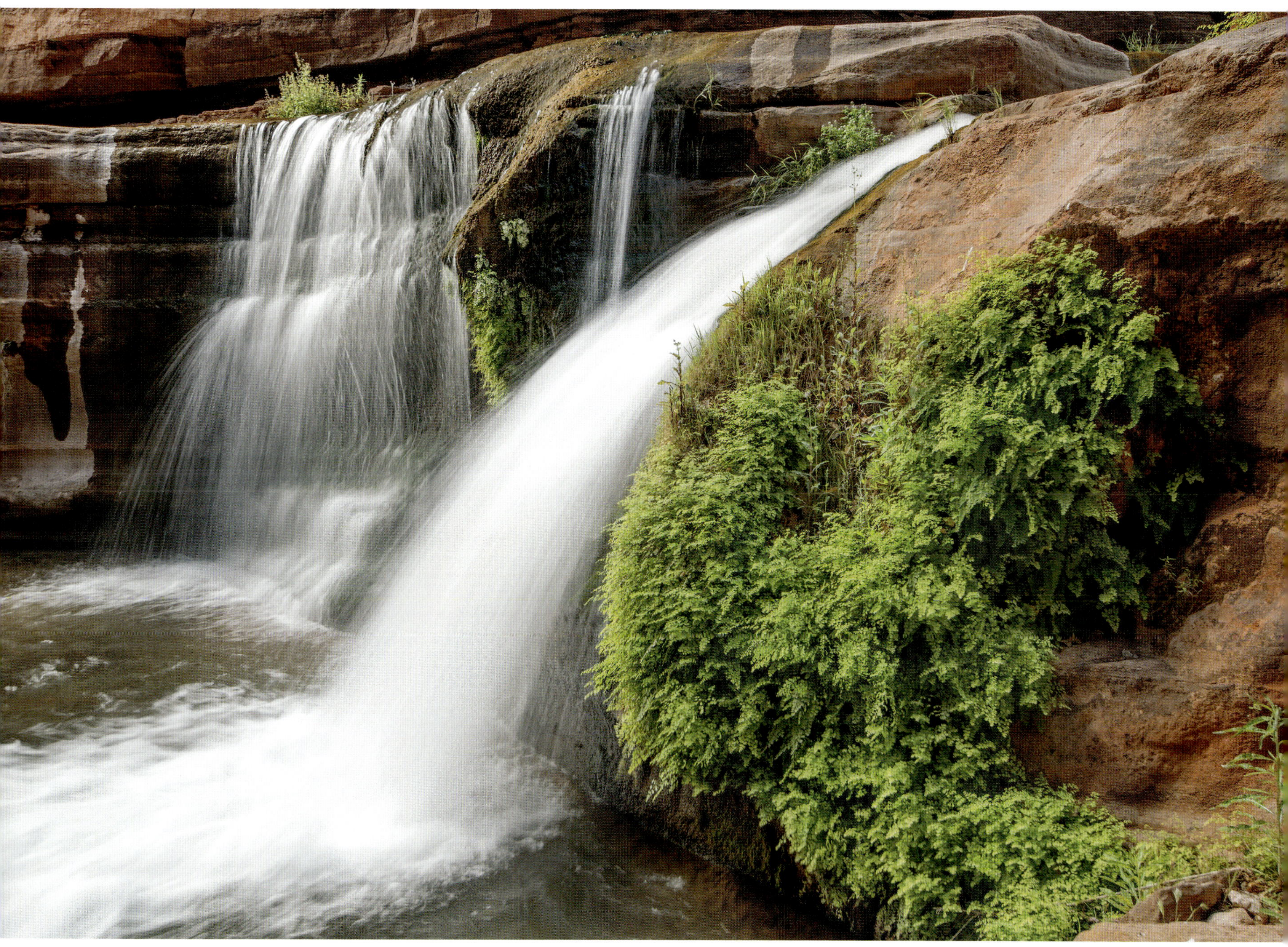

◀ Desert four o'clock flowers at sunset, Deer Creek Camp ▲ Waterfall at the patio, Deer Creek Canyon

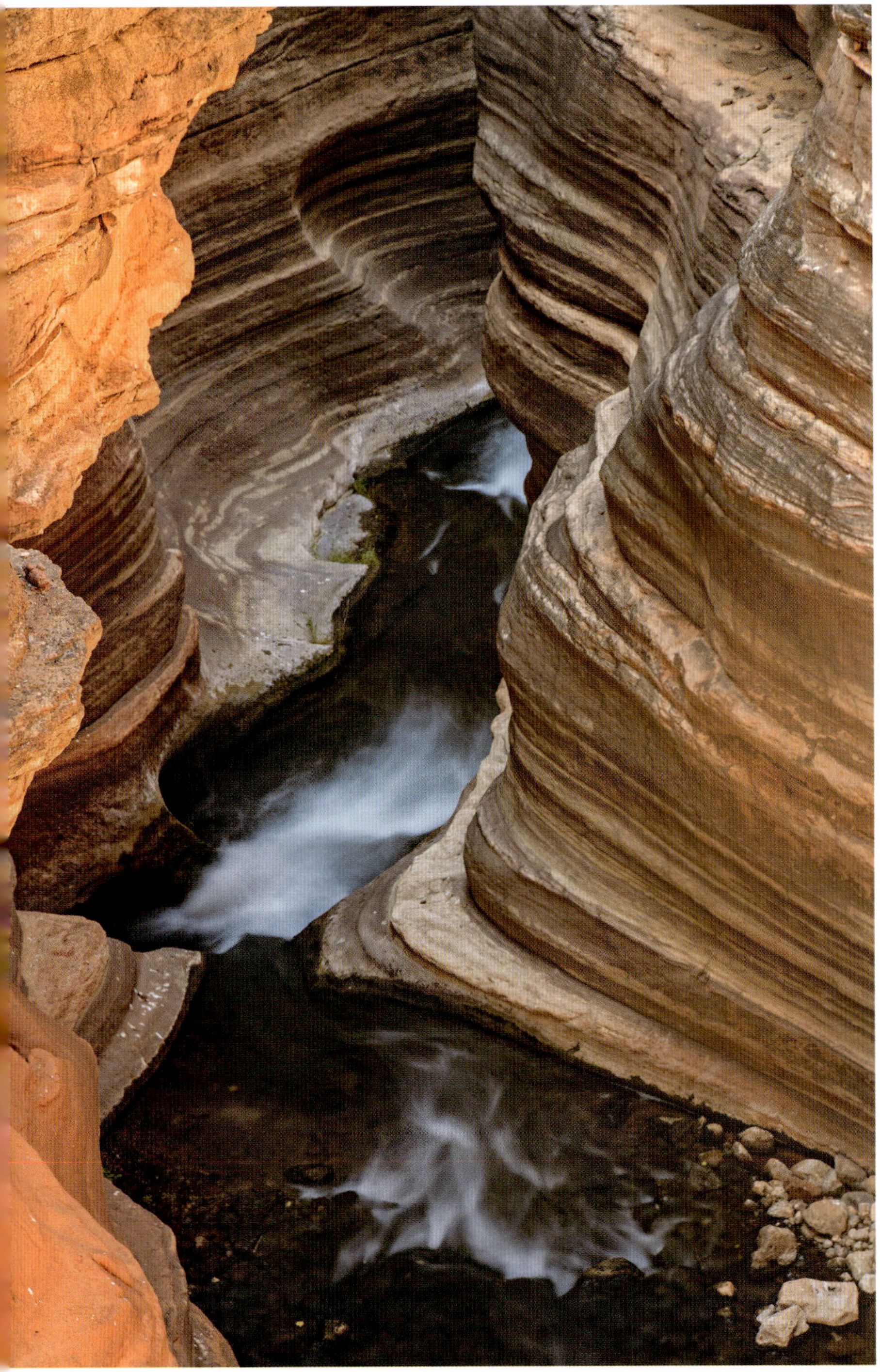

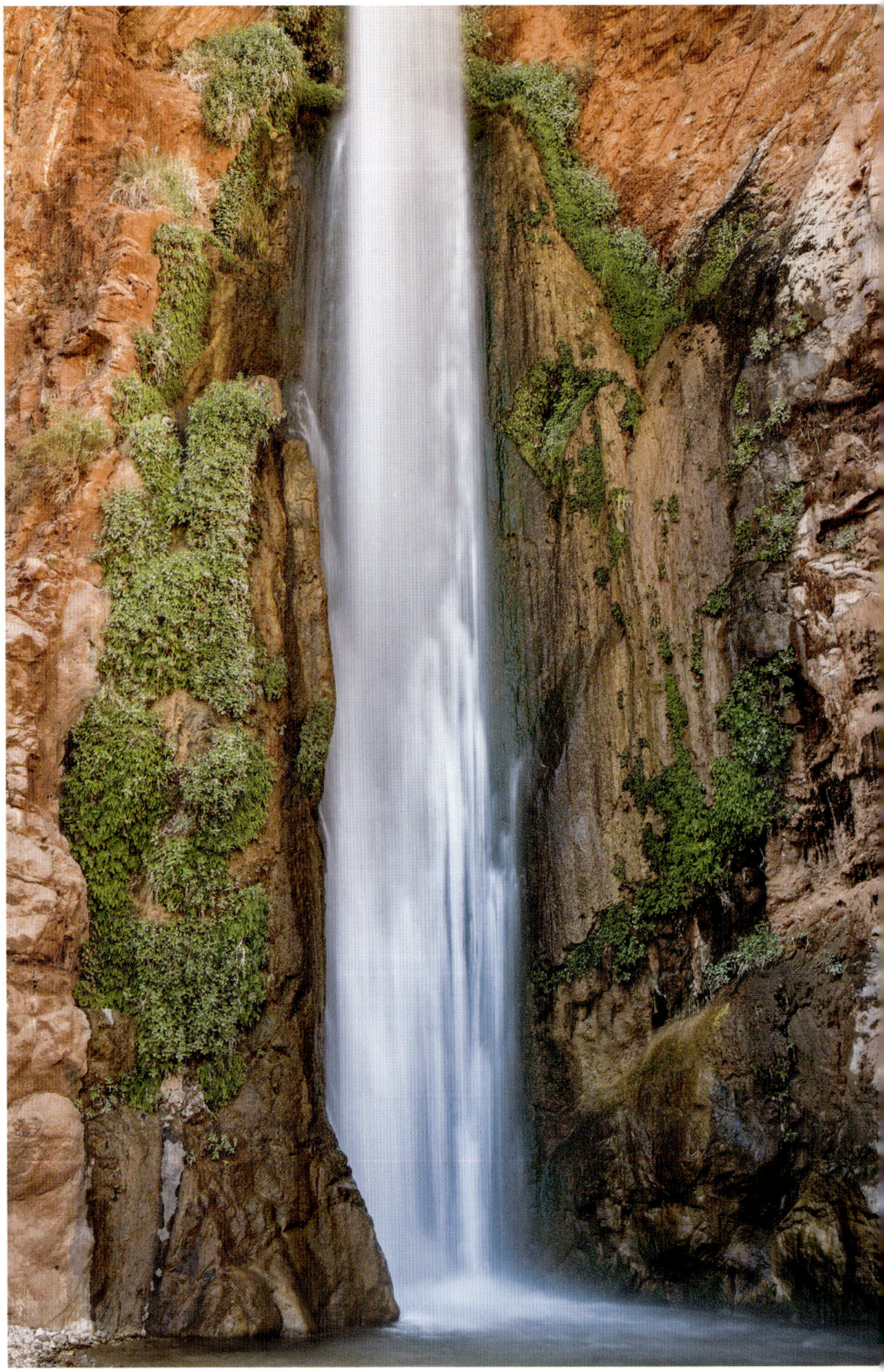

▲ Deer Creek Canyon (left) and waterfall (right) ▶ View downriver at sunset from Deer Creek Camp

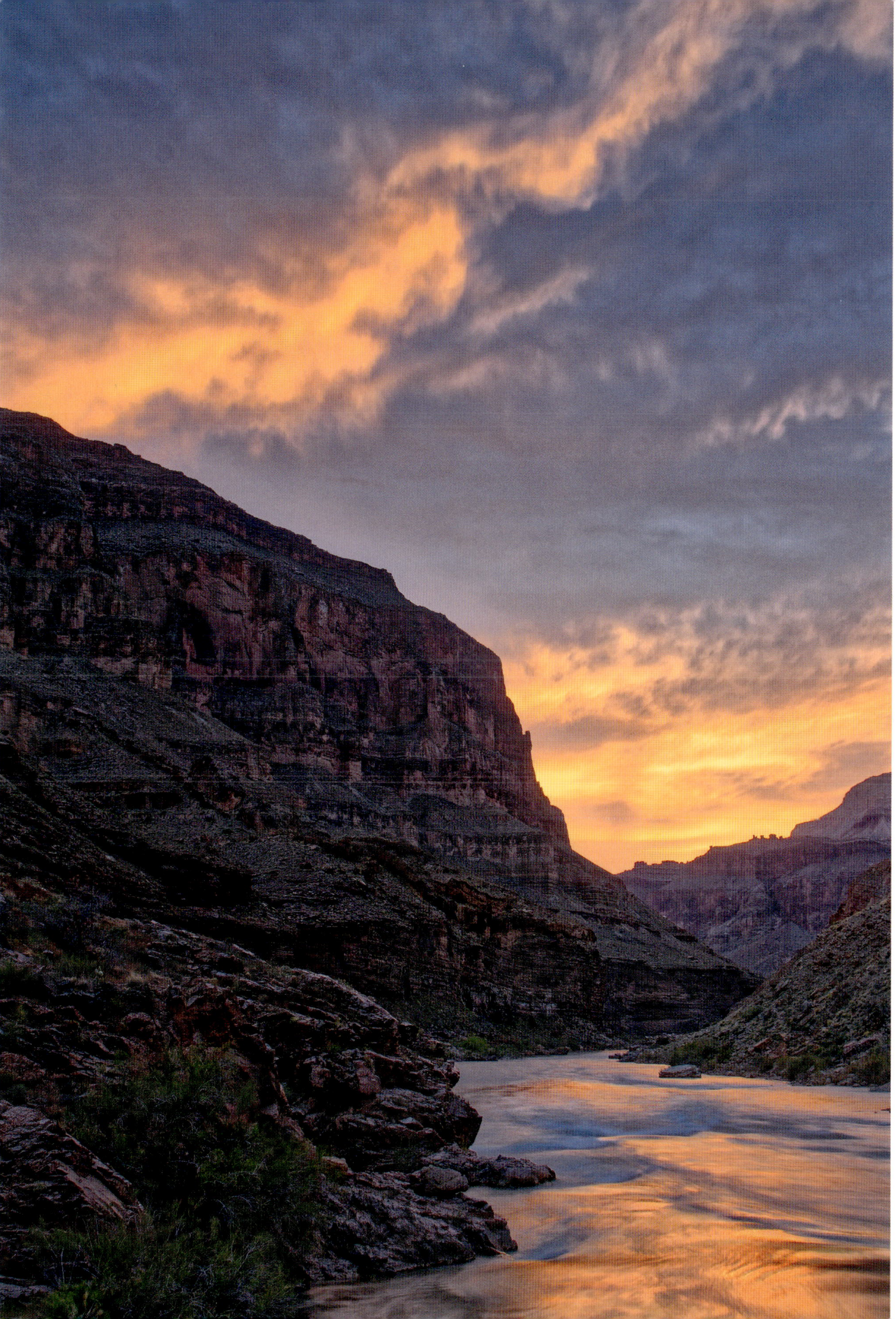

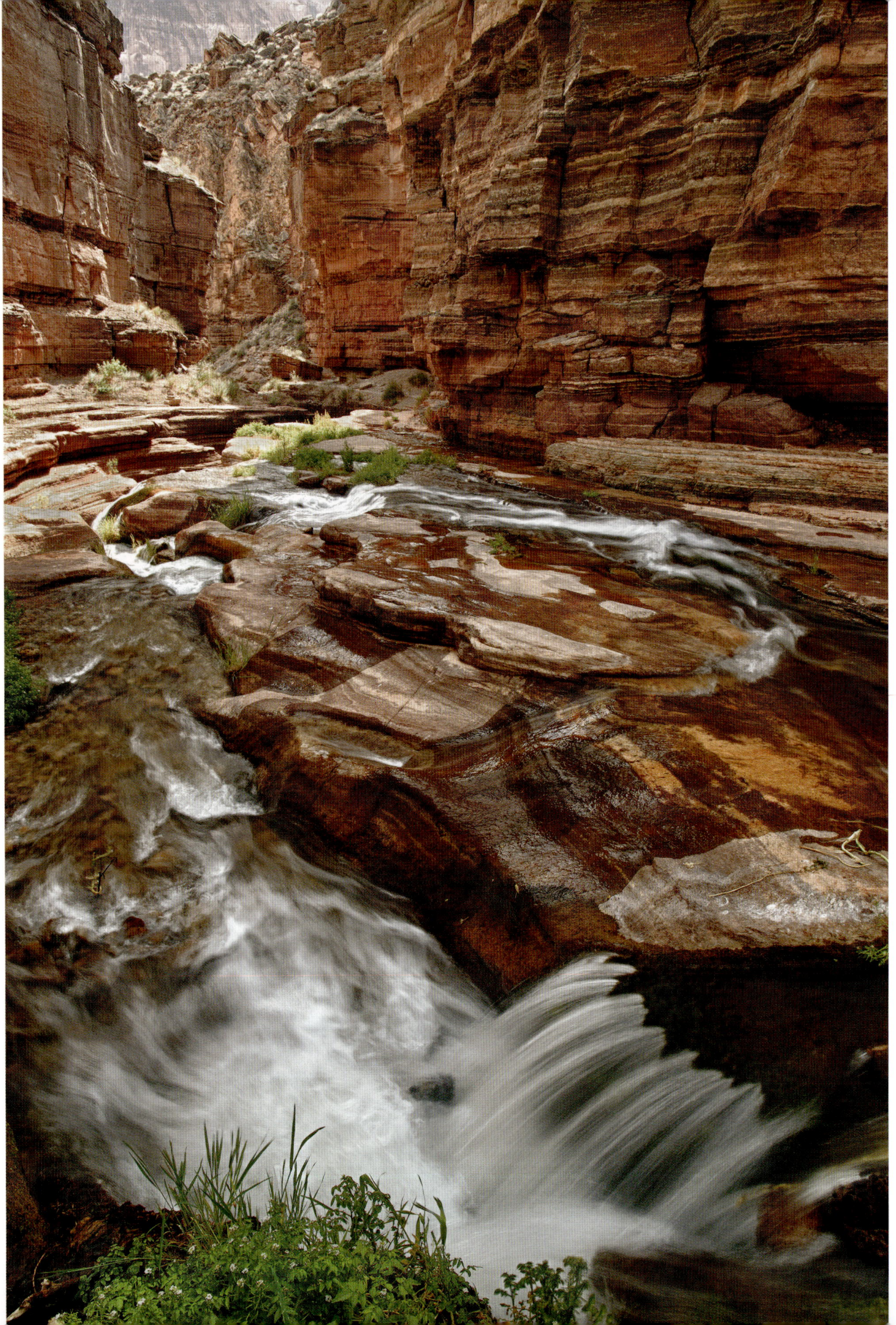

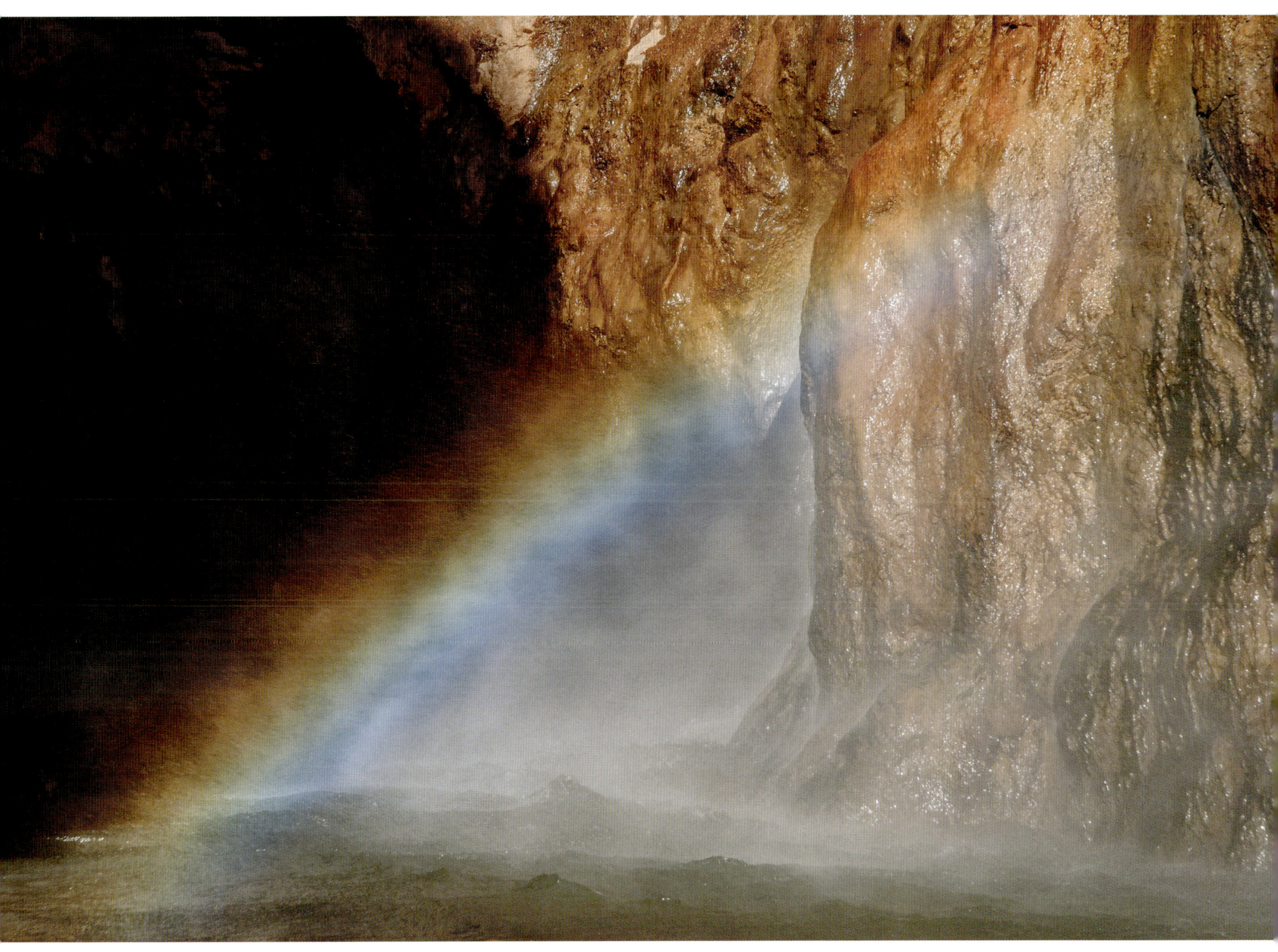

◀ Top end of Deer Creek Canyon ▲ Rainbow at base of Deer Creek waterfall

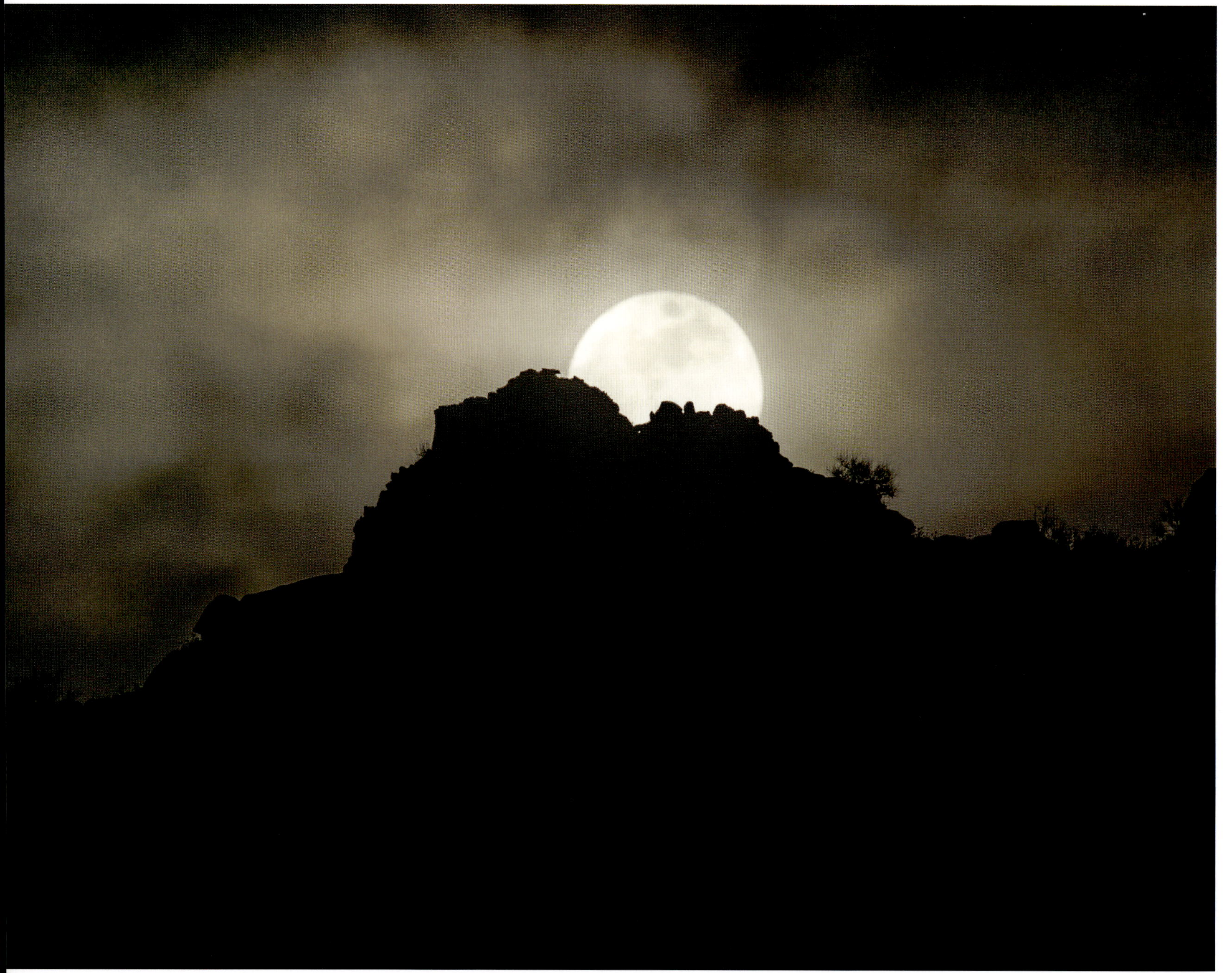

▲ Moonrise over canyon wall, Deer Creek Camp ► Claret-cup cactus, Deer Creek Camp

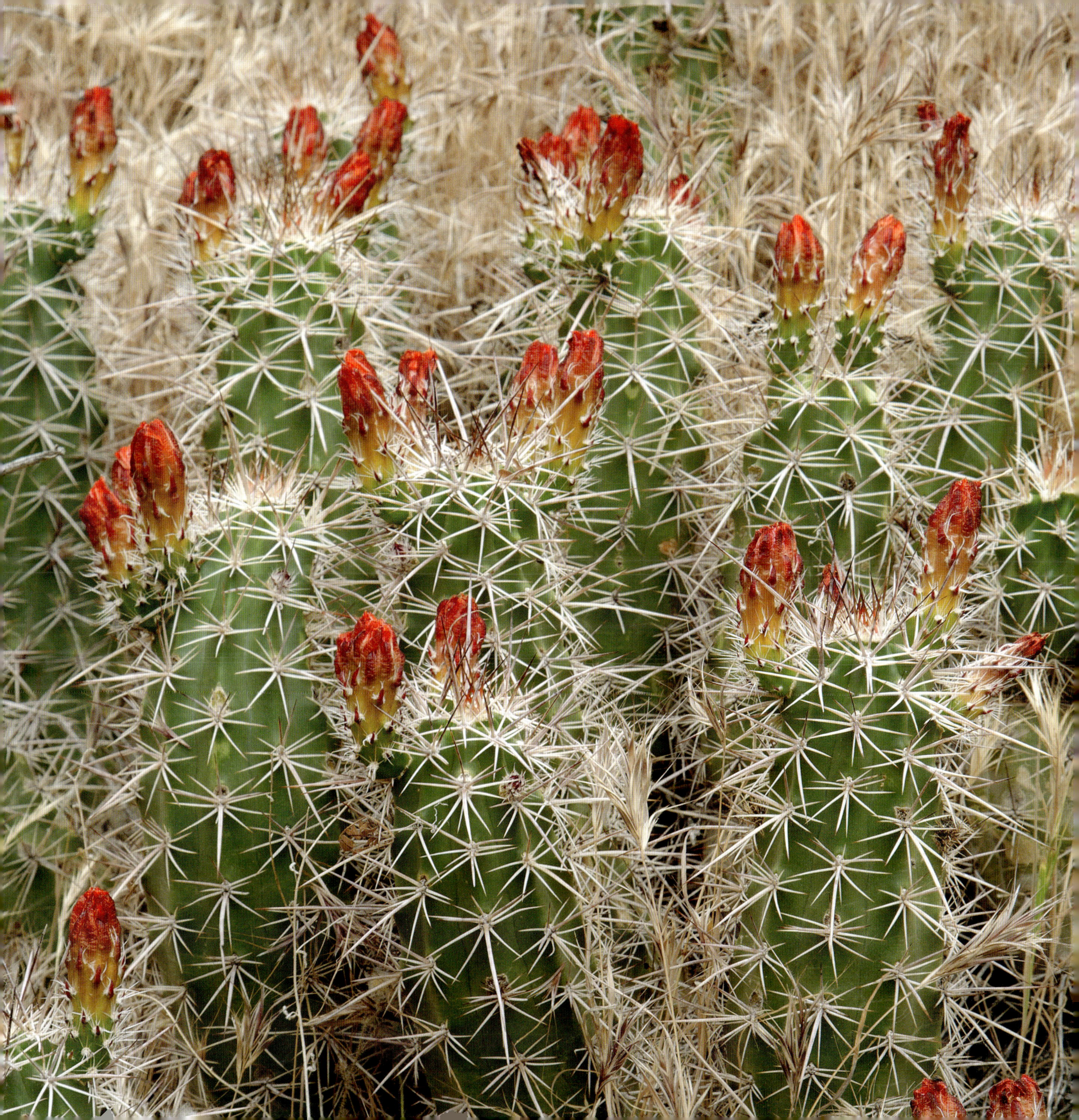

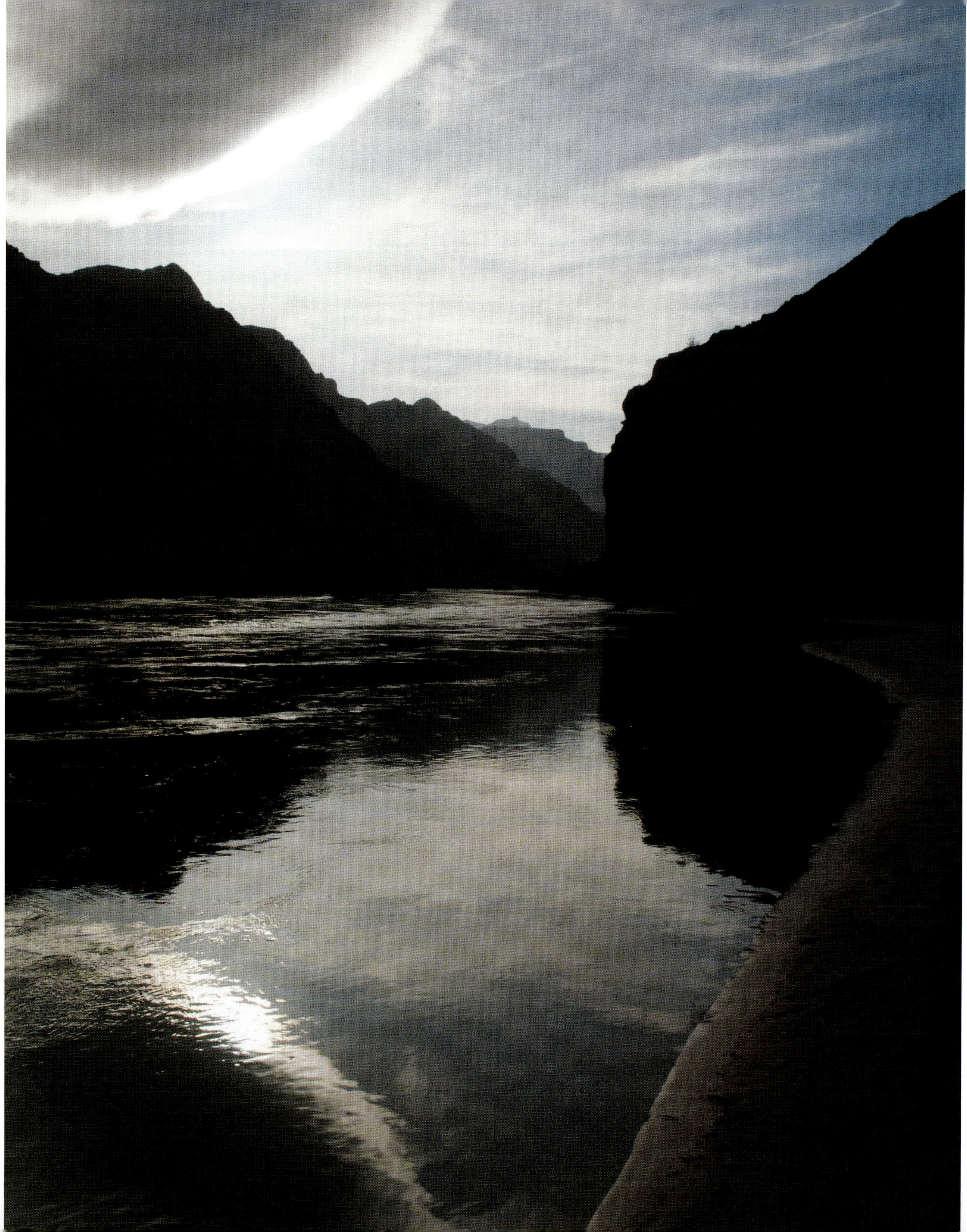

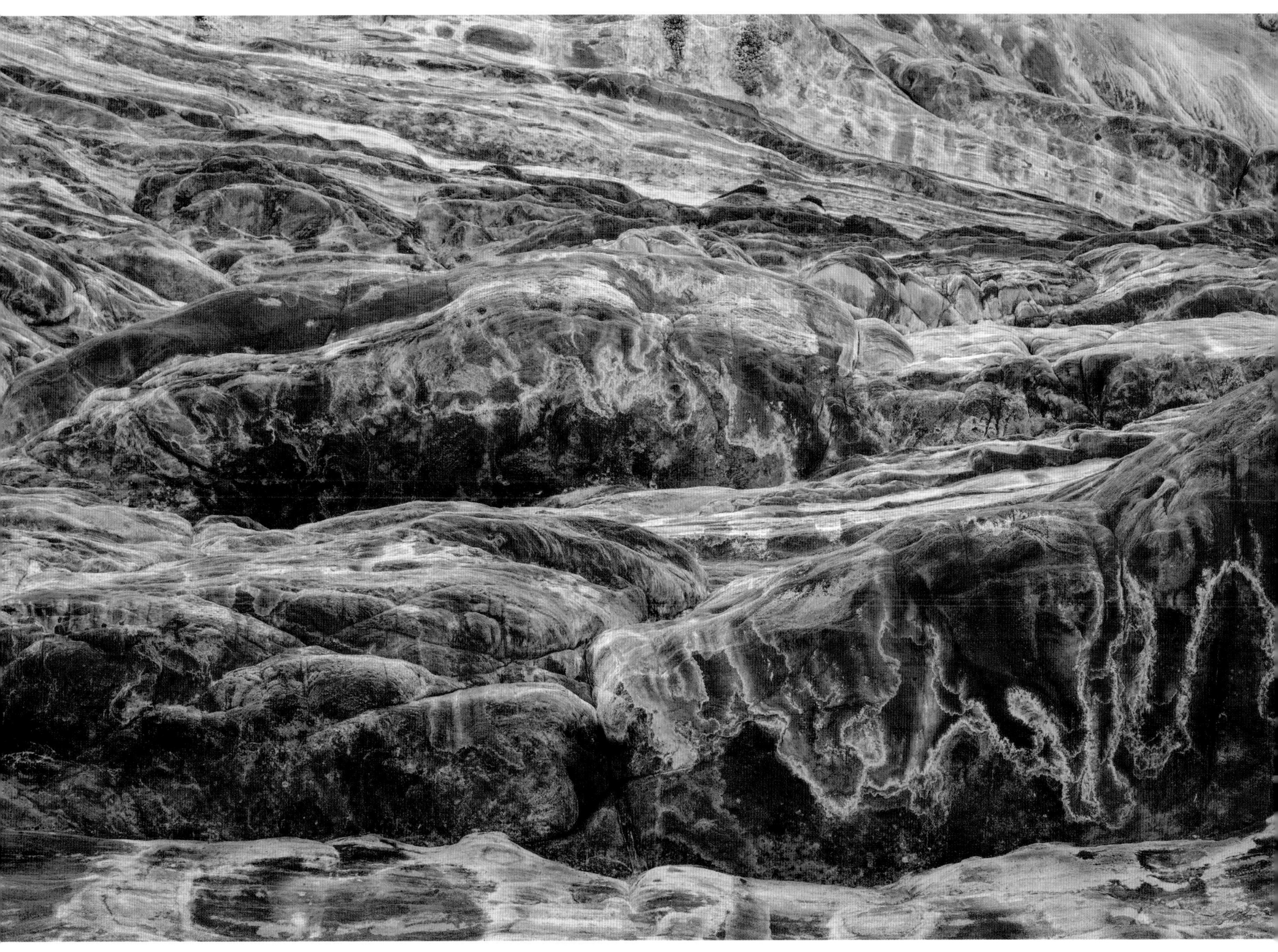

◀ View upriver from 137 Mile Camp ▲ Layered rock patterns, Pancho's Kitchen

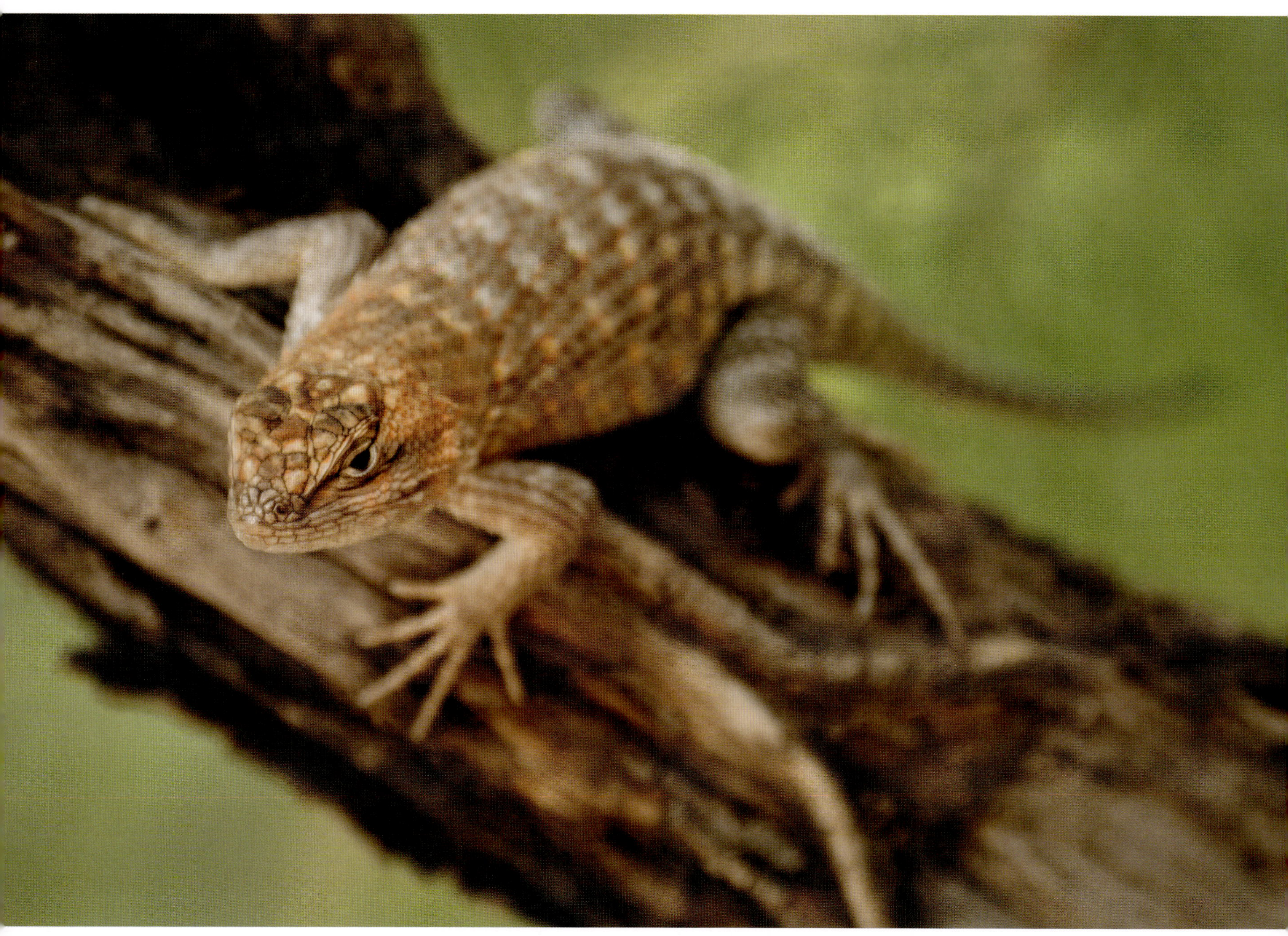

▲ Desert spiny lizard, Pancho's Kitchen ▶ Cliff with half moon, Pancho's Kitchen

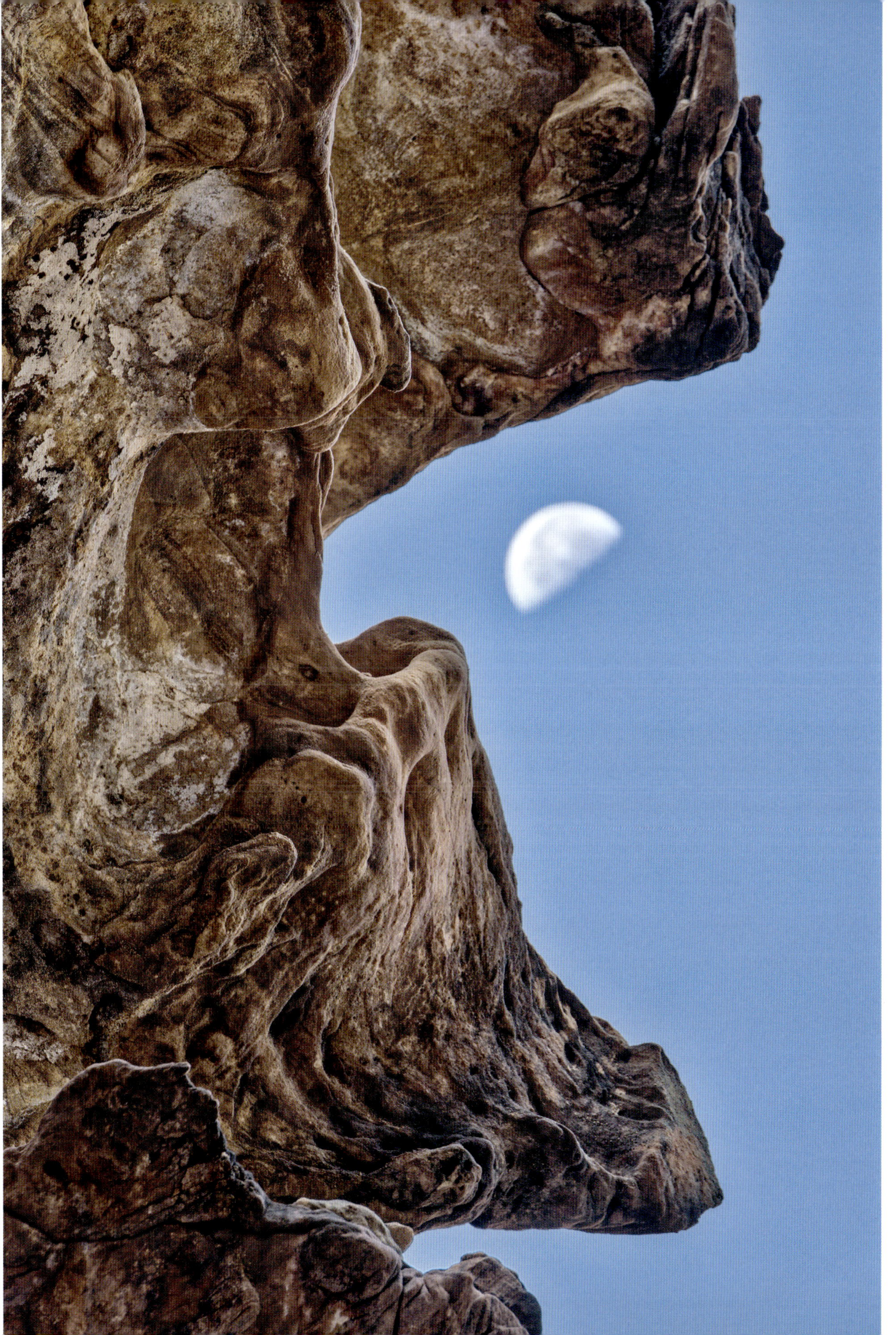

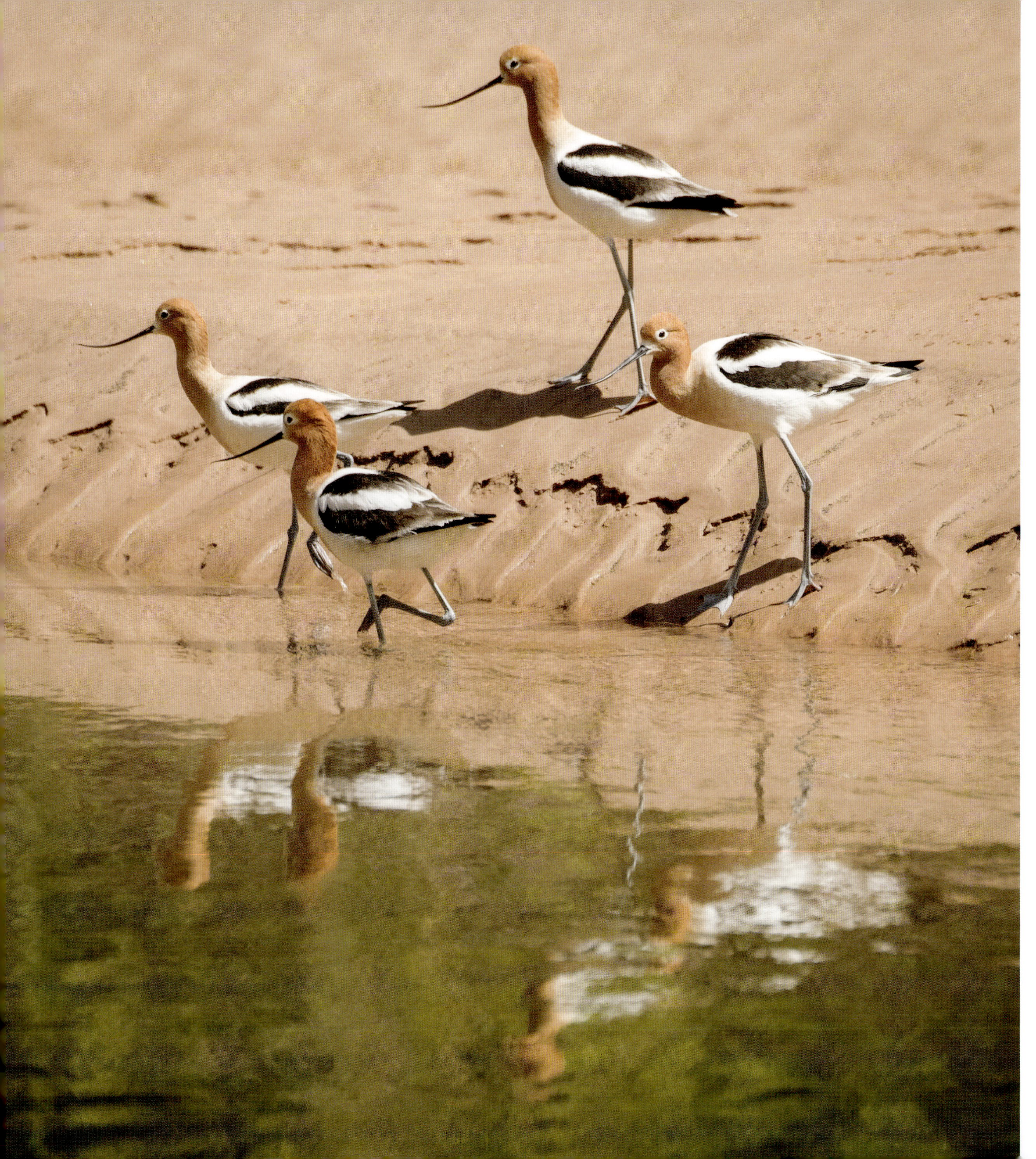

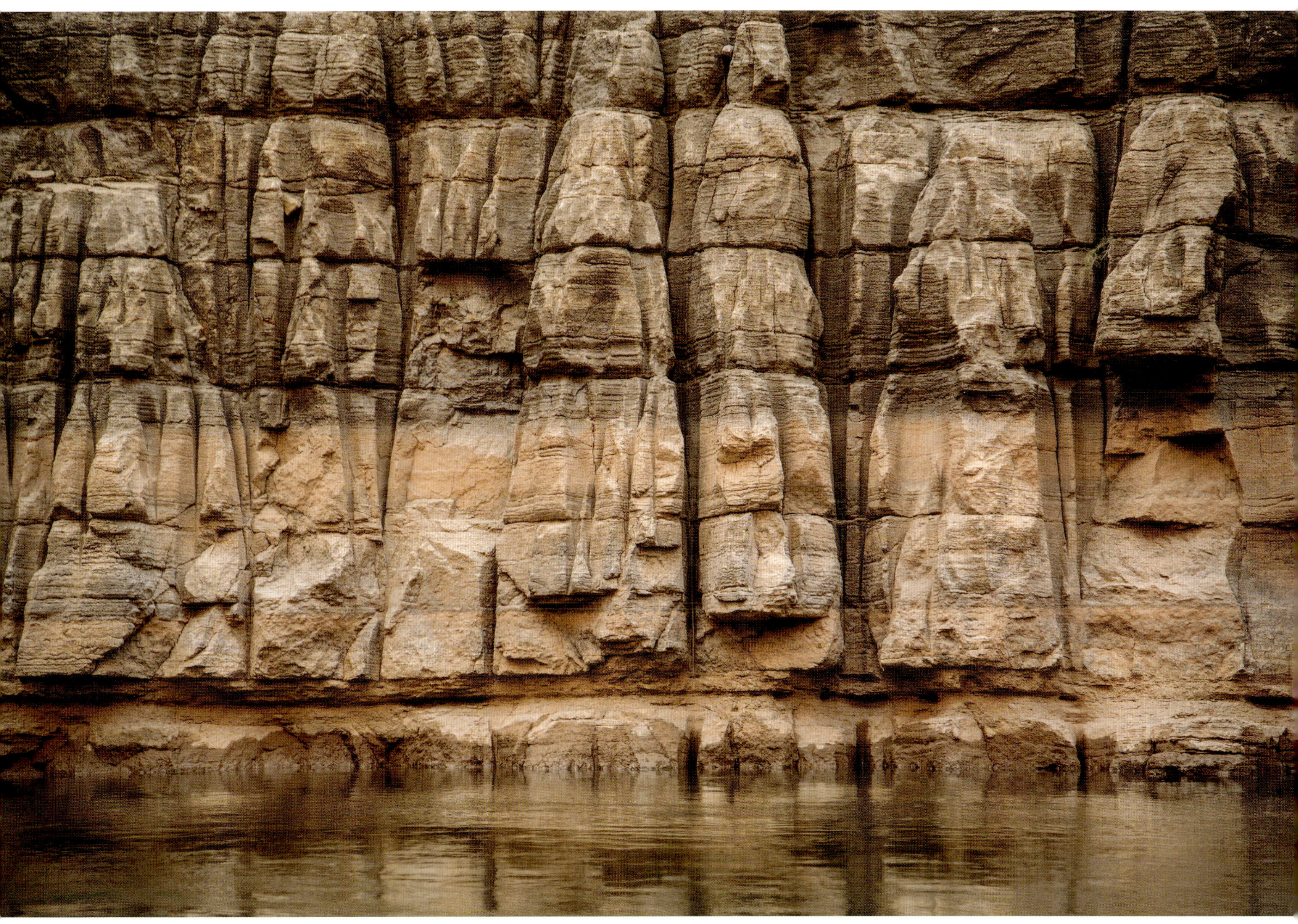

◄ American avocets ▲ Canyon wall at river's edge, approximately mile 147 ▼ View downriver from mile 147

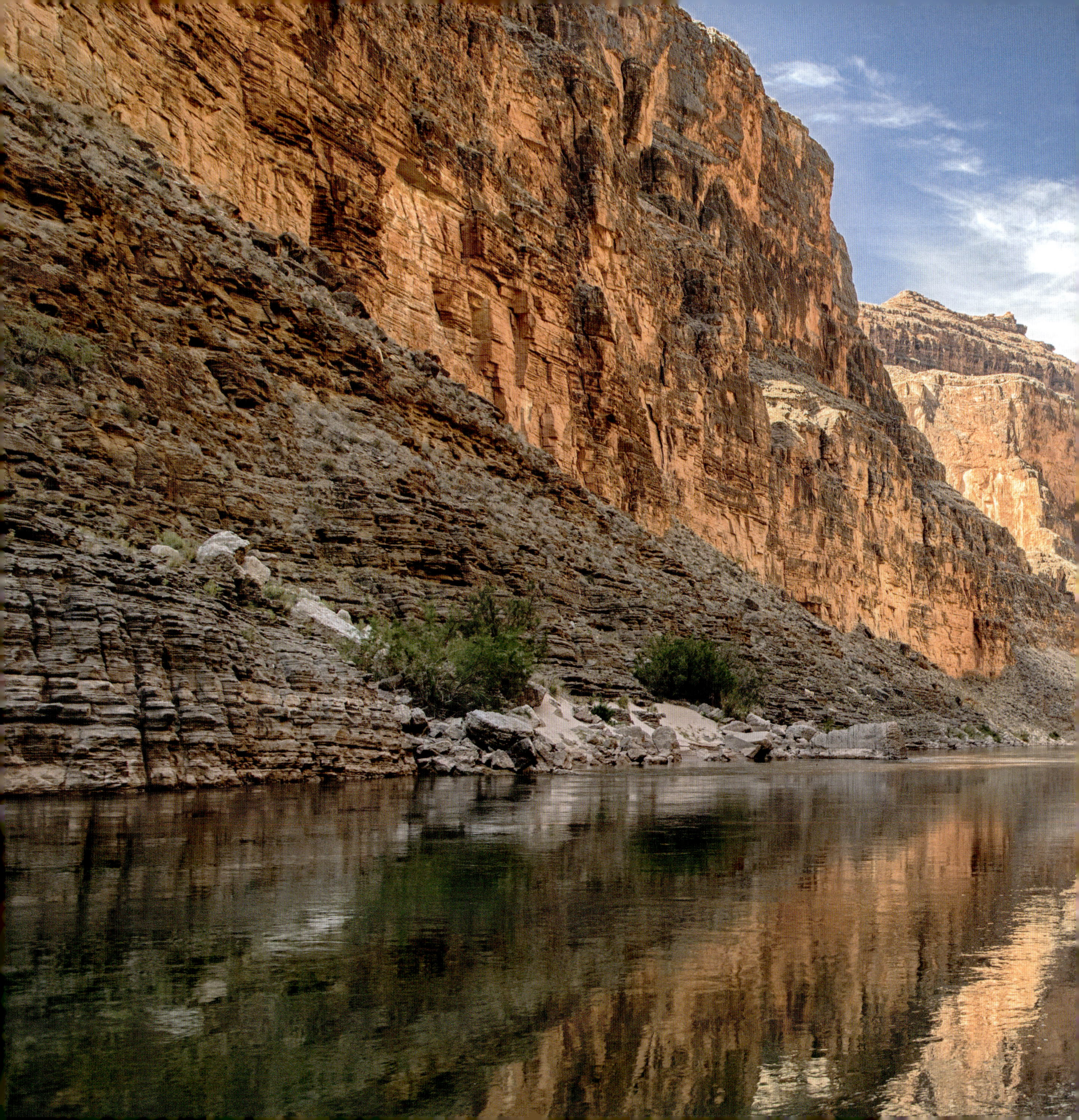

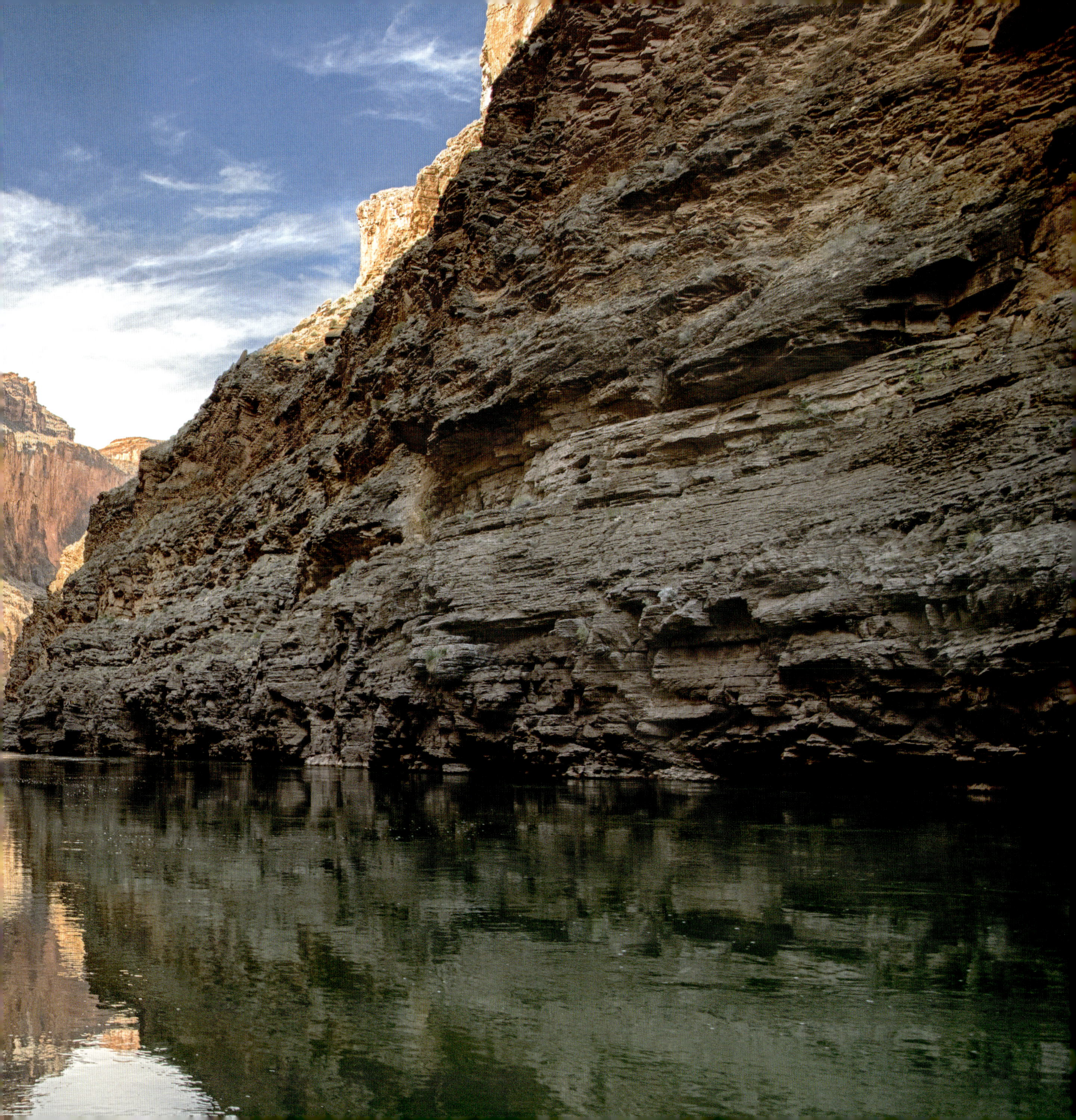

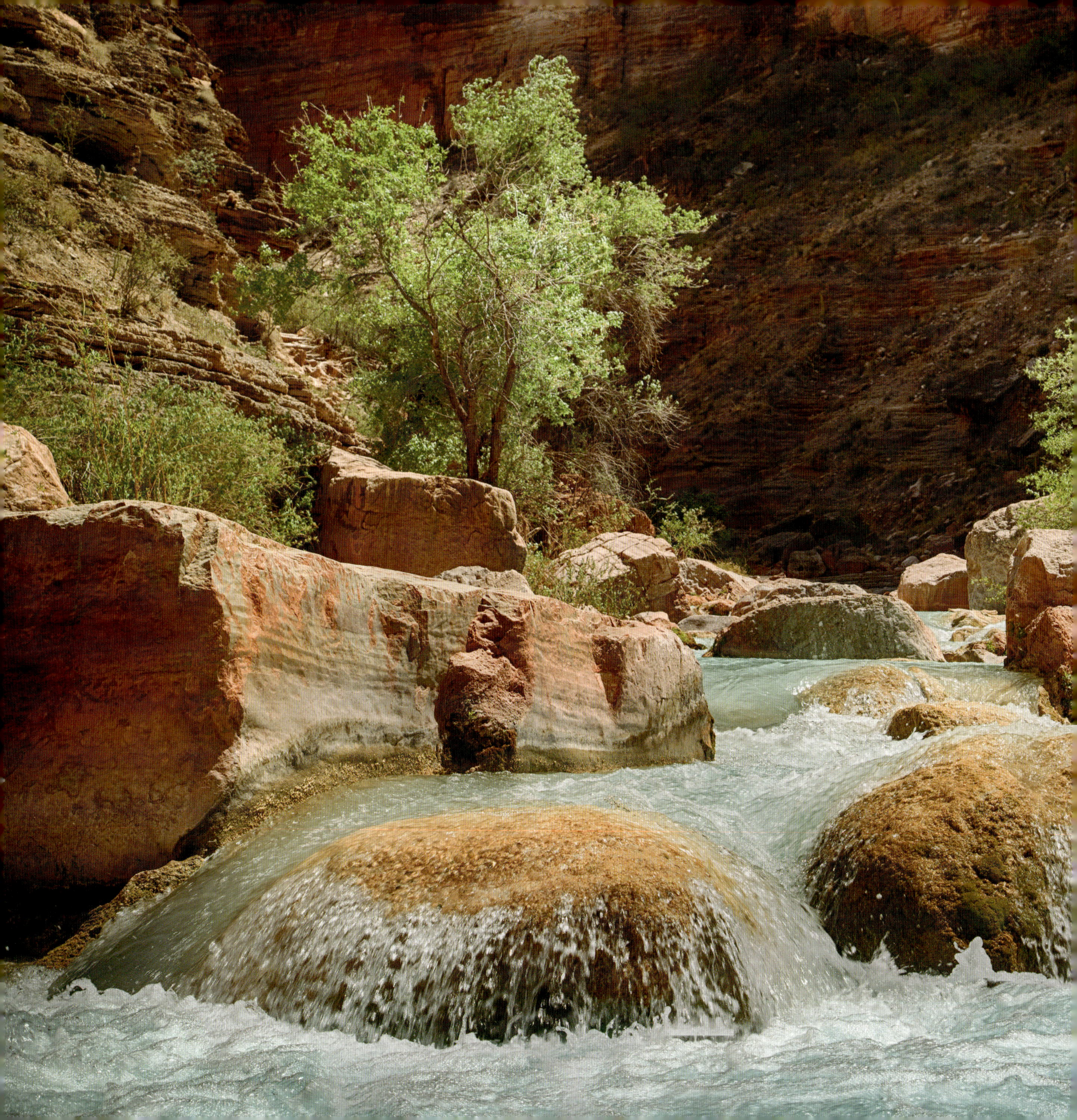

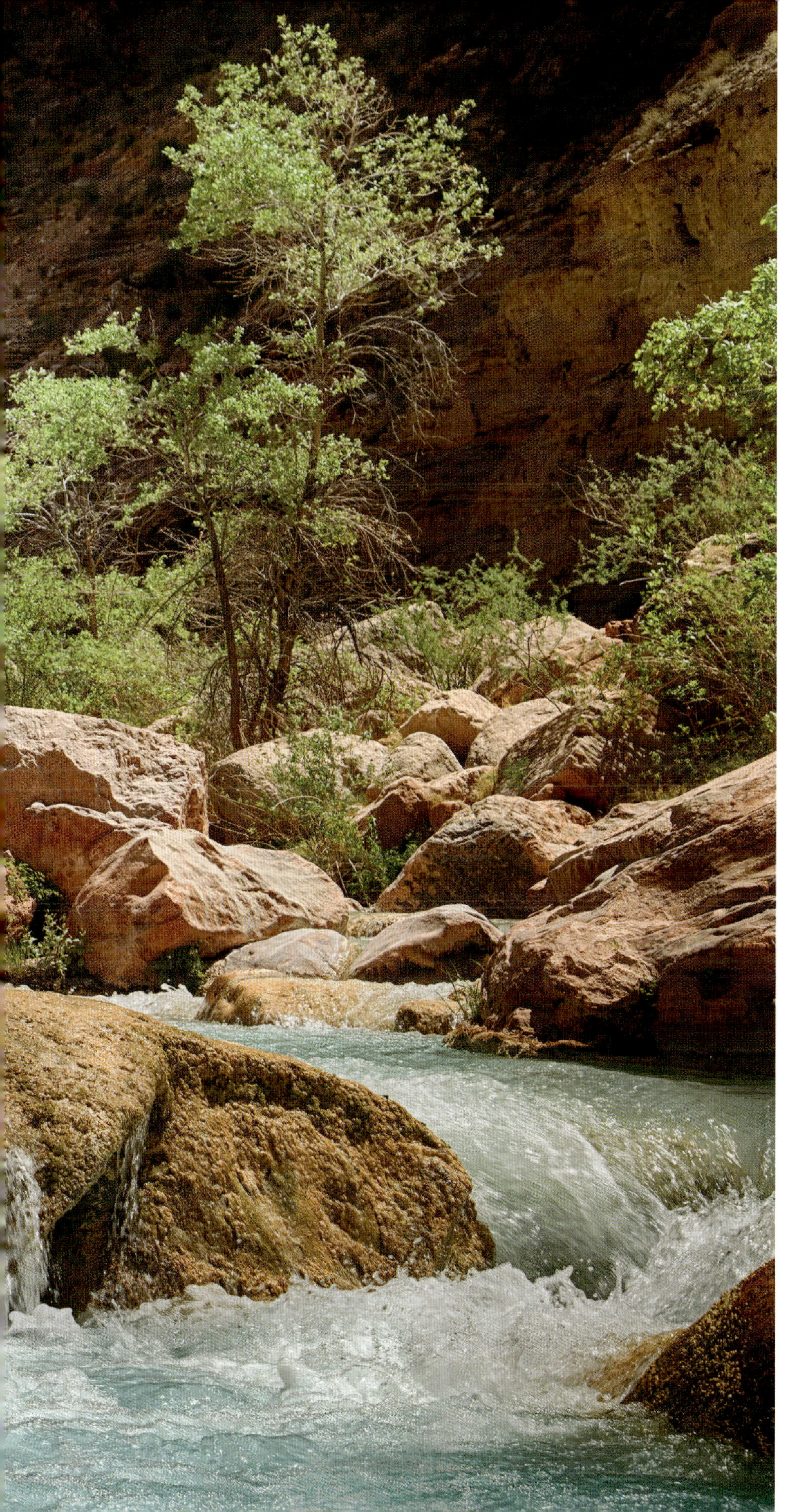

◀ Havasu Canyon

▼ Rock portal along Havasu Creek (left) and Havasu Canyon at the mouth of the creek (right)

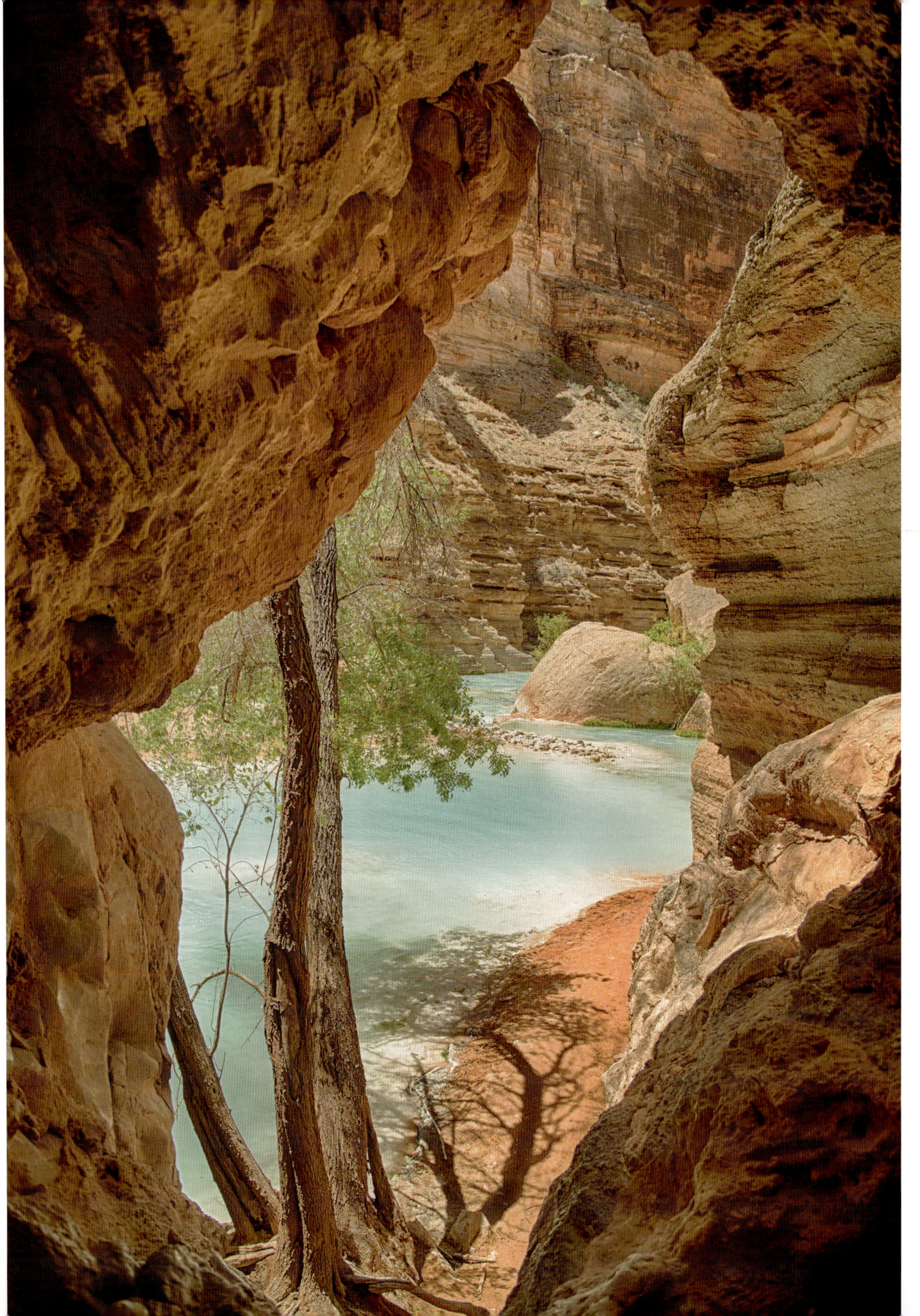

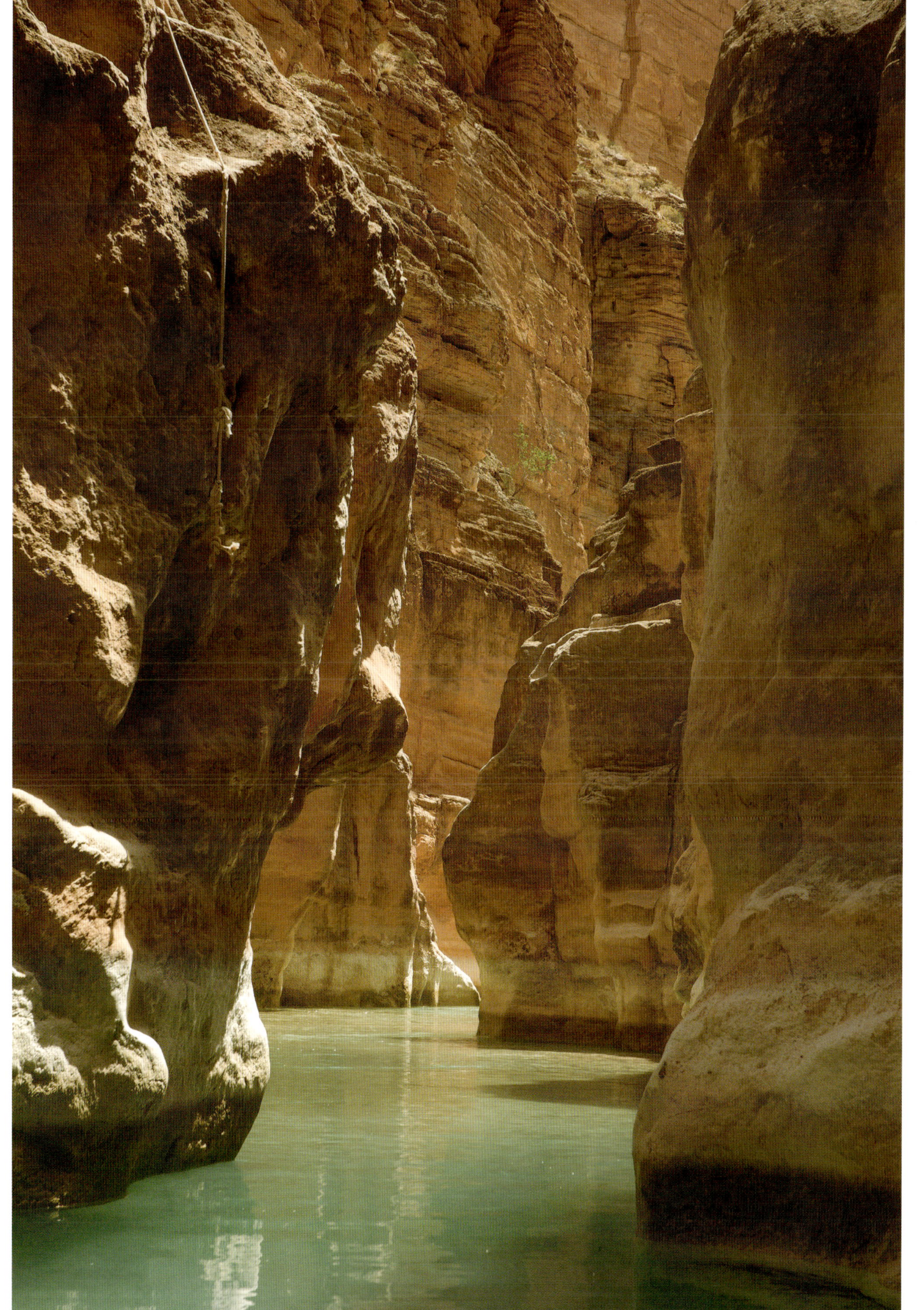

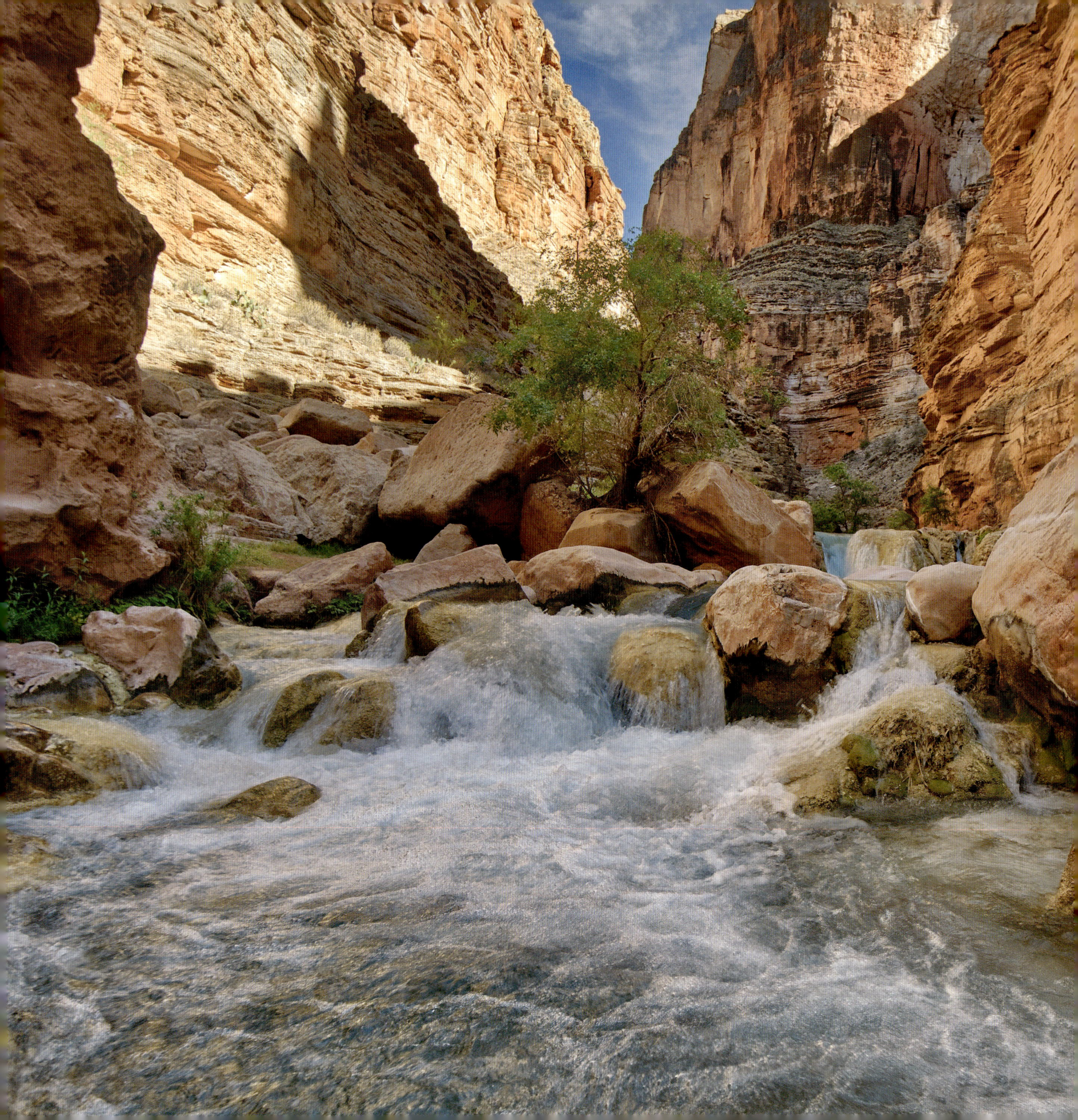

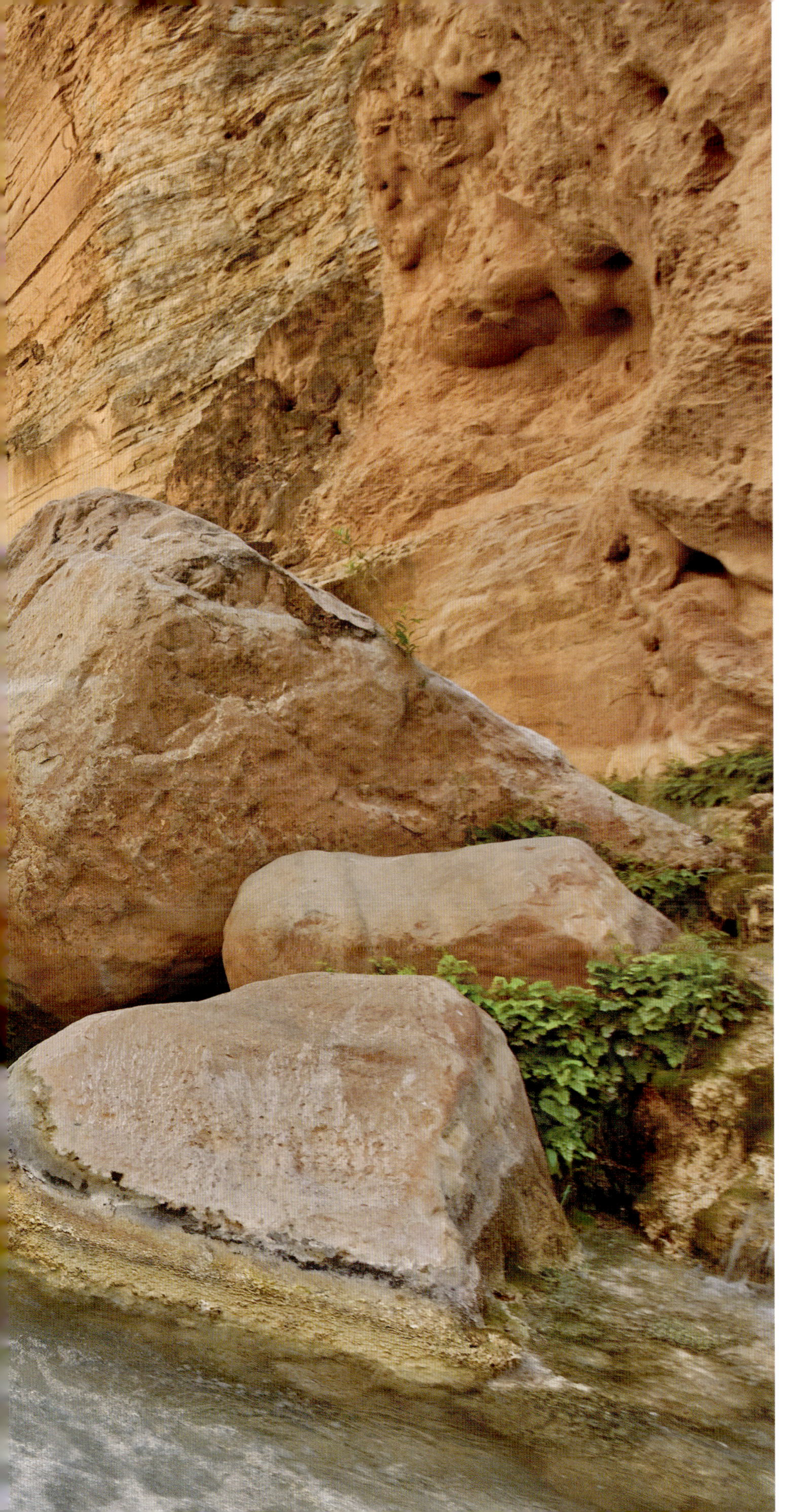

◀ Havasu Creek

▼ Flannelmouth suckers schooling in Havasu Creek (left, top), claret-cup cactus in Havasu Canyon (left, bottom), and gray fox on Havasu Canyon wall (right)

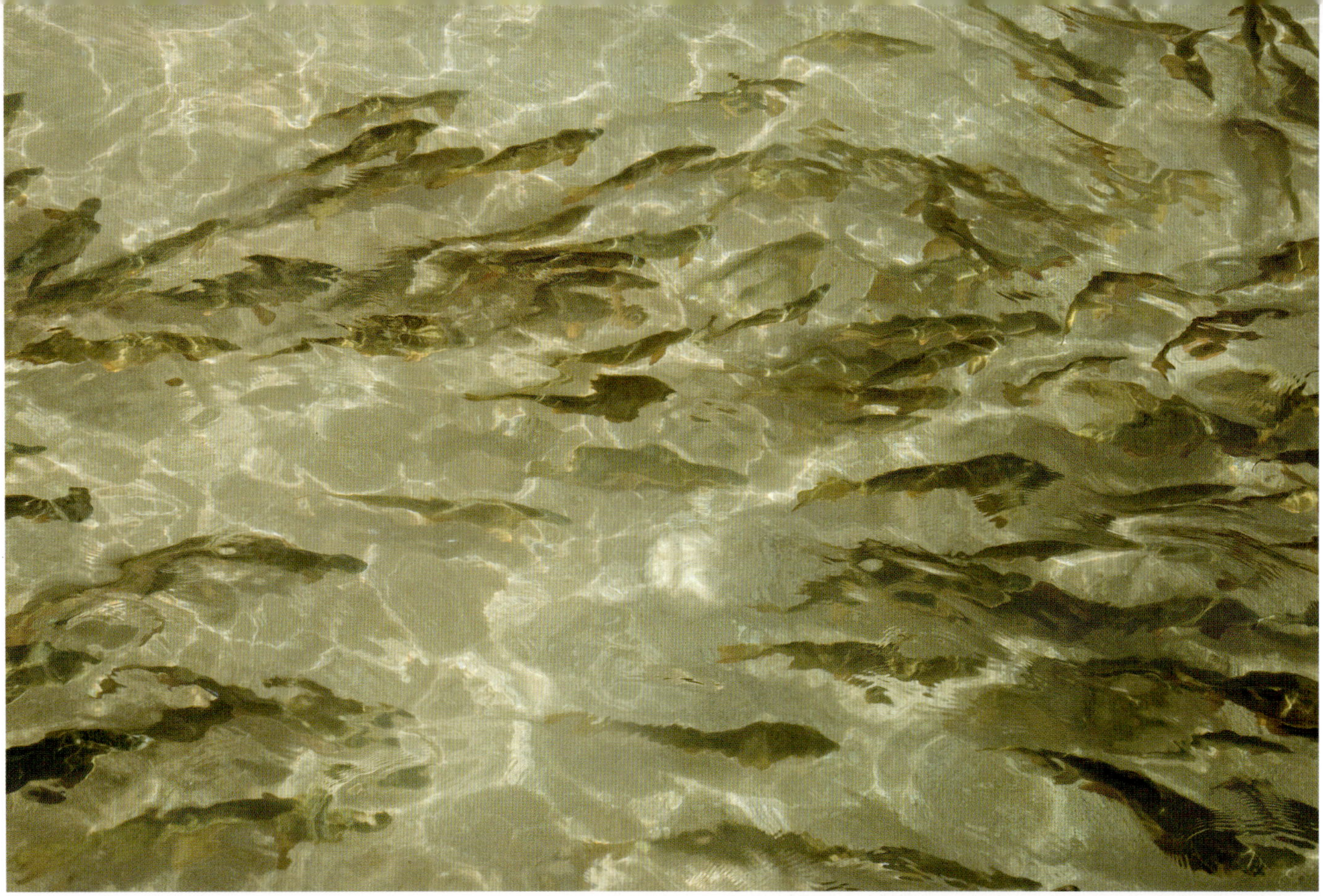

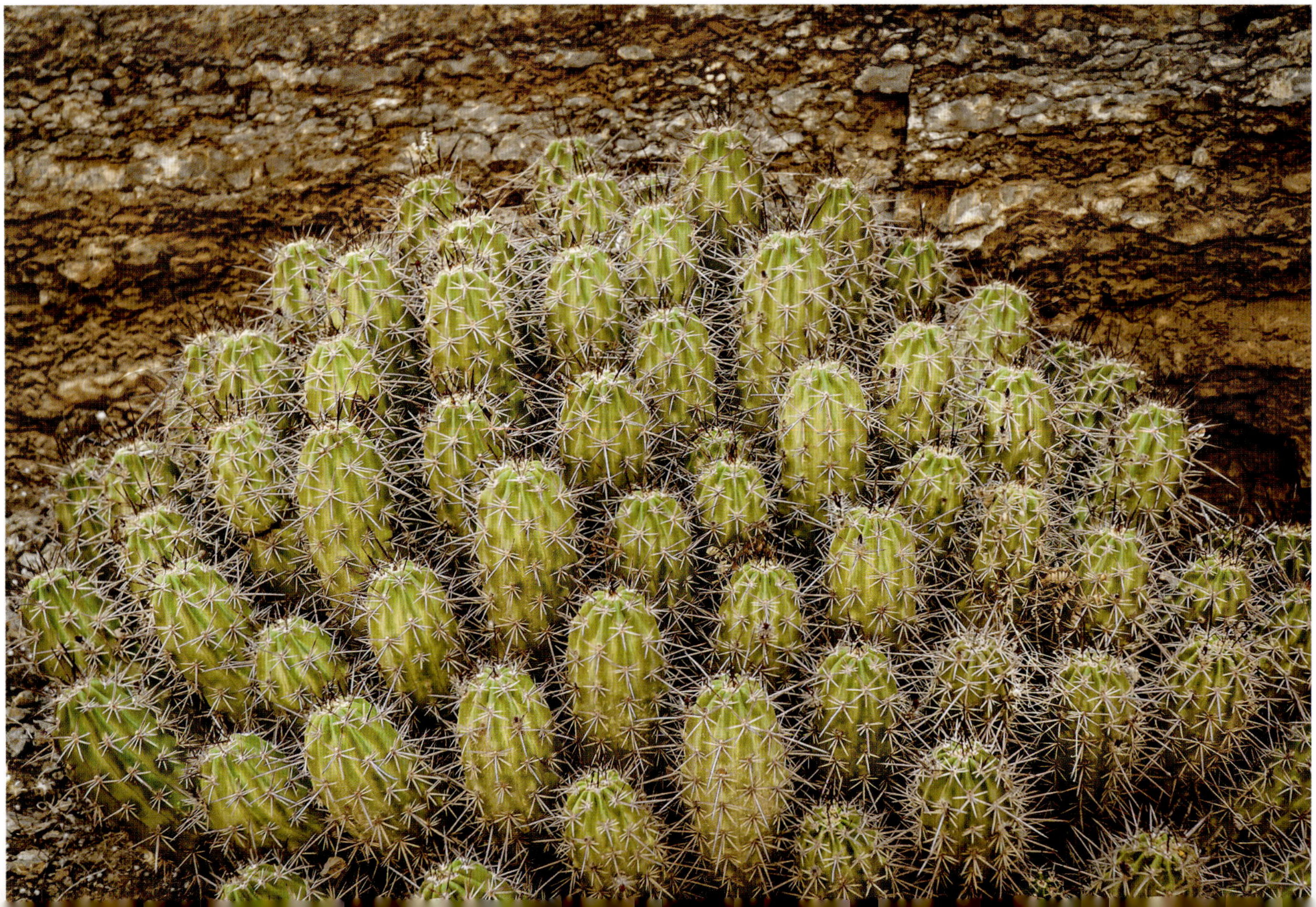

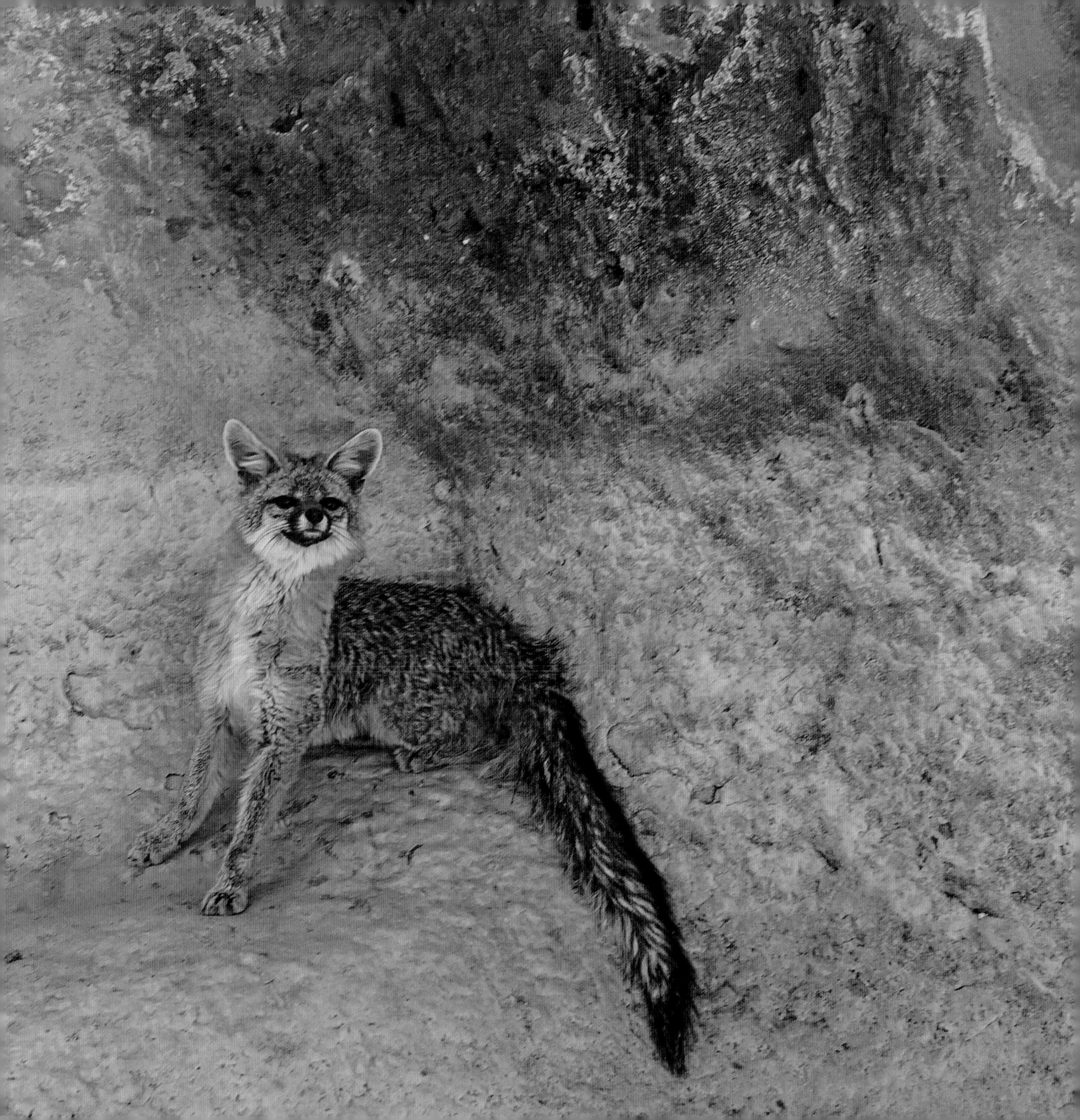

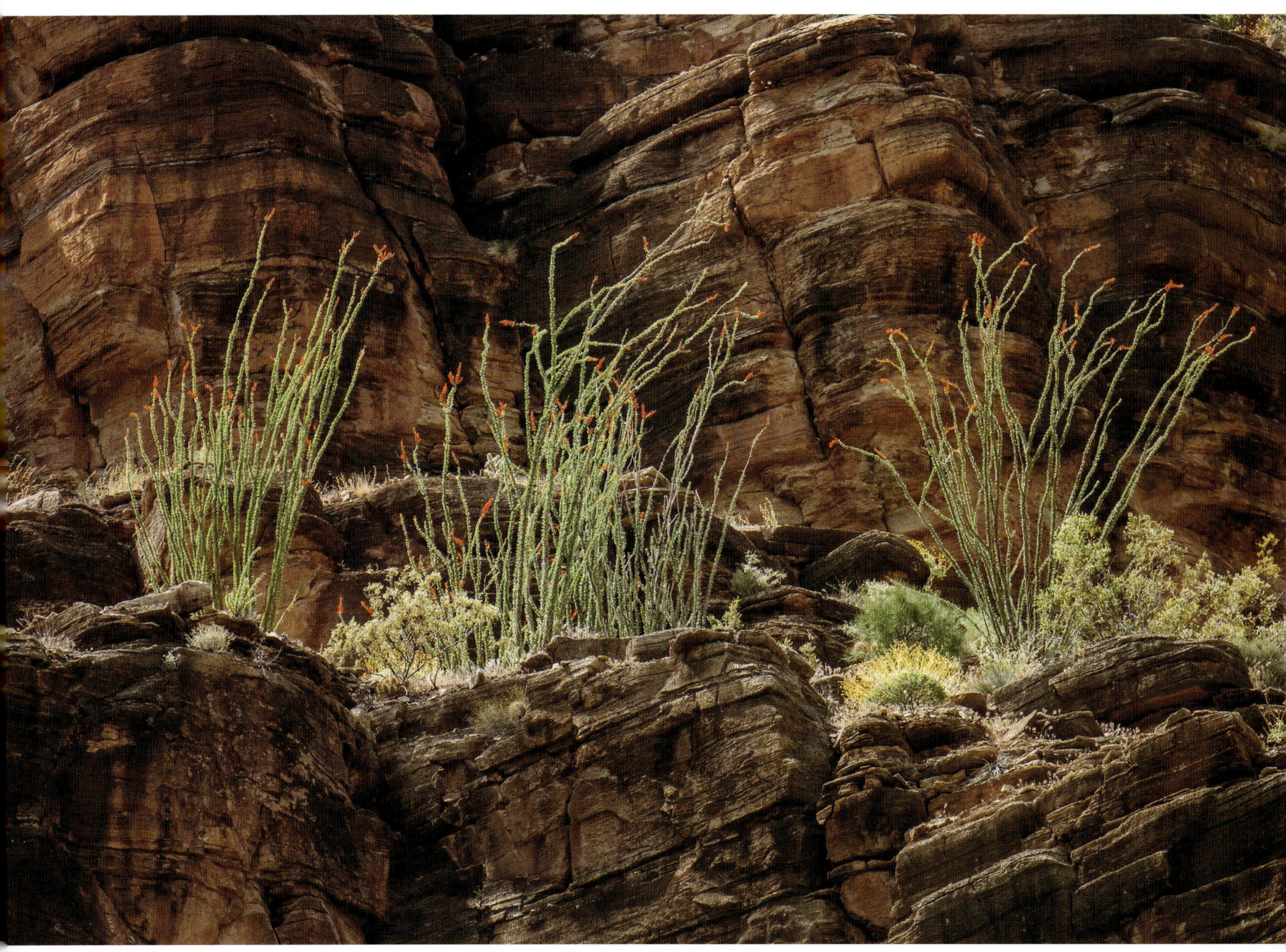

▲ Ocotillo in bloom, Havasu Canyon cliff ▶ Havasu Creek

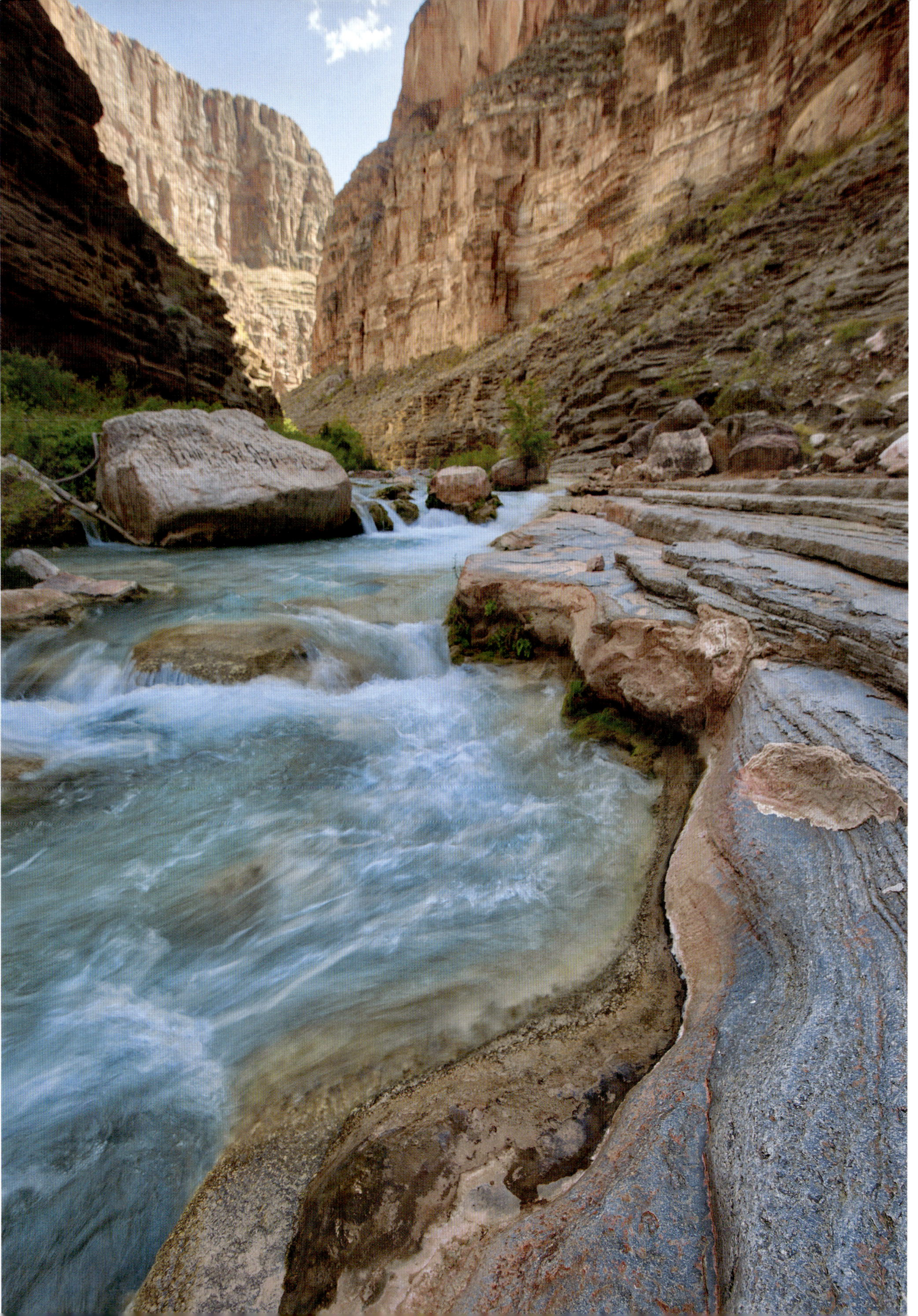

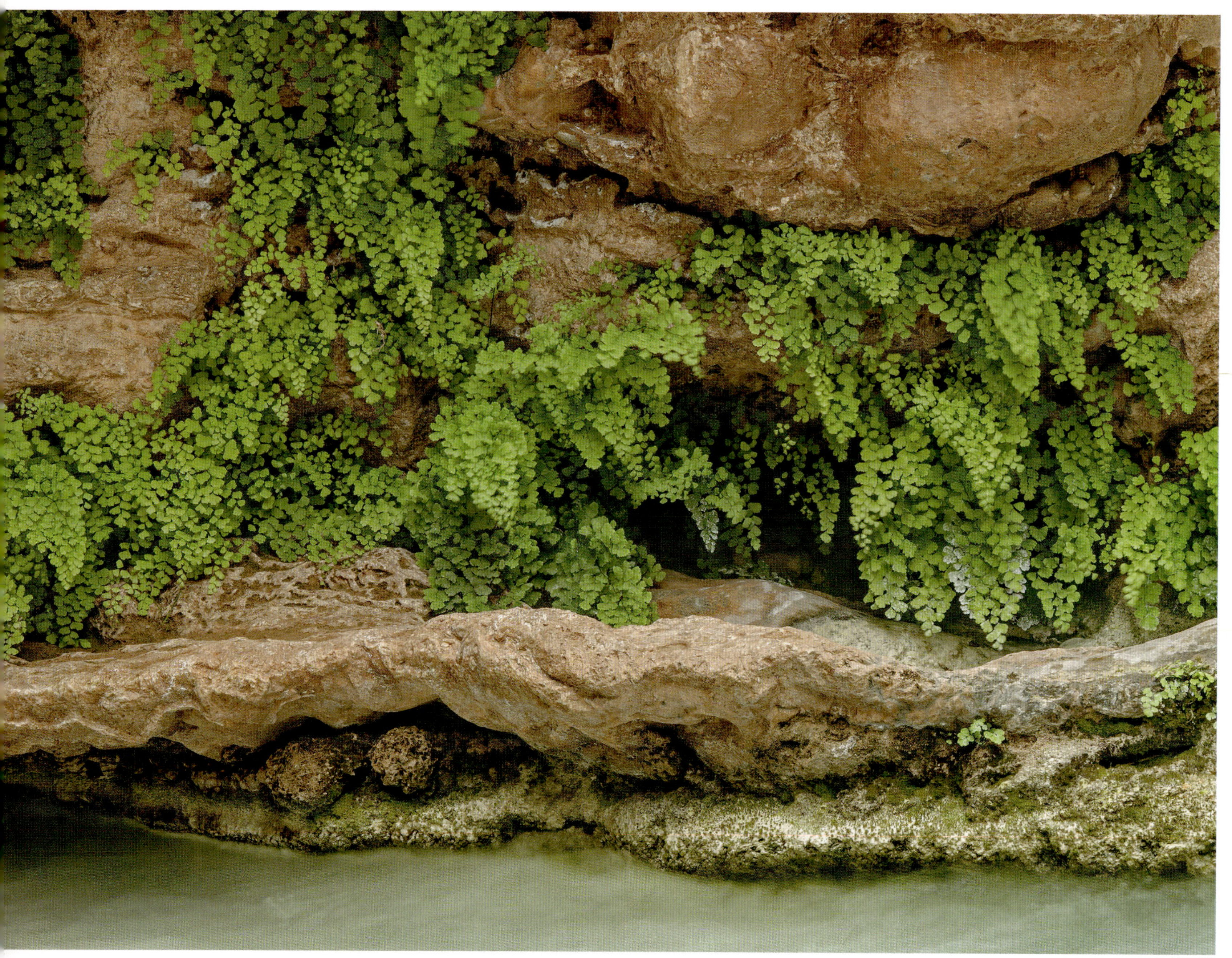

Ferns along Havasu Creek

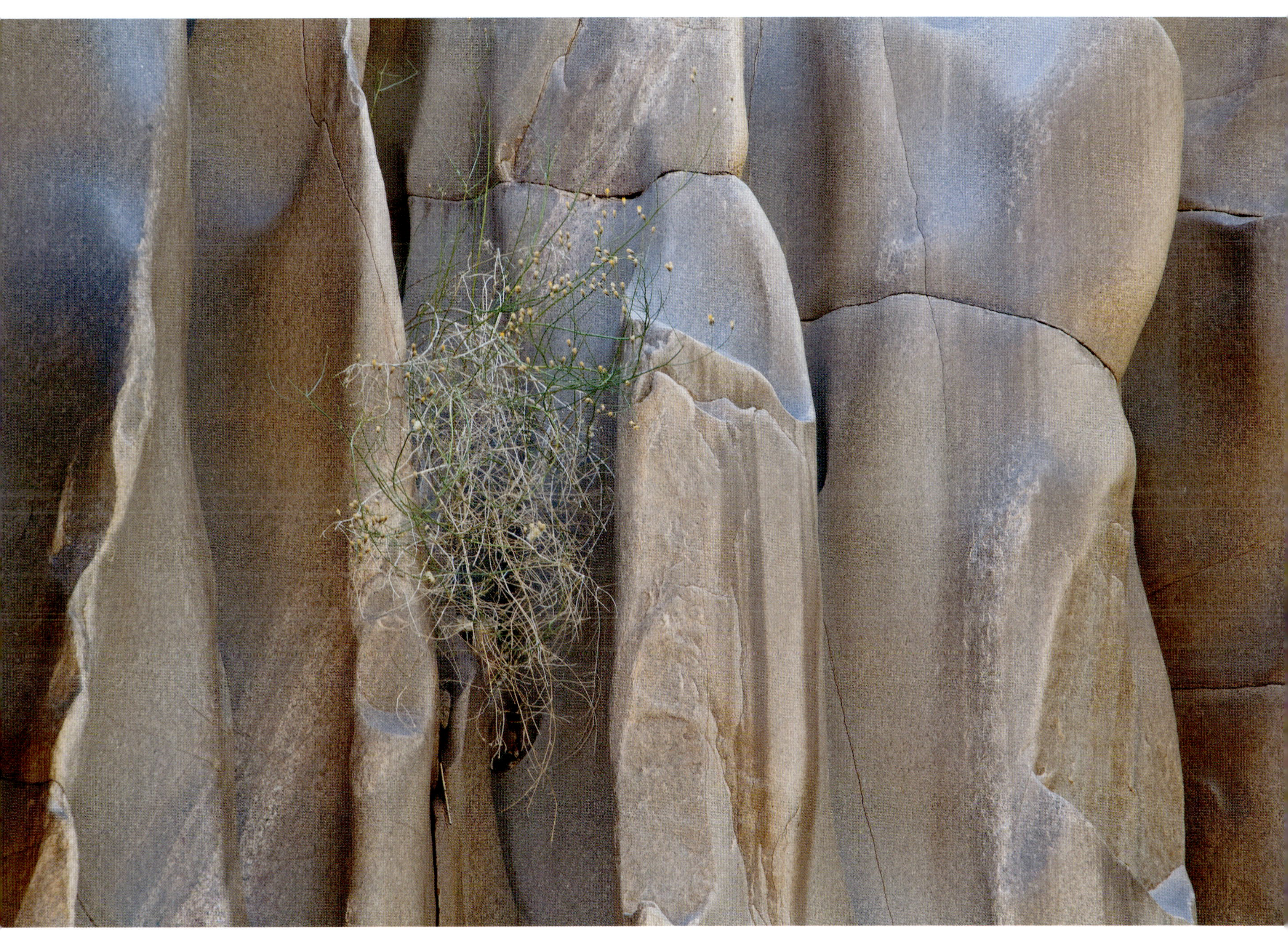

Fluted Vishnu schist at river's edge

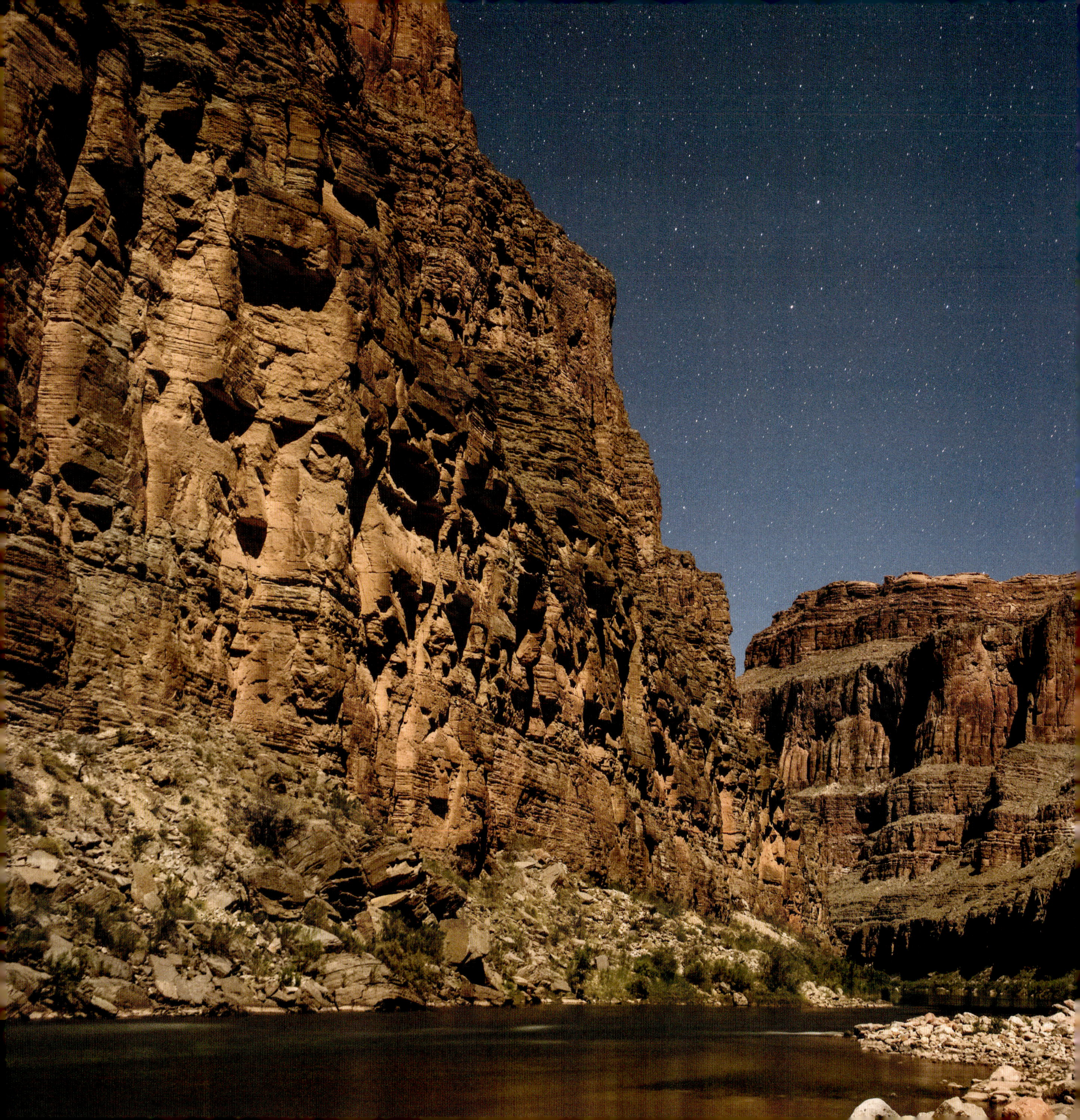

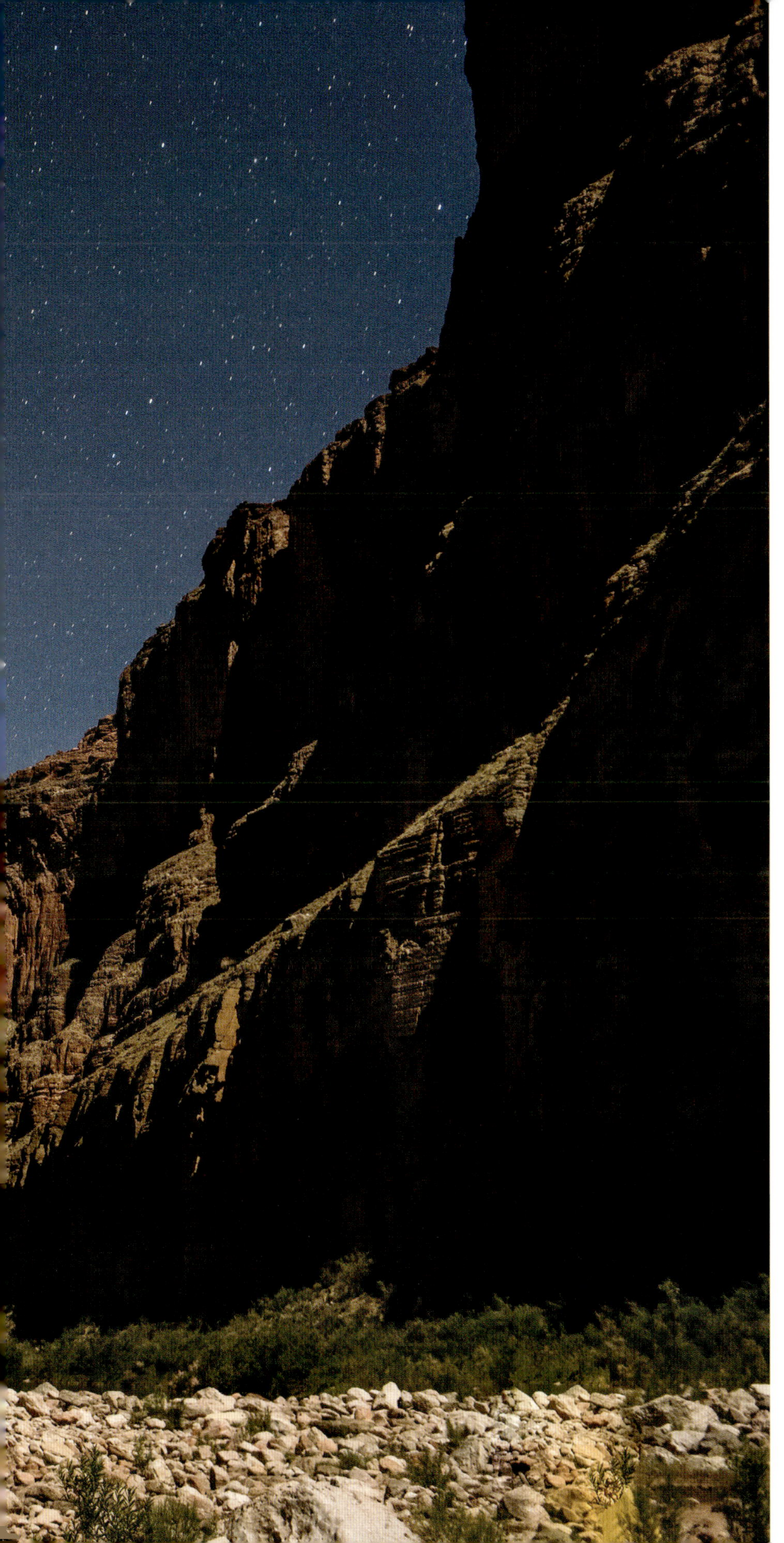

◀ Moonlit view upriver, National Canyon Camp

▼ National Canyon (left and right)

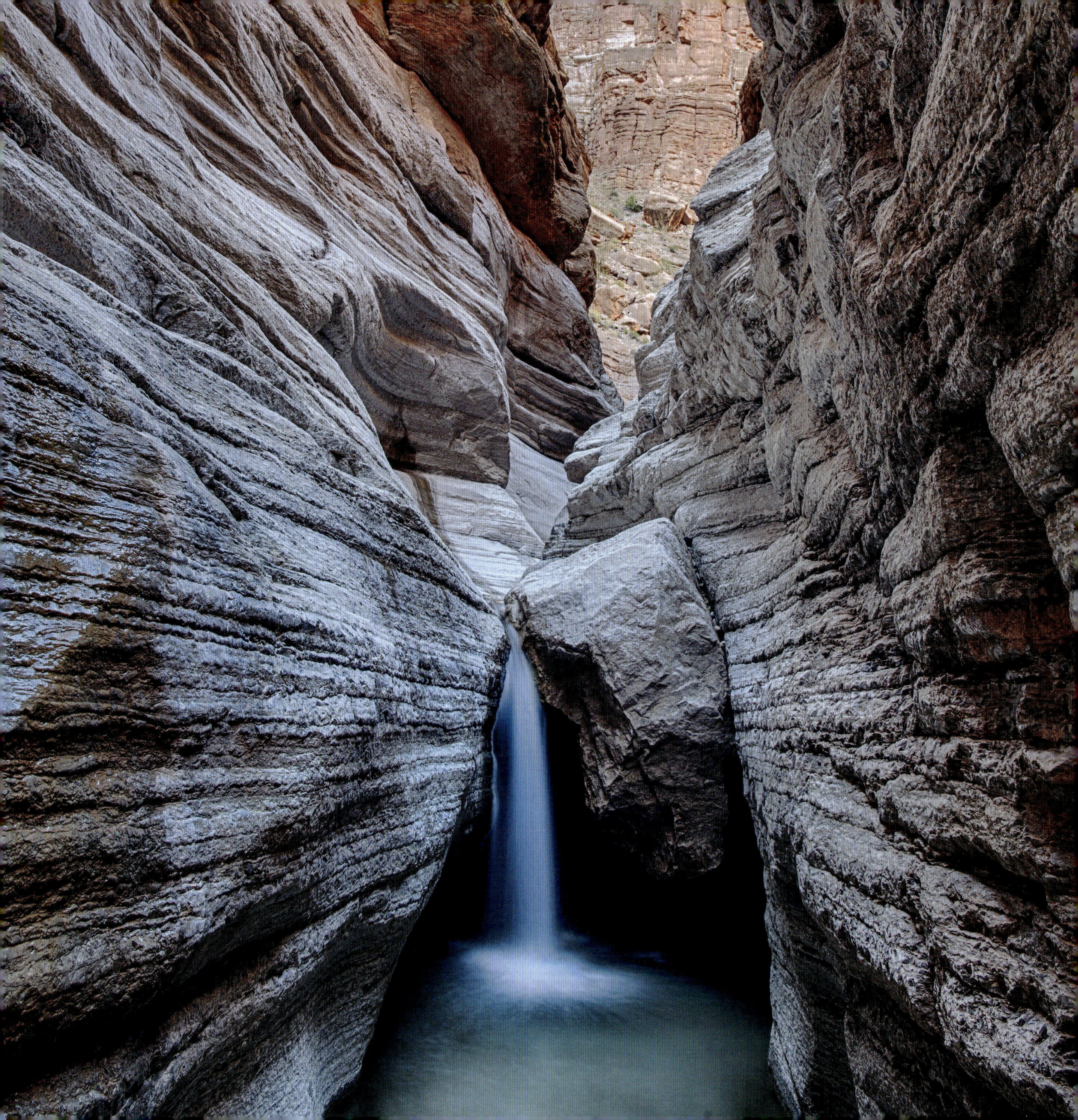

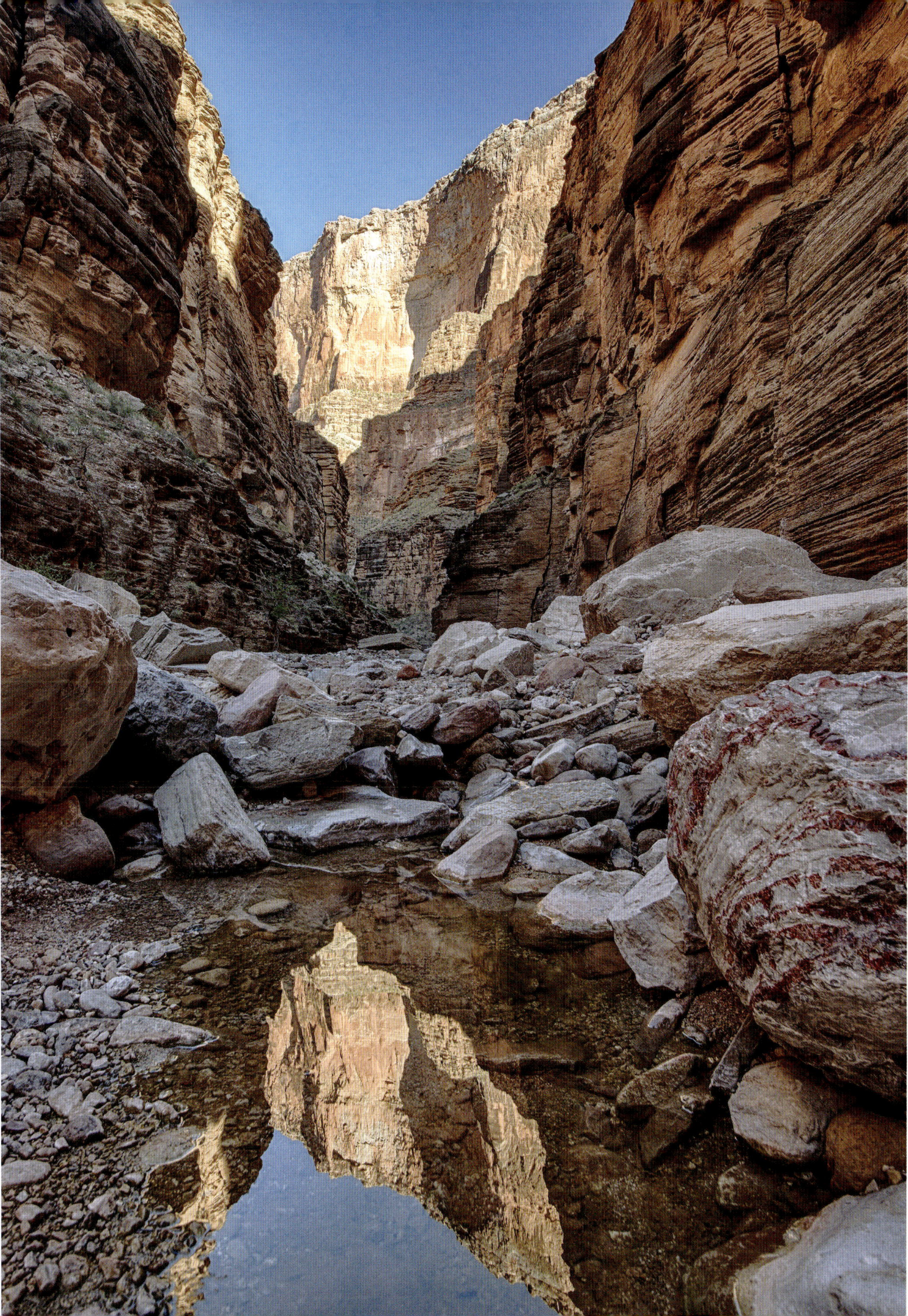

Sunset from National Canyon Camp

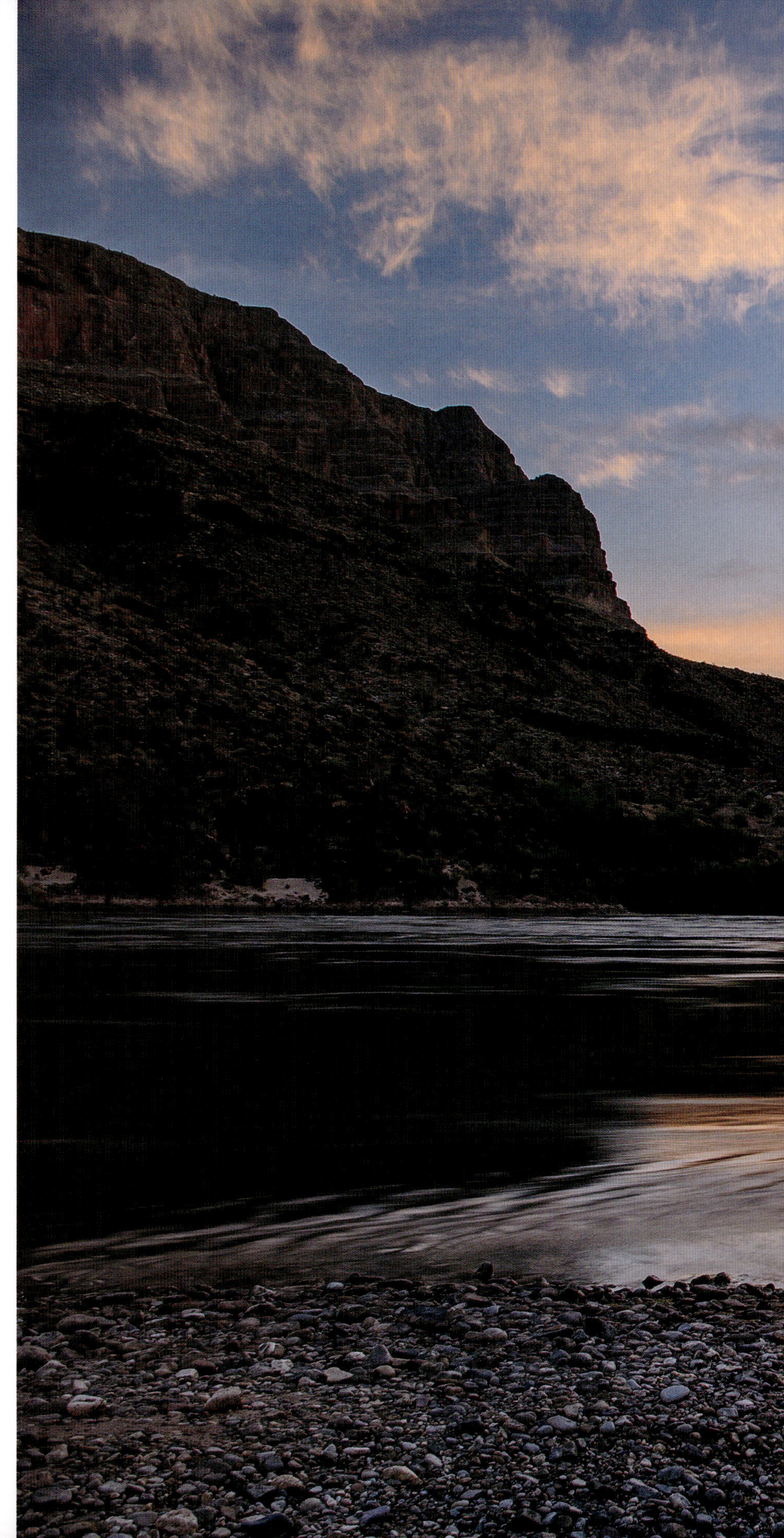

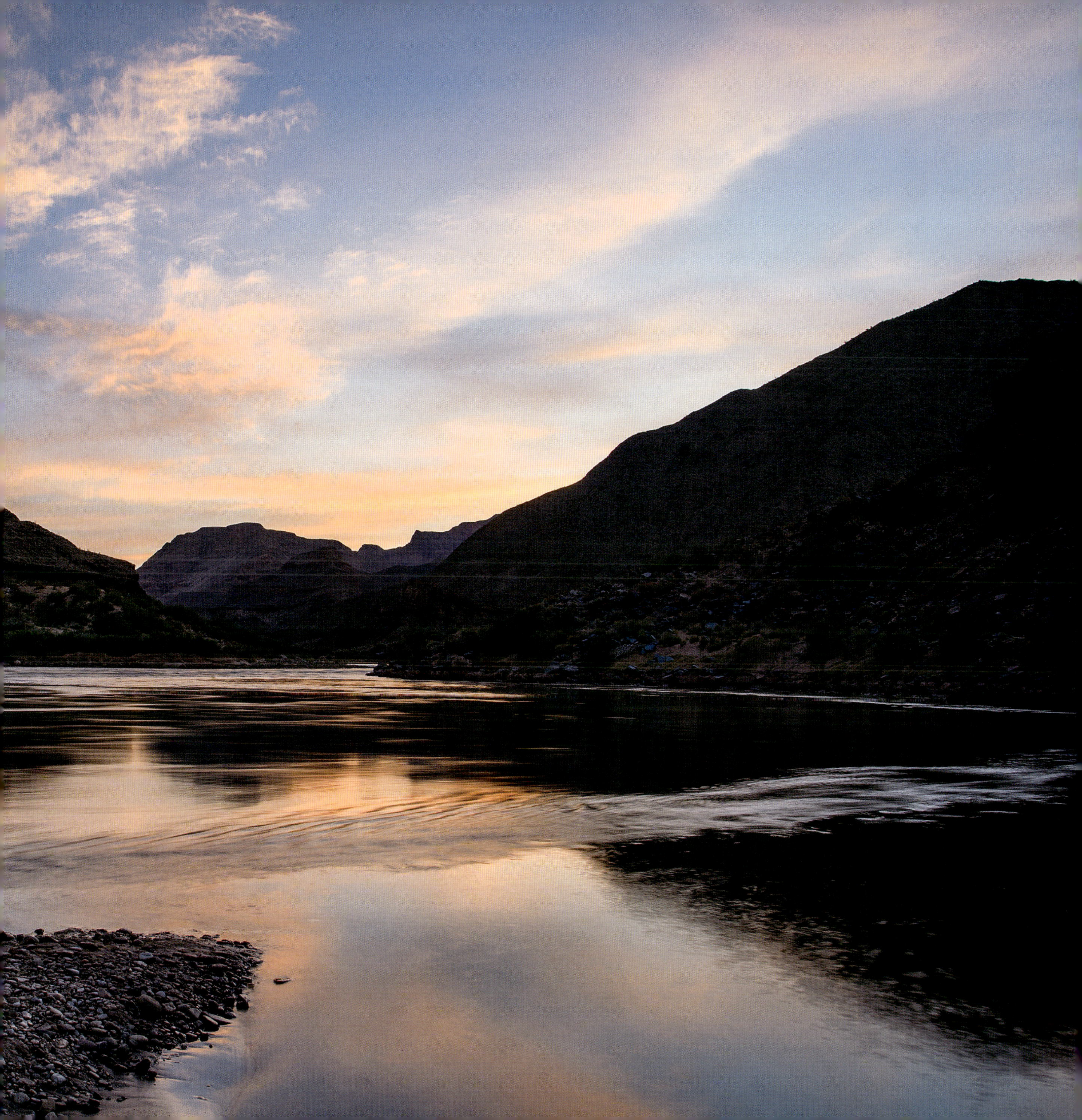

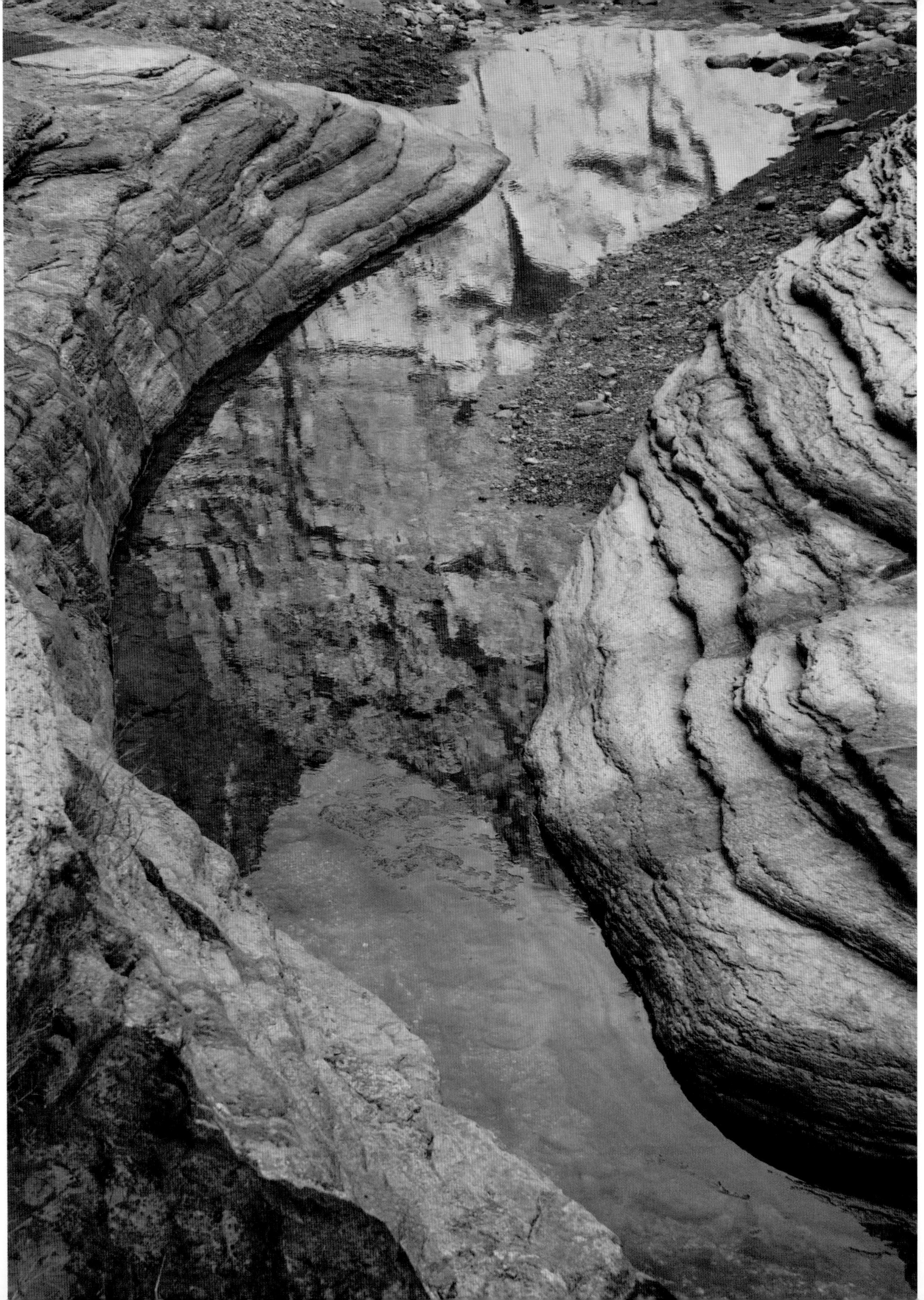

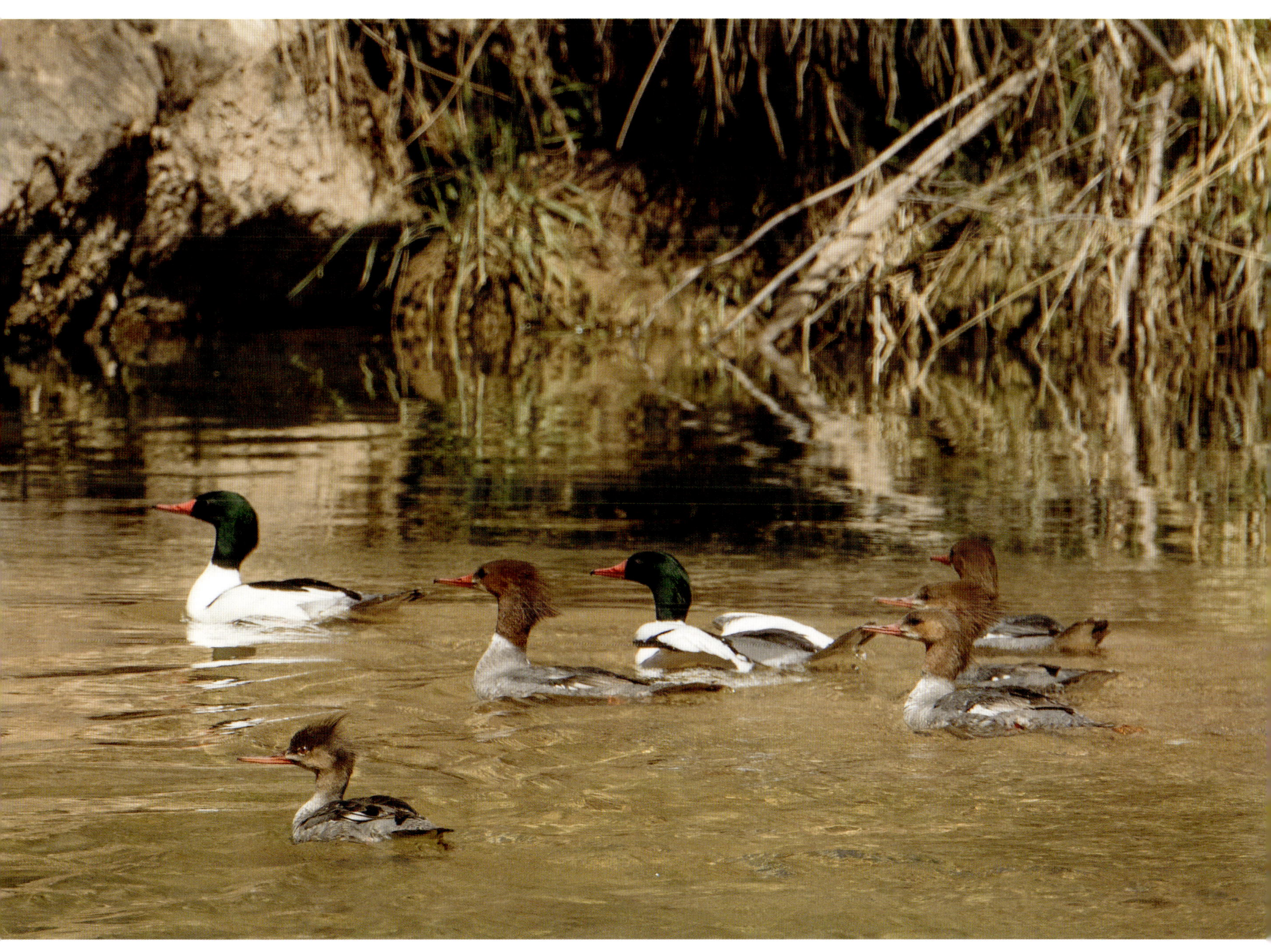

◀ Rocks and stream reflection, Matkatamiba Canyon ▲ Common mergansers

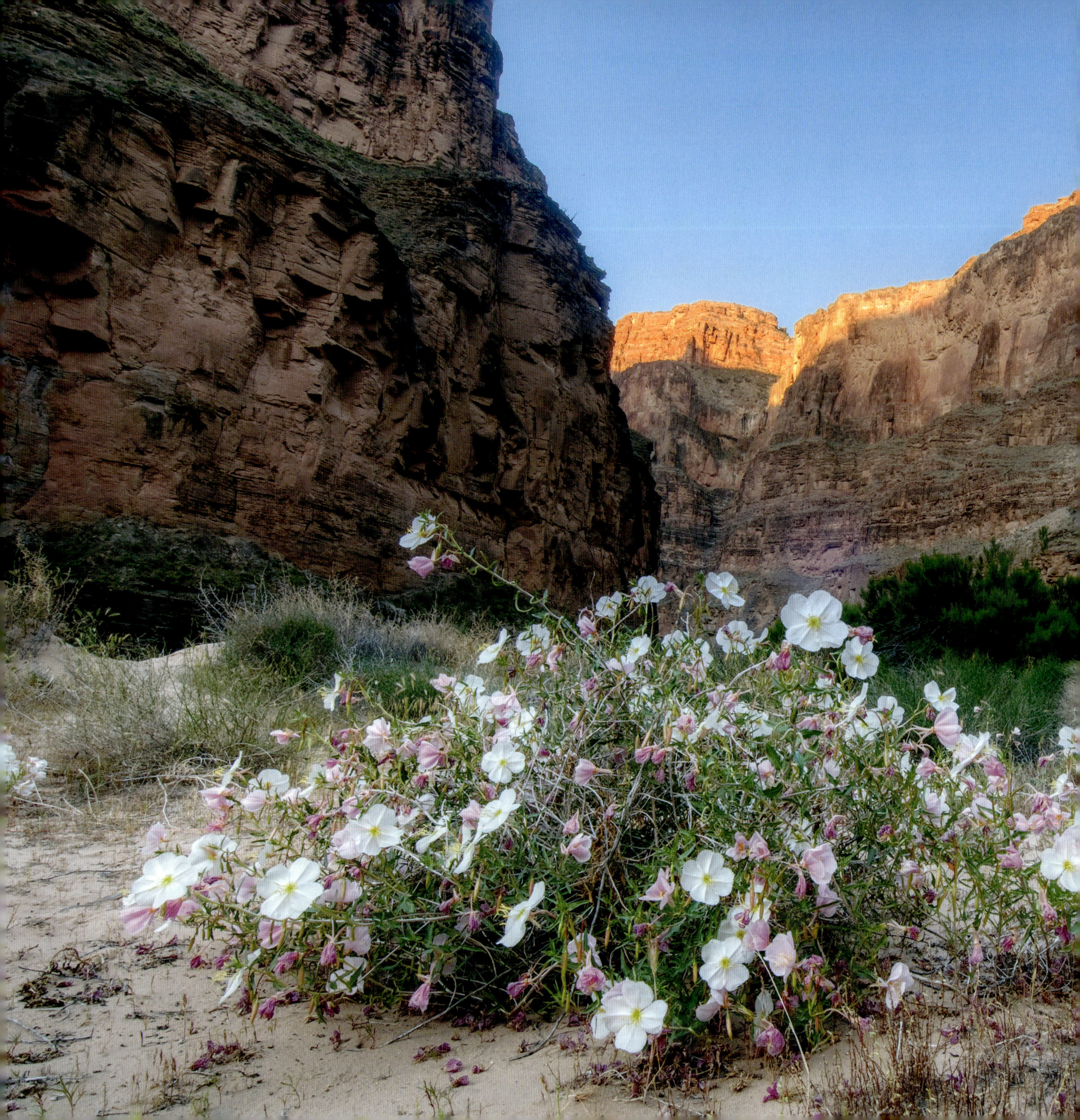

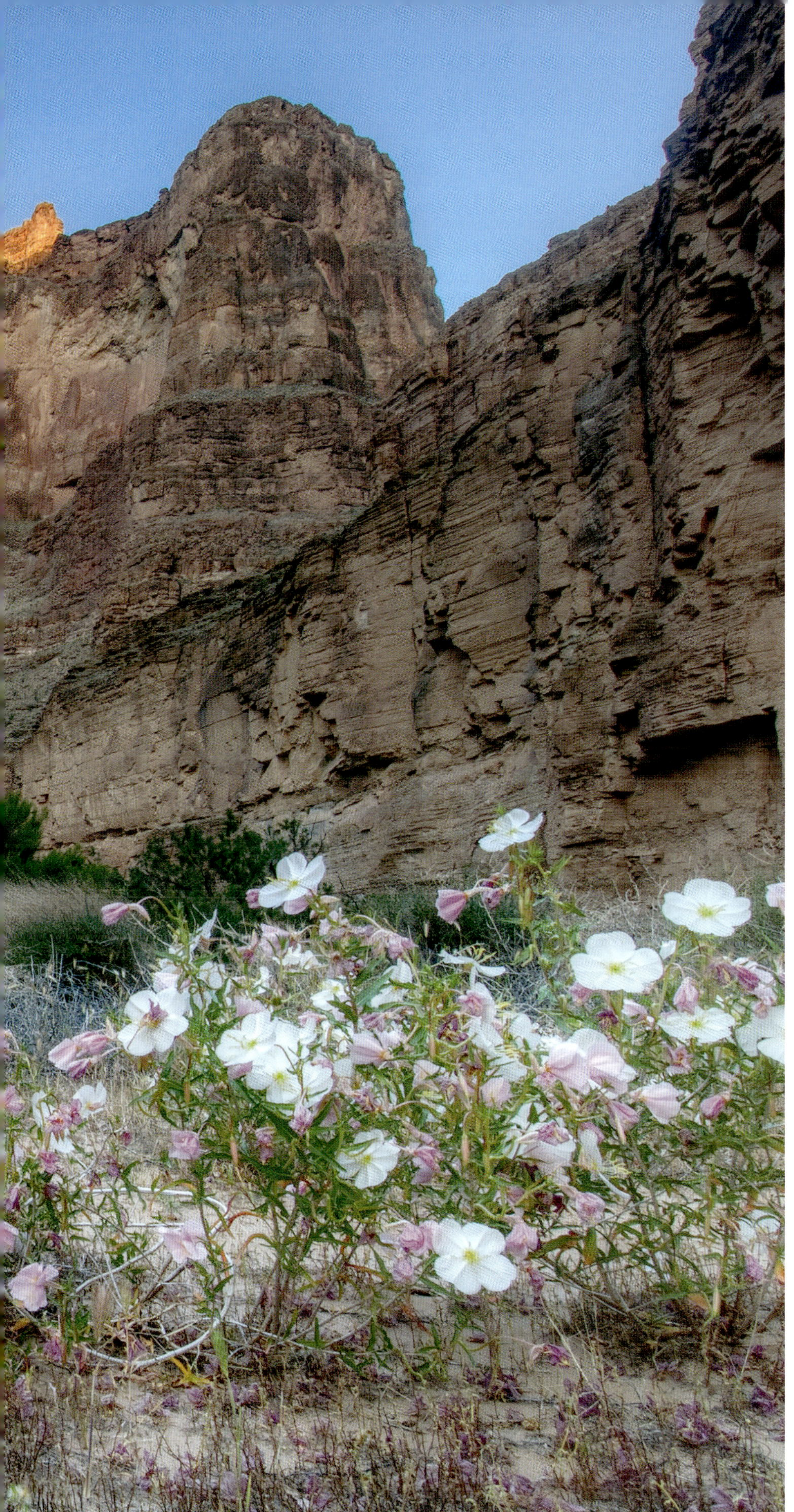

◀ Pale evening-primrose, Fern Glen Canyon

▼ Waterfall at amphitheater (left) and giant chock stone (right), Fern Glen Canyon

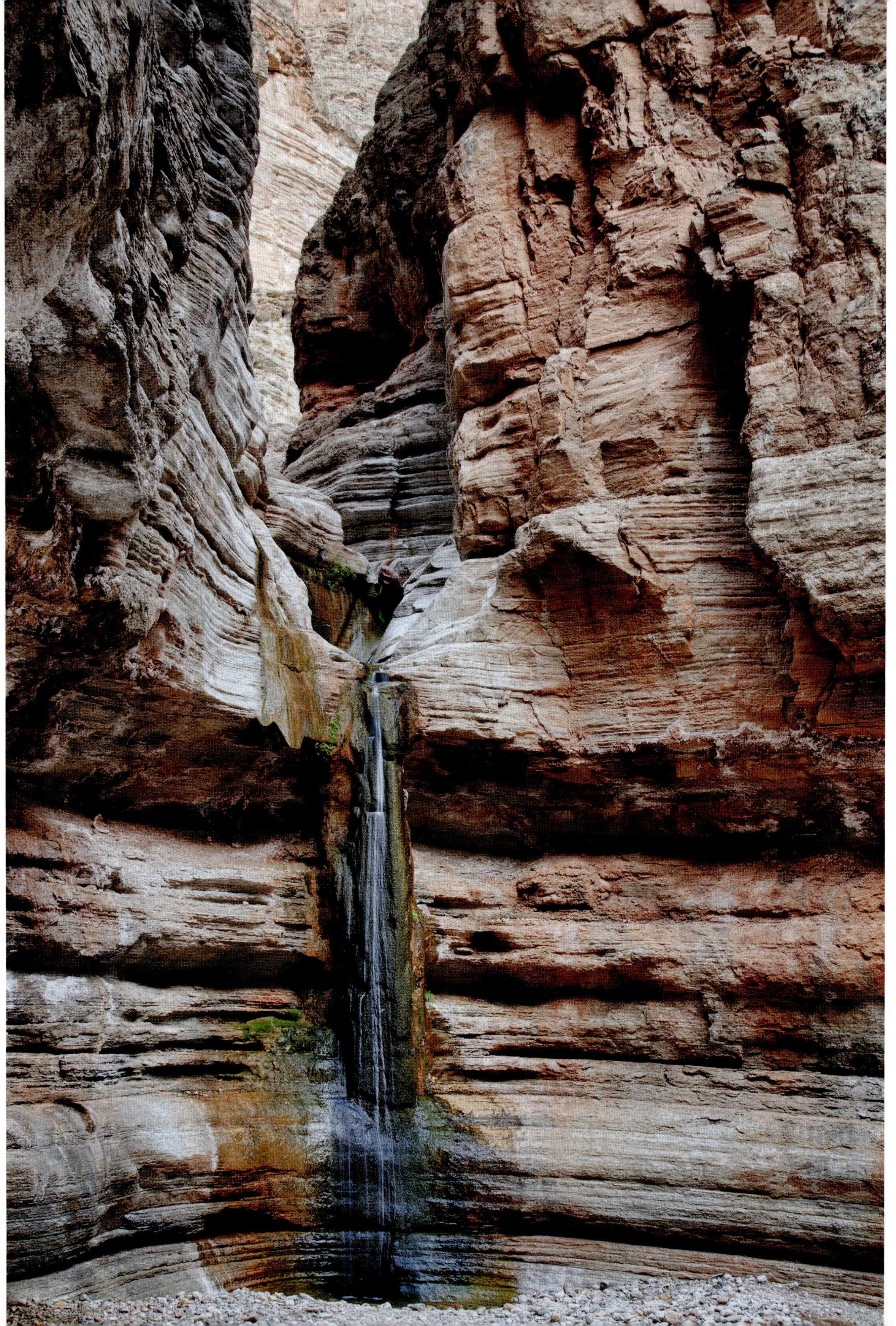

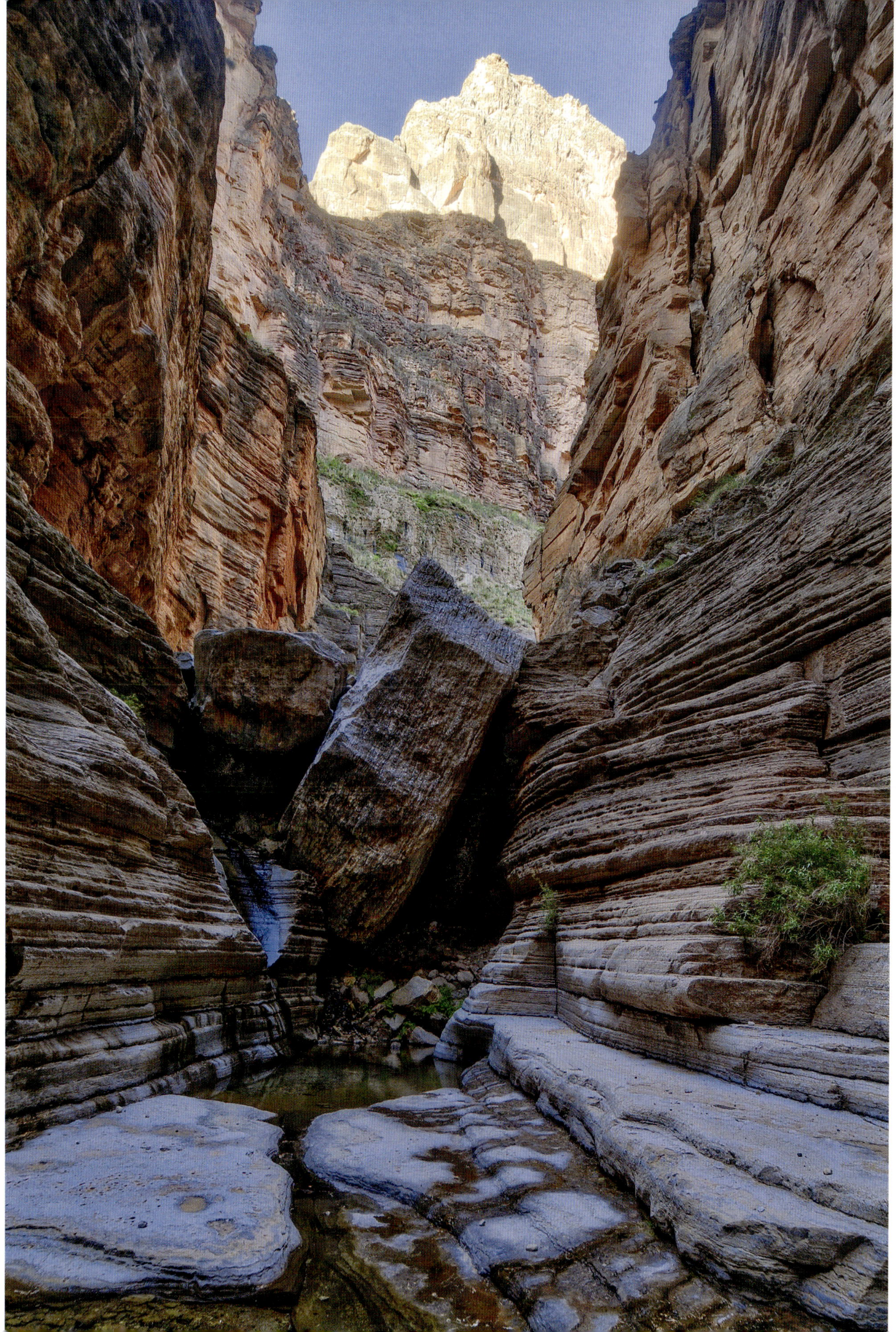

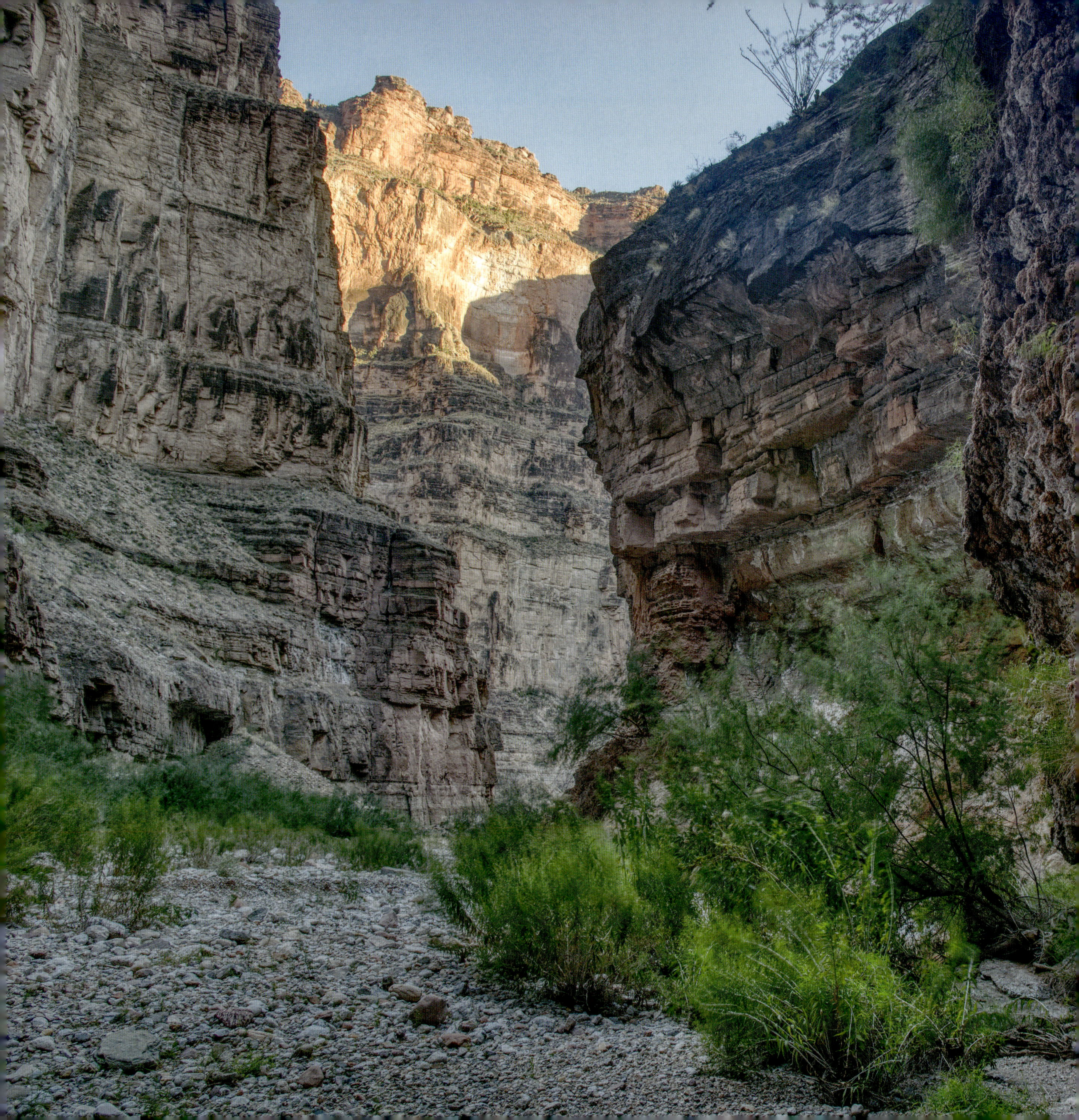

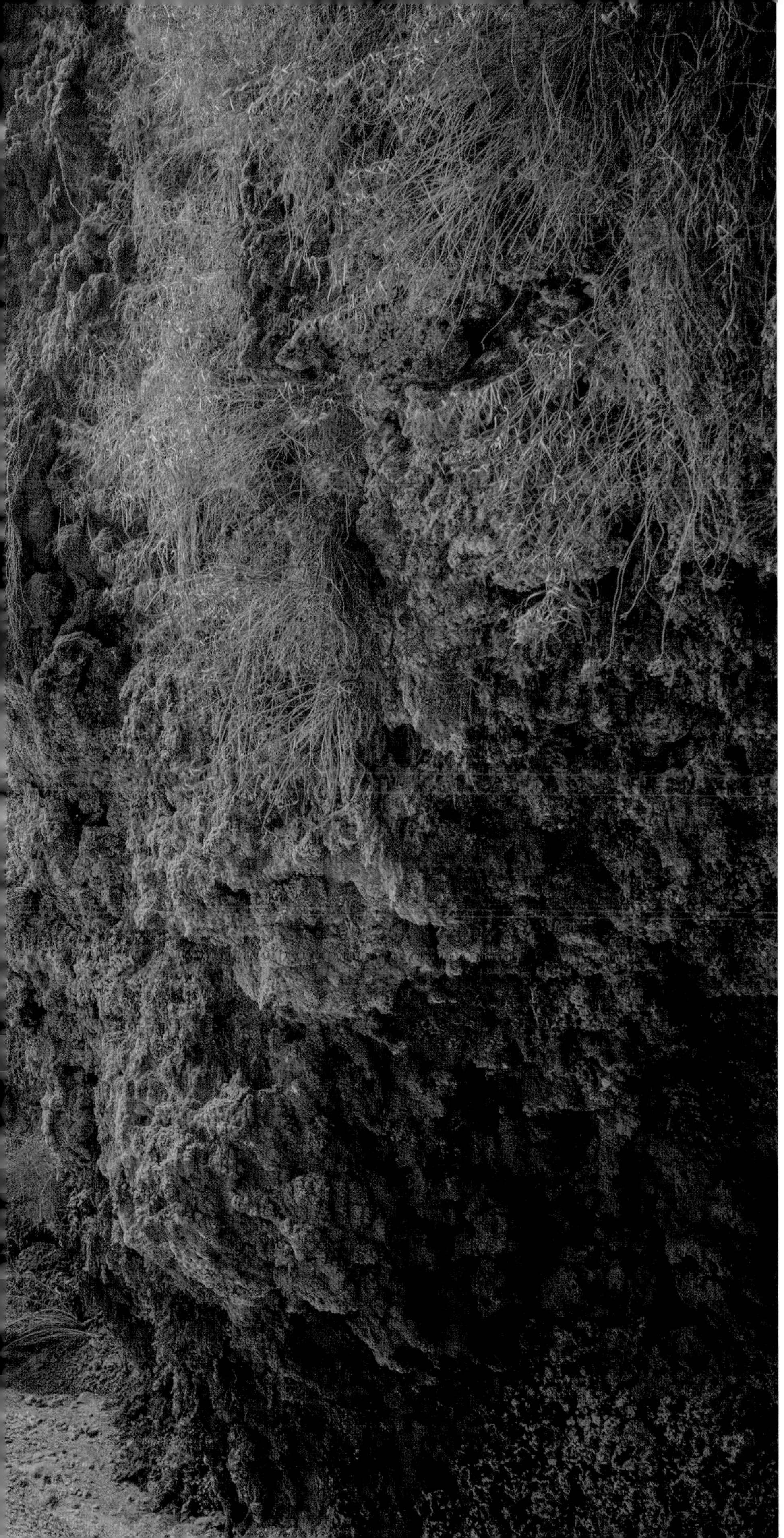

Cove Canyon

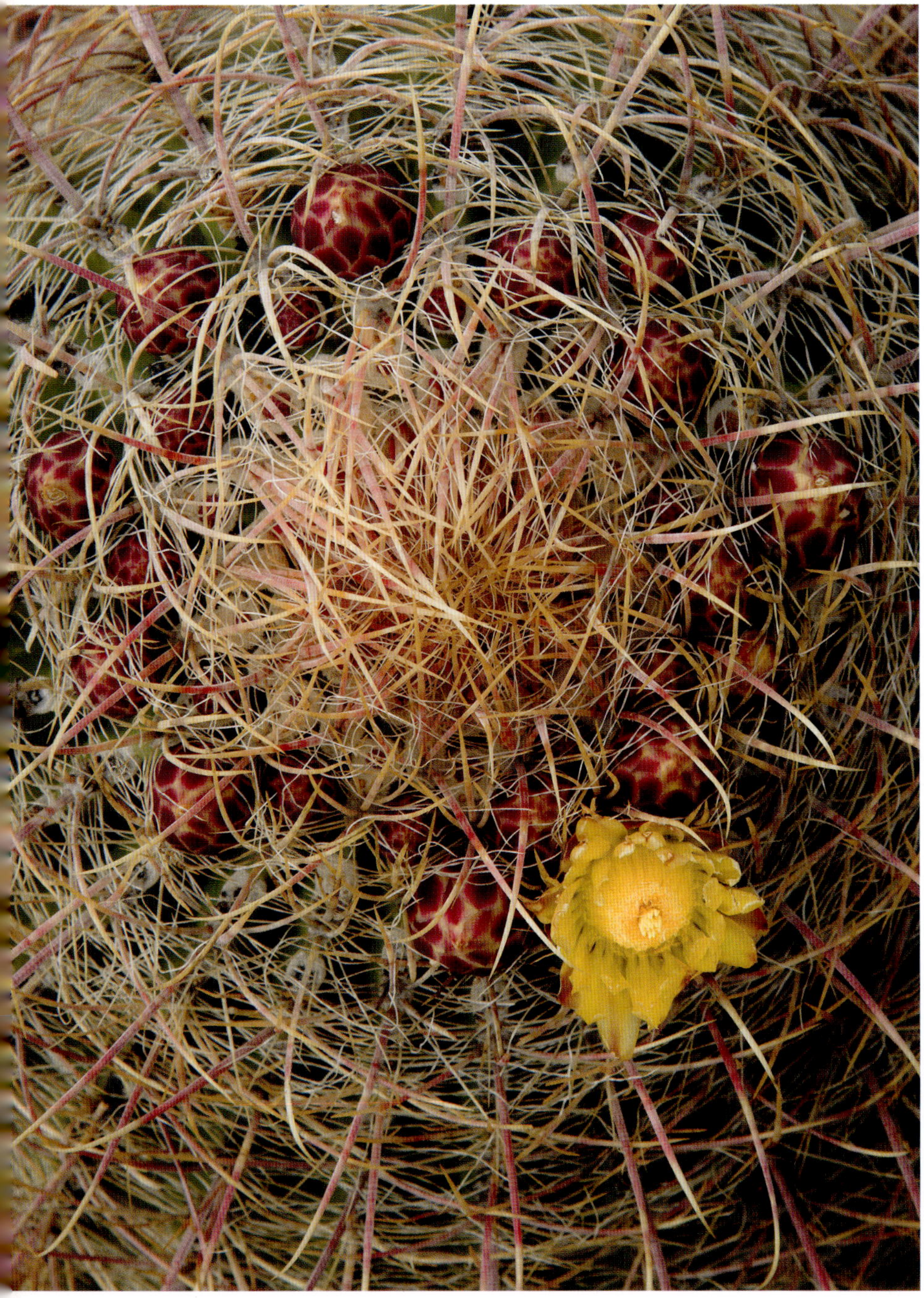

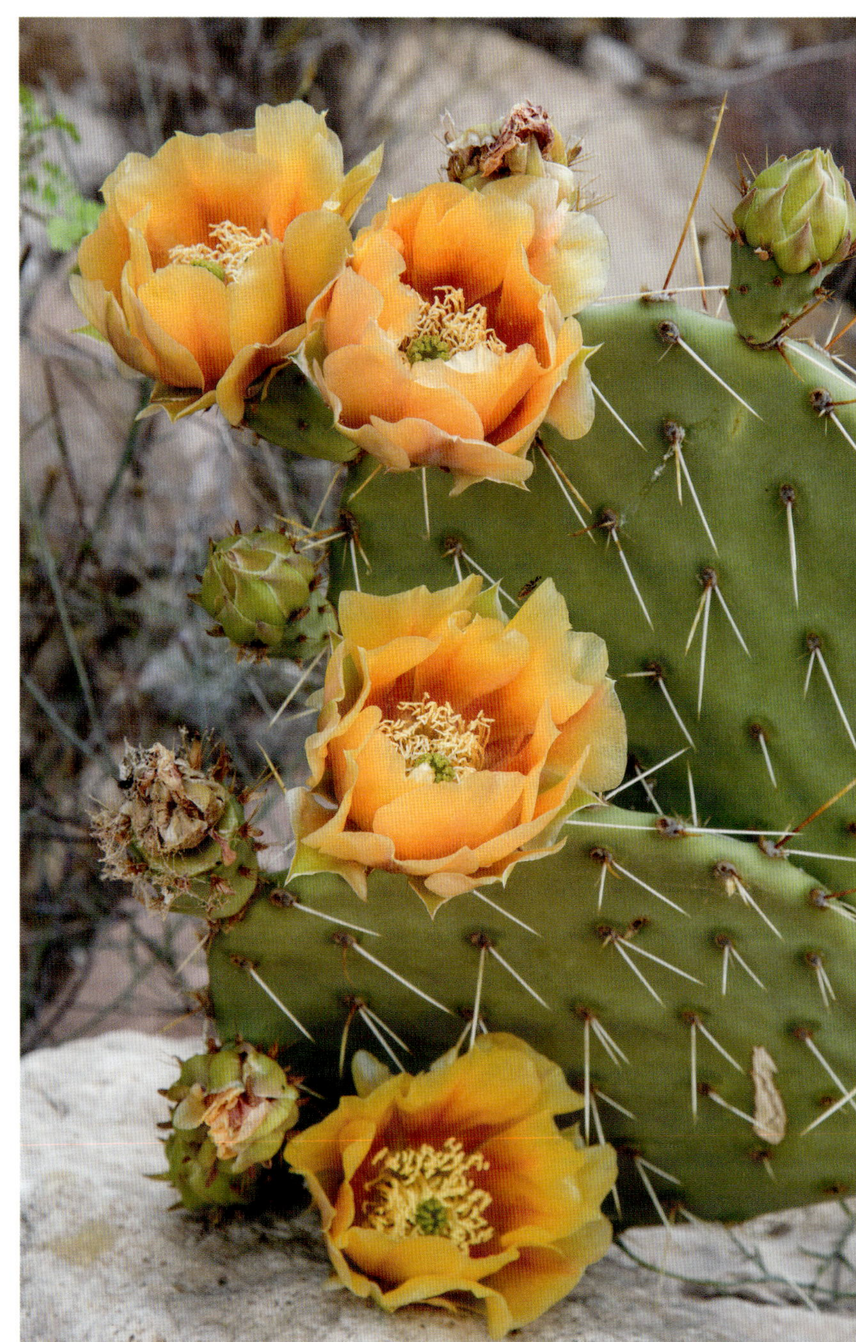

▲ Barrel cactus (left) and Engelmann prickly-pear cactus (right), Cove Canyon ▶ Raven

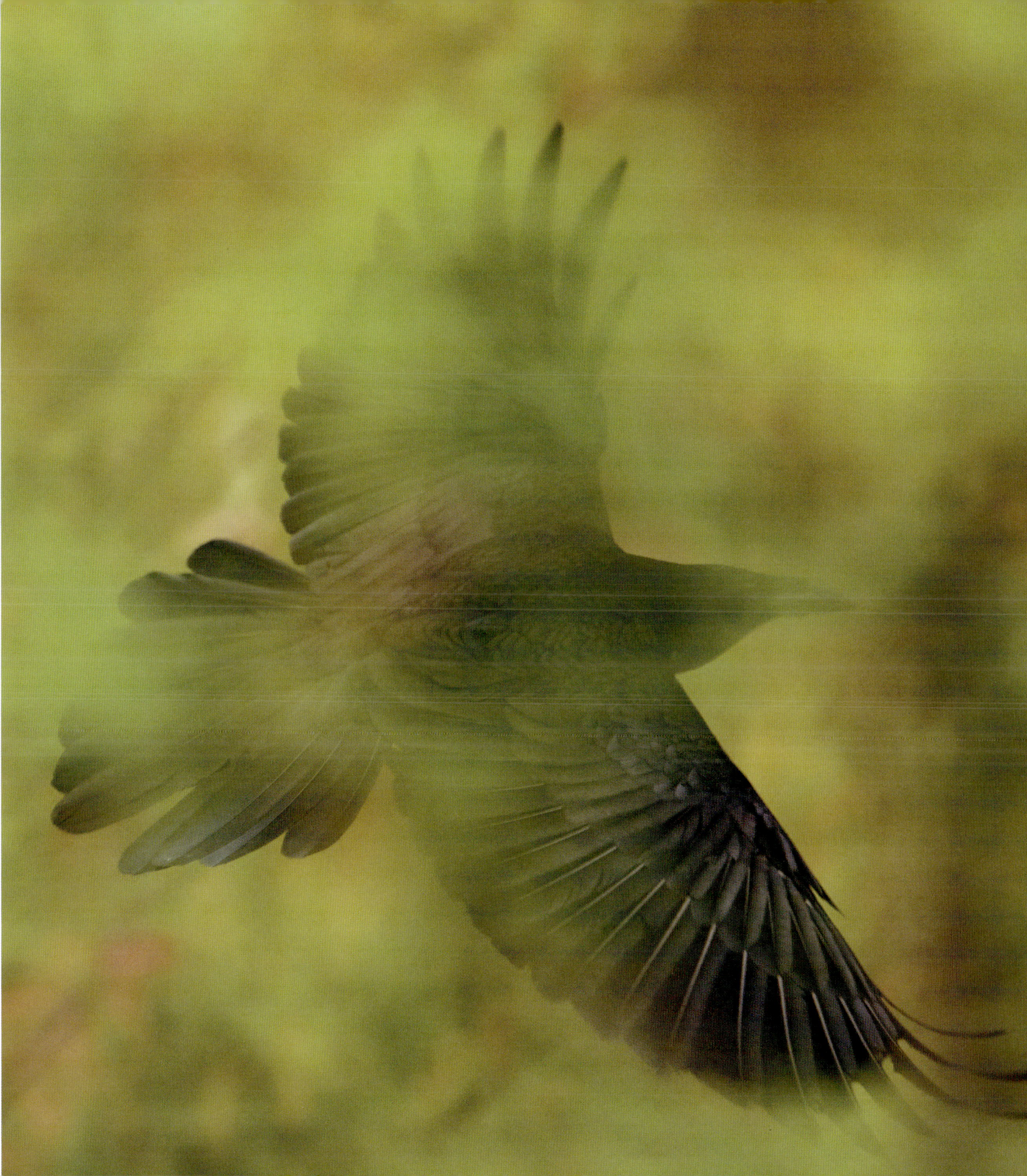

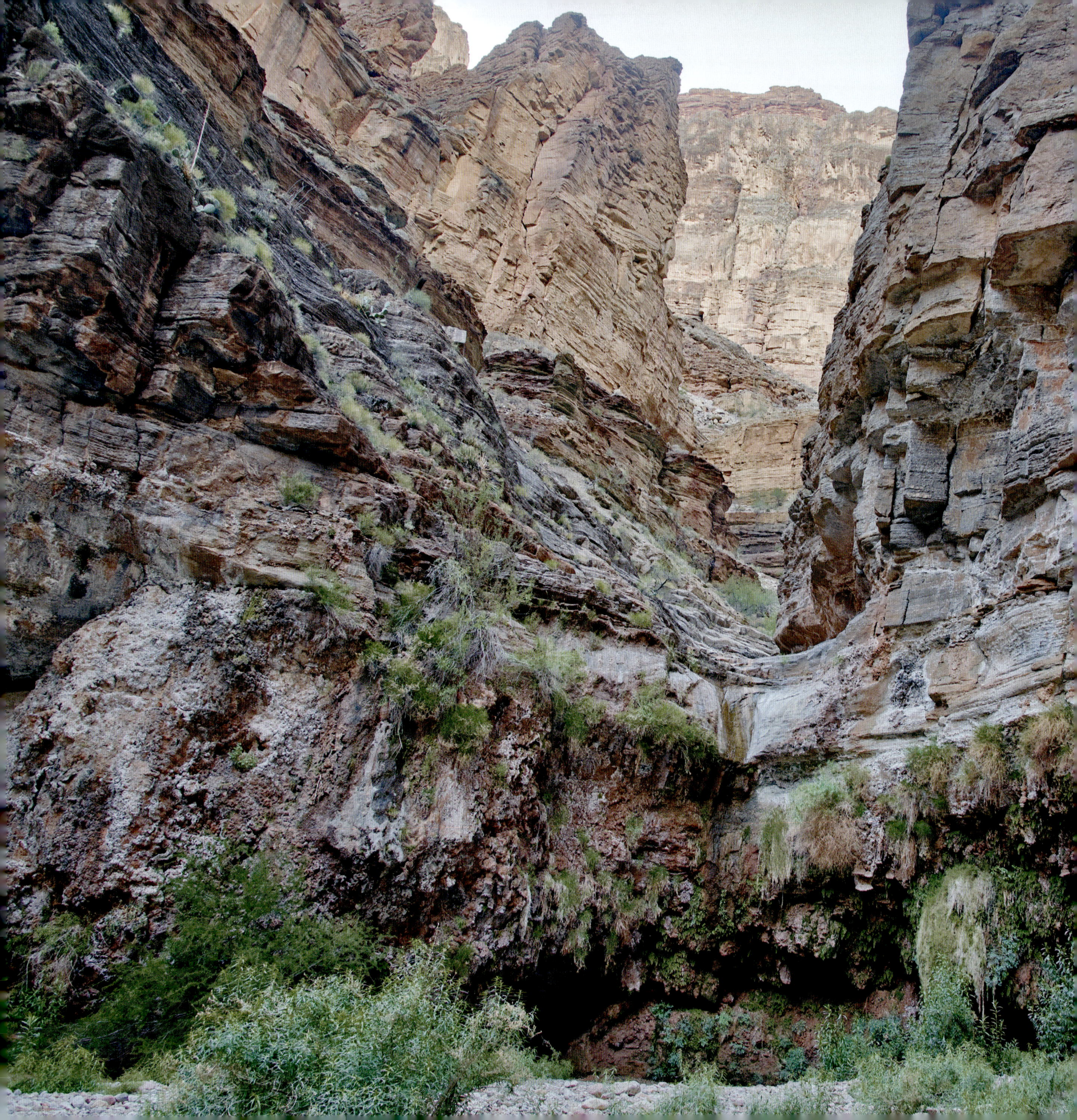

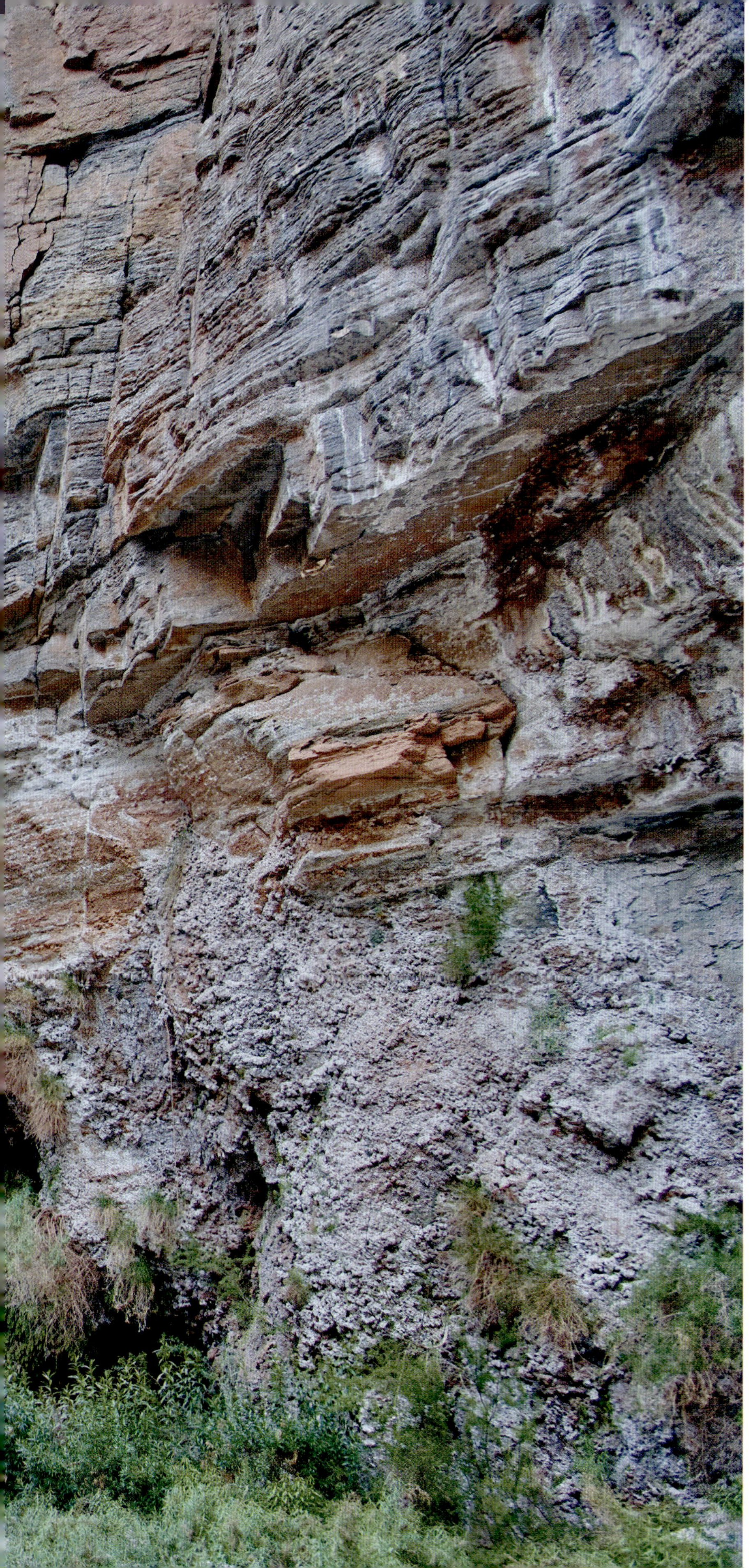

Grotto seep, upper end of Cove Canyon

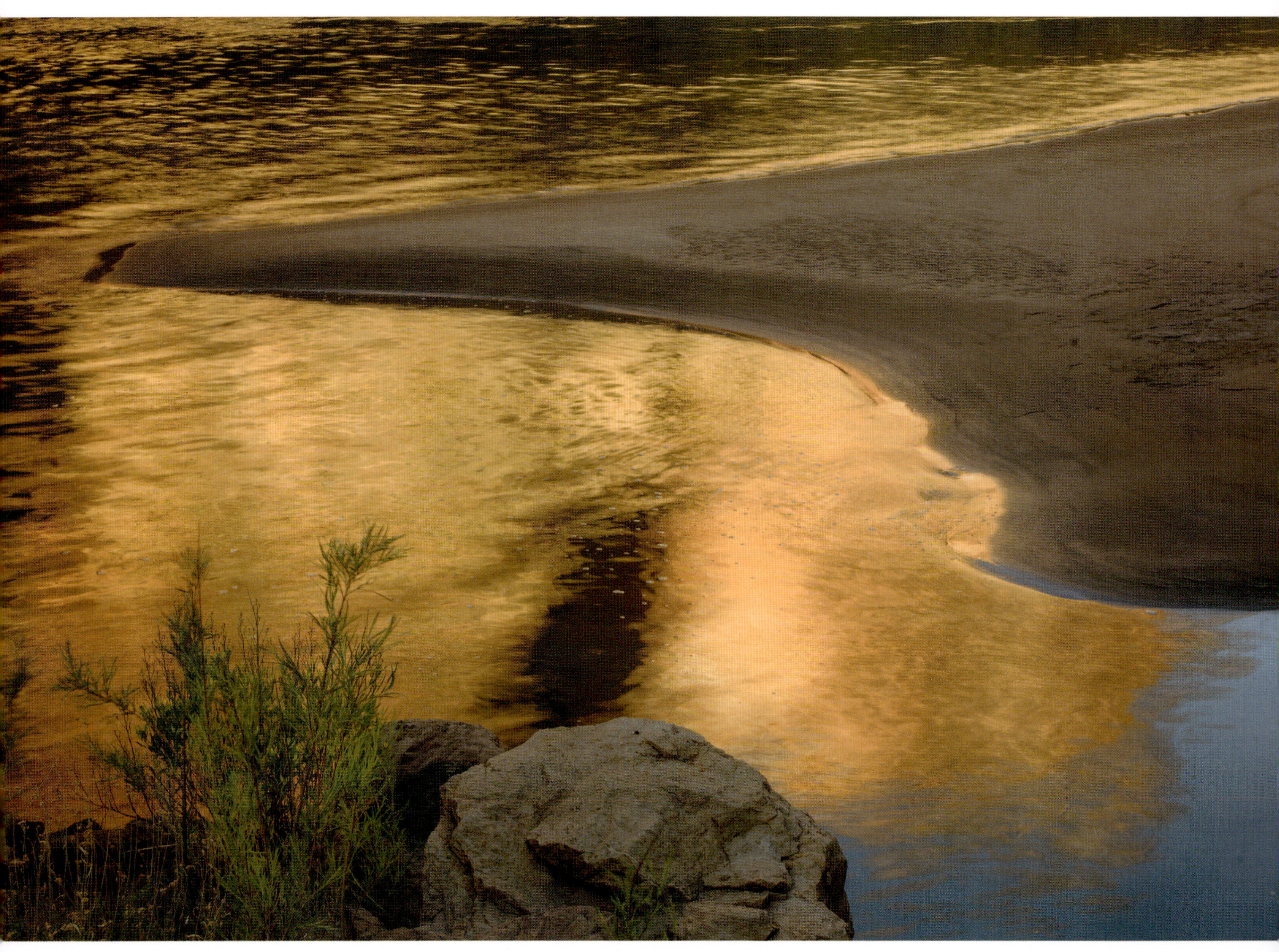

▲ River sandbar and reflections ▶ Engelmann hedgehog cactus

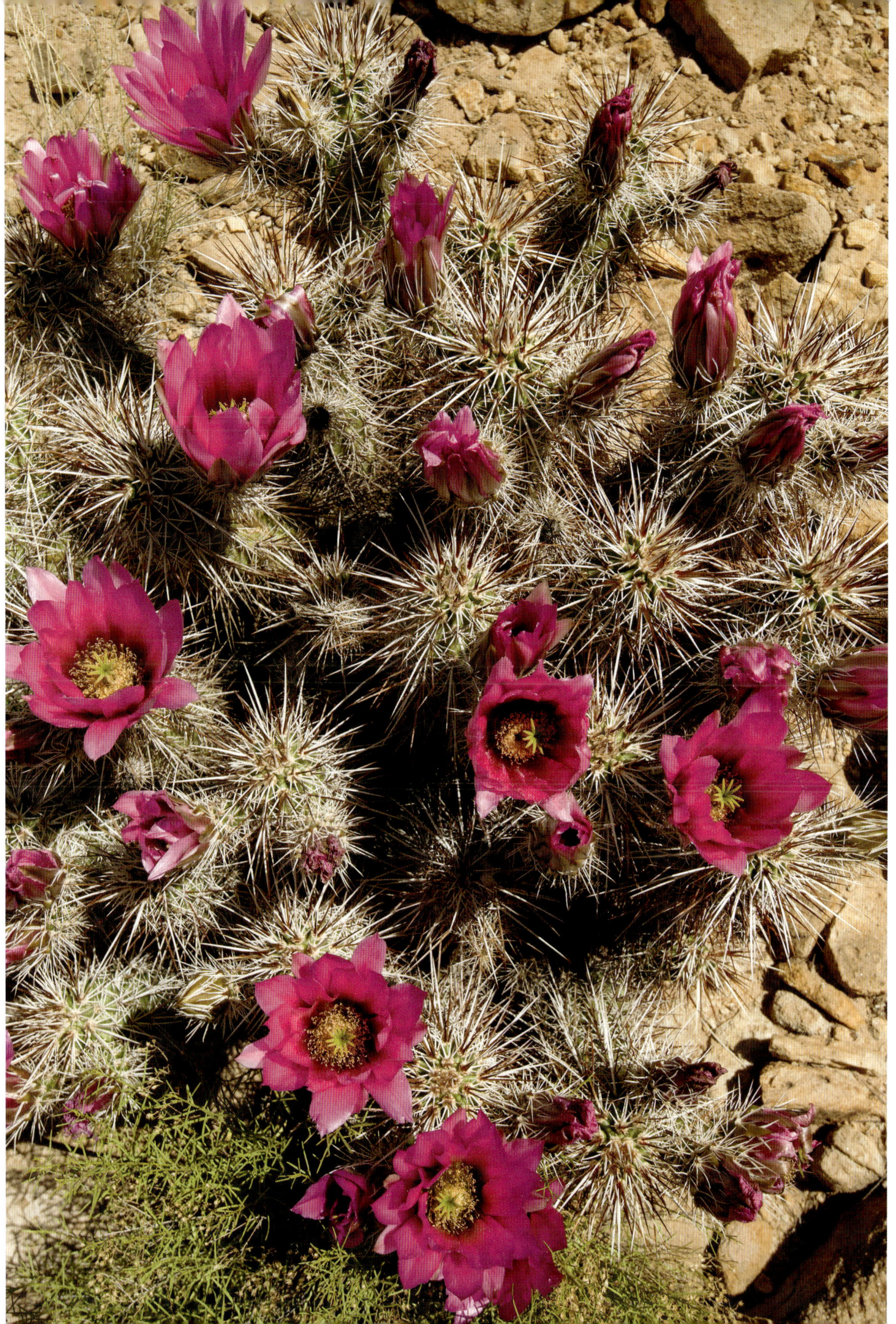

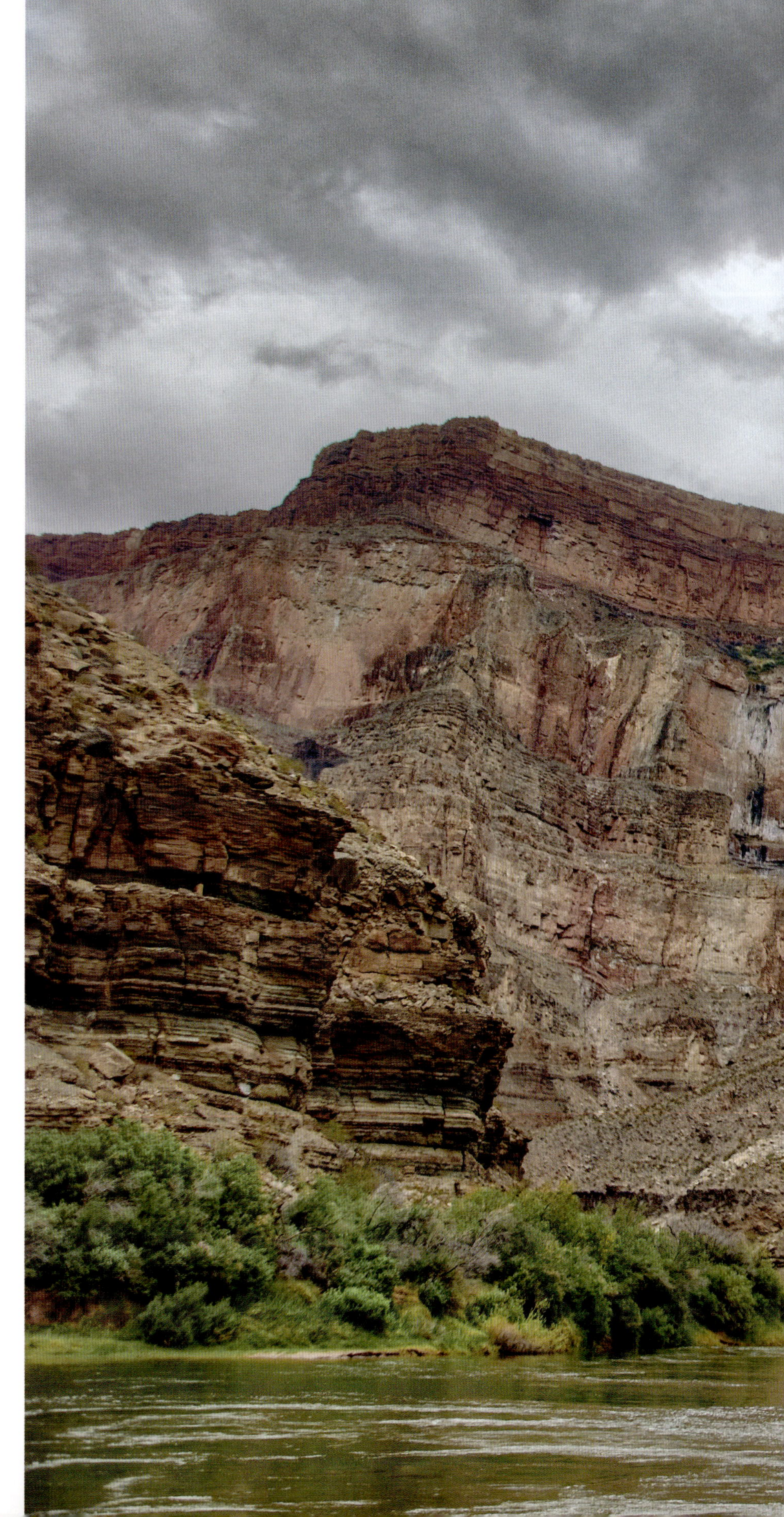

Vulcan's Anvil above Lava Falls Rapid

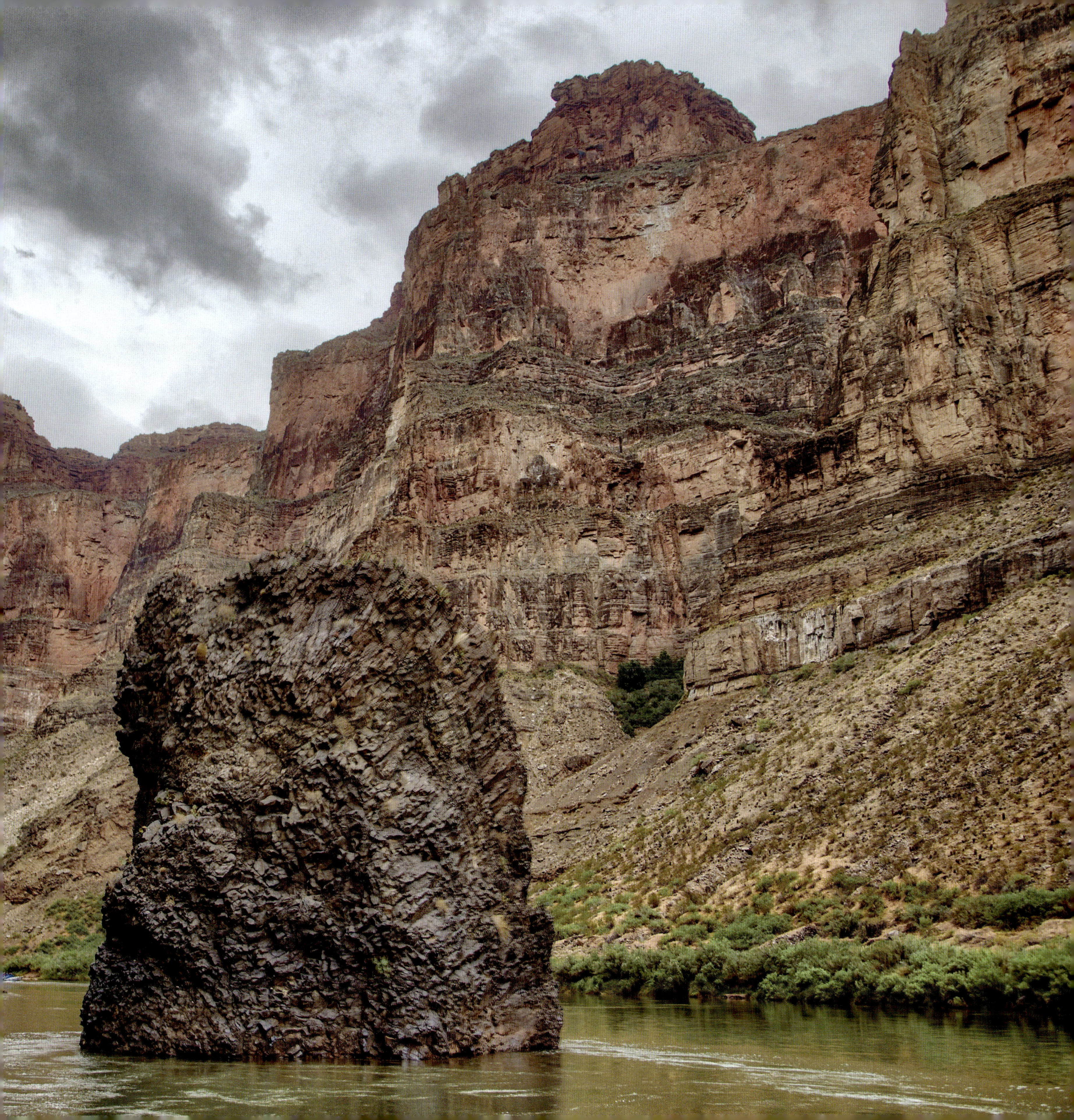

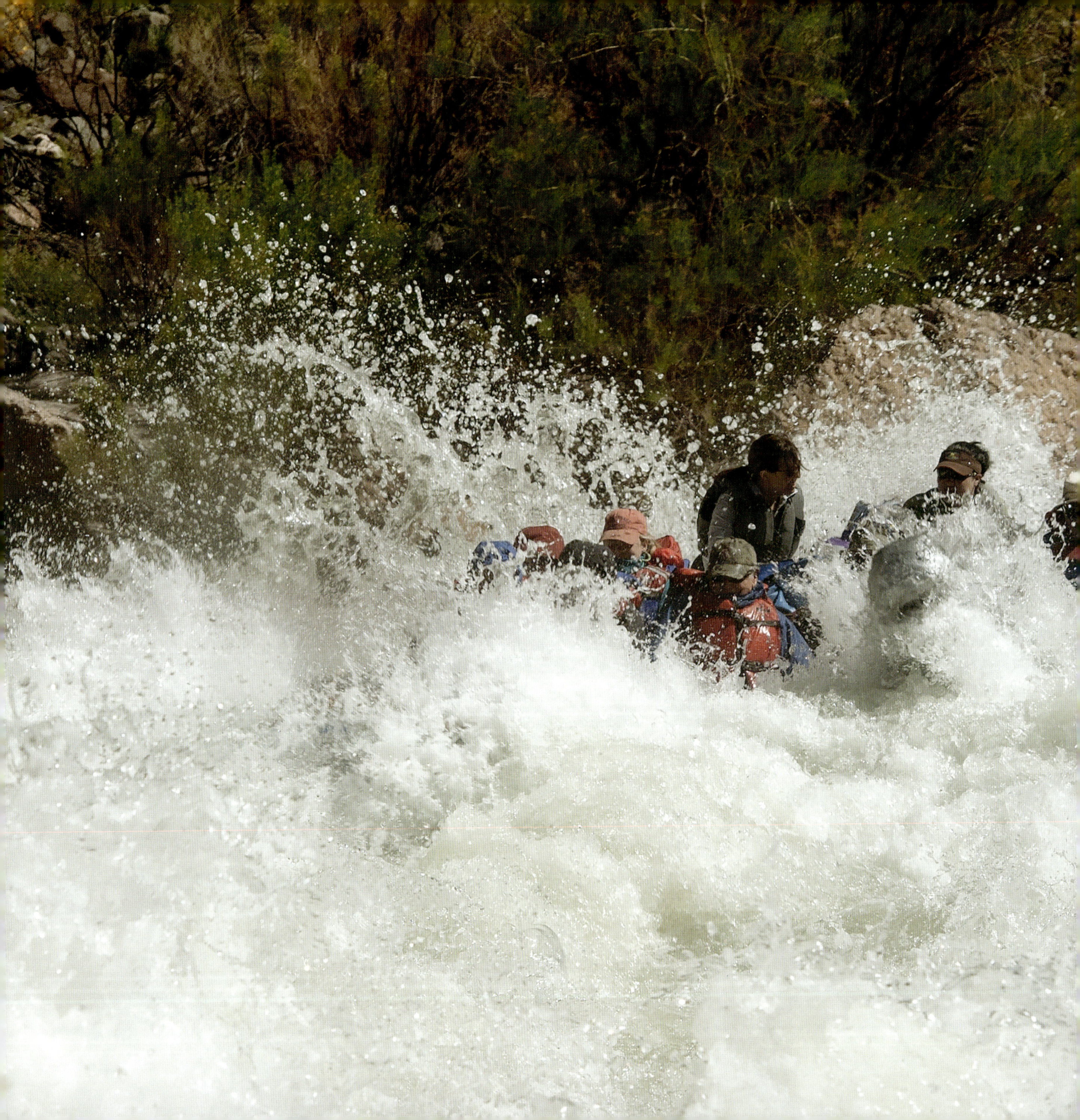

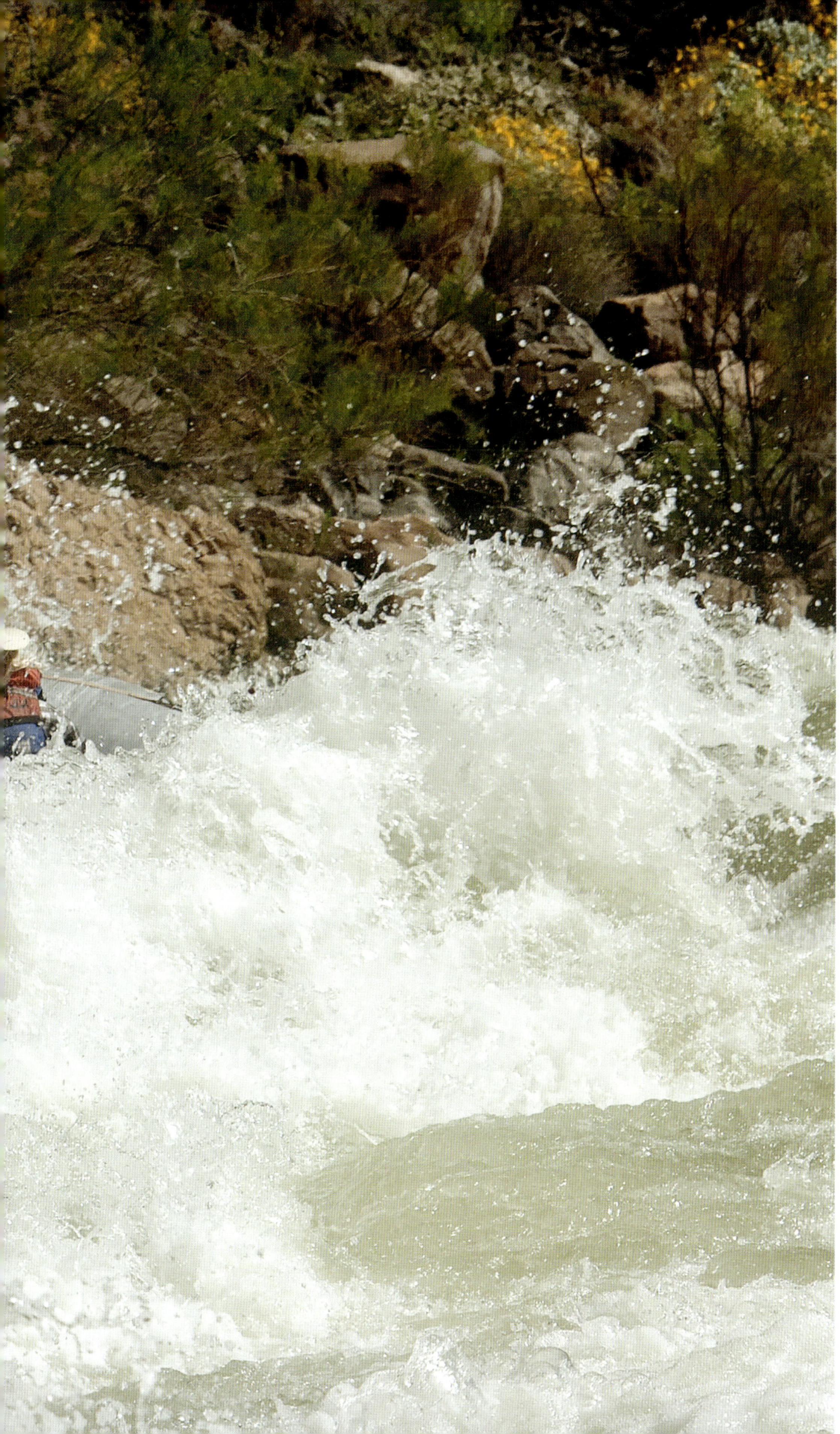

Lava Falls Rapid

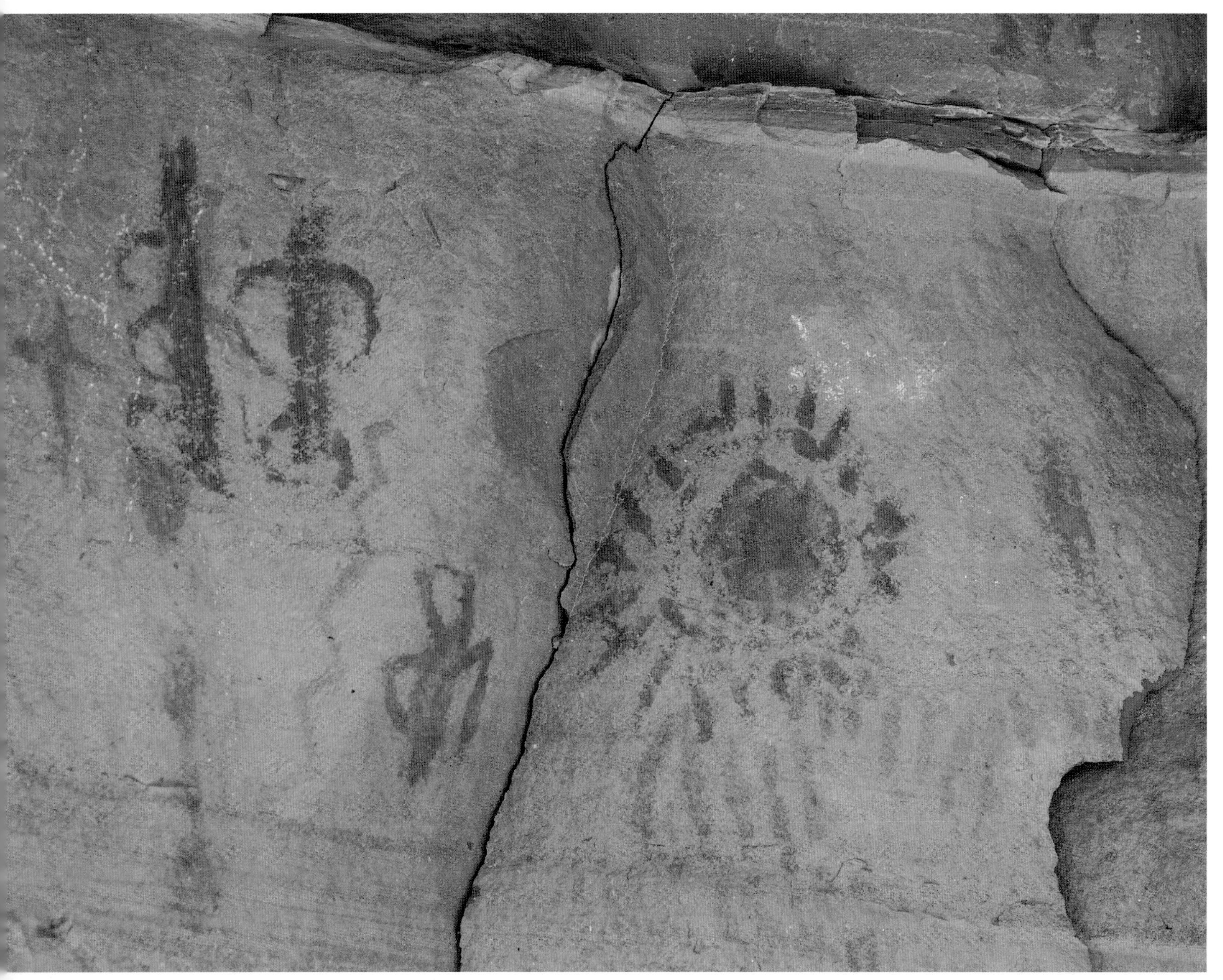

▲ Whitmore pictographs ► Lava boulders, mile 214

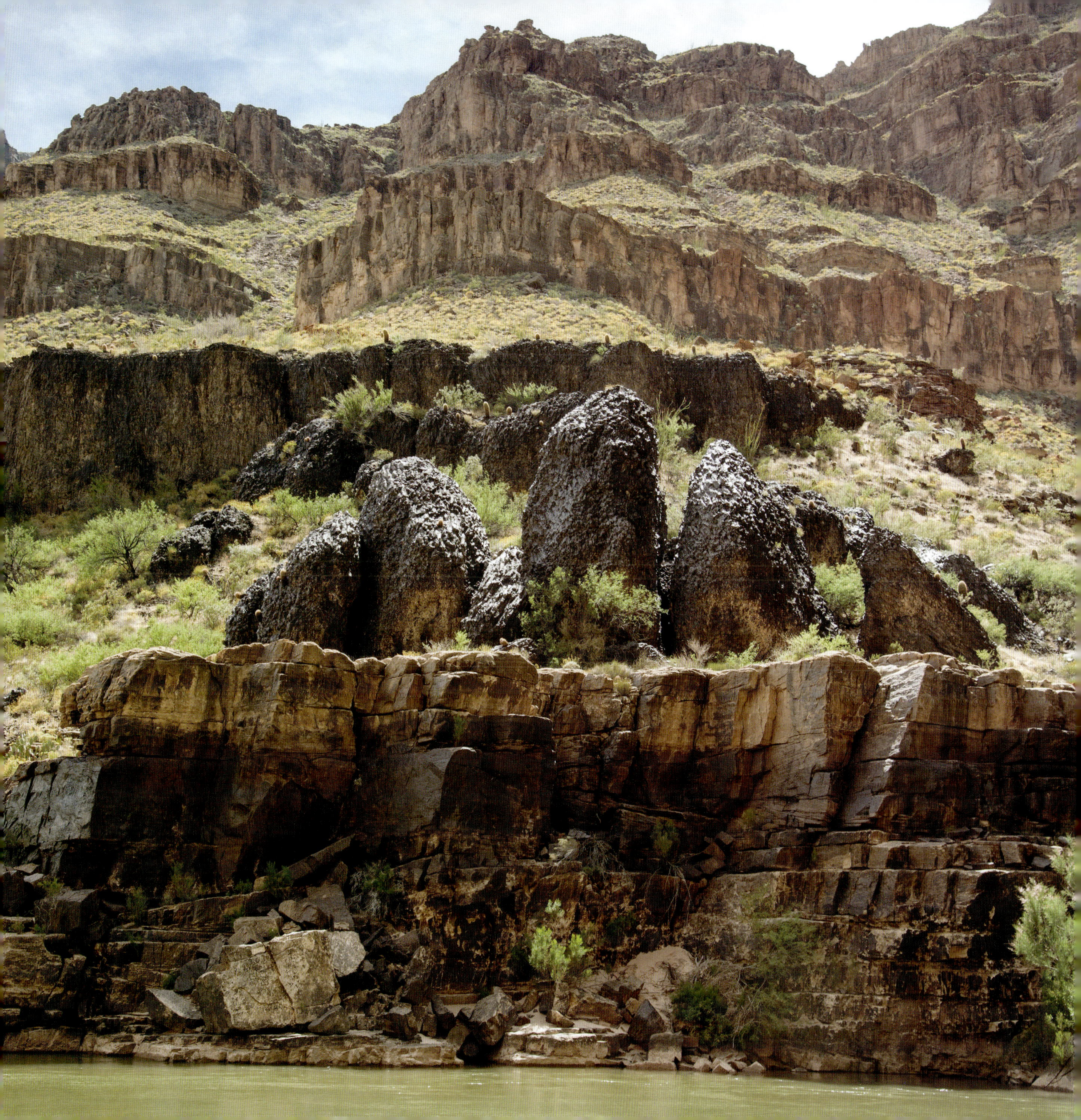

▶ Roderick Nash on oars with approaching storm

▼ Rapids splashing bow

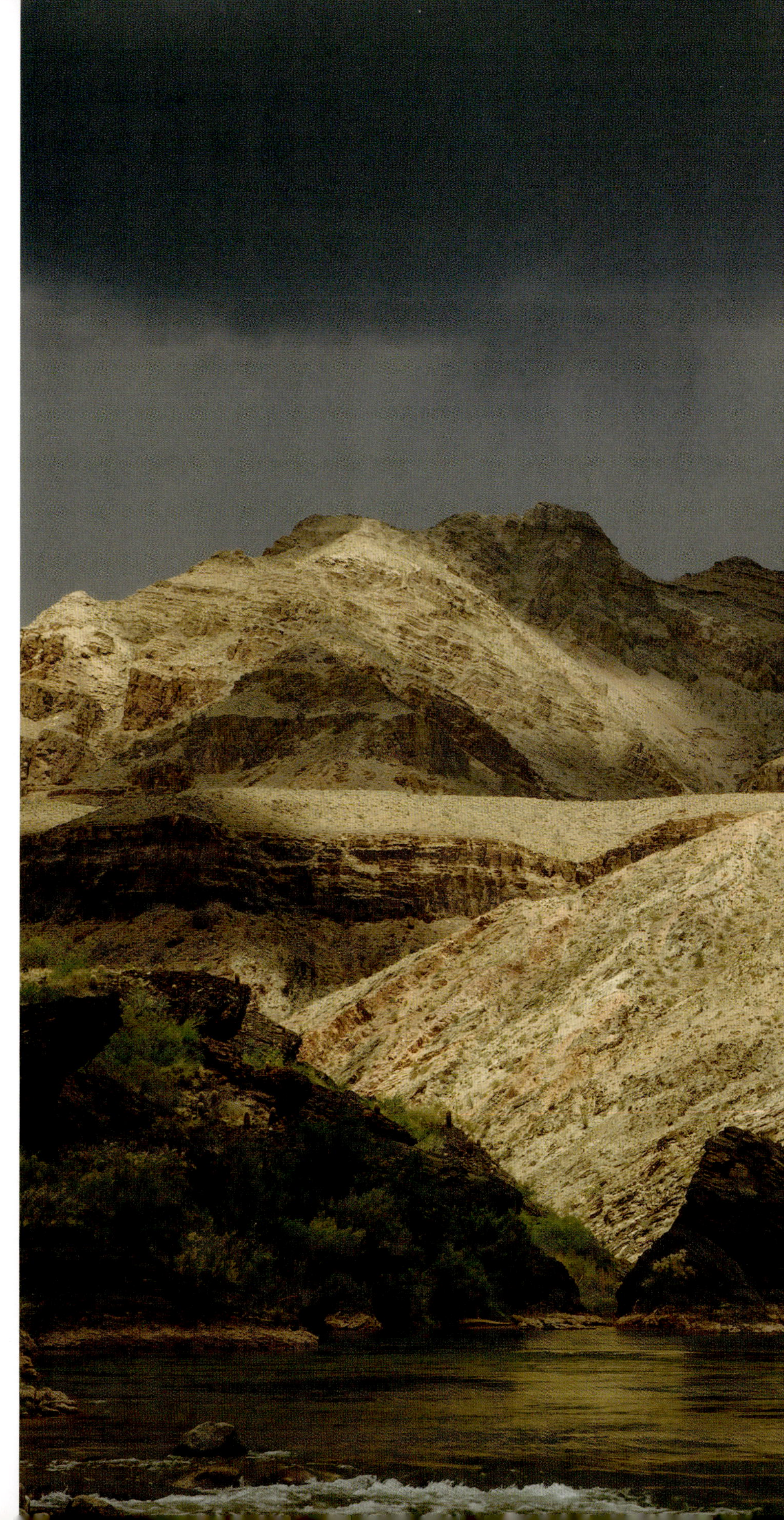

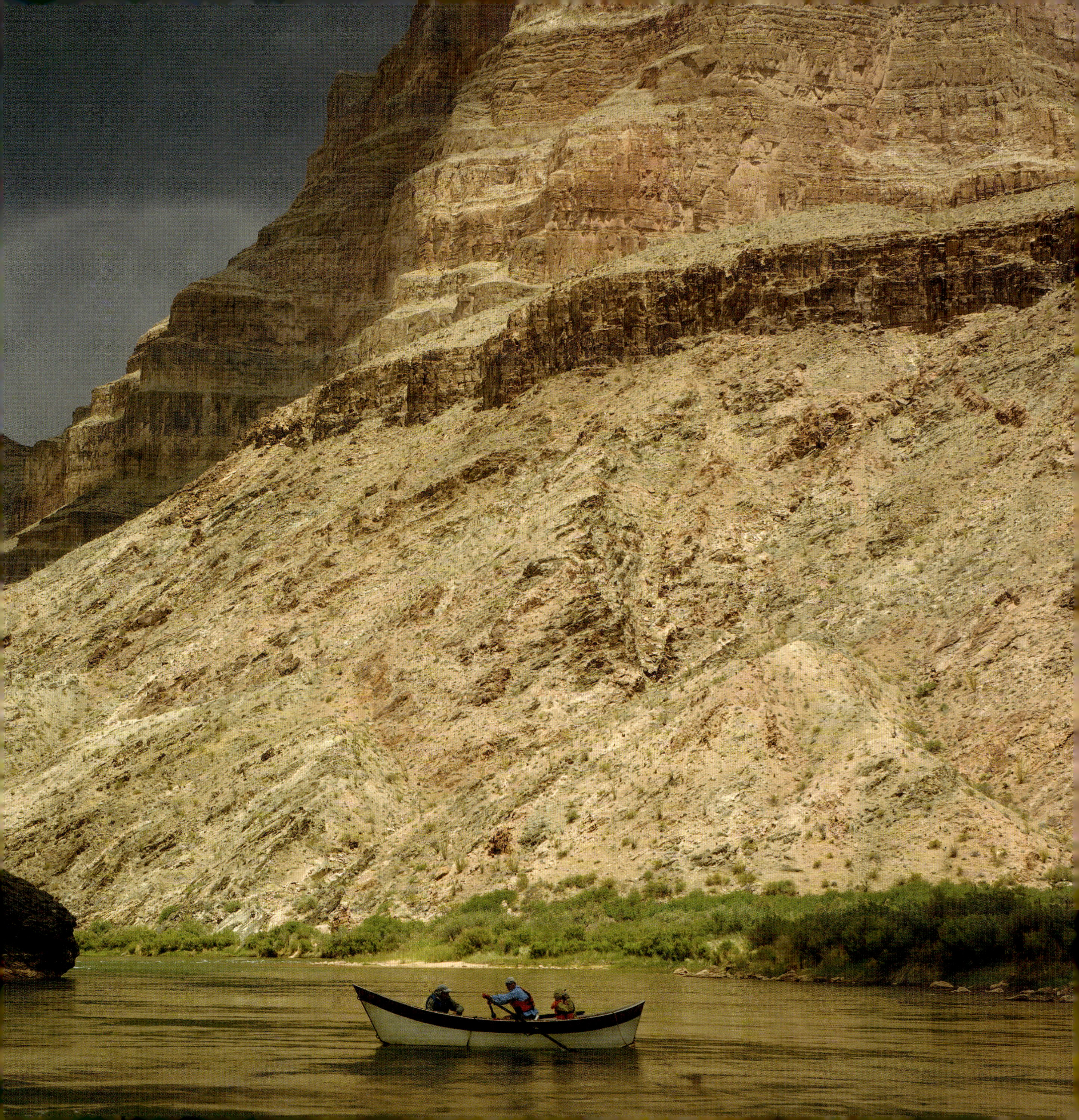

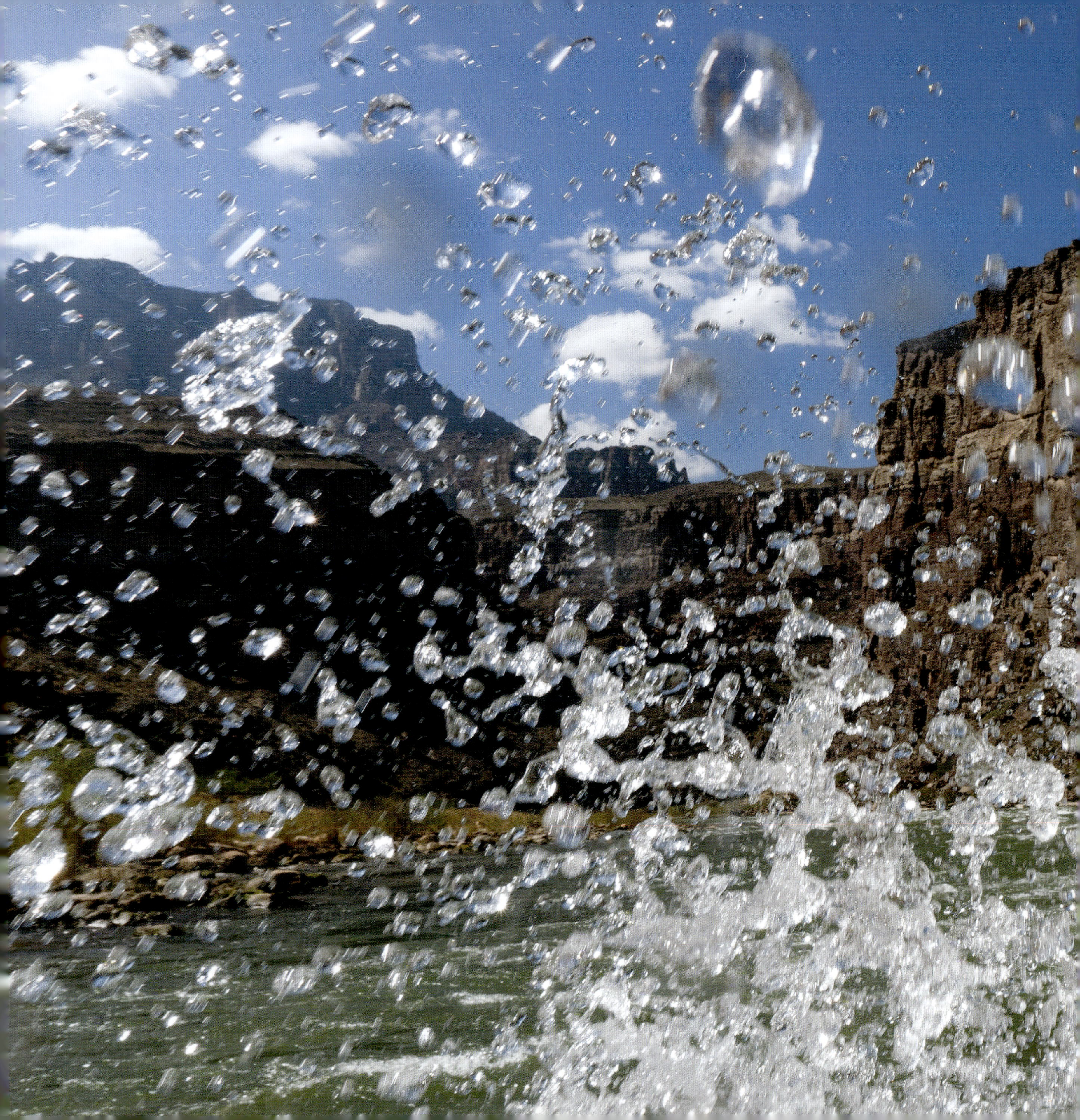

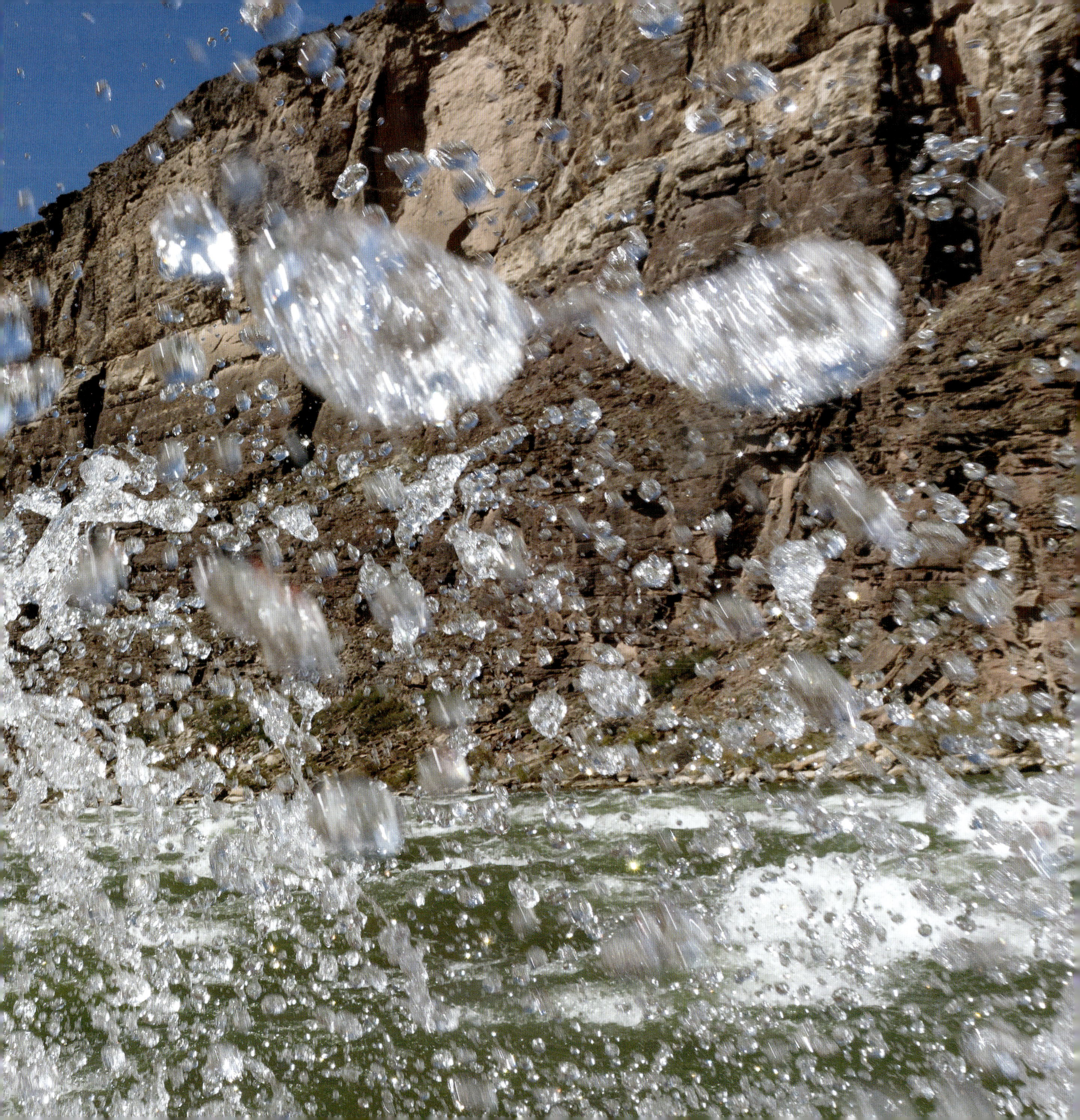

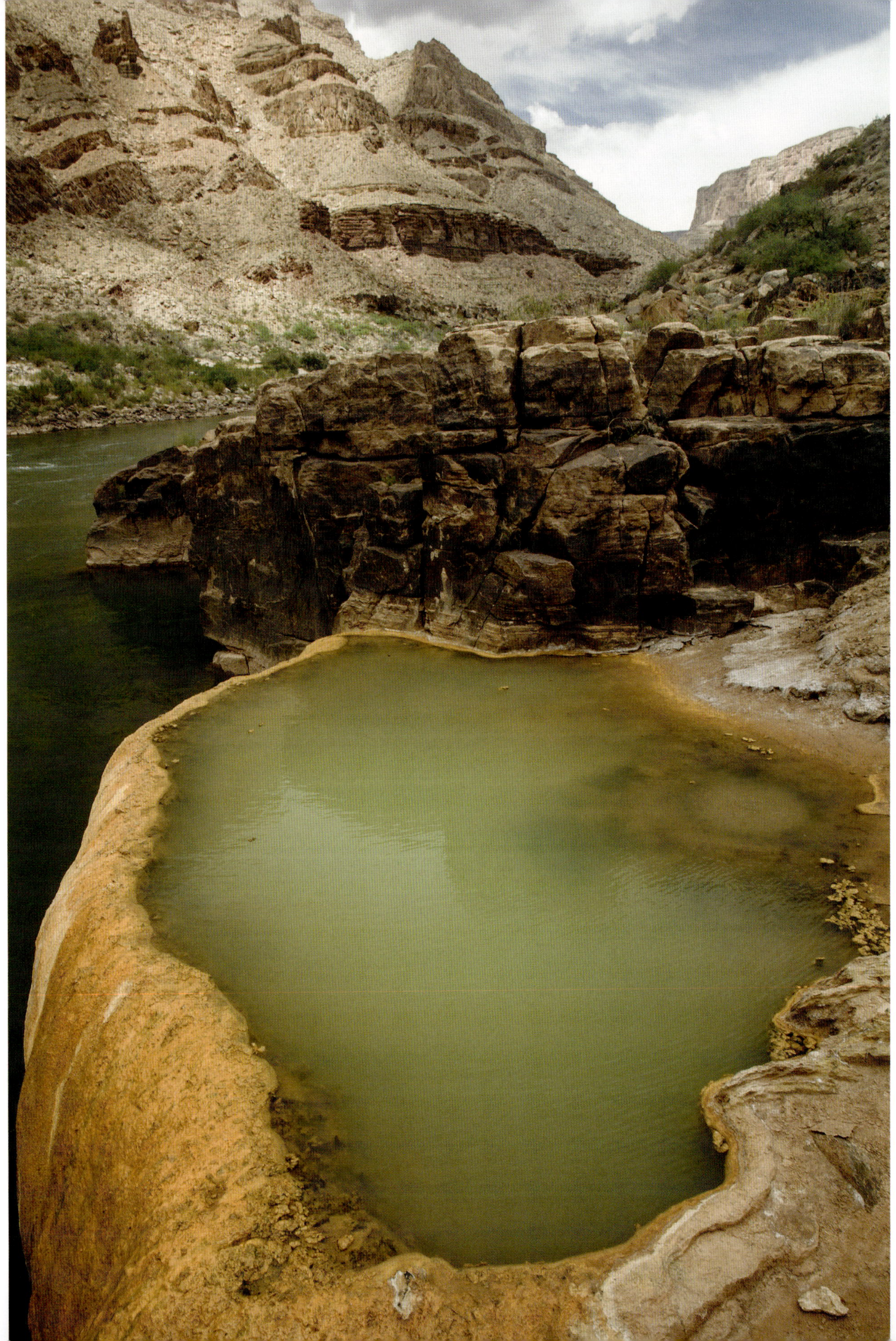

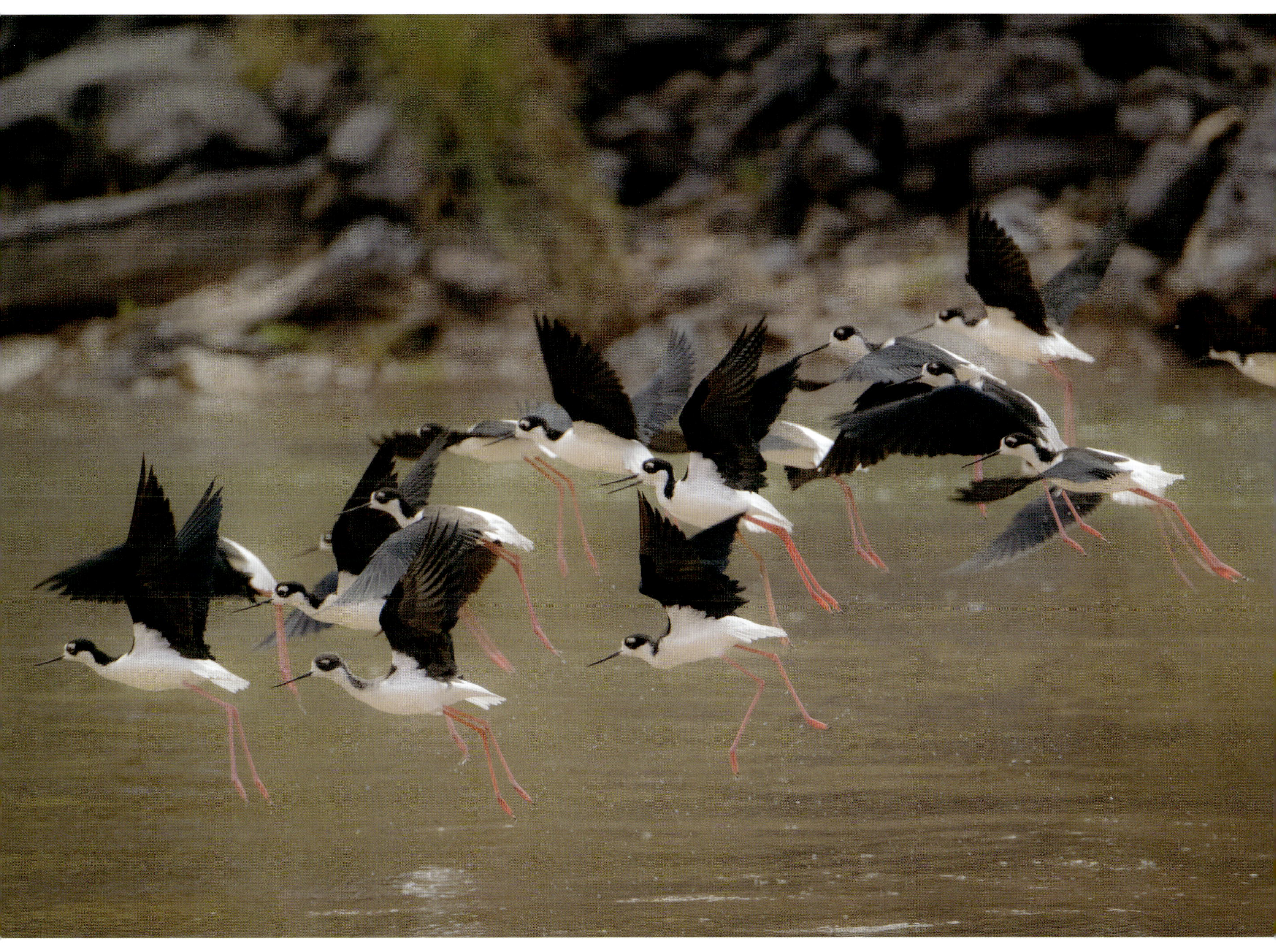

◀ Pumpkin Spring ▲ Black-necked stilts

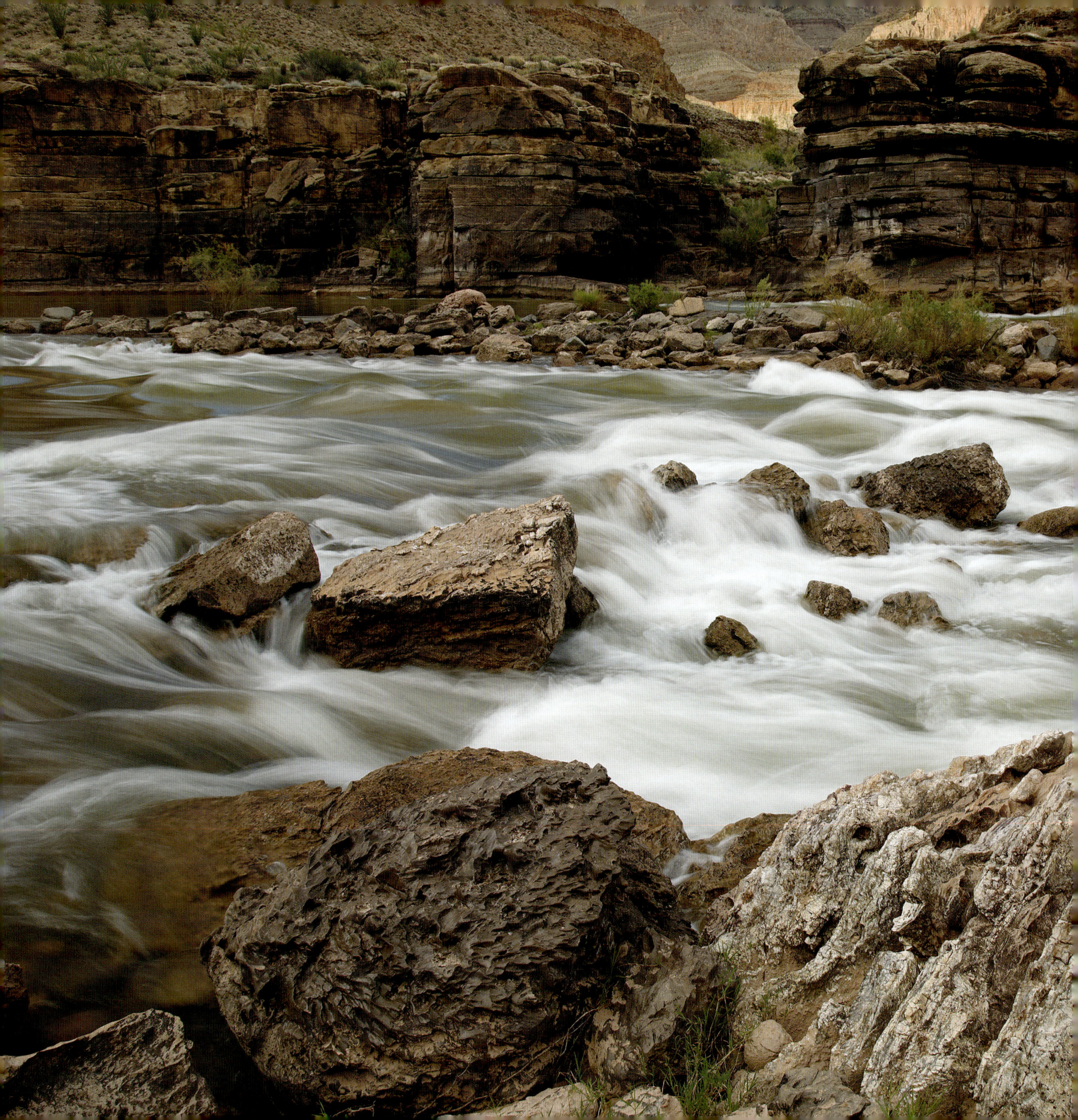

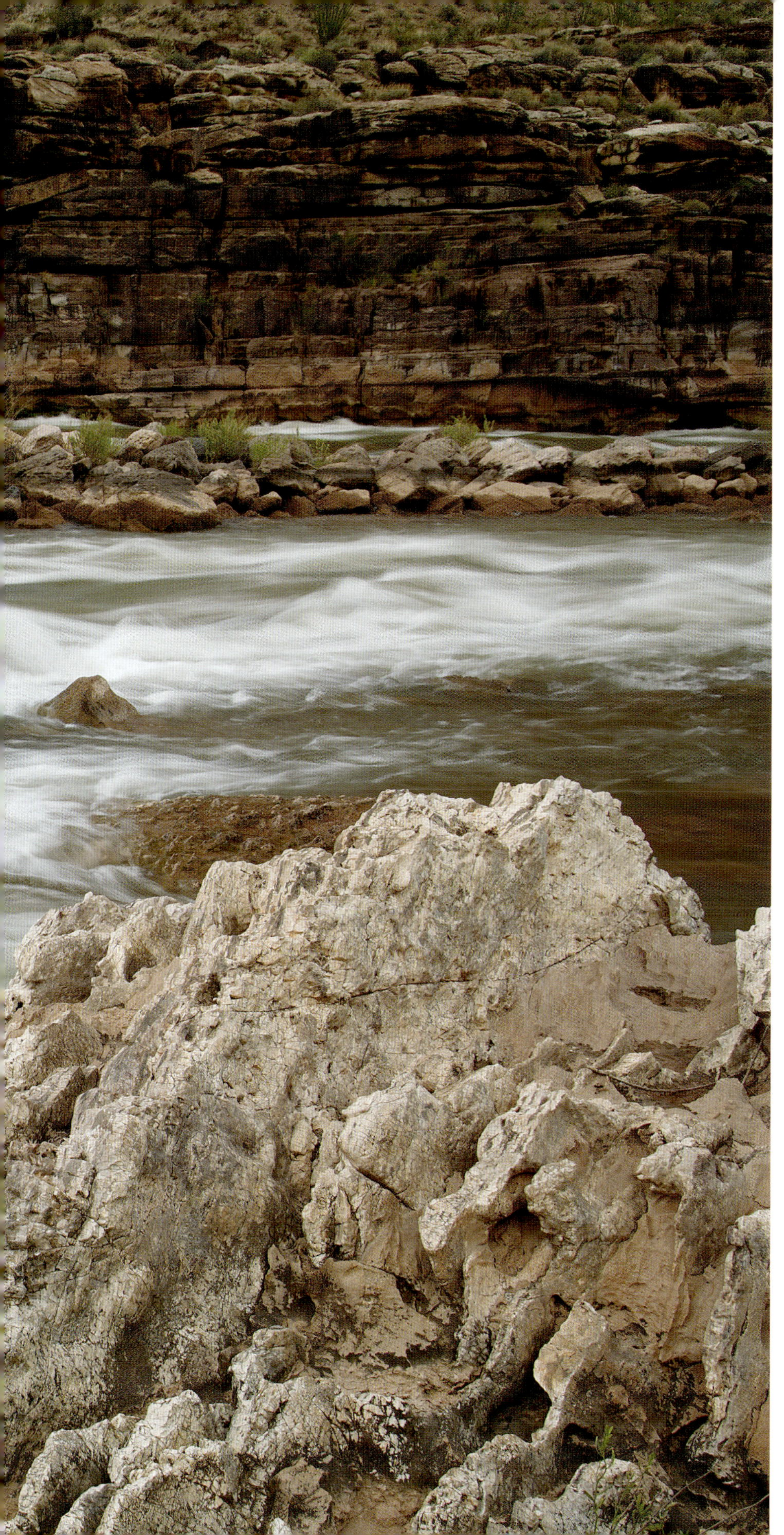

◀ Three Springs Camp

▼ Male side-blotched lizards fighting (left), osprey (right, top), and river rapid reflections (right, bottom), Three Springs

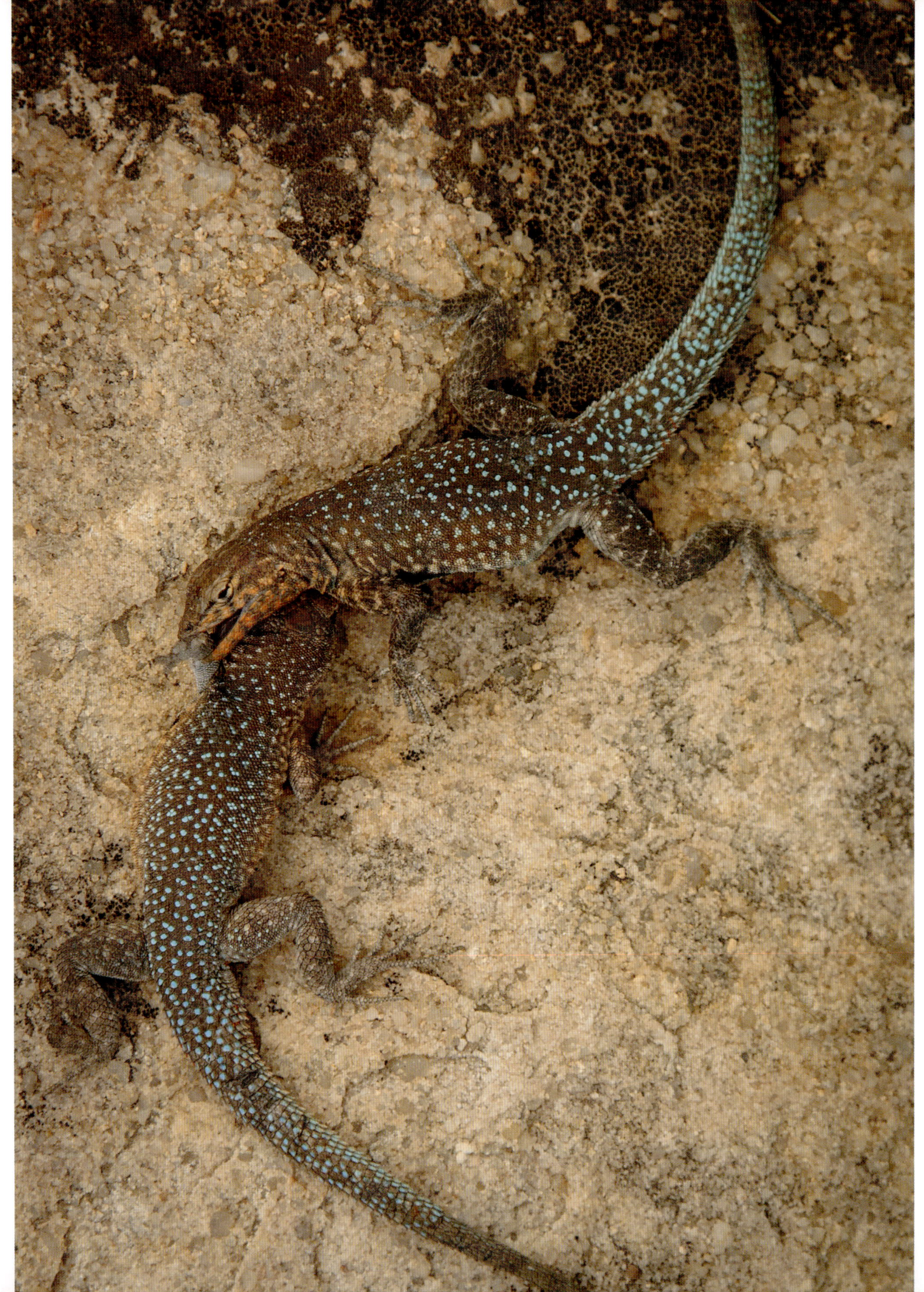

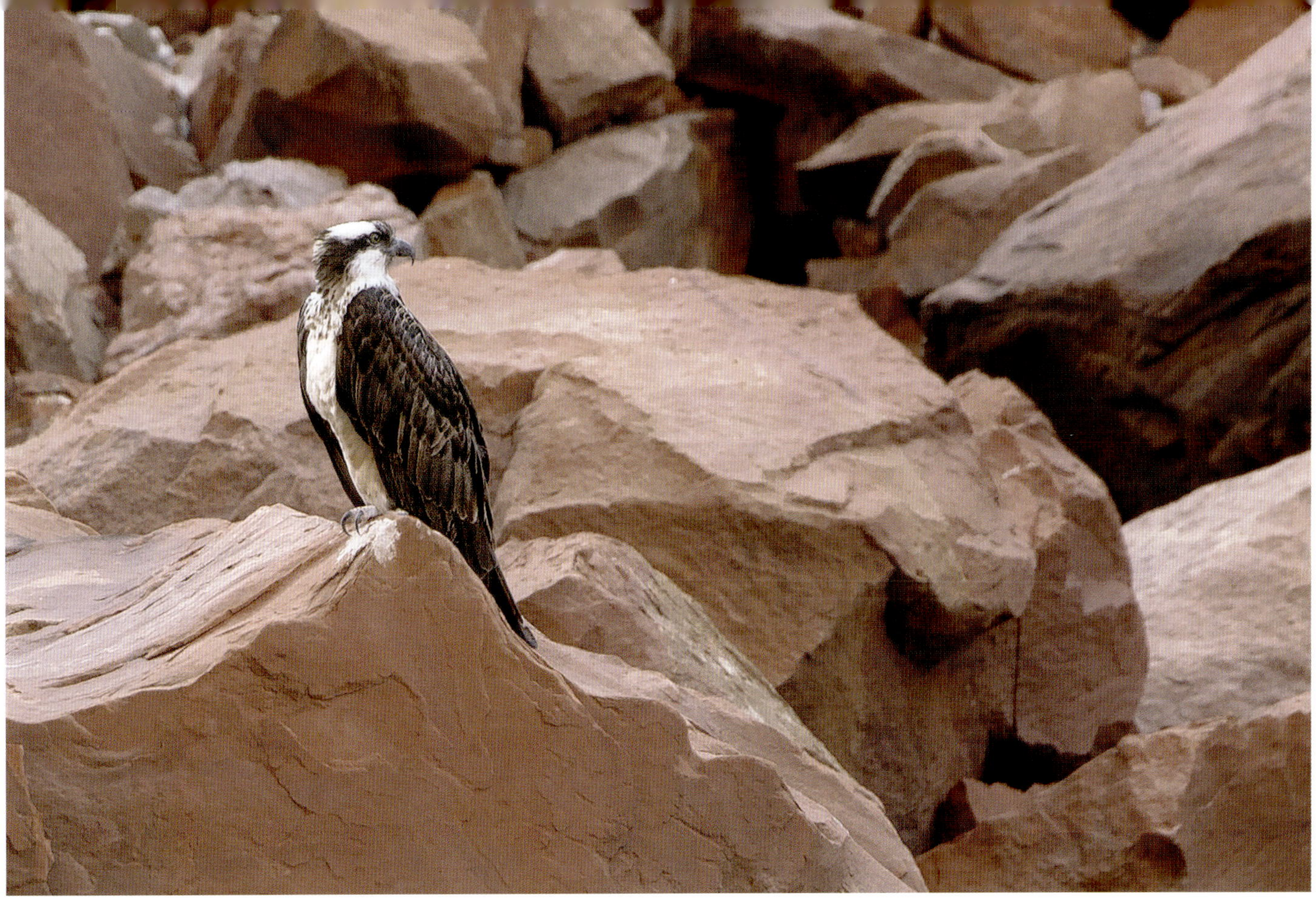

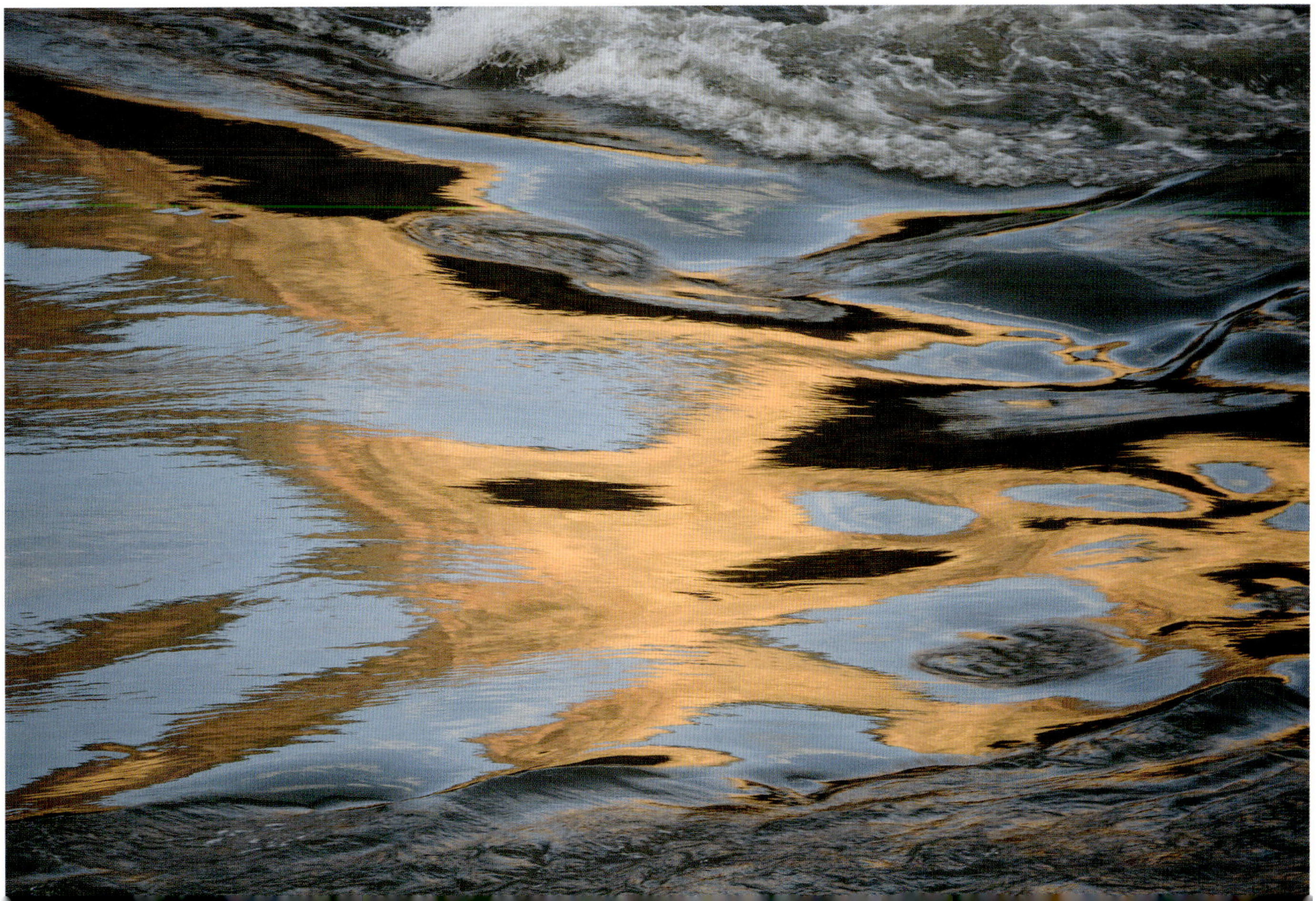

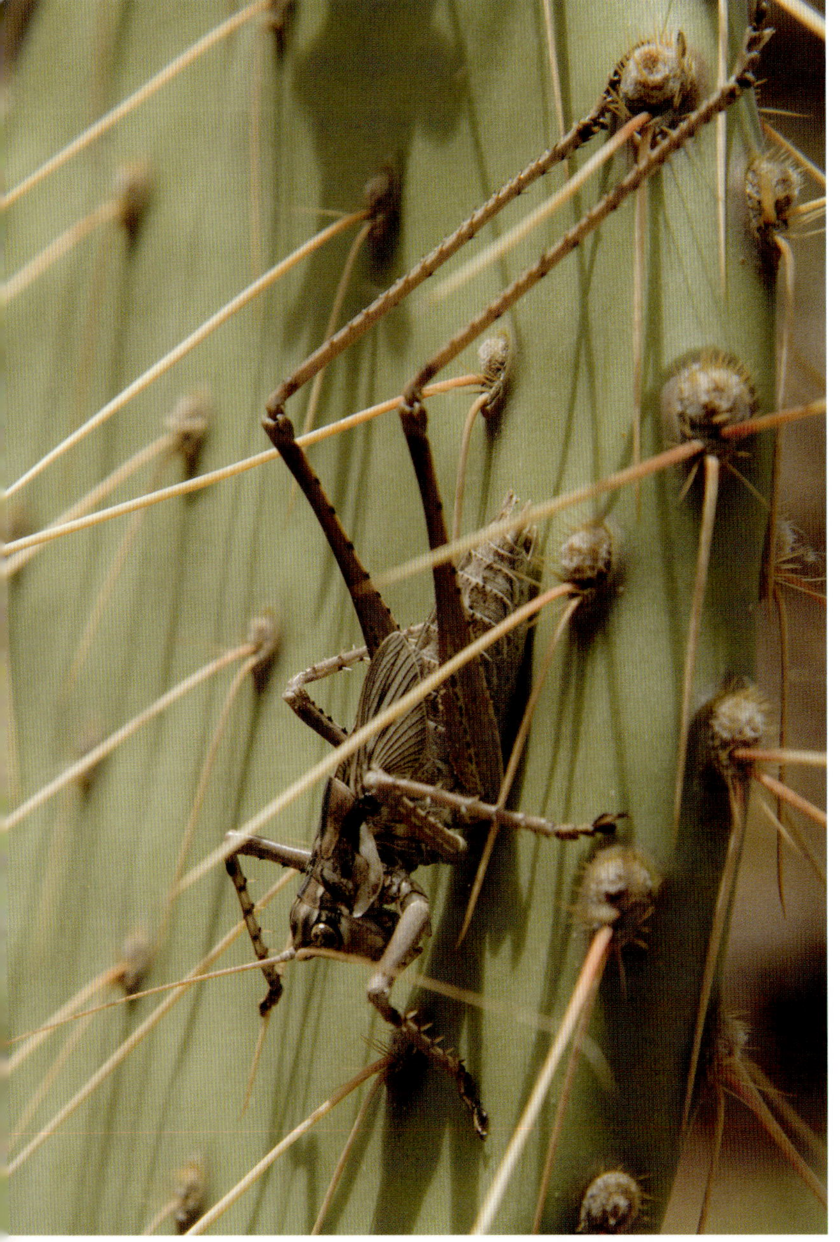

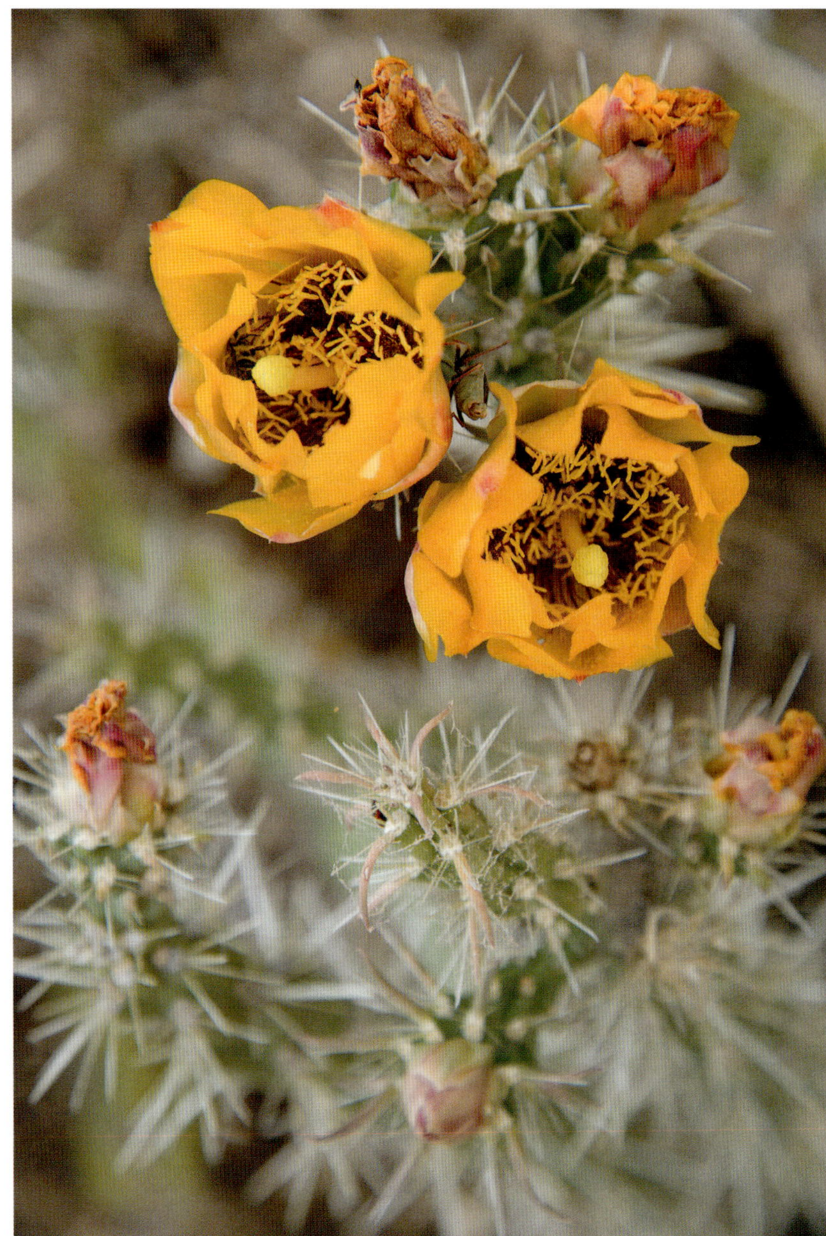

▲ Grasshopper (left) and Buckhorn cholla cactus blooms (right) ▶ Buckhorn cholla cactus, 222 Mile Camp

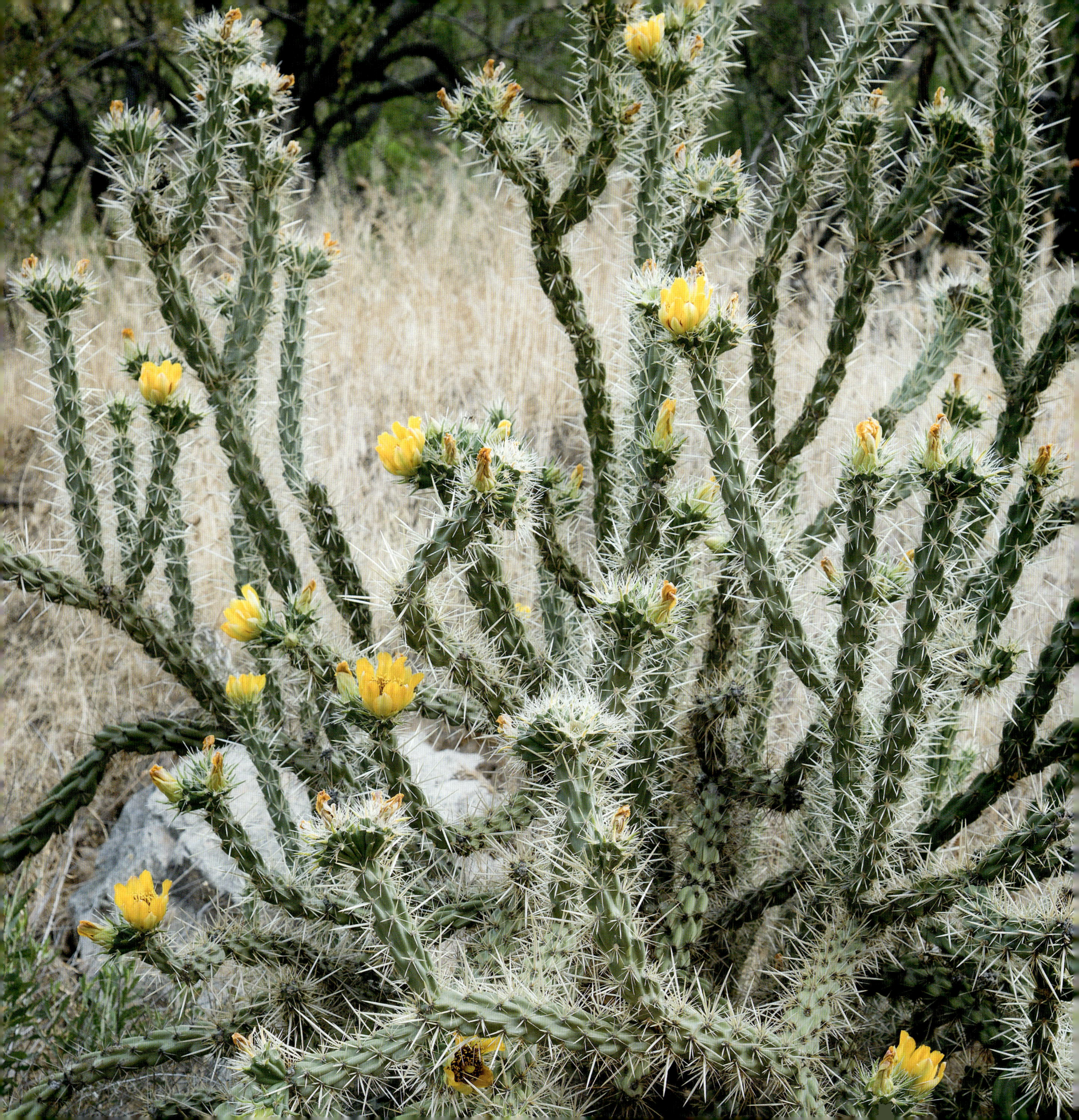

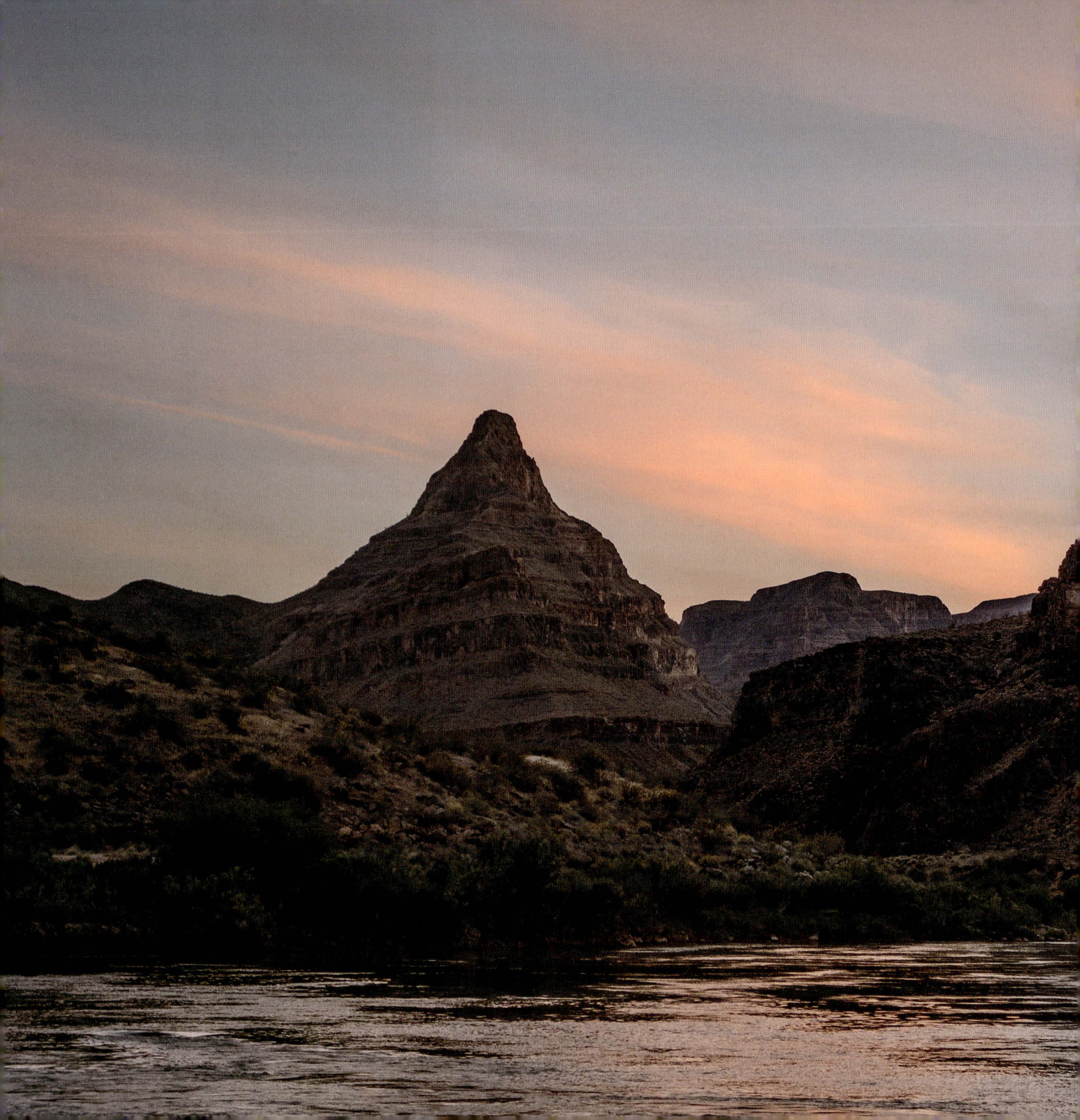

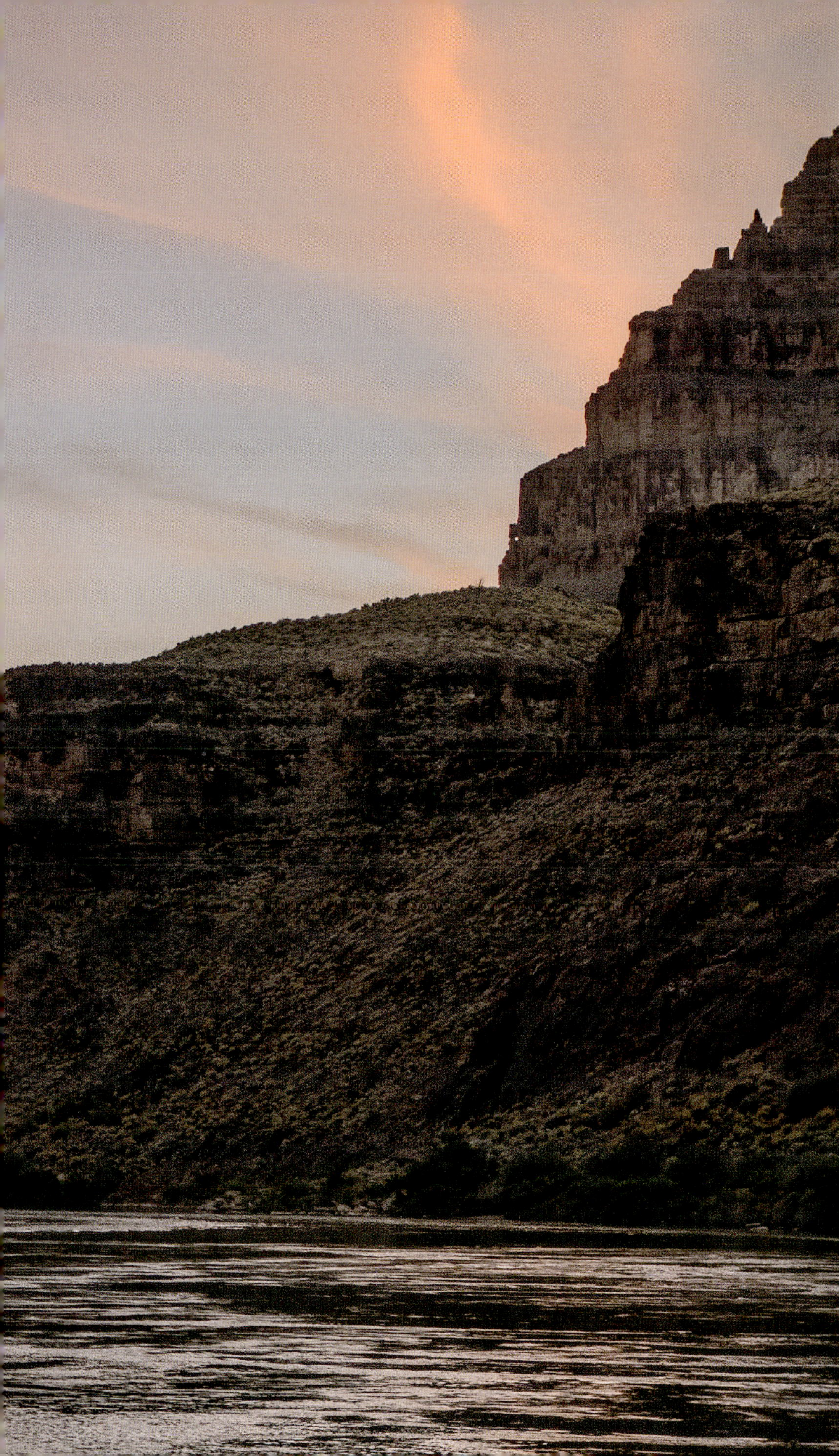

Diamond Peak at sunset, 222 Mile Camp

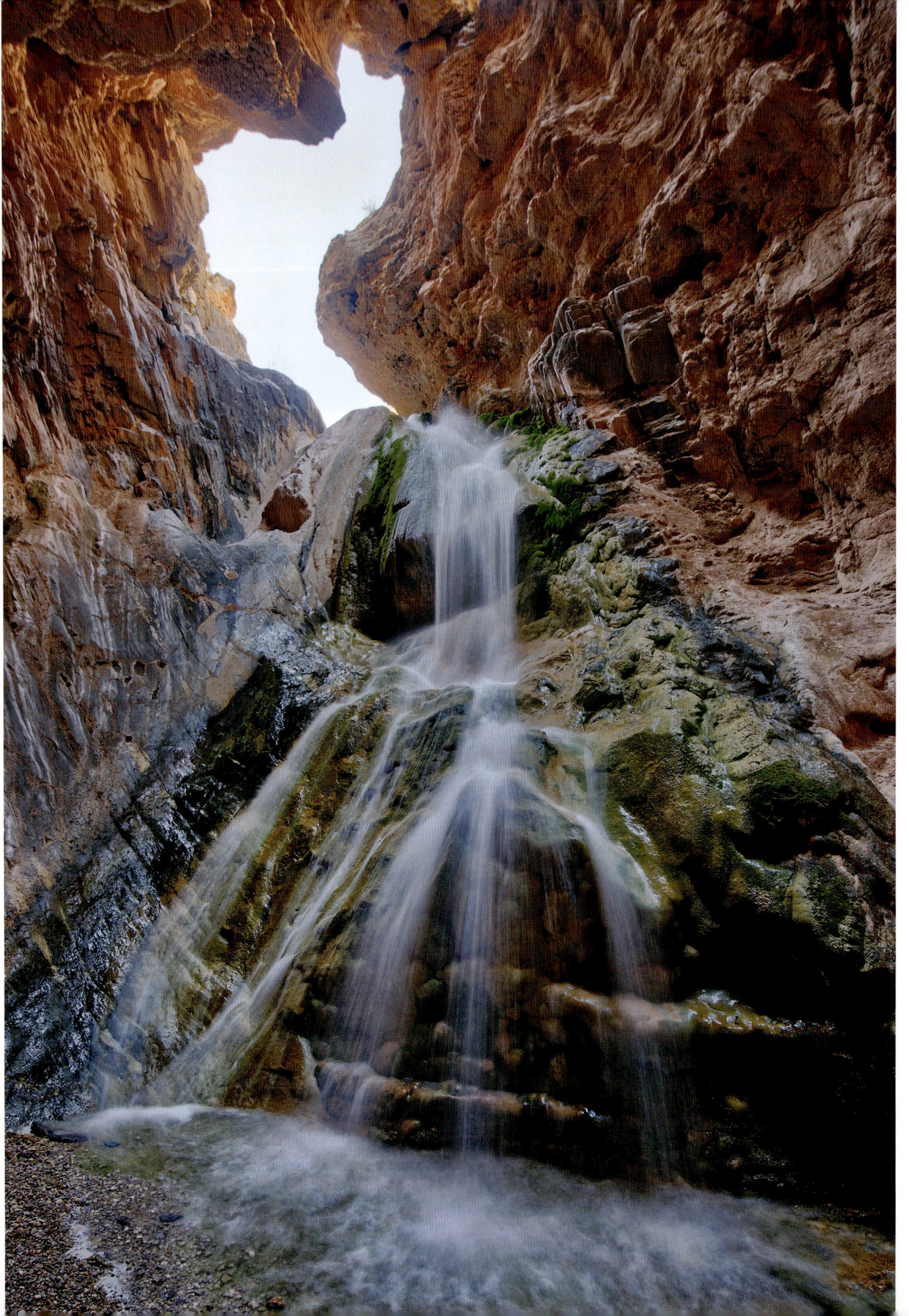

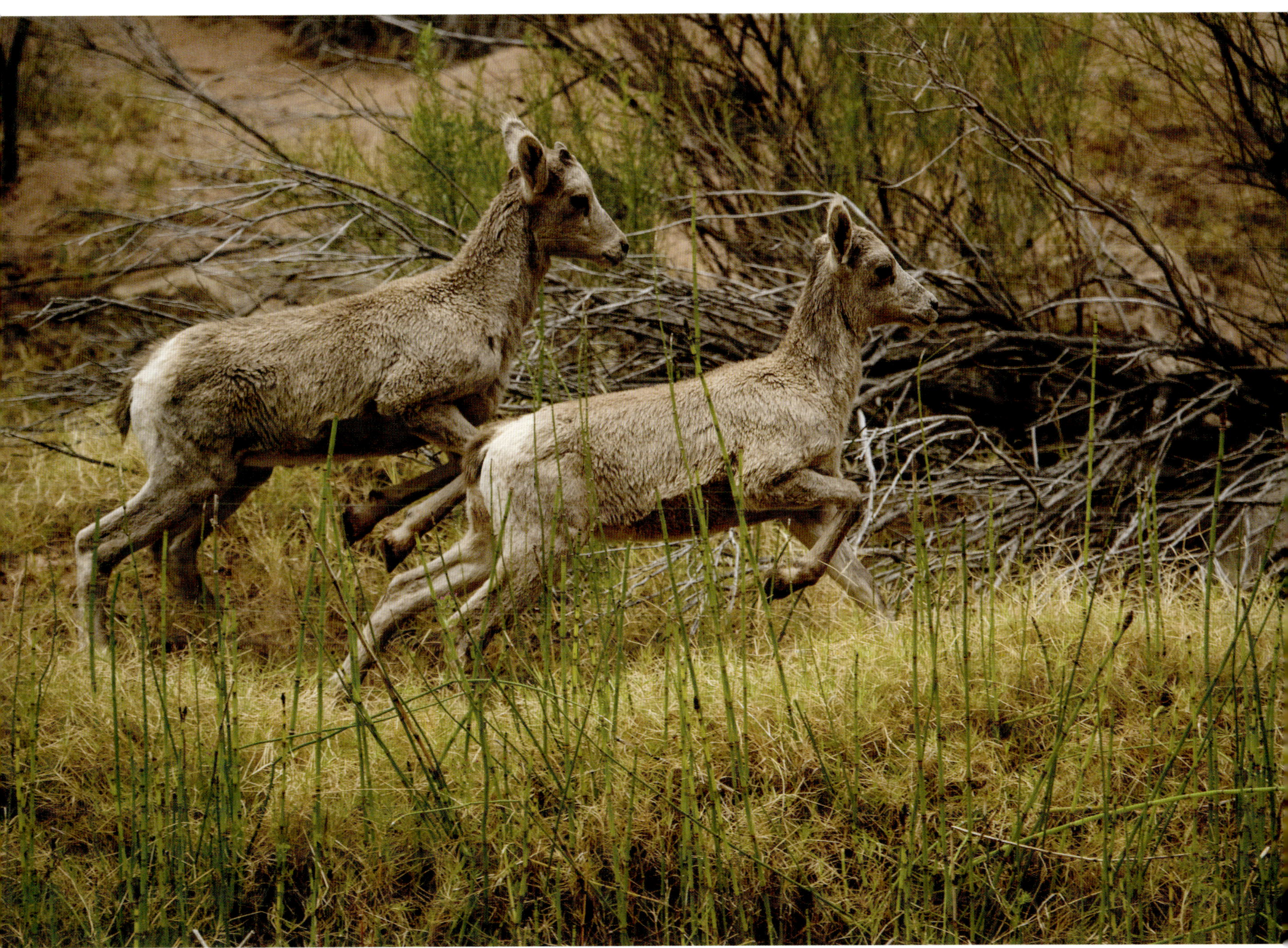

◀ Travertine Grotto ▲ Desert bighorn lambs

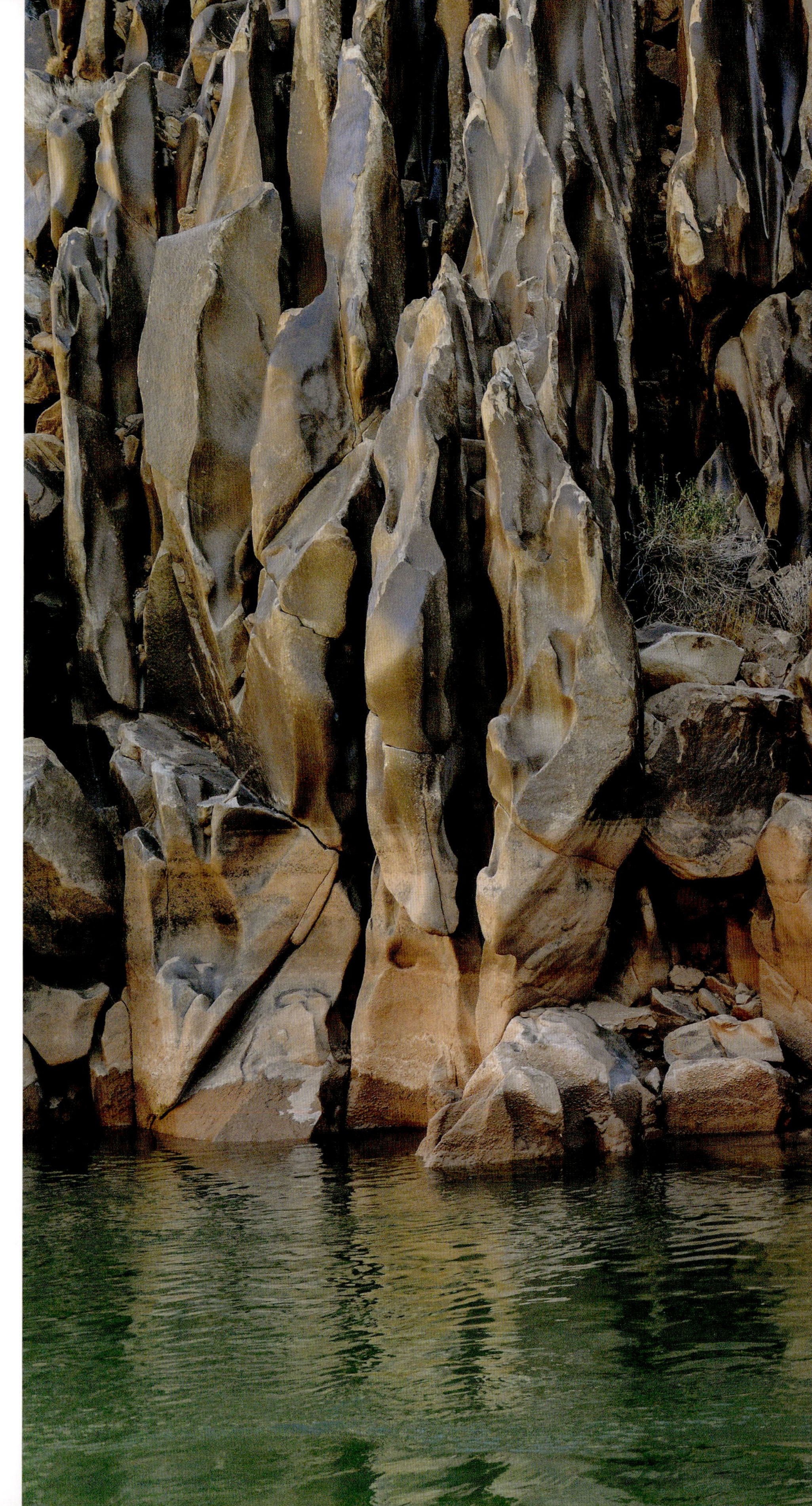

Waterworn cliffs at river's edge, Lower Granite Gorge

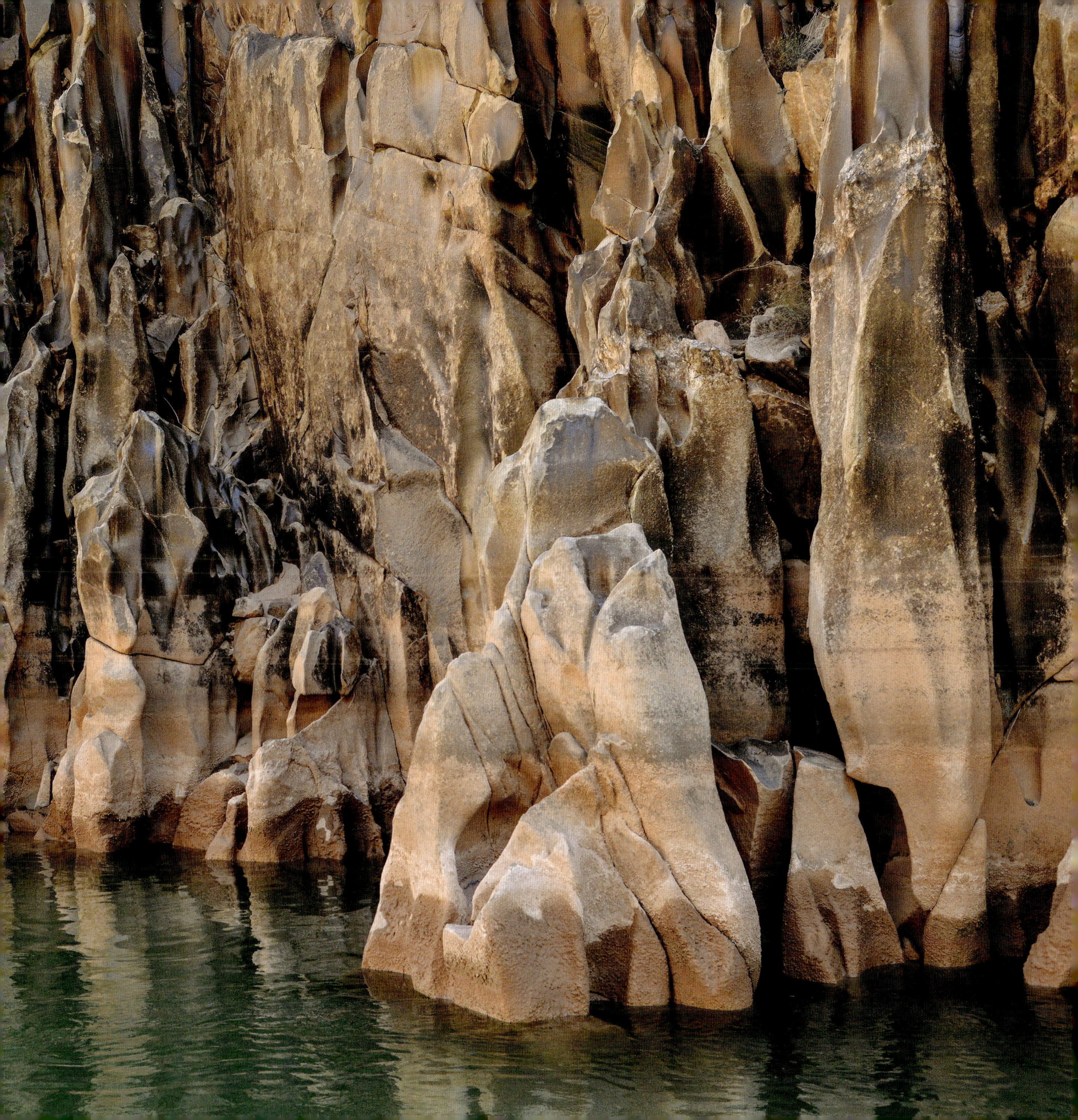

Notes on Photography

Photographing the Grand Canyon has been one of the greatest privileges of my life. That said, it has also been one of the greatest challenges. As a landscape photographer, I tend to embrace an approach that is slow and contemplative, mostly using a tripod. Photographing on the Colorado River in the Grand Canyon brought me, by necessity, totally out of my comfort zone. Everything seems to be moving, even rocks that have been there for a billion years. I had to adapt my style to the almost constant motion of the boat and be ready to shoot with camera in hand or arm's reach the very instant I saw something worthwhile—not an easy predicament with frequent splashing and intermittent dunking from massive rapids.

All the images in this book were taken with digital cameras, the versatility of which proved invaluable with the demands of working fast and constantly adjusting shutter speeds and ISOs. For my entire career I've been a loyal Nikon shooter. The project of photographing for this book spans a period of 12 years and, consequently, runs through a series of Nikon bodies: D810, D800, D500, D7000, and D300. With the constraints of keeping gear to a minimum I usually carry two camera bodies, plus a backup, and only three lenses, all Nikon: 16-35mm f4, 24-120mm f4, and 80-400mm f5.6. For night shots, I also take a Sigma 24mm f1.4 for the extra speed. For a rig that is totally waterproof, I use a Sony a6300 with a 16-50mm lens in a Meikon underwater housing. My tripod is a Really Right Stuff (RRS), model TVC-24L, with a B50 ballhead.

I've witnessed many a camera casualty in the Grand Canyon (fortunately none of them mine) to water, heat, and sand and dust. I've had great success placing the bulk of my gear in a hard Pelican waterproof case strapped down near me, which allows for fast access. In addition, I have numerous light, waterproof rolltop bags into which I temporarily slide the camera I'm holding when going through moderate rapids. In attempts to photograph the rapid, I dress the camera in a waterproof "Storm Jacket" with just the front of the lens exposed or shoot with the Sony in the underwater housing. If aiming the camera forward, the deluge of water usually obscures the lens after the first few drops, especially with the small cameras that have a tiny front element. Better results are obtained from shooting out the side or from behind the splash range.

For the frequent hikes and explorations, I keep a pouch belt at the ready and quickly transfer the gear and grab my tripod as soon as we stop. The tripod is invaluable in many of the locations, which tend to be narrow canyons that are exceedingly dark and impossible to shoot without one. The digital technique of HDR plus tripod allows unprecedented capture of these extreme contrast situations. Adequate battery power is essential on any Grand Canyon rafting trip. Some people are willing to cope with a solar charger or a supplementary battery hub, but I prefer to just bring a heap of camera batteries.

The Grand Canyon's landscape is beyond a scale to which most images can do justice. We become so enthralled with its grandiosity that it's easy to overlook the subtle details, especially of textures and abstract patterns. The rocks themselves embody an entire library of abstract images. With the canyon walls and curving river, there is always an angle of optimum light. Even at midday, the light is striking the cliffs at a low angle. I'll concentrate my vision toward the most expressive light and keep looking in that direction for compositions, working fast and shooting from the hip, because the perspective is constantly changing.

White pelican

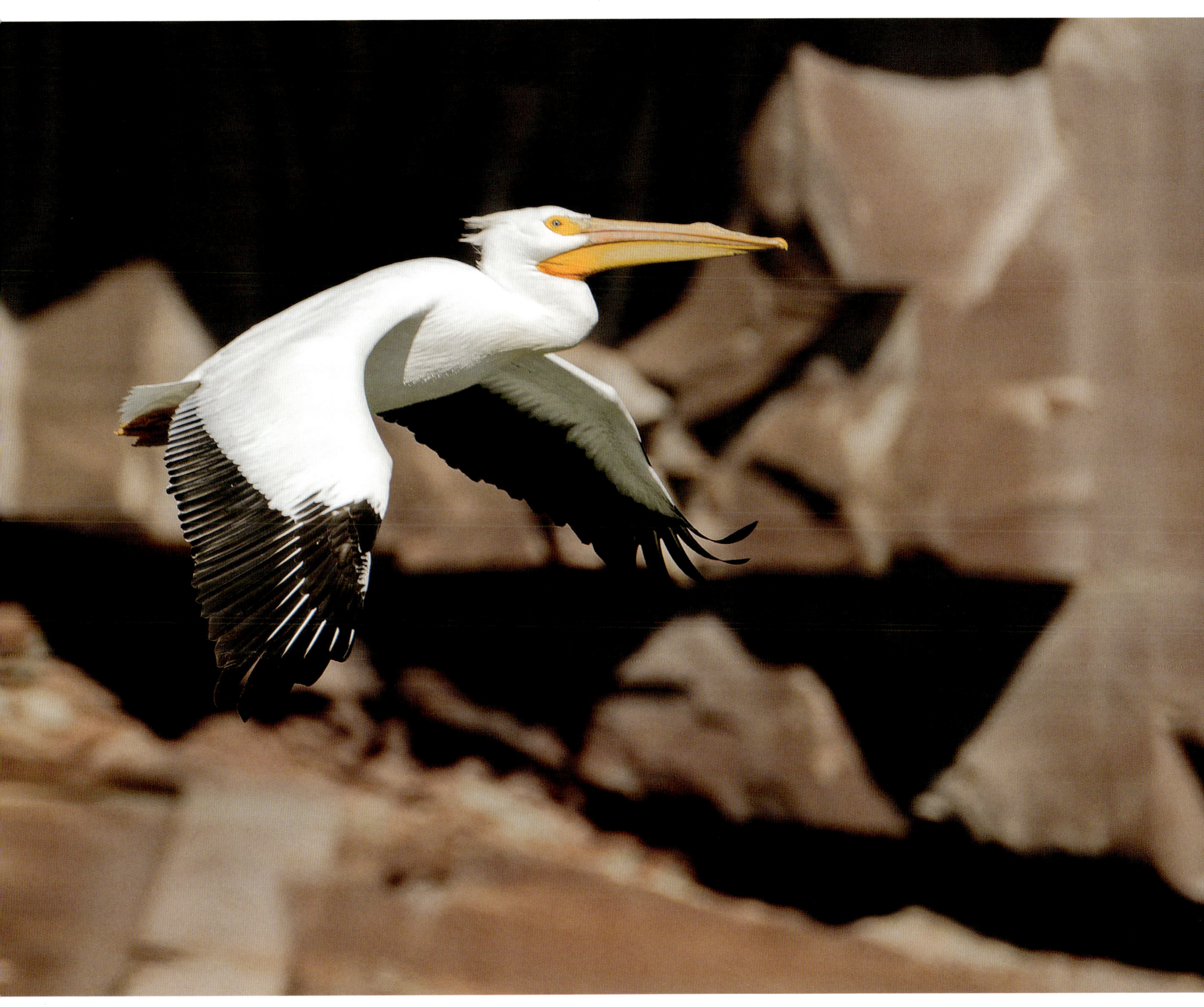

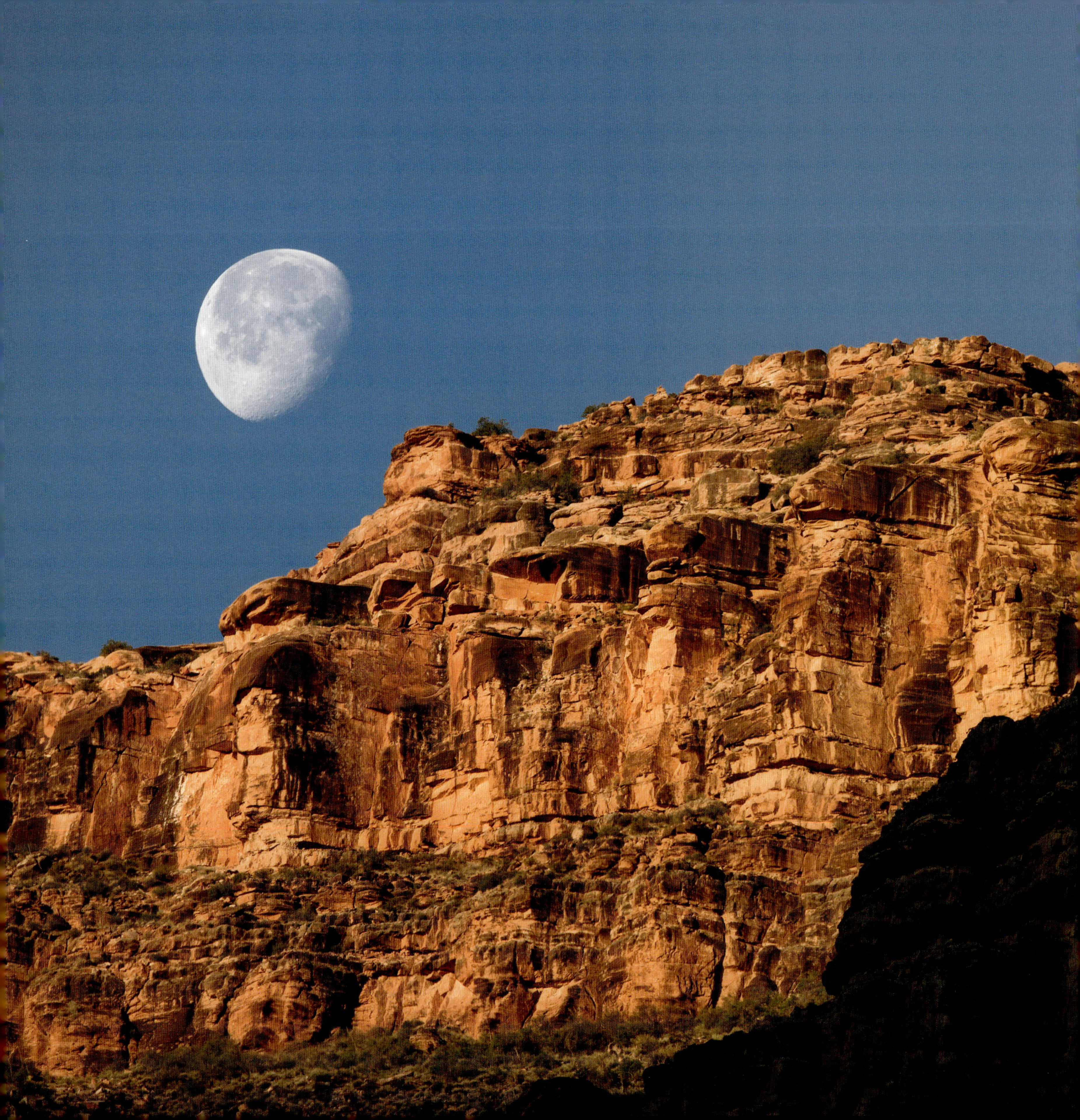

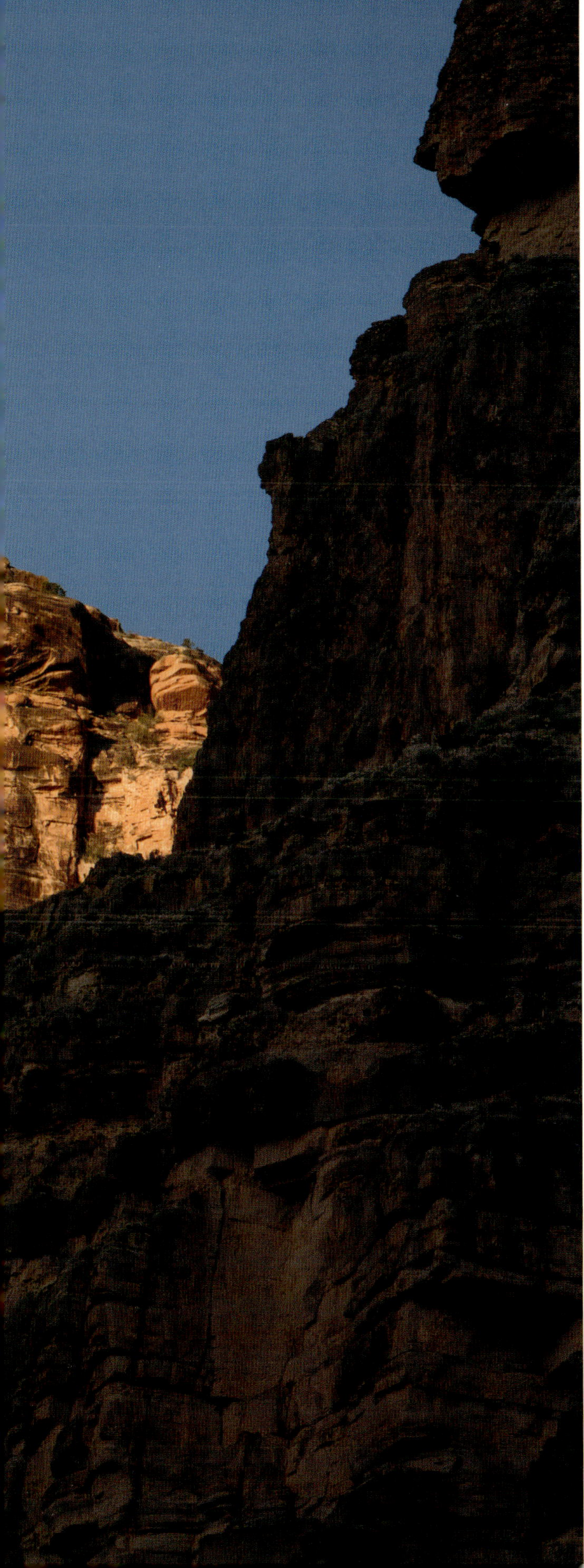

Photographing wildlife is an even bigger task. The large, fast telephotos are too unwieldy and hard to protect on the raft. Most of the birds and animals are totally unpredictable encounters that ideally require the camera and proper lens to be already in hand. Many of the bird opportunities are split-second passing flight shots. I keep a wildlife rig at the ready consisting of my Nikon D500 with the 80-400mm lens. The smaller APS-C sensor gives me the equivalent of up to 600mm. This larger telephoto is also excellent for taking isolated sections and details of the canyon walls. On the boat my full-frame Nikon usually carries the 24-120mm lens for landscapes.

The quality and color of light in the Grand Canyon is like nothing I've ever experienced. The light is not only pure much of the time, but also reverberates off the canyon walls like a giant reflector, absorbing more color each time. A shadowed wall opposite a sunny cliff will have twice the saturation from the hues bouncing off the sunny side. I seek this interplay of light and shadow, pastels and rich tones. Sometimes I even had to desaturate the colors in post-processing because they looked too unreal. Another similar resonant theme is the reflection on the river's surface created by light off the canyon walls. The effect is strongest when the water is in shadow and the opposite wall in sunlight. The challenge is to apply enough shutter speed to freeze the water and enough depth of field to keep it all in focus . . . or go with a slow shutter and let it blur impressionistically.

Photographing the Grand Canyon, as formidable and rewarding as it may be, is secondary to the immense power of the experience itself. Everyone comes away with striking images, but the magnitude of the Canyon and its effect on our psyche is far beyond what we can capture in imagery. I don't let the photographic results dictate the quality of the experience. I hope, though, that the images herein inspire you to take that journey, defined by river time and embraced by ancient rock.

Moonrise above canyon wall

Acknowledgments

The photography for this book would not have been possible if not for a wonderful relationship that started in 2008 with Grand Canyon Expeditions (GCE), for which I have since been leading annual photography trips rafting the Colorado River through the Grand Canyon. The cumulative body of images led not only to this book, but also to a generous sponsorship on behalf of GCE toward its publication. I'm extremely grateful to GCE's owners, Mike Denoyer and especially Marty Mathis for his loyal support, encouragement, and friendship. The various boatmen and "swampers" with whom I've worked over the years have embraced my cause and welcomed me into their rarified world. I particularly want to extend my appreciation to those boatmen who have tolerated me for multiple trips: Denalie McCormick, Irv Callahan, Emily Dale, Jared "Beav" Weaver, Art Thevenin, and especially Roger Patterson, with whom I've made the majority of my trips and whose friendship and guidance are an integral part of this book. I also want to thank Art for his knowledge of natural history and significant help with the captions.

My Grand Canyon odyssey began, however, in 2006, when I was invited on a private oar trip with renowned Colorado photographer John Fielder, my former publisher for numerous books, and Rod Nash, author of the foreword to this book, noted dory oarsman, and professor emeritus at USC Santa Cruz. I had the thrill of running the river with them through the Canyon in small oar boats. I was hooked on the experience and left wanting more. But how? Good fortune prevailed when C. C. Lockwood, a friend and award-winning conservation photographer from Louisiana, asked me to substitute instruct for him on GCE's photography trip. I jumped at the chance. C. C., who had been rafting the Canyon with GCE for decades, ultimately passed the torch to me with GCE's approval—thus starting my deep relationship with both the Canyon and GCE. My sincere gratitude goes to C. C. for opening that door.

When I started leading photography trips for GCE, I had no idea it would eventually lead to this book. At the time, I was pursuing another book, on Acadia National Park, for Rizzoli International Publications. Due to the success of that book and my wonderful working relationship with Rizzoli, we have once again teamed up for this publication. I have the great privilege of not only partnering with one of the finest art book publishers, but also working with the same trusted team: Jim Muschett, the associate publisher; Susi Oberhelman, the designer; and Candice Fehrman, the editor. I'm indebted to them for extending me creative flexibility and editorial input on the project.

Theresa Chamberlain and Grand Canyon Conservancy receive my gratitude as another valued partner in this book project, and I am thankful for their support and protection of the Grand Canyon.

I cannot name the many friends and photographers who have taken this journey with me, but a part of them is embodied in this book and these images. We all share and are inspired by one another's enthusiasm and creative energy. The power of the experience affects us all and infuses both the quality of the trip and our resulting photographs. I want to thank my wife, Lynn, for enriching my experience on three of these trips and for her tireless and astute editorial input.

Last, I want to acknowledge Nikon for producing excellent equipment that has served me for more than 40 years without a catastrophic failure. The reliability and optical performance together are unsurpassed. I consider photographing in the Grand Canyon one of the ultimate gear tests, and Nikon passed with flying colors.

Royal Arches

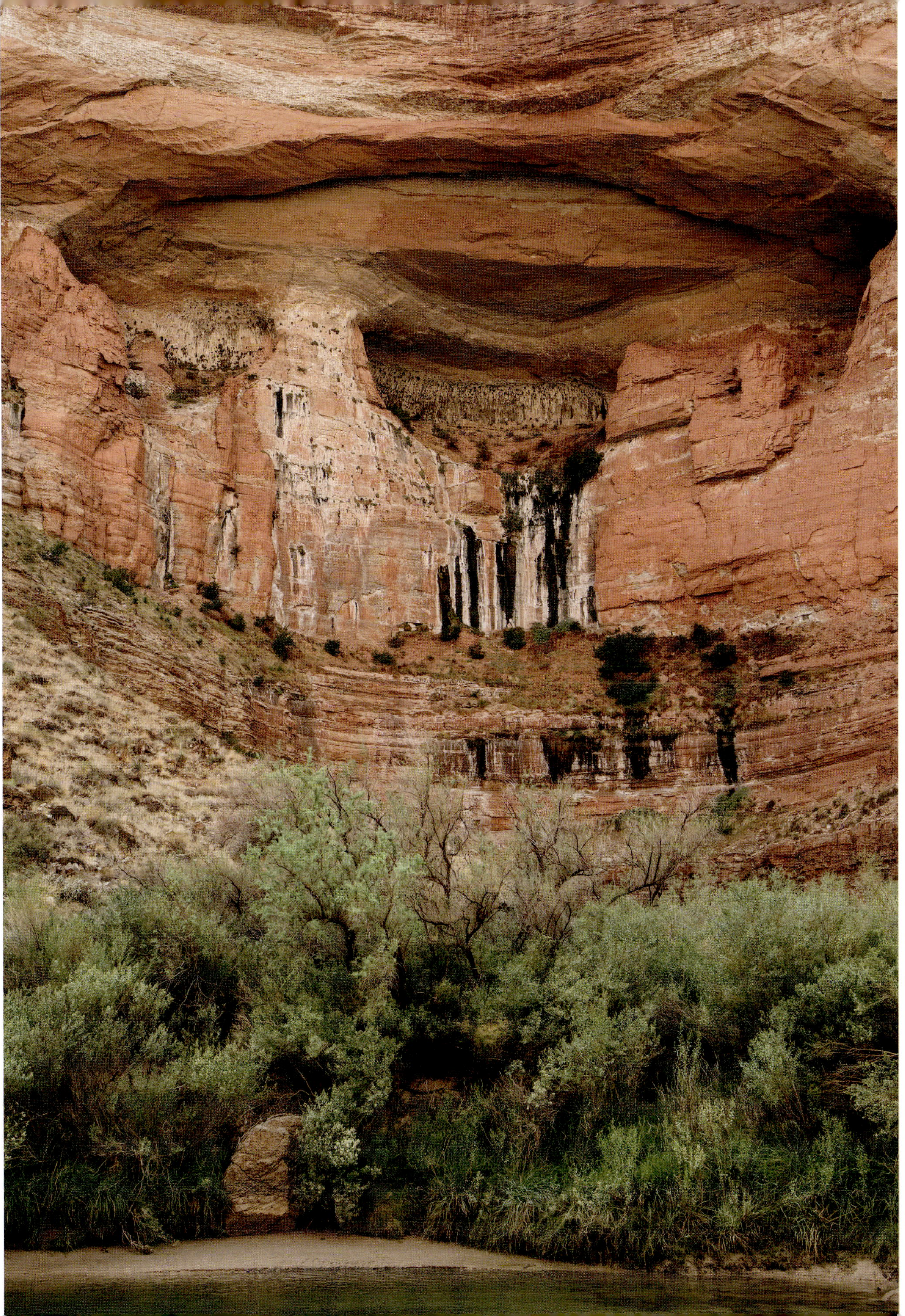

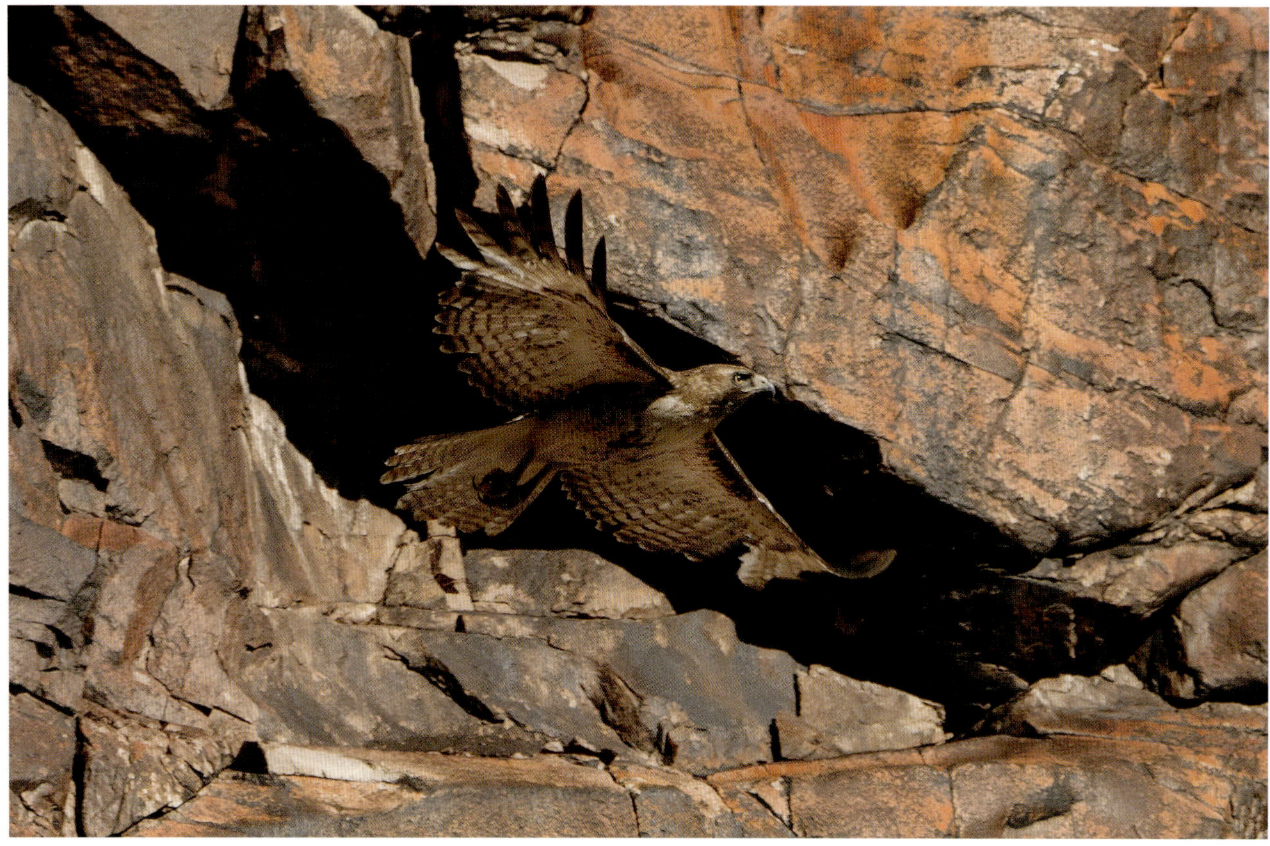

THIS BOOK IS DEDICATED TO MY WIFE, LYNN, AND DAUGHTER, SARAH.

First published in the United States of America in 2019 by
Rizzoli International Publications, Inc. • 300 Park Avenue South • New York, NY 10010 • www.rizzoliusa.com

 • Foreword by Roderick F. Nash

Associate Publisher: James Muschett • Project Editor: Candice Fehrman • Book Design: Susi Oberhelman
Endpaper Map: *Belknap's Waterproof Grand Canyon River Guide*, © Westwater Books 2019

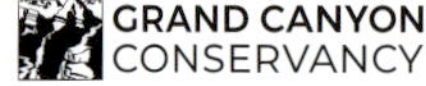

Grand Canyon Conservancy is the official nonprofit partner of Grand Canyon National Park. For more information, please visit www.grandcanyon.org.

2019 2020 2021 2022 / 10 9 8 7 6 5 4 3 2 1 • Printed in China • ISBN-13: 978-0-8478-6640-3 • Library of Congress Catalog Control Number: 2018959830

Pages 2–3: Havasu Canyon; Pages 4–5: Downriver below Blacktail Canyon; Above: Red-tailed hawk

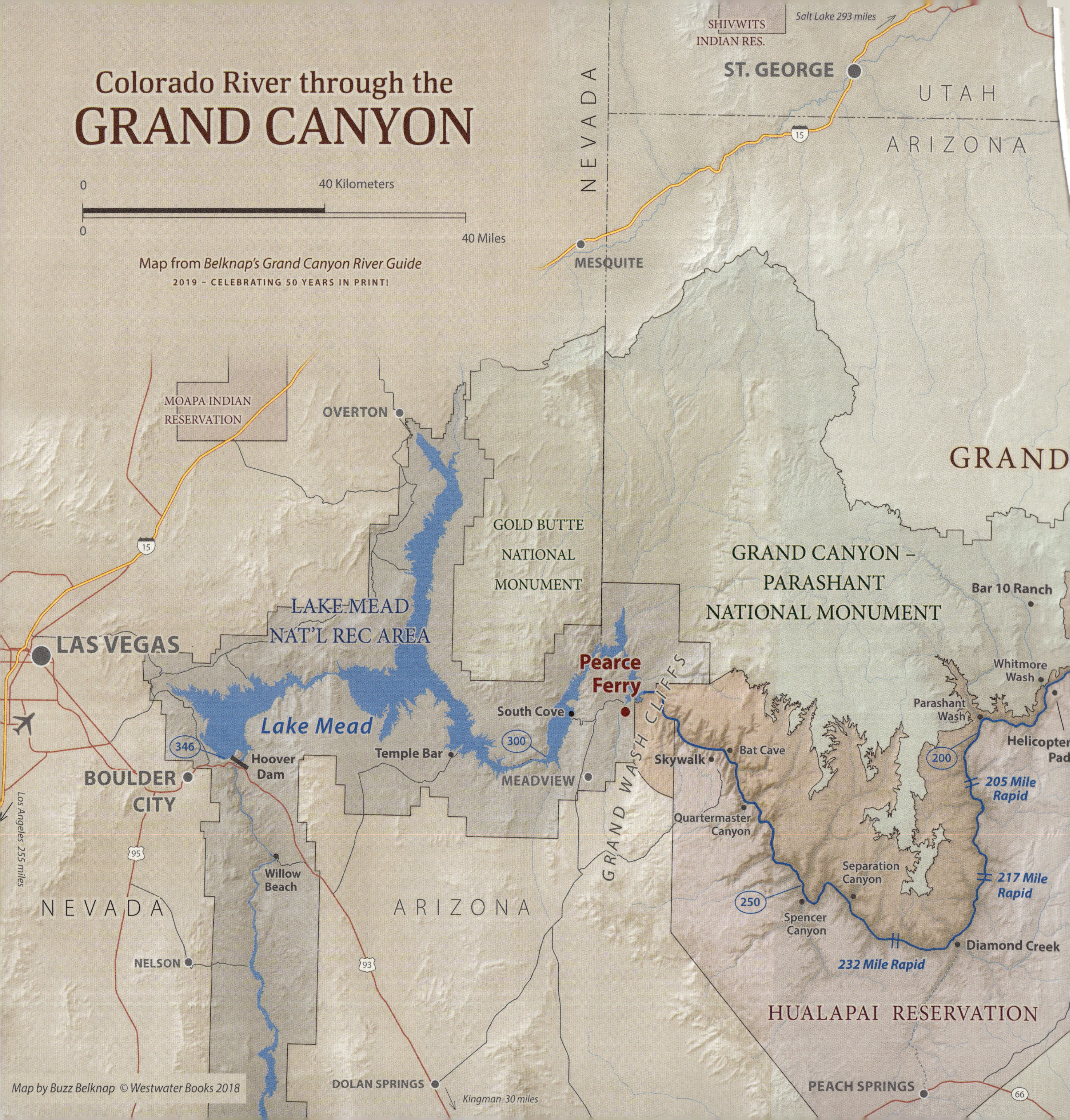

Colorado River through the
GRAND CANYON
0
40 Kilometers
0
40 Miles
Map from Belknap's Grand Canyon River Guide
2019 – CELEBRATING 50 YEARS IN PRINT!
SHIVWITS INDIAN RES.
Salt Lake 293 miles
ST. GEORGE
UTAH
ARIZONA
NEVADA
15
MESQUITE
MOAPA INDIAN RESERVATION
OVERTON
GRAND
GOLD BUTTE NATIONAL MONUMENT
GRAND CANYON – PARASHANT NATIONAL MONUMENT
Bar 10 Ranch
LAKE MEAD NAT'L REC AREA
LAS VEGAS
Pearce Ferry
Whitmore Wash
Parashant Wash
Helicopter Pad
South Cove
Lake Mead
300
346
Hoover Dam
Temple Bar
Skywalk
Bat Cave
200
BOULDER CITY
MEADVIEW
GRAND WASH CLIFFS
205 Mile Rapid
Quartermaster Canyon
95
Willow Beach
Separation Canyon
217 Mile Rapid
Los Angeles 255 miles
250
Spencer Canyon
NEVADA
ARIZONA
Diamond Creek
232 Mile Rapid
NELSON
93
HUALAPAI RESERVATION
Map by Buzz Belknap © Westwater Books 2018
DOLAN SPRINGS
Kingman 30 miles
PEACH SPRINGS
66